Evolutionary Economics and Social Complexity Science

Volume 32

The Japan Association for Evolutionary Economics (JAFEE) always has adhered to its original aim of taking an explicit "integrated" approach. This path has been followed steadfastly since the Association's establishment in 1997 and, as well, since the inauguration of our international journal in 2004. We have deployed an agenda encompassing a contemporary array of subjects including but not limited to: foundations of institutional and evolutionary economics, criticism of mainstream views in the social sciences, knowledge and learning in socio-economic life, development and innovation of technologies, transformation of industrial organizations and economic systems, experimental studies in economics, agent-based modeling of socio-economic systems, evolution of the governance structure of firms and other organizations, comparison of dynamically changing institutions of the world, and policy proposals in the transformational process of economic life. In short, our starting point is an "integrative science" of evolutionary and institutional views. Furthermore, we always endeavor to stay abreast of newly established methods such as agent-based modeling, socio/econo-physics, and network analysis as part of our integrative links. More fundamentally, "evolution" in social science is interpreted as an essential key word, i.e., an integrative and /or communicative link to understand and re-domain various preceding dichotomies in the sciences: ontological or epistemological, subjective or objective, homogeneous or heterogeneous, natural or artificial, selfish or altruistic, individualistic or collective, rational or irrational, axiomatic or psychological-based, causal nexus or cyclic networked, optimal or adaptive, micro- or macroscopic, deterministic or stochastic, historical or theoretical, mathematical or computational, experimental or empirical, agent-based or socio/econo-physical, institutional or evolutionary, regional or global, and so on. The conventional meanings adhering to various traditional dichotomies may be more or less obsolete, to be replaced with more current ones vis-à-vis contemporary academic trends. Thus we are strongly encouraged to integrate some of the conventional dichotomies. These attempts are not limited to the field of economic sciences, including management sciences, but also include social science in general. In that way, understanding the social profiles of complex science may then be within our reach. In the meantime, contemporary society appears to be evolving into a newly emerging phase, chiefly characterized by an information and communication technology (ICT) mode of production and a service network system replacing the earlier established factory system with a new one that is suited to actual observations. In the face of these changes we are urgently compelled to explore a set of new properties for a new socio/economic system by implementing new ideas. We thus are keen to look for "integrated principles" common to the above-mentioned dichotomies throughout our serial compilation of publications. We are also encouraged to create a new, broader spectrum for establishing a specific method positively integrated in our own original way.

Editors in Chief

***

Norio Tokumaru • Chino Yabunaga •
Yuriko Shibayama
Editors

Creative Co-evolution of the Economies and Welfare States in the Nordic Countries

Springer

Editors
Norio Tokumaru
Faculty of Policy Studies
Kansai University
Suita-shi, Osaka, Japan

Chino Yabunaga
Faculty of Global and Regional Studies
Toyo University
Bunkyo-ku, Tokyo, Japan

Yuriko Shibayama
Department of Nordic Studies
Tokai University
Hiratsuka-shi, Kanagawa, Japan

ISSN 2198-4204 ISSN 2198-4212 (electronic)
Evolutionary Economics and Social Complexity Science
ISBN 978-981-97-8568-1 ISBN 978-981-97-8569-8 (eBook)
https://doi.org/10.1007/978-981-97-8569-8

This Springer imprint is published by the registered company Springer Nature Singapore Pte Ltd.
The registered company address is: 152 Beach Road, #21-01/04 Gateway East, Singapore 189721, Singapore

Preface

While researchers have persistently questioned the sustainability of the welfare state, including the Nordic welfare states since the 1970s, they have in fact survived through a series of reforms. As a result, the Nordic countries have managed to maintain high levels of well-being, as the *World Happiness Report* has repeatedly shown, as well as the high labour productivity. This fact reminds us of a concept that has become popular in recent years: *resilience* as the capacity of a system to return to its original state. This concept, however, is not necessarily appropriate to characterize the dynamic nature of the Nordic welfare states because they have *not* simply returned to their original state by overcoming problems *but* have constantly renewed themselves by developing new services and inventing new ways of providing social services.

Until the financial crisis, it had been highly relevant to discuss the "comparative institutional advantage" of each country by comparing institutions among developed countries, as in the *Varieties of Capitalism* (VoC) thesis. However, in the current situation of developed countries, which have also fallen into secular stagnation after the financial crisis, the relevance of the comparison of performance and its institutional underpinnings practiced by the studies influenced by the VoC thesis seems to be rapidly diminishing. In this context, it seems more important to examine the *dynamic* capability of countries to renew oneself than to *statically* compare efficiency and advantage.

The same is true of the Nordic countries, which are the focus of this book. The Nordic countries have been highly regarded for their social and economic achievements, which are unquestionable. However, especially after the financial crisis, some of these achievements have begun to fade. Faced with this reality, it is an urgent task to introduce a new perspective that makes it possible to assess the *dynamic* process of adaptive change and the social capabilities behind it, rather than the *static* assessment of social and economic performance.

It is in these contexts that the concept of *evolution*, on which this book is based, becomes more relevant than it has ever been before. First, unlike the concept of resilience, the concept of evolution includes the emergence of novelty. Second, evolution is a fundamental concept in clarifying the dynamic capability for change in any country.

The aim of this book is to show how actors in the Nordic welfare states, especially in Finland, are trying to adapt to the multifaceted pressures on welfare states, such as industrial change, globalization, and the demographic maturation of the ageing population, by making creative use of existing resources and institutions. In particular, we focused on the high resistance of universalist welfare states to pressure by means of creative, adaptive changes and attempted to evaluate the adaptive capacity of Nordic welfare states. How do welfare states evolve creatively under different pressures, and what are the factors that make evolution possible? This book aims to shed new light on these questions from a variety of perspectives over a long period of time, covering the past, present, and future of post-industrial society.

As explained in detail in Chap. 1, we have chosen Finland as an appropriate case to examine the adaptive capacity of the Nordic countries. In this sense, this book is intended to be a study of the development of the Nordic welfare states, with Finland as the main case. At the same time, however, it should be emphasized that the book pays sufficient attention to the uniqueness of Finland as a latecomer to the Nordic welfare state.

We hope that the chapters in this book can convincingly demonstrate the effectiveness of an evolutionary perspective in comparative welfare state studies and comparative political economy. We also hope that this book will serve as a starting point for a systematic study of the socio-economic systems of the Nordic countries from the perspective of evolutionary social sciences.

Osaka, Japan — Norio Tokumaru
Tokyo, Japan — Chino Yabunaga
Kanagawa, Japan — Yuriko Shibayama
August 2024

Acknowledgement

We are deeply grateful to the participants in the sessions organized by the editors at the *Japan Association of Northern European Studies* and the *Public Policy Studies Association Japan* for their insightful comments.

The editors greatly appreciate the generous assistance provided by the interviewees during the site visits. This work was supported by JSPS KAKENHI Grant Number 19H04368.

Contents

Chapter 1
Introduction

Norio Tokumaru, Chino Yabunaga, and Yuriko Shibayama

Abstract Welfare states have always been under constant pressure to reform, especially since the 1970s when the "golden age of capitalism" ended, which includes the Nordic countries that have maintained both high-performing economies and well-developed welfare states. This pressure has been particularly pronounced during the economic stagnation following the Great Financial Crisis. The pressure to reform may have been even stronger in the Nordic countries than in other countries because they have maintained high levels of social outcomes and social spending despite deepening economic stagnation and the resulting fiscal constraints. Finland, in particular, has maintained higher social outcomes than, say, Sweden, despite facing deeper economic stagnation and more severe fiscal constraints. Consequently, the need for creative adaptation to pressures for reform is likely to be greatest in Finland. This book examines critical cases of such creative evolution, with Finland as the primary example, to shed new light on the current potential of Nordic welfare states and their *evolutionary learning capability*. This dynamic capability allows them to develop new services to meet emerging needs, deliver existing services without compromising quality or increasing costs, and reinterpret existing services. This introductory chapter outlines the evolutionary perspective and evolutionary learning capability that underpin this book and introduces the contents of the following chapters.

Keywords Creative evolution · Welfare state reform · Nordic welfare state · Stagnation · Austerity · Evolutionary learning capability

N. Tokumaru (✉)
Faculty of Policy Studies, Kansai University, Osaka, Japan
e-mail: norio-t@kansai-u.ac.jp

C. Yabunaga
Faculty of Global and Regional Studies, Toyo University, Bunkyo-ku, Tokyo, Japan
e-mail: yabunaga@toyo.jp

Y. Shibayama
Department of Nordic Studies, School of Cultural and Social Studies, Tokai University, Hiratsuka, Kanagawa, Japan
e-mail: ys@tokai.ac.jp

N. Tokumaru et al. (eds.), *Creative Co-evolution of the Economies and Welfare States in the Nordic Countries*, Evolutionary Economics and Social Complexity Science 32, https://doi.org/10.1007/978-981-97-8569-8_1

1.1 Nordic Welfare States Under Neoliberalism and Societal Transformation

All advanced capitalist economies have largely maintained their status as welfare states, albeit in diverse forms, as Esping-Andersen (1990) persuasively demonstrated. To secure sufficient resources to ensure the provision of public social services and benefits, welfare states require economies with a high capacity to increase productivity and create new jobs while transforming their industries. Since the end of the "golden age of capitalism" (Marglin & Schor, 1990) in the early 1970s, welfare states have often been seen as unproductive systems that extract too many resources from the economies to be sustained. In particular, since the 1990s, attempts have been made to curb the increase in social spending by tightening eligibility for services and benefits and increasing the supply of services by the private sector. It was during this period that welfare state scholars began to talk about the "retrenchment" of the welfare state (Pierson, 1994, 1996), including conducting empirical studies of whether, to what extent, and how the retrenchment of the welfare state has been realized (e.g., Collington, 2022; Greve, 2020). While subsequent research has shown that it is not appropriate to describe changes in the welfare state simply as overall retrenchment,[1] clearly, the pressure for *reform* has always existed (Karsbergen et al., 2014).

At the same time, the different "worlds" of the welfare state (Esping-Andersen, 1990) face different reform pressures and have different reform agendas, mainly due to the different constellations of political coalitions and support for service provision. According to Pierson (2001), the *social democratic* regime of the welfare state (i.e., the Nordic welfare states) have high political support and moderate reform pressure, resulting in *cost-containment* and *rationalization* of existing services as the main reform agenda, where reforms have been "negotiated, consensual, and incremental" (Pierson, 2001, p. 455), compared to the *liberal* and *conservative* regimes, where reform agendas such as *re-commodification* and *updating* of services are needed, which require non-incremental changes (Table 1.1).

Table 1.1 Different reform agendas in the different regimes

	Liberal	Social democratic	Conservative
Political support for welfare state	Moderate	High	High
Adjustment pressures	Moderate	Moderate	High
Reform agenda	Re-commodification/ Cost-containment	Cost-containment/ Rationalization	Cost-containment/ Updating

Source: Pierson (2001, p. 455)

[1] It can be argued that while across-the-board retrenchment is politically infeasible because of the strong public support for service provision (Pierson, 2001), it is also theoretically unlikely because the capitalist economy inevitably requires the welfare state to ensure social reproduction, as Polanyi's (1944) seminal argument for social protection against the free market strongly implied.

Despite the differences between them, the Nordic welfare states exhibit striking similarities. According to Greve (2007, p. 45), who reviewed the comparative welfare state literature, the distinctive features of the Nordic welfare model are the following: "Extremely decentralised and at the same time complex structure regarding both regulations as well as financing; High degree of equality; Active labour market policy with high level of employment (also for women) and low level of wage differentiation; High level of taxes; Family friendly in the sense that the public sector has been actively involved in delivery of day care for children, leaves schemes for parents and a high level compared to other welfare states of economic support for families with children." Greve (2007) adds that the Nordic welfare model can be characterized as a "service welfare state" because of its emphasis on the public provision of social and health services. The "Nordic model" of the socioeconomic system is a broader and more encompassing concept. According to Andersen et al. (2007, pp. 13–14), the main features of the Nordic model are as follows: (1) "a comprehensive welfare state […] financed by taxes which are high notably for wage income and consumption," (2) "a lot of public and/or private spending on investment in human capital, including child care and education as well as research and development," and (3) "a set of labour market institutions that include strong labour unions and employer associations, significant elements of wage coordination, relatively generous unemployment benefits and a prominent role for active labour market policies."

It has been argued that the Nordic welfare state has shown superior adaptability to the social challenges of the twenty-first century, including the transition from an industrial to a knowledge-based economy, globalization, an aging and mobile population, and changing family structures (e.g., Armingeon & Bonoli, 2006; Bonoli & Natali, 2012; Hemerijck, 2013; Taylor-Gooby, 2004). Especially in the early twenty-first century, there has been much discussion about the *social investment welfare state*, with some arguing that the welfare state can enhance economic growth by promoting skill formation and labor mobility through generous social investment while ensuring the basic security of life (Crouch, 2013; Hemerijck, 2017; Morel et al., 2012). Similarly, another related argument emphasizes "enabling" aspects of the Nordic welfare state in the sense that it encourages people to take risks and make innovative efforts (Kristensen & Lilja, 2011; Miettinen, 2012). Indeed, the "flexicurity" model of Denmark and other countries, which attempts to combine labor market flexibility, active labor market policies, and unemployment security in a productive way, has been praised and positioned as one of the keys to achieving the goals of the "Lisbon Strategy," the European Union's growth and jobs strategy for 2000–2010.

It should be noted that the Nordic welfare states have traditionally sought to reconcile economy and welfare, and it has been their basic strategy to develop social policies that contribute to economic performance, which, in turn, finances the welfare state. In fact, the Nordic model of the welfare state and socioeconomic system has been emphasized as a driver of innovation and economic growth. While "democratic corporatism" has been argued to be an effective way to coordinate the adjustment of the economies, especially the small ones, through economic crises

(Katzenstein, 1985), Ornston (2012) coined the concept of "creative corporatism" and understood it as an effective system for rapidly changing the allocation of resources to enable innovation in particular sectors. Similarly, Thelen (2021) showed that Sweden was able to move into high-tech manufacturing and services at least partly because of its coordination mechanisms institutionalized for wage determination, compared to Germany and the Netherlands. Centralized wage setting in the Nordic countries, supported by high trade union density, has also led to wage compression among workers, which has promoted the elimination of low-productivity industries and firms and the growth of high-productivity ones, thereby enhancing the productivity growth of the economies (Erixon, 2008, 2018; Maliranta et al., 2010).

Despite these high expectations that both the Nordic model of the welfare state and socioeconomic system can be a driving force for innovation and economic growth, it is also true that the economy has stagnated, especially since the great financial crisis (GFC) in 2007–08, as the following data show, exposing the limitations of the above expectations.

On the one hand, Table 1.2 shows that while all three Nordic countries—Denmark, Finland, and Sweden—had better employment records than Germany before the GFC, their unemployment rates increased more than Germany's after the GFC. As shown in Tables 1.3 and 1.4, while all advanced economies have had a

Table 1.2 Unemployment rate (% of labor force)

	2002–2007	2008–2013	2014–2019
Denmark	4.52	7.34	5.65
Finland	7.86	8.15	8.10
France	8.04	9.34	9.21
Germany	9.51	6.02	3.80
Japan	4.40	4.44	2.81
Sweden	6.52	8.12	7.10
United Kingdom	5.17	7.56	4.52
United States	5.27	8.24	5.03

Source: OECD Labor Statistics

Table 1.3 GDP growth (%: annual average)

	1976–86	1987–97	1998–2008	2009–2021
United States	3.51	3.12	2.82	1.71
United Kingdom	2.39	2.72	2.42	1.09
Japan	4.18	2.99	0.80	0.27
Germany	2.36	2.44	1.57	0.95
France	2.47	2.26	2.23	0.80
Italy	3.06	2.04	1.28	−0.38
Sweden	1.77	1.59	3.10	1.85
Finland	3.01	2.08	3.53	0.39

Source: OECD National Accounts at a Glance

Table 1.4 Growth of labor productivity (%: annual average)

	1964–74	1975–85	1986–96	1997–2007	2008–18
United States	2.05	1.22	1.43	2.14	1.14
United Kingdom	3.79	3.15	2.09	2.05	0.24
Japan	7.61	3.26	3.17	1.68	0.79
Germany	5.21	3.28	2.52	1.30	0.83
France	5.90	3.58	1.76	1.76	0.82
Italy	6.79	2.81	2.37	0.39	0.08
Sweden	4.12	1.40	1.51	2.20	0.86
Finland	5.27	2.53	3.00	2.74	0.57

Note: Calculated as GDP divided by total hours worked, evaluated in 2010 US dollars
Source: Long-Term Productivity Database (Bergeaud et al., 2016)

Table 1.5 Structural change parameter

	Period I (1998–2008)	Period II (2008-)[a]
Japan	0.50	0.28
Germany	0.48	0.30
France	0.23	0.25
Sweden	0.52	0.42
Finland	0.56	0.38
United Kingdom	0.47	0.47
United States	0.35	0.35

Source: Authors' calculations using the OECD STAN Database. See Appendix for further details
[a]Japan, Sweden, and Finland: 2008–17/Germany and France: 2008–16/United Kingdom: 2008–15/United States: 2008–18

long-term stagnation trend since the mid-1970s, Sweden and Finland outperformed the other countries in terms of economic and productivity growth in the period just before the GFC. However, after the GFC, their performance deteriorated and became similar to that of other countries.

The nature and pace of industrial structural change have been key to understanding economic and productivity growth, as the growth of high-productivity industries contributes to the economic and productivity growth of an economy, which has underpinned the growth performance of the Nordic countries (Barth et al., 2014; Erixon, 2008, 2018; Iacono, 2018; Perraton, 2018). The structural change parameter in Table 1.5, where the higher the number, the more rapid the pace of industrial structural change, shows that although Sweden and Finland had much more rapid structural changes than all other countries before the GFC, their pace of change also stagnated along with other countries and converged to the level of other countries. This may be due, at least in part, to stagnant capital accumulation despite the high expected rates of return (Perraton, 2018).

On the other hand, even after the GFC, social outcomes in the Nordic countries were generally better than those in other developed countries, as measured by poverty rates and income inequality (Table 1.6), and the level of social spending was still higher than in other developed countries (Fig. 1.1).

Table 1.6 Income inequality and poverty (2018)

	Gini coefficient[a]	P90/P10[b]	Poverty rate[c]
Denmark	0.263	3.0	6.4
Finland	0.269	3.1	6.5
Germany	0.289	3.6	9.8
Japan	0.334	5.2	15.7
Sweden	0.273	3.3	8.7
United Kingdom	0.366	4.5	11.7
United States	0.393	6.3	18.1

Source: OECD Income Distribution Database
[a]Gini coefficient of disposable income
[b]P90/P10 disposable income decile ratio
[c]Poverty rate based on 50% of the national median disposable income

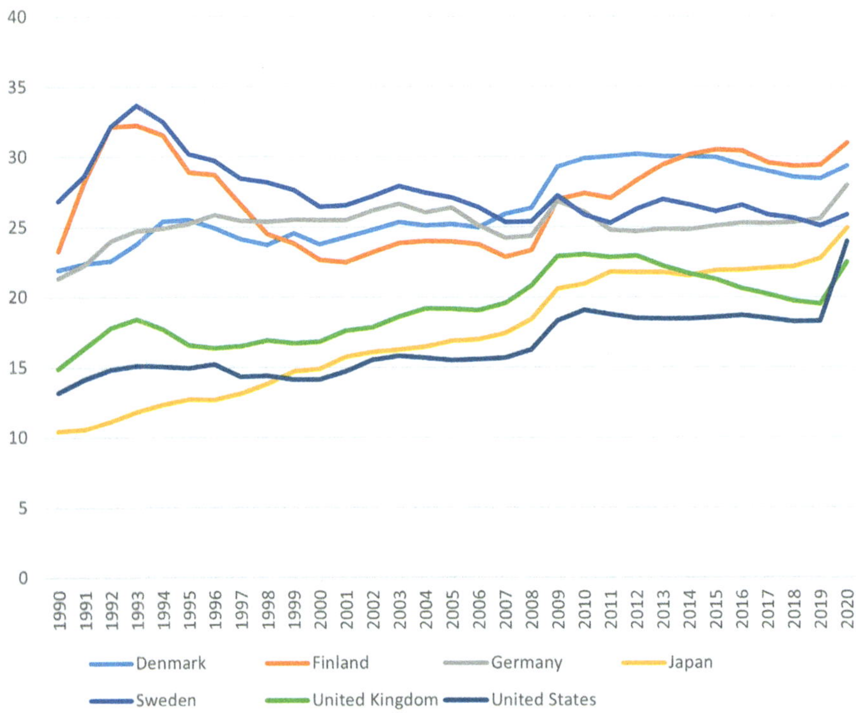

Source: OECD Data Explorer

Fig. 1.1 Public social expenditure (% of GDP). Source: OECD Data Explorer

The fact that social outcomes have remained high despite social spending being maintained at a certain level, even in the face of increased demand for social services, strongly suggests that *creative adaptation* has been unavoidable and has been attempted, such as experimenting with innovative service delivery, developing novel programs in response to new challenges, and adopting new technologies and

Table 1.7 Societal capacity for innovation

Country	Score
Denmark	149.2
Sweden	145.9
Finland	145.6
Netherlands	139.6
Belgium	136.4
Austria	130.0
Germany	127.8
Luxembourg	127.1
Ireland	125.6

Note: *Summary Innovation Index* is a composite variable with a simple average of 32 indicators. The original indicators consisted of four main categories: framework conditions, investments, innovation activities, and impacts. It measures the institutional conditions, inputs, processes, and outputs of innovation
Source: European Commission (2023)

organizational structures. From an *ex-post* perspective, adaptations are *creative* when they develop new services to meet new or unmet needs, find ways to deliver existing services without compromising quality or increasing costs, and develop new interpretations of existing services. The proposal of the social investment welfare state concept and the emphasis on active labor market policies in the 2000s can also be seen as examples of the creative adaptation of the welfare state. The high scores of Denmark, Sweden, and Finland on the European Commission's (2023) *Summary Innovation Index*, a measure of societal capacity for innovation, suggest that these Nordic countries have retained their societal capacity for creative adaptation (Table 1.7).

1.2 The Aim and Subject of This Book

How has the Nordic welfare state evolved? How was the creative adaptation made possible? What kind of new forms of organizations, services, and ideas are currently emerging, and how? This book addresses these questions by examining both historical and contemporary cases and aims to shed new light on the current potential of the Nordic welfare state and provide clues to understanding its adaptive capacity.

We believe it is appropriate that this book focuses primarily on Finland to identify the creative adaptive capacity of the Nordic welfare state and socioeconomic system. This is because while Finland, along with Denmark, remains at the top of OECD countries in terms of social outcomes and social expenditure, the Finnish economy suffered the most in the aftermath of the GFC, resulting in the most severe fiscal constraints among the Nordic countries. This implies that the Finnish welfare state has faced the greatest adaptive pressures among the Nordic countries, as the following data show.

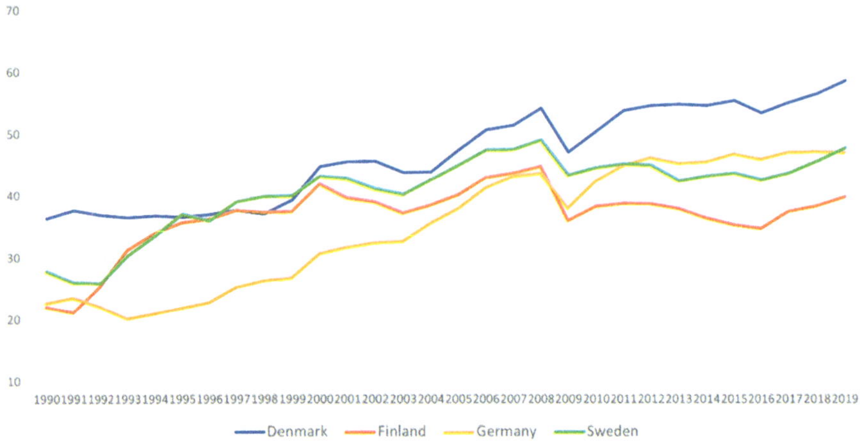

Source: OECD National Accounts at a Glance

Fig. 1.2 Export of goods and services (% of GDP). Source: OECD National Accounts at a Glance

First, in terms of social outcomes, Finland ranked second in income equality and poverty reduction (Table 1.6). Fig. 1.1 shows that public social spending in Finland and Denmark has been the most intensive since the GFC although it plausibly reflect the severe depression. It should be noted that both in terms of social outcomes and spending, Sweden has lagged behind Finland and Denmark in the post-GFC period.

Second, although the economic performances of Finland and Sweden were quite similar in the decade leading up to the GFC (Tables 1.3 and 1.4), Finland's post-GFC economic recovery was slower than that of Sweden and Denmark, as evidenced by the higher unemployment rate in 2014–19 (Table 1.2) and slower economic growth (Table 1.3) and productivity growth (Table 1.4). In addition, while exports in Sweden and Denmark recovered to pre-GFC levels by the end of the 2010s, Finland's exports had not yet recovered (Fig. 1.2). Since the GFC, industrial structural change has stagnated more in Finland than in Sweden (Table 1.5). Overall, due, in part, to the rapid decline of the ICT sector, the economic situation in Finland has been hit harder than that in Sweden since the GFC (Honkapohja, 2015).

Third, the fiscal constraints in Finland after the GFC are considered more severe than those in Sweden and Denmark, which can be explained by stagnation and fiscal austerity. Although government expenditures in all four countries increased sharply (Denmark, Finland, and Germany) or moderately (Sweden) after the GFC, only Finland has not recovered to pre-GFC levels (Fig. 1.3). Only in Finland has the government's primary balance remained negative (Fig. 1.4). Despite the decline since 2016, the increase in Finland's gross government debt since the GFC has been more pronounced than that in Sweden and Denmark (Fig. 1.5). Despite the apparent contradiction with the above data, it should be noted that Finland began to adopt fiscal austerity as one of its main policy responses to the GFC as early as 2011 (Harjuniemi & Ampuja, 2019), which could deepen the recession (Andersen, 2012;

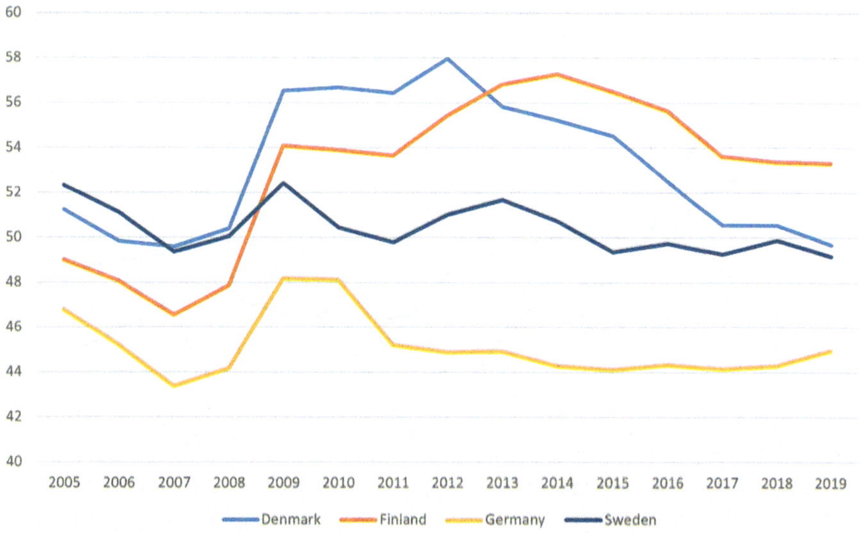

Source: OECD National Accounts at a Glance

Fig. 1.3 Expenditure of general government (% of GDP). Source: OECD National Accounts at a Glance

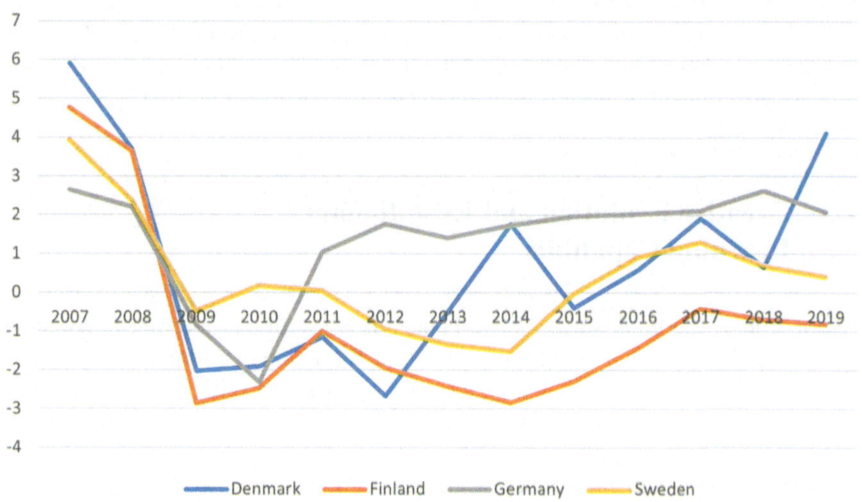

Source: OECD Government at a Glance

Fig. 1.4 Government primary balance. Source: OECD Government at a Glance

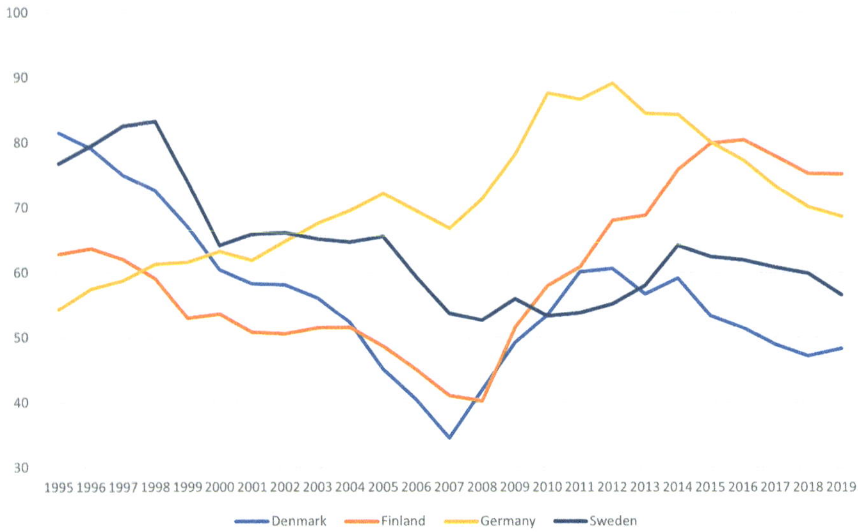

Source: OECD National Accounts at a Glance

Fig. 1.5 Gross debt of general government (% of GDP). Source: OECD National Accounts at a Glance

Stockhammer et al., 2019),[2] resulting in sluggish GDP growth and lower tax revenues. This means that the general government expenditure-to-GDP ratio (Fig. 1.3) and the general government debt-to-GDP ratio (Fig. 1.5) are likely to rise, while the primary government balance is unlikely to become positive (Fig. 1.4).

1.3 Creative Evolution and Evolutionary Learning Capability

As the title of the book suggests, we believe it is useful and relevant to adopt an evolutionary perspective to understand the transformation of complex entities such as the Finnish welfare state, where the authors focus on critical aspects in each chapter. Interpreting socioeconomic change through an evolutionary lens can be justified because the "subtle relationship between the complexity of our problems and our own skills and capabilities" (Shiozawa, 2019, p. 3) makes it implausible to view change solely as the result of rational calculation. In other words, because

[2] There is well-established evidence that the fiscal multiplier, which measures the impact of public spending on national income, is larger during recessions than at other times (Blanchard & Leigh, 2014; Delong & Summers, 2012; Gechert & Rannenberg, 2018). In line with this evidence, Blyth (2013) also shows several important cases in which austerity measures during a recession exacerbated the recession.

three of our abilities—namely, perception, judgment, and execution—are limited (Shiozawa, 2019, pp. 19–20),[3] it is extremely difficult to precisely define problems, calculate optimal solutions, and act accordingly. Consequently, it is often irrelevant to view changes as the result of rational calculations. Instead, changes should be seen as evolutionary processes.

Basically adopting Darwin's theory of evolution by natural selection,[4] most evolutionary theories in social sciences have explained change through the combination of the following three mechanisms (Shiozawa, 2019): (1) *Retention*: Like genes in biological entities, there are artifacts ("replicators") in both tangible and intangible forms that retain basic information and are subject to evolutionary change. (2) *Mutation*: Replicators mutate in an adaptive, non-optimizing manner. (3) *Selection*: Among the diverse sets of mutated replicators, only the better-adapted replicators are retained, according to certain criteria. Specifying the mechanisms of retention, mutation, and selection is expected to explain changes, especially the emergence of well-functioning organizations and social systems, in a *non-functional, non-teleological* way.

It follows that changes that are entirely based on prior rational planning or are the result of rationally planned and optimal adaptations to environmental changes, cannot be characterized as evolution. It goes without saying that in human society, where action is essentially purposeful, mutations are not completely random, as they are in biology. In this regard, it should be noted that we must have a different conception of mutation from the standard biological theory of evolution, which explains evolution exclusively in terms of random variation (Fujimoto, 1999, pp. 279–285; Penrose, 1952).

It should be noted that we adhere to the idea of *universal Darwinism*, which holds that Darwin's theory of evolution is a *generic* theory, i.e., it can explain changes also in areas other than biology (Hodgson & Knudsen, 2010; Metcalfe, 2002). In fact, universal Darwinism has been widely adopted to explain social change in many fields, including economics (Andersen, 1994; Bowles, 2004; Fujimoto, 1999; Hodgson, 1996; Metcalfe, 2002; Nelson & Winter, 1982), political economy (Yagi, 2021), politics (Steinmo, 2010), economic history (Mokyr, 2002), and geography (Boschma & Martin, 2010).

Therefore, how did the *creative evolution* of the Finnish welfare state occur when the term "creative" is used in the same sense as "creative adaptation"? Fujimoto (1999) proposed the concept of *evolutionary learning capability*, defined as "an organization's overall ability to evolve competitive routines even in highly episodic and uncertain situations," which "encompasses making good decisions, learning from mistakes, and grasping the competitive benefits of unintended consequences" (p. 5). Note that here, as in other evolutionary theories of the firm (e.g., Nelson &

[3] It should be noted that "bounded rationality," which means that our ability to calculate is limited (Simon, 1996), is only one of Shiozawa's (2019) three limited abilities, namely judgment.

[4] The concept of evolution does not imply progress. Rather, it is understood here as a neutral logic that explains change. Needless to say, understanding social change from a Darwinian evolutionary perspective does not imply endorsing "social Darwinism."

Winter, 1982), because organizations are understood as consisting of multiple routines, evolutionary learning is *non-routinized* learning to generate new routines.

Applying the concept of evolutionary learning capability, originally defined at the *organizational* level, to the *societal* level is a natural extension. Thus, questions such as how evolutionary learning capability is socially distributed and organized, how it is mobilized and demonstrated, and what it consists of are important to fully understand the creative evolution of the Finnish welfare state. Although this book does not aim to answer these questions directly, it seeks to examine the nature of the evolutionary learning capability of the Finnish welfare state. The historical and contemporary cases of Finland and other comparable countries examined in the following chapters will provide important clues to answering these important questions from different angles by exploring how particular cases of evolution occur.

1.4 The Outline of This Book

The chapters in this book are organized as follows.

Part I, entitled "The Historical Evolution of the Welfare State," consists of three chapters that explain Finland's evolutionary path to a Nordic welfare state. In particular, these chapters emphasize the relevant context of this evolutionary path, including delayed industrialization, pressures from neighboring powers, and other factors that made the evolutionary path unique and distinctive. In addition, all three chapters in Part I underscore the importance of complicated political processes for understanding the historical evolutionary path of complex social systems like the Finnish welfare state.

Chapter 2, "The Making of the Welfare State in Finland," by Pauli Kettunen, provides a detailed political history of the Finnish welfare state and examines how it rapidly transformed from a poor agrarian society into a well-developed welfare state. In particular, he carefully demonstrates how crucial events and periods in Finnish history since independence, namely the Civil War, the Second World War, the post-war high-growth period, and the post-Cold War neoliberal globalization, have significantly shaped the evolutionary path towards a full-fledged welfare state. However, this evolutionary path has been far from straightforward. In fact, as he points out, it took quite a long time for social policies to materialize due to complicated political processes, including severe conflicts and compromises, which often resulted in unique social security systems different from the Swedish one. At the same time, however, the "Nordic welfare state" has served as a frame of reference for the construction of a national identity and institutions in Finland. Although the Finnish welfare state has currently been reformed in response to the emphasis on competitiveness and security issues, the public's support for the welfare state remains strong, as reflected in the popular political argument of "saving the Nordic welfare state," which is used for a wide range of political purposes.

Chapter 3, "Agrarian Party and Kela: Evolutionary Development of Finnish Social Policy" by Yuriko Shibayama, shows that the Centre Party, an agrarian power, was important in building the Finnish welfare state. The construction of welfare states in Scandinavia, represented by Sweden, was led by the Social Democratic Party and was driven by cooperation between the conservative party and agrarian party. However, the driving force behind the construction of the welfare state in Finland was the conflict between the Social Democratic Party and the Agrarian Party, as well as the dominance of the Agrarian Party. The first major social policy reform was the Social Democratic Party's call for the introduction of social insurance for wage earners, but the Agrarian Party rejected this and instead established a national pension for all citizens in 1937. To manage the national pension, Kela (Kansaneläkelaitos) has been established directly under the parliament. Currently, Kela is the main organization that provides basic income security in Finland. This section explains how the Agrarian Party and Kela influenced Finland's social policy through their interactions. In particular, it shows that the Agrarian Party's intention was strongly recognized in the areas of national pensions and health insurance, and that the Social Democrats and Conservatives built complementary systems by avoiding the Agrarian Party and Kela, leading to the formation of Finland's unique and complex system.

Chapter 4, "Family and the Evolutionary Development of the Welfare States: A Comparison of the Discourse on Child and Family Policy in Finland and Japan" by Chino Yabunaga, discusses Finnish and Japanese family policies from the perspective of placing institutions in a broader historical and evolutionary process, with an emphasis on the "context" in which they function, operate, and shape polity choices. The process through which the two countries chose different family policies is examined from an evolutionary perspective, focusing on contingency and adaptation. Although the two countries, located in the East and West, appear to have contrasting cultural norms regarding the family, both countries actually share a similar history of dominant conservative rural values and an emphasis on the maternal role of women. This chapter traces the history of family policies in the two countries and examines when and how they diverged, focusing on the dominant discourses and political choices. During the 1970s, care policies in the two countries began to substantially differ. While in Finland different arguments reached compromised conclusions within the political power structures from the 1970s onwards, in Japan one of the different arguments was reinforced or transformed by the political power structures.

Part II, entitled "Industrial Transformation and the Welfare State," consists of four chapters that shed new light on the conditions and foundations of industrial transformation and innovation in the Nordic welfare states and other comparable countries from different, complementary perspectives.

Chapter 5, "Industrial Transformation, Innovation, and the Enabling Roles of the Nordic Welfare State" by Norio Tokumaru, addresses the important question of how the institutional features of the Nordic model can contribute to industrial restructuring following Nokia's exit from the mobile phone business and the subsequent development of the digital healthcare industry in Oulu, Finland. Because improving productivity and restructuring industries are essential for the economic sustainability of welfare states, this question is important for understanding the economic sustainability of the Nordic welfare states. The author emphasizes two points: First, welfare state institutions and their reform can promote the creation of new industries and innovation by creating new demand for new industries. Second, local governments and intermediary organizations can play active roles as catalysts in stimulating and shaping innovation. These emphases can be contrasted with those in previous studies on the economic significance of the Nordic welfare state models, which have primarily focused on investment in education and training for individuals, highlighting the Nordic model's impact on the supply side of individual and collective capabilities. However, the experience in advanced economies since the 2000s has shown that policies aimed at strengthening the supply side, such as policies to promote skill formation, have not been as effective as expected. In contrast, this chapter focuses on how the institutional features of the Nordic model can affect the demand for these capabilities, shifting the focus to the potential of the demand side to promote industrial structural change and innovation.

Chapter 6, "The Potential of the Co-Creation Approach to Create Innovation to Meet Better the Needs of Communities" by Kazue Haga, highlights that the private sector, beside the conventional actors for handling social challenges (e.g., government), is increasingly involved in solving social problems. However, the complexity of society and the bounded rationality of individual actors make it difficult to believe that social problems can be solved by a single entity. Moreover, the fact that social problems are both ill-defined and embedded in social contexts makes them even more difficult to solve. Social innovation has been proposed as a promising solution for these problems. Participation of stakeholders from the community, in particular, residents there, is considered crucial to developing suitable solutions to challenges in the target communities. Previous research has understood innovation as a product of collective effort, whereas in social innovation, the Living Lab is actively practiced as a methodology for organizing collective effort. This chapter aims to shed light on the possibility of a collective approach to the creation of social innovations that can solve social problems by examining several cases of Living Labs in Japan and Denmark.

Chapter 7, "Understanding the Change of the Finnish Digital Health and Welfare Ecosystems" by Marika Iivari, Minna Pikkarainen, Julius F. Gomes, Jouni Kaartinen, and Parisa Gazerani, based on an empirical study of digital health experts in Finland, explores the concept of digital health through the lens of complex adaptive systems and identifies several key capabilities that are essential for advancing digital health, enabling resilient and adaptive approaches to both the long-term development of healthcare services and the response to abrupt crisis situations. The development of ICT and the availability of relevant data enable the digitalization of healthcare practices and provide new opportunities for the development of digital healthcare industries. Finland has the ambition to be a pioneer in the digitalization of healthcare by reforming processes and digitalizing services and, together with other Nordic countries, has embraced the concept of value-based care, emphasizing the creation of value for citizens mainly through personalized care with the intensive use of data. This can be a source of increased complexity in healthcare delivery, involving multiple stakeholders with different values, and requiring a collaborative ecosystem approach to healthcare delivery. According to their in-depth review of information gathered through interviews with various practitioners, a critical factor was the need for timely access to useful information. At the national level, policymakers need to pay more attention to data-driven decision-making and invest in interoperability between different systems to better utilize future AI-based digital services and the increasing amount of health data. There is also a need to leverage non-medical and heterogeneous data to support better treatments and clinical decision-making. At the organizational level, both healthcare providers and technology companies require leadership to support healthcare professionals and policymakers. They emphasize the need for deeper collaboration between relevant stakeholders from different sectors, which means that an innovative ecosystem-driven approach has been and will continue to be central to advancing digital health in Finland.

Finally, Chap. 8, entitled "Innovation and Social Capital in Nordic Welfare States: The Advantages of Nordic Societies in a Modern Economy" by Mayuko Kitai and Tatsushi Waragai, examines the nature of social capital in Nordic countries and its impact on innovation by considering the varying nature of social capital and the type thereof supporting innovation systems. Innovation is becoming increasingly important in the modern welfare states of knowledge-based economies. According to the authors, social factors, including the informal institutional context (i.e., norms, trust, and routines), play a critical role in the interactive learning processes that are essential for innovation. They utilize the concept of social capital and examine how it relates to innovative outcomes. By classifying countries into four clusters of social capital types and generalized and particularized trust, Kitai and Waragai analyze the effects of each social capital category on innovation. Their findings show that social capital, characterized by high generalized trust and high particularized trust, has the greatest positive effect on innovation. Notably, another important finding is that the Nordic countries have a hybrid type of social capital with high levels of both generalized and particularized trust. Overall, these results confirm that the functioning of innovation systems in the Nordic countries is underpinned by the hybrid type of social capital, while simultaneously providing new evidence that each type of social capital has a significantly different effect on innovative performance.

In short, all four chapters in Part II emphasize the importance of collaboration and ecosystems for industrial transformation and innovation, in contrast to the conventional, individualistic understanding of entrepreneurship. In particular, the uniqueness of Chap. 5 lies in its identification of the institutional conditions (decentralization, catalysts, and the need to eliminate the influence of vested interests) for collaborative relationships to lead to industrial change and innovation, as well as the benefits of collaborative relationships for industrial change. While Chap. 6 shares the emphasis on the collaborative nature of the innovation process with other chapters, this chapter's uniqueness lies in its emphasis on the variability of the collaborative effort for innovation, depending on whether and to what extent deliberately collaborative members are gathered, which may be influenced by the social capital endowment of each society. Chapter 7 is compelling in that it uses a specific example of digital healthcare to illustrate why and how collaboration and an ecosystem approach are important. It is also noteworthy that the authors highlight the importance of the idea behind the Nordic welfare state for innovation, as embodied in value-based care and MyData, for example. Finally, Chap. 8 is theoretically and empirically novel in that it convincingly demonstrates how different types of social capital underlying collaborative, interactive learning make innovation possible. This chapter is also instructive as a complement to the other chapters in that it shows how the Nordic countries can be characterized in terms of social capital.

Part III of the volume, entitled "The Evolution of the Welfare State and New Welfare Governance," discusses the transformation and future of the Finnish welfare state system.

In Chap. 9, "Creative Evolution of Finnish Regional Governance" by Pekka Valkama and Lasse Oulasvirta illustrate the historical development of Finnish regional governance, identifying four distinct phases. Both nationally organized reforms and municipal bottom-up arrangements have enabled regional variations in joint-municipal organizations (JMOs) and inter-municipal collaborative contracts. Through systems of inter-municipal collaboration (IMC), municipalities have been able to avoid some overlapping investments, improve economies of scale, and share risks associated with the ownership of modern service institutions, such as hospitals and educational institutions. Regional governance based on IMC has also jointly pursued the respective policy objectives of individual municipalities, reduced mutual competition, and coordinated local actions. According to Valkama and Oulasvirta, the creative evolution of regional governance in Finland has been unpredictable and sporadic, lacking a long-term vision of how to agree on and define the optimal division of labor between local communities and regions. The ultimate purpose and societal functions of regional public law authorities have been somewhat unstable, while the role of regional public policymaking has developed through contradictions that have sustained fragmentary regional structures. However, the authors also demonstrate that the new wellbeing service counties established in 2023 unified the regional governance of social, health, fire, and rescue services on the Finnish mainland, excluding the city of Helsinki.

In Chap. 10, "The Evolution of Finnish Welfare State and its Structural Reforms of Welfare Provision," Chino Yabunaga also focuses on the local and subnational systems and discusses the reforms of Finnish welfare provision and its system as an evolutionary process. Yabunaga attempts to analyze recent reforms of the local government system mainly from the 1980s and to trace the context of the four new emergent initiatives undertaken by the municipalities and their coalitions as well as top-down reforms. This chapter shows that several advanced cases and attempts have experienced successes and failures in the context of different interest structures, interactions between actors, and at different times, while the local system has intermittently changed to one in which new initiatives are more likely to emerge.

Chapter 11, entitled "Adaptation of Finnish Welfare State to a Post-Industrial Society: Practicing 'The Consensus Model of Democracy' through Formation of Diverse Coalition Governments" by Yuriko Shibayama, explains how the Finnish welfare state has adapted to the post-industrial stage of socioeconomy, focusing on the Finnish political system, particularly its party politics. Finland, based on the basic system of social security established in the 1930s, has been constructing a comprehensive welfare state similar to the ones in its other Nordic neighbors since the 1960s as it transitioned to an industrialized society, and from the 1970s to the 1980s, it has achieved a level similar to that of Nordic countries. Social policy, higher education policy, and economic policy, especially with an emphasis on promoting science and technology that have been developed since the 1960s, have been strongly linked since the 1980s and have strengthened the characteristics of a social investment-based welfare state. These changes were accelerated when parliamentarianism began to function as the extremely strong presidential power ended. Since 1983, stable coalition governments have been in power every 4 years. In Finland, the formation of a majority or even oversized cabinets is common, and no dominant party has been running the government for a long time. Finland has formed a variety of coalition governments while the leading party has changed. The leading party chooses different partners, large and small, depending on the goals of the different governments, including new parties established through new cleavages. It can be said that they are practicing the "consensus democracy" mentioned by Lijphart (1999), which gives them policy flexibility.

In Chap. 12, "The Future(s) of the Welfare State," Aleksi Neuvonen explores the future of the welfare state in the 2030s and 2040s. The primary focus is on the possible directions, tensions, and ethical dilemmas of the welfare states in the wider context of the development of human civilization. This chapter first maps the current well-known tensions that welfare state institutions grapple with. It then advances towards investigating the ethical foundations of the twenty-first century welfare state by examining issues such as growth dependency, the state vs. market dichotomy, and people-centrism. It eventually re-evaluates the claim made after the 1980s onwards by Pekka Kuusi, a great Finnish welfare state theorist, on the urgency to transform the prevailing worldviews held in modern societies to better grasp humans as "children of the Earth" instead of mere "brain creatures." Thus, the article suggests the discovery of a new basis for welfare states for a century characterized by a poly/meta-crisis and the era of the Anthropocene.

In Part III, the first two chapters describe how the institutions of the Finnish welfare state have undergone ad hoc, haphazard, and piecemeal changes rather than integrated development based on a long-term vision. Looking at the individual processes, however, it can be seen that the welfare state has tolerated the diversity of municipalities in the course of reforms, both bottom-up initiatives and top-down institutional changes. While central government has drawn up an overall picture of welfare state service provision, it has left room for individual choices rather than defining local authority responsibilities in detail (initially forced by financial constraints, and since the 1990s intentionally). As a result, local authorities have chosen to avoid the duplication of investment and share risks in their relationships with different actors, even though optimal overall distribution and sharing were not intended. Through trial and error, good practice has also been transferred. In other words, it can be understood that the welfare state and its local governments have adapted and changed in response to the changing environment in Finland, and that the central government has played a facilitating role in the evolutionary process, providing essential direction and encouraging the adaptation efforts of the municipalities. As illustrated in Chap. 11, coalition governments resulting from elections based on proportional representation tolerated diversity because of repeated changes in the government. Membership in the EU has also encouraged the survival of individual regions, rather than a centripetal, powerful, single state (Chaps. 9 and 10). Contrary to the previous three chapters, Chap. 12 lists the factors that will be important to the process of mutation, replication, and selection of the welfare state in the future. As shown in Part III, the evolution of the welfare state to date has been strongly influenced by economic survival and the development of the functions expected of the welfare state. In contrast, Chap. 12 focuses on the ethical foundations. It proposes a redefinition of the fundamental values of the welfare state based on the welfare state as a powerless entity that cannot be deliberately changed through policy design and implementation, but rather as a vulnerable entity that cannot resist overall changes, including those in the global environment, and on altruistic humanity as a social entity.

Appendix

The structural change parameter in Sect. 1.1 was calculated as follows. The value added for each year was calculated by taking the moving average of the value added per industry data obtained from the *OECD STAN Database* for the 3 years before and after the year in question. If the share of value added of industry i at time t is w_i^t, the magnitude of the change in industrial structure in an economy between time t_1 and t_2 can be expressed as $\frac{\sqrt{\sum_{i=1}^{n}\left(w_i^{t_2}-w_i^{t_1}\right)^2}}{T}\times 100$, where $T = t_2 - t_1$ (Yoshikawa & Matsumoto, 2001).

References

Andersen, E. S. (1994). *Evolutionary economics: Post-Schumpeterian contributions*. Pinter Publishers.

Andersen, T. M. (2012). The welfare state and the great recession. *Intereconomics, 47*(4), 206–211.

Andersen, T. M., Holmström, B., Honkapohja, S., Korkman, S., Söderström, H. T., & Vartiainen, J. (2007). *The Nordic model: Embracing globalization and sharing risks*. The Research Institute of the Finnish Economy (ETLA).

Armingeon, K., & Bonoli, G. (2006). *The politics of post-industrial welfare states: Adapting post-war social policies to new social risks*. Routledge.

Barth, E., Moene, K. O., & Willumsen, F. (2014). The Scandinavian model: An interpretation. *Journal of Public Economics, 117*, 60–72.

Bergeaud, A., Cette, G., & Lecat, R. (2016). Productivity trends in advanced countries between 1890 and 2012. *Review of Income and Wealth, 62*(3), 420–444.

Blanchard, O. J., & Leigh, D. (2014). Learning about fiscal multipliers from growth forecast errors. *IMF Economic Review, 62*(2), 179–212.

Blyth, M. (2013). *Austerity: The history of a dangerous idea*. Oxford University Press.

Bonoli, G., & Natali, D. (2012). *The politics of the new welfare state*. Oxford University Press.

Boschma, R., & Martin, R. (Eds.). (2010). *The handbook of evolutionary economic geography*. Edward Elgar.

Bowles, S. (2004). *Microeconomics: Behavior, institutions, and evolution*. Princeton University Press.

Collington, R. (2022). Disrupting the welfare state? Digitalisation and the retrenchment of public sector capacity. *New Political Economy, 27*(2), 312–328. https://doi.org/10.1080/13563467.2021.1952559

Crouch, C. (2013). *Making capitalism fit for society*. Polity Press.

Delong, J. B., & Summers, L. H. (2012). Fiscal policy in a depressed economy. *Brookings Papers on Economic Activity, 2012*(1), 233–297.

Erixon, L. (2008). The Swedish third way: An assessment of the performance and validity of the Rehn-Meidner model. *Cambridge Journal of Economics, 32*, 367–393.

Erixon, L. (2018). Progressive supply-side economics: An explanation and update of the Rehn-Meidner model. *Cambridge Journal of Economics, 42*, 653–697.

Esping-Andersen, G. (1990). *The three worlds of welfare capitalism*. Princeton University Press.

European Commission. (2023). *European innovation scoreboard*. European Commission Directorate-General for Research and Innovation.

Fujimoto, T. (1999). *The evolution of a manufacturing system at Toyota*. Oxford University Press.

Gechert, S., & Rannenberg, A. (2018). Which fiscal multipliers are regime-dependent? A meta-regression analysis. *Journal of Economic Surveys, 32*(4), 1160–1182.

Greve, B. (2007). What characterise the Nordic welfare state model. *Journal of Social Sciences, 3*(2), 43–51.

Greve, B. (2020). *Austerity, retrenchment and the welfare state: Truth or fiction?* Edward Elgar.

Harjuniemi, T., & Ampuja, M. (2019). Established ideas from established institutions: Austerity and structural reforms in the Finnish economic policy debate. *Critical Policy Studies, 13*(4), 451–469.

Hemerijck, A. (2013). *Changing welfare states*. Oxford University Press.

Hemerijck, A. (2017). *The uses of social investment*. Oxford University Press.

Hodgson, G. M. (1996). *Economics and evolution: Bringing life back into economics*. University of Michigan Press.

Hodgson, G. M., & Knudsen, T. (2010). *Darwin's conjecture: The search for general principles of social and economic evolution*. The University of Chicago Press.

Honkapohja, S. (2015). Challenges to the Nordic model: The case of Finland. In T. M. Andersen, U. M. Bergman, & S. E. H. Jensen (Eds.), *Reform capacity and macroeconomic performance in the Nordic countries*. Oxford University Press.

Iacono, R. (2018). The Nordic model of economic development and welfare: Recent developments and future prospects. *Intereconomics, 53*, 185–190.

Karsbergen, K., Vis, B., & Hemerijck, A. (2014). The great recession and welfare state reform: Is retrenchment really the only game left in town? *Social Policy and Administration, 48*(7), 883–904.

Katzenstein, P. J. (1985). *Small states in world markets: Industrial policy in Europe*. Cornell University Press.

Kristensen, P. H., & Lilja, K. (Eds.). (2011). *Nordic capitalisms and globalisation: New forms of economic organization and welfare institutions*. Oxford University Press.

Lijphart, A. (1999). *Patterns of democracy: Government forms and performance in thirty-six countries*. Yale University Press.

Maliranta, M., Rouvinen, P., & Ylä-Anttila, P. (2010). Finland's path to the global productivity frontier through creative destruction. *International Productivity Monitor, 20*, 68–84.

Marglin, S. A., & Schor, J. B. (Eds.). (1990). *The golden age of capitalism: Reinterpreting the postwar experience*. Oxford University Press.
Metcalfe, J. S. (2002). *Evolutionary economics and creative destruction*. Routledge.
Miettinen, R. (2012). *Innovation, human capabilities, and democracy: Towards an enabling welfare state*. Oxford University Press.
Mokyr, J. (2002). *The gifts of Athena: Historical origins of the knowledge economy*. Princeton University Press.
Morel, N., Palier, B., & Palme, J. (Eds.). (2012). *Towards a social investment welfare state? Ideas, policies and challenges*. Polity Press.
Nelson, R. R., & Winter, S. G. (1982). *An evolutionary theory of economic change*. The Belknap Press of Harvard University Press.
Ornston, D. (2012). *When small states make big leaps: Institutional innovation and high-tech competition in Western Europe*. Cornell University Press.
Penrose, E. T. (1952). Biological analogies in the theory of the firm. *American Economic Review, 42*(5), 804–819.
Perraton, J. (2018). Social corporatism and capital accumulation: The fate of the Nordic model. *Intereconomics, 53*, 196–201.
Pierson, P. (1994). *Dismantling the welfare state? Reagan, Thatcher and the politics of retrenchment*. Cambridge University Press.
Pierson, P. (1996). The new politics of the welfare state. *World Politics, 48*(2), 143–179.
Pierson, P. (2001). Coping with permanent austerity: Welfare state restructuring in affluent democracies. In P. Pierson (Ed.), *The new politics of the welfare state*. Oxford University Press.
Polanyi, K. (1944). *The great transformation: The political and economic origins of our time*. Beacon Press.
Shiozawa, Y. (2019). Microfoundations of evolutionary economics. In Y. Shiozawa, M. Morioka, & K. Taniguchi (Eds.), *Microfoundations of evolutionary economics*. Springer.
Simon, H. (1996). *The sciences of the artificial* (3rd ed.). The MIT Press.
Steinmo, S. (2010). *The evolution of modern states: Sweden, Japan, and the United States*. Cambridge University Press.
Stockhammer, E., Qazizada, W., & Gechert, S. (2019). Demand effects of fiscal policy since 2008. *Review of Keynesian Economics, 7*(1), 57–74.
Taylor-Gooby, P. (Ed.). (2004). *New risks, new welfare: The transformation of the European welfare state*. Oxford University Press.
Thelen, K. (2021). Transitions to the knowledge economy in Germany, Sweden, and The Netherlands. In A. Hassel & B. Palier (Eds.), *Growth and welfare in advanced capitalist economies: How have growth regime evolved?* Oxford University Press.
Yagi, K. (Ed.). (2021). *From reproduction to evolutionary governance: Toward an evolutionary political economy.* Springer.
Yoshikawa, H., & Matsumoto, K. (2001). Changes of industrial structure and economic growth [In Japanese]. *Financial Review, 58*, 121–138.

Part I
The Historical Evolution of the Welfare State

Chapter 2
The Making of the Welfare State in Finland

Pauli Kettunen

Abstract With good reason, the success stories of Europe's northern periphery commonly point out the active role and strong legitimacy of the nation-state in the making of the so-called Nordic model. Coping with the tension between the international economy and the national society was the nexus of the politics shaping the nation-state as a welfare state. This also applies to the discourse on Finland's path from poverty to welfare. However, Finland was, even in intra-Nordic comparison, a latecomer in urbanization and industrialization as well as in social policies and industrial relations. Structural changes began late but were very rapid. Finland appears to be a good case not only for comparative historical analysis but also for recognizing comparative and historical reflexivity as an integral dimension of national politics. This chapter underscores the importance of the Nordic framework of international comparison, communication, cooperation, and competition for the formation of the welfare state in Finland. Since the 1990s, welfare policies have been revised through reinforced emphases on competitiveness and security. However, in present-day Finland, political rhetoric reflects the strong support of the welfare state among ordinary people. "Rescuing the Nordic welfare state" is a popular argument for a wide range of policy objectives, including the cuttings of social policy spending.

Keywords Welfare state · Nordic · Periphery · Conflicts · Consensus · Universalism · Income security

P. Kettunen (✉)
University of Helsinki, Helsinki, Finland
e-mail: pauli.kettunen@helsinki.fi

N. Tokumaru et al. (eds.), *Creative Co-evolution of the Economies and Welfare States in the Nordic Countries*, Evolutionary Economics and Social Complexity Science 32, https://doi.org/10.1007/978-981-97-8569-8_2

2.1 Introduction

"There is no automatic connection between growth and the lack or elimination of absolute poverty," the German development researcher Dieter Senghaas concluded in the early 1980s. What was required was a combination of world market integration and an internally consolidated national economy. This was most successfully demonstrated by "the Scandinavian development path," especially "Finland's remarkable development" between the late nineteenth century and the 1980s. A constitutive factor was the formation of national political, economic, and cultural identity as well as "considerable political control over domestic and external economic processes, in order to prevent export growth from making society more oligarchic and producing a sort of rentier capitalism" (Senghaas, 1985, pp. 71–94).

The success stories of Europe's northern periphery, such as the one told by Senghaas, commonly point out the active role and strong legitimacy of the nation-state in the making of the so-called Nordic model. With good reason, this also appears in the discourse on Finland's path from poverty to welfare (Ojala et al., 2006). However, Finland is rarely seen as a typical example of a Nordic pattern of change and reform. While all five Nordic nation-states—Denmark, Finland, Iceland, Norway, and Sweden—are different forms of "a model with five exceptions" (Christiansen & Åmark, 2006), Finland appears to be an especially exceptional one.

The Finnish specificities most often referred to in Nordic welfare state histories include, firstly, that Finland was, even in intra-Nordic comparison, a latecomer in urbanization and industrialization as well as in social policies and industrial relations (Christiansen & Markkola, 2006). Historians have emphasized that structural changes began late but happened swiftly (Koponen & Saaritsa, 2019). Secondly, those labeling the Nordic welfare state as a social democratic project have had reservations concerning Finland and Iceland, recognizing that the social democracy in these countries never achieved such a political hegemony as it did especially in Sweden and Norway (Castles, 1979; Christiansen & Markkola, 2006). A third specific aspect of the Finnish case is the role played by internal and external conflicts—including the Civil War of 1918 and the two wars with the Soviet Union during World War II—in the shaping of national experiences, practices, memories, and narratives (Kettunen, 2018).

For a study trying to avoid the trap of exceptionalism, the case of Finland might inspire the development of a comparative perspective. On the one hand, all Nordic countries, including Finland, share institutional and ideational features with other small Western European states that have been highly dependent on world markets and exposed to crises and conjunctures (Katzenstein, 1985). On the other hand, many Finnish specificities are associated with the country being one of the nations that achieved sovereignty through the collapse or transformation of the multinational Eastern European empires at the end or in the aftermath of World War I (Alapuro, 1988).

However, Finland is a good case not only for problematizing the frames of reference employed in comparative historical analysis but also for recognizing the importance of comparison as an element of the activities that created the welfare state. Not only researchers but also the actors under scrutiny have made comparisons. Comparing "us" and others and relating "our" experiences to our expectations—that is, comparative and historical reflexivity—are constitutive aspects of social action. "Comparative imagination" (Fredrickson, 2000; Sluga, 2004) played an integral role in the building of nations as "imagined communities" (Anderson, 1983). In the nineteenth century, the agency of a nation was incorporated into the modern view of history as development and progress. While having an own unique history was a core element of being a nation, nations in general were conceived of as the agents of world history. Connected by their economic, cultural, and political rivalries and interdependencies, nations lied were in different stages of development. This spatialized and temporalized view of world history and world order became an active part of nation building and the making of the welfare state, most notably when it was associated with a "peripheral" and "latecomer" self-image, as it clearly was in Finland (Kettunen, 2011).

Coping with the tension between the international economy and the national society was crucial in the politics shaping the nation-state as a welfare state. Comparative and historical reflexivity was an integral dimension of this politics. In what follows, the historical formation of the Finnish welfare state is examined from this angle. This chapter highlights the importance of the Nordic framework in the making of Finland as a nation-state and a welfare state. This framework has been used for international comparison, communication, competition, and cooperation in various fields of social knowledge and for constructing a national identity and national institutions.[1]

2.2 The Peripheral Gaze Towards the Centers of Modernization

Sweden lost its Eastern provinces in the Russo-Swedish War of 1808–1809, which was linked with the Napoleonic Wars; they were reshaped as the Grand Duchy of Finland under the Russian Empire. In the nineteenth century, the Grand Duchy developed into an autonomous nation-state. In the borderlands of the Russian Empire, old Swedish legal and religious (Lutheran) institutions and traditions persisted, utilized by and intertwined with the new Finnish nationalism that was long compatible with the Russian imperial interest of promoting the separation of Finland from Sweden.

In the loyal Grand Duchy of Finland, the old Swedish four-Estate Diet (composed of nobility, clergy, burghers, farmers) was re-introduced in 1863, the year of the Polish uprising against the Russian Empire that led Poland to lose its autonomy.

[1] The chapter draws heavily on my earlier works, especially Kettunen (2001, 2006a, 2011, and 2018).

Space for political debate and civic organization opened up in the 1860s. "The people" emerged in the debates of educated elites as a target for education and "national awakening" and as the source of political legitimacy. Conflicts tended to be shaped as struggles for the right way and the privilege to speak in the name of "the people." This was evident in the controversies between the so-called Fennomans and the so-called Liberals from the 1860s onwards concerning the role of language, culture, and constitution in the making of the nation; it was also characteristic of later political conflicts concerning the right ways to defend Finland's autonomy and to handle social class divisions (Alapuro, 1988; Klinge, 1993; Pulkkinen, 1999).

The state was the central agent in the integration of Finland in expanding industrial capitalism as it was in other Nordic countries, too. The interest of the bureaucracy in increasing the revenue of the state motivated market-promoting reforms, and the political and economic elites adopted a state-centered image of a national economy that, since the 1860s, had its own currency, customs, and state railways. Economic reforms in the 1860s and 1870s, removing mercantilist privileges and regulations, created preconditions for market integration through commercial agriculture and the rise of the wood processing industry.

The reforms also gradually induced the principle of a free labor market. Accordingly, the *Bill of Poor Relief* was revised in 1879 in accordance with the liberalist work-discipline spirit of the *English Poor Law* of 1834, imported to Finland via the *Swedish Bill of Poor Relief* that had been revised a few years earlier (Satka, 1995, pp. 19–27). Poor relief as well as sick care was included in the tasks of municipalities that in 1865 were separated from the parishes of the Lutheran church. However, at the time, Finland was a poor rural country in which extreme natural conditions imposed major economic constraints. The last nation-wide famine in 1866–1868, and associated diseases killed approximately 150,000 people, about 8% of the population (Häkkinen & Forsberg, 2015).

From the second half of the nineteenth century onwards, international comparisons, oriented towards modernization as "the horizon of expectation" (Koselleck, 1979), became integral to the way the educated elites analyzed society and defined socio-political tasks. It was considered important to learn from both the solutions and mistakes of these countries so as to be able to exploit "the advantages of backwardness" (Gerschenkron, 1962, pp. 356–363). It was a question not only of imitating the "more civilized" countries but also deliberately attempting to anticipate social problems by taking on board experiences from them, above all from Germany, to a somewhat lesser extent from Britain and, in matters relating to labor efficiency, the United States. One may characterize this mode of thought and action as the avant-gardism of the intellectual elite of a peripheral country. For this pattern of thinking, the outside world provided a framework of external preconditions and constraints, hopes and threats, impulses but also alarming ideas, models but also unpleasant examples, and points of reference but also limits as to what was possible.

A good example is a series of articles which appeared in 1874 and which placed "the labor question" on the Finnish political agenda. They were written by Yrjö Koskinen (Georg Zachris Forsman), one of the foremost leaders of the "Fennoman" faction of the Finnish nationalist movement. Koskinen argued that efforts should be made to forestall threats to social stability by examining Finnish conditions "from a European perspective," i.e., by trying to learn from what was happening in those countries that were more highly developed than Finland. Koskinen's articles also showed that the threat, socialism, and economic system that provided a breeding ground for socialism through its inherent conflicts between capital and labor were perceived as international phenomena (Kettunen, 2006a, pp. 40–42).

Many ideas and impulses were transferred to Finland via Sweden, but it was only in the 1930s and especially after World War II that Sweden was seen as representing the forefront of modernization. Nevertheless, contact with Sweden and the established forms of intra-Nordic communication in different fields of social knowledge since the late nineteenth century made "Nordic" embody an active, future-oriented peripheral perspective towards the varying centers of modernity.

Representatives of all groups with professional knowledge or aspirations to professional status travelled abroad in the late nineteenth and early twentieth centuries with the support of the Finnish government and their professional organizations. In this regard, the close connection between professionalization and the consolidation of the Finnish nation-state was of great importance (Hietala, 1987, 1992). The *national* mission to which these professional groups were dedicated was to acquire, through their *international* contacts, *transnational* (e.g., technical, medical, hygienic, socio-political) knowledge to be in a position to identify—on the basis of a comparative perspective—opportunities for applying this knowledge in a domestic context.

Such a mode of action and thought led to contradictory tendencies. Political rhetoric sometimes stressed Finland's backwardness in the same breath as there was a strong tendency to describe current conditions as a projection of anticipated modernization, and in this way to exaggerate the existing level and speed of the country's modernization. A long period often elapsed from defining a social problem and its solution with the help of imported ideas to the practical application of these definitions (Kalela, 1989).

However, as early as the 1880s and 1890s—when the far-from-democratic system of the Estates still operated and there was no proper labor movement—two in principle important acts were adopted: the *Act on the Protection of Industrial Workers* (1889), which established the institution of factory inspection, and the *Workers' Compensation Act* (1895). Finland was not a laggard when it came to the statutory regulation of industrial work; indeed, it was not even a latecomer among the Nordic countries. Thus, for example, the adoption of a special female factory inspectorate was launched in Finland in 1903, 10 years earlier than in Sweden (Kettunen, 1994, pp. 32–91).

At the turn of the twentieth century, the consolidation of Finland as an autonomous political, economic, and cultural unit openly collided with the reinforced Russian effort to promote stronger administrative unity of the Empire. However, imperial integration policies temporarily lost much of their force as the Empire was weakened by its defeats in the Russo-Japanese War of 1904–1905. In connection with revolutionary turmoil in Russia, a breakthrough of mass politics and the labor movement took place in Finland. After the General Strike of 1905, representation through the Estates was suddenly replaced by the most democratic representative system in Europe. Although restricted by the re-established authority of the Emperor, after 1906, Finland had a political system based on a universal franchise that included women (Jussila, 1999, pp. 79–91).

National integration with its economic, political, and cultural dimensions (Alapuro, 1988, pp. 92–110) greatly contributed to the development of class conflicts. The nation, as an imagined community, provided socially subordinated groups with criteria for the critique of prevailing circumstances and with a frame of reference in which they could politically interpret and generalize their local experiences of injustice. In one of the most rural countries in Europe, one of the largest (in relative terms) labor movements emerged by succeeding to create an alliance between urban workers and rural landless workers and tenant peasants.

The discourse of the "social question" included several "questions": a "labor question," a "tenant question," and a "landless population question." Controversies between the Socialists and the bourgeois parties were evident, yet social policy reforms were—in varying ways and with divergent intentions—included in the programs of all parties. Laws concerning labor protection, the regulation of labor relations, and unemployment funds were legislated by Parliament (*Eduskunta*) before World War I. However, very few of these policies were actually implemented as the Parliament's legislative power was restricted by the authority of the Russian Emperor, who frequently refused to confirm acts.

2.3 The Civil War and the Strategies of National Integration

Finland did not directly become a battlefield of World War I, yet through the connection with Russia, the war greatly affected the economy, society, and the state. It was experienced as the extended presence of Russian military units; restrictions on civic activities by martial law; the reorganization of industrial production to serve the needs of Russian warfare; large fortification works and associated labor mobility; and vast unemployment after the end of these works. Inflation accelerated, and finally, there were food shortages. The declaration of Finland's independence in December 1917 and the Civil War from January to May of 1918 took place in connection with World War I and the Russian revolution (Alapuro, 1988; Upton, 1980).

After Russia's February revolution in 1917, two major political questions emerged. One was the question of what body would assume supreme authority after the Emperor ceased to rule, and the other concerned the organization of the coercive power of internal order and security after the replacement of a police force that had been largely "Russified" in previous years (Alapuro, 1988). Closely linked with different phases of the Russian revolution, these two unresolved questions gave impetus to mass mobilization and conflicts, resulting in a confrontation between two armed political forces that emerged in a weakly coordinated fashion on the basis of the earlier established class-based political divide.

After the October revolution, the achievement of full national sovereignty became an urgent issue for all Finnish parties. For the Social Democrats, a decisive factor was that the Bolsheviks, now in power, had been the only party in Russia that had declared willingness to approve Finland's independence, whereas, among the bourgeois groups, the fear of Socialist revolution urged for separation from Russia. In December 1917, Finland was declared independent and the Bolshevik government recognized this independence. This did not, however, prevent the escalation of political confrontation into a full-scale Civil War at the end of January 1918, with the left forming the Red Government and assuming revolutionary power.

The Red Guards, a poorly trained army with hardly any military expertise, received arms from Russia and were assisted by Russian soldiers, yet the withdrawal of Russian troops from Finland continued and the peace treaty between Soviet Russia and Germany in March 1918 further diminished this source of support. The White Government in turn received support from Germany, which sent to Finland a first-rate military unit, the Baltic Division, which played a significant role in the last phase of the war. On May 16, 1918, a victory parade of the White Army marched through the city of Helsinki. Among the 38,000 casualties of the Civil War, 75% were on the Red side.

Despite the counter-revolutionary outcome of the Civil War, Finland was, by the constitution of 1919, established as a parliamentary republic. Again, this solution had its antecedents in international transformations. The alliance of the White winners with the German Empire lost its basis when Germany not only lost World War I, but the Empire itself was also dissolved through revolution. In Finland, the parliamentary form of democracy persisted throughout the 1920s and 1930s, even though it was threatened and limited by right-wing pressure, especially in the early 1930s. The persistence of democratic forms of government made Finland exceptional among the new nation-states created through the collapse of multi-ethnic empires at the end of World War I. Any explanation of this exceptionality must recognize that Nordic political traditions had played a crucial role in Finnish nation-building.

The outcomes and memories of the Civil War became an integral part of social, political, and cultural structures. To the White winners, the free land-owning peasant symbolized the White army as the antithesis of the harmful Red alliance between urban workers and the rural landless population. A free independent peasantry constituted the ideological center around which "social peace" had to be "rebuilt" and defended against the threats associated with the collectivism of wage workers (Kettunen, 1986, Ch. 6). Based on previous plans, land reforms were carried out rapidly after the Civil War. These reforms made tenants into land-owning, small-scale farmers and facilitated the colonization of the landless rural proletariat. The mode of thought and action according to which social peace should be rooted in political democracy and an independent freeholder peasantry as the core of the nation was especially characteristic of the Agrarian Party, which in the 1920s gained a powerful position in the political system.

However, efforts to foster national reconciliation after the Civil War also included legislative reforms concerning industrial working life. Together with the Social Democratic Party that was reorientated under the leadership of reformist socialists, politicians and civil servants representing social liberal traditions took up earlier plans of regulating individual employment contracts and collective interest conflicts. Inspiration was taken from the International Labour Organization (ILO), founded in 1919 as an autonomous part of the League of Nations, and from the established Nordic social policy cooperation (Kettunen, 2013; Petersen, 2006).

The act of establishing an 8-h workday was an achievement of the labor movement in the revolutionary year of 1917, and even though employers managed to postpone its implementation, the norm was widely in practice by the start of the 1920s. In the early 1920s, the Parliament passed acts on employment contracts, collective agreements, and the mediation and arbitration of industrial conflicts. These reforms were meant to facilitate a shift towards the comprehensive regulation of labor relations by collective agreements between trade unions and employers. Nevertheless, this vision was not realized prior to World War II, as employers—especially in the wood processing and textile industries and other manufacturing sectors—successfully adhered to a policy rejecting collective agreements while utilizing repressive, ideological and paternalist company welfare means against the influence of trade unions. The ideology that made "the will to work" of the independent farmer the foundation of social peace provided ideological legitimization for the policies of industrial employers (Kettunen, 1990).

Labor law reforms were not costly. A much more expensive social reform—also urged for by the integrative conclusions drawn from the Civil War—was compulsory education. The act was passed in 1922 and increased the responsibilities of municipalities, in which decision-making had been democratized by the legislative reform of 1917. The new *Bill for Poor Relief* of 1922 included more modest changes in municipal practices. Taxation was reformed in the early 1920s at the state and municipality levels, and the state level taxation bill of 1920 established the progressive taxation of income (Lindberg, 1934; Linnakangas, 2015).

Discussion on and planning of social insurance had begun in the 1880s, but before the 1920s, only workers' accident insurance had been introduced (1895) and extended (1917). The first act regulating and facilitating voluntary funds was passed in 1897, with a focus on sickness. In 1917, an act permitting voluntary unemployment funds established by trade unions was passed, the origin of the so-called Ghent system in Finland. In post-Civil War debates on options to extend social insurance, the relative priority of sickness insurance and old-age insurance became an issue of dispute. While the sickness insurance of wage workers was the first priority of the Social Democrats, the Agrarian Party disliked social benefits that were targeted only at wage workers and put old-age and disability insurance before sickness insurance. After much debate, the Old-age and Disability Insurance Scheme was legislated in 1937 after compromises between the coalition partners of the new government: the Social Democrats and the Agrarian Party. An act on sickness insurance was not enacted until 1963 (Kettunen, 2001).

After the abortive revolution, the Finnish labor movement was divided between Social Democrats and Communists. The Communist Party was illegal until 1944 and its leaders, the former leaders of the Red Government of 1918, lived in exile in the Soviet Union. Most were killed in Stalin's purges in the late 1930s. In the 1920s,

Communists and their sympathizers had, nevertheless, opportunities to act in public labor organizations, most notably in the trade union movement in which they had the leading position in the 1920s, and even in the Parliament. In 1930, those categorized as Communists were excluded from public political life. In terms of electoral support, the Social Democratic Party was still the largest political party in Finland in the 1920s and 1930s. However, in different ways, both major wings of the labor movement were preconditioned by the post-Civil War regime, which did not provide a favorable context for comprehensive political projects that would include less than the achievement of a socialist society but more than single piecemeal social policy reforms.

The Social Democrats could not attain the leading position in defining the political agenda in the manner that occurred in Denmark, Sweden, and Norway in the 1930s. This remained true after World War II. The Social Democrats faced the Communists as their fierce rivals in the labor movement after the Civil War and still more after the end of the Finnish-Soviet war in 1944 and the rise of Communism from illegality to a major political force. The Agrarian Party (from 1965 onward, it was known as the Center Party) played an influential role in the political system and in social policies after World War II as an opponent and coalition partner of working-class parties. Agricultural policies were closely connected with social policies; these two kinds of policies partially represented competing views on the problems of social order. Until the 1960s, the power of cultural conservatism still reflected the heritage of the counter-revolutionary White victory of 1918, a continuity that was far from totally broken by the post-World War II political shift.

2.4 Nordic Democracy

Reflecting the class structures and drawing on the experiences of the Great Depression and the expansion of fascism in Europe, in the 1930s, politics in Nordic countries were reoriented by the force of new class compromises. These included political coalitions of Social Democrats and agrarian parties and—true, in Finland only after World War II—the consolidation of the practice of collective negotiations and agreements concerning industrial labor markets. The compromises implied a shared confidence in a positive-sum game between conflicting interests and were supported by theoretical arguments for the possibility of virtuous circles between the objectives of economic progress, social security, and broadening democracy within a national society.

While the compromises indicated an ideational change, they were related to the old international discourse on the tension between the international economy and national society (Kettunen, 2006a). They deviated from the justifications of capitalism, according to which a capitalist economy would produce market-based and company-level solutions to the social problems it had caused. The compromises also deviated from the Marxist assumption that capitalism would generate the force (i.e., the revolutionary working class) that would overthrow it. Other arguments stemming from the nineteenth-century discourse on the "social question" were put into practice in the Nordic class compromises (Kettunen, 2006a).

According to an old argument, social policies were needed to diminish the threat of class conflicts caused by the international capitalist economy. Notwithstanding, the feasibility of reforms was questioned by claiming that they would weaken the nation's economic competitiveness. This view, in turn, faced counter-arguments. One of them was advocating for international social norms that would be binding for all competing countries and firms. Another way of solving the tension between national society and the international capitalist economy appeared at an early stage in the discourse. It claimed that national social policies would in fact support the success of the national economy by improving the quality and productivity of labor power and by increasing purchasing power. This argument for social policies played an important role in the 1930s Nordic class compromises and the associated reorientation of economic policies.

In Finland, the Great Depression did not result in the adoption of new contracyclical economic policy views as it did in Sweden, Denmark, and Norway. This is an obvious difference regardless of the fact that in these countries (even in Sweden), the practical significance of the "active crisis policy" (Möller, 1938)—including the "new employment policy"—was limited (Gustafsson, 1993). The coalition of the Social Democrats and the Agrarian Party in Finland after 1937 was not an outcome of conclusions drawn from the Great Depression to the same degree as the corresponding earlier solutions in other Nordic countries. Nor did the Finnish political coalition prove to be a similar step for the Social Democratic Party to attain a position of dominant political power although its electoral support in the late 1930s almost reached the "Scandinavian" level. One element of the Nordic class compromises was strikingly absent in Finland in the 1930s as Finnish employers (especially in the manufacturing sector) were still able to maintain a policy of opposing collective agreements with trade unions.

In addition to the class compromises and the new confidence in a positive-sum game, an orientation called "social rationalization" or "social engineering" is often referred to as another Nordic novelty of the 1930s (Andersson, 2006; Hirdman, 1997). To the extent that this orientation appeared in Finland, it was less shaped by social democracy than it was in Sweden. In Finland, as elsewhere, the leaders of the labor movement shared a deep trust in the need to rationalize the economy and society (and the possibility of this occurring). However, the role of the labor movement was rather marginal in defining the agenda of rationalization; there were no preconditions for active social democratic visions of social engineering like those of Alva and Gunnar Myrdal in Sweden (cf. Hirdman, 1997).

The Great Depression, accompanied by a wave of right-wing politics, contributed to the rationalized treatment of poverty and the poor in the spirit of preventive criminal law, including a more systematic social categorization and intensified and centralized social control. These were crucial features in the new acts on social care in the mid-1930s concerning children in need of protection, vagrancy, and alcoholics as well as in the related *Act on Sterilization* (1935), which in itself was far from exceptional in the Nordic context (Satka, 1995, pp. 101–104; Mattila, 1999).

"Nordic" was adopted as an attribute of Finnish society, but its meaning was a matter of political struggle, partially concerning the position of the Swedish language in Finland but also stemming from the Civil War. In the White heritage of the Civil War, "Nordic" was associated with the idealized tradition of the free Nordic peasant and local community, whereas for the Social Democrats, "Nordic" in the 1930s began to represent democracy in contrast to authoritarian regimes and also in contrast to the prevailing state of industrial relations in Finland. The concept of Nordic democracy, as it was defined in the cooperation of the Nordic Social Democrats in the 1930s (Kettunen et al., 2015; Kurunmäki, 2011), included a combination of parliamentary political democracy and institutions of collective negotiation and agreement in labor markets. In the 1930s, Finland's social democratic trade union leaders argued that Finland was a Nordic society but did not fulfill the democratic criteria inherent in the term "Nordic" (Kettunen, 2006a, pp. 56–59).

In any case, for the development of the notion of Finland as a Nordic democracy, the coalition of the Social Democratic Party and the Agrarian Party in the late 1930s was important. The Scandinavian-type coalition of "the worker and the farmer" crossed the line between the Red and White heritage of the Civil War and contributed to national integration and the stabilization of parliamentary democracy although the limits of democracy were marked by the illegality of the Communist Party until 1944. The so-called Nordic orientation of Finnish foreign policy in the late 1930s became associated with the concept of "Nordic democracy," a way defining Finland's position in a world of threatened democracy and the increasing danger of war.

2.5 The Legacies of the Second World War

Finnish responses did not meet the demands the Soviet Union made in Autumn 1939 after the Molotov-Ribbentrop Pact and the British and French declarations of war on Germany after its invasion of Poland. With the Soviet invasion of Finland on November 30, 1939, the war later called the Winter War began. The Finnish resistance proved stronger than Stalin had expected, both militarily and in terms of national unity. The Winter War ended with the Moscow Peace Treaty on March 13, 1940. Finland had to cede one tenth of its territory and a naval base to the Soviet Union. The population of the ceded territories, about 410,000 Finnish Karelians, or 12% of the total population of 3.7 million, was relocated throughout the rest of Finland.

After the Winter War, Finnish political decision-making was influenced by further Soviet pressure, fears caused by the Soviet annexation of the Baltic countries, and wishes of recovering what had been lost in the Winter War, partially inspired by visions of right-wing nationalists about a Great Finland that would extend to Eastern Karelia that had never belonged to Finland. Finland gradually moved closer to Germany, and in late June of 1941, Finland was again at war with the Soviet Union.

The war was described as the Continuation War, implying that it was a defensive continuation of the Winter War with a distinctly Finnish-Soviet rationale, yet Finland was now in fact allied with Nazi Germany and contributing to Hitler's Operation Barbarossa. After the German defeat at Stalingrad, Finnish political and military leaders began to seek a way out of the war, and the powerful Soviet offensive in June of 1944 urged for a solution. In September, an armistice treaty was signed between Finland, the Soviet Union, and the United Kingdom, which in 1941 had also declared war on Finland, without subsequent military action. A most urgent obligation of the treaty was expelling German forces from Finland. The so-called Lapland War began in September 1944 and ended in April 1945 when all German troops had withdrawn.

The control commission of the Allies, dominated by the Soviet Union, controlled the implementation of the treaty of armistice until its conditions were confirmed by the Peace Treaty of Paris in 1947. Territorial losses included even somewhat more than those ceded to the Soviet Union after the Winter War. A naval base close to Helsinki was rented to the Soviet Union for 50 years yet it left it during the so-called first détente in 1956. Finland had to pay large war reparations and to put wartime leaders on trial. Prison sentences were handed down to eight political leaders. However, Finland was one of the few countries participating in World War II that was never occupied. In international comparison, the share of civil casualties was low: Among the 95,000 Finns who died in World War II, 2000 were civilians.

The treaty of armistice in 1944 implied political changes. Organizations categorized as fascist or anti-Soviet were banned. The banned organizations included the vast paramilitary Civil Guard that had been built on the basis of the White guards in 1918 and its sister organization, Lotta Svärd, a very important entity mobilizing women in the war effort. The Communist Party ceased to be illegal, and the Finnish People's Democratic League, which the Communists founded together with their left-wing Socialist allies, became a major political force.

Controversial accounts of the experiences and outcomes of the wars were an integral part of politics in post-war Finland (Aunesluoma, 2013; Kettunen, 2018). Instead of celebrating and defending national wartime solidarity, many contemporaries and later commentators (most clearly Communists, yet not only them) identified the end of the Continuation War in 1944 as the beginning of a new democratic era. In the late 1940s, the concept of a "Second Republic" was coined by the advocates of new policies. It did not refer to any constitutional change—the constitution of 1919 remained untouched—but was meant to point to the post-1944 changes of foreign policy, notably in relations with the Soviet Union, and the broadening of democracy, indicated by the legitimacy of Communism, the new strength of trade unions, and the breakthrough of collective agreements in labor relations. This narrative gained widespread popularity, especially in the 1960s and 1970s.

After the collapse of the Soviet Union, the interpretation pointing to the positive value of the post-war political shift and drawing from the lessons of the lost war was pushed into a margin. The post-Cold War neo-patriotic narrative argued in favor of the legitimacy, correctness, and necessity of Finnish wartime decisions. To be sure, this was no new account of the causes, experiences, and consequences of the wars.

This view had existed side by side with the critique of pre-war and wartime politics, expressing that wartime efforts and sacrifices had made it possible to keep the country unoccupied, independent, democratic, Nordic, Western, and neutral, although within the limits of a special relationship to the neighboring Soviet Union. The treaty of armistice had begun a period of injustice and danger, but Finland had survived the Soviet-based threat of Communism.

In the post-war visions of future social policies, the experiences of wartime national unity and the post-war political shift were intertwined. The self-understanding of the academic discipline of "social policy" was developed by individuals active in various wartime social policy initiatives, especially Heikki Waris, the first Professor of Social Policy at the University of Helsinki starting in the late 1940s. He interpreted wartime problems and solutions as the decisive reinforcement of social solidarity and the legitimacy of social policy, realized through the close ties established between voluntary organizations cooperating across political borders and government authorities at the central, provincial, and local levels (Waris, 1973, pp. 24–26; Urponen, 1994, pp. 213–216) as well as through closer interactions between workers and employers.

Waris later praised the so-called January Engagement during the Winter War as the "historically most important" social policy achievement of the wartime period (Waris, 1973, pp. 24–25). It was a short joint declaration in which the peak organizations of trade unions and industrial employers promised to negotiate on common issues in the future. Employers were now ready to soften their views on trade unions as it was important to convince the Nordic and Western public opinion that the target of Soviet aggression was a democratic Nordic country. The practice of mutual negotiations was institutionalized by corporatist representation in wartime economic regulation. After the Continuation War, a time of rapidly increasing power of trade unions, this practice was modified into a national system of collective labor-market agreements, decades later than in Denmark, Sweden, or Norway.

Wartime and immediate post-war experiences influenced ways of defining social problems and solutions. These experiences enhanced the understanding of a modernizing nation-state society in which the objectives of economic rationalization, social integration, and individual self-discipline intersected. The functionalist idea of a national society that could and should be steered and rationalized by means of scientific knowledge was strengthened. New and old elements were mixed in attempts to structure society as a target of knowledge and reform, and in the views of the state as an agent of rational planning.

Concerns about the quantity and quality of the population gained much attention (Bergenheim, 2020). Women's associations played a significant role in initiating and implementing wartime population and family policies. Many of their leading figures advocated for urban middle-class family ideals but with limited success. In a rural society such as Finland, the gendered division of labor never followed male-breadwinner ideals; women (even married women) had also worked in manufacturing (Åmark, 2006; Suoranta, 2009). The role of female labor power nevertheless increased significantly in all sectors of the economy during the course of the war.

This change in the gendered division of labor was only in part a temporary wartime phenomenon.

The quantity and quality of the population came to be an effective argument for rational societal planning. It was interlinked with the issue of how to fit individuals into the functions of society, an urgent problem on the wartime agenda of politics and administration. Classifications of jobs were developed according to the amount of food and calories needed as well as categorizations of people according to their occupational skills and political loyalty. A classification of medical practices was needed in the treatment and employment of disabled soldiers, and the development of psychiatric methods was fostered by the need to somehow recognize the most acute and obvious forms of psychological damage (Kivimäki, 2013).

Wartime experiences inspired institutional novelties such as the Institute of Occupational Health. The decision to set up this institution was made in 1945, and the institute was in full-scale action starting in 1951. It was initiated by young doctors and organized through the cooperation of government authorities, employer organizations, and trade unions. In the activities of the institute, physicians, engineers, and psychologists combined their knowledge. Models came not only from Sweden but also the United States. The American pragmatist orientation inspired an attempt to combine different fields of scientific knowledge in seeking solutions to work-life problems. The Rockefeller Foundation gave significant economic support to the institute (Kettunen, 1994, pp. 378–392).

The ethos of economic and societal rationalization implied a reinforced legitimacy of the state as an economic actor, regulator, redistributor, and provider. In reforms of taxation, responses to immediate wartime needs also implied long-term changes. For example, the collection of income tax was made more effective in 1943 by adopting a pay-as-you-earn system in which the employer withholds the tax.

In Finnish wartime debates, the New Deal, the Beveridge Plan, and Nazi social policies were all referred to as evidence of the state's new active role in the future post-war world. After the war, the definition of national necessities and the content of state intervention became a matter of political controversy. Yet even the Communists shared much of the way of thinking emphasizing economic rationalization as an urgent national task, not least due to their view that reparations to the Soviet Union—a crucial economic necessity for Finland until 1952—were an anti-fascist and democratic national duty. Both the Communists and the Social Democrats interpreted their divergent socialist goals as a transition to true national economic rationality.

Finland did not join the Marshall Plan as the Soviet Union was opposed. However, the Western—and especially, American—connections played an important role, not only in terms of international post-war social aid but also for the ideological and practical flavor they gave to how social problems were defined as targets of science-based knowledge. The American lessons of management became connected with the efforts of science-based societal planning and mixed with conclusions drawn from wartime experiences (Kettunen, 1994, pp. 355–361).

Between the broader society and different individuals, there was a third level that wartime experiences helped define as a target of problem-solving knowledge: a social sphere that could neither be reduced to the norms and institutions of the societal system, nor to the properties of individual people. Sociological studies identified group dynamics as a force with autonomous laws in wartime army units and post-war working life (Kettunen, 1997, pp. 163–165). Most influentially, Väinö Linna's novel *The Unknown Soldier* (1954) told about disobedience and conflicts between official and unofficial norms that seemed to be characteristic of Finnish culture, and especially to have a positive impact on organizational operations. This line of thinking gained new strength in the 1960s in sociological studies and political discourse. By recognizing conflicts and institutionalizing them, the efficiency and cohesion of society could be improved. This assertion achieved considerable influence in the politics of social policy, but it was still connected with the framing idea of the nation-state society as a historical agent that by means of its internal will and capacity responds to external challenges and threats.

2.6 National Necessities

Until the early 1950s, the post-war years were a period of urgent responses to the economic and social problems caused by the war, including care, pensions, and compensation to disabled soldiers and the widows and children of fallen soldiers; the relocation of the population of the territories ceded to the Soviet Union; extensive reparations made to the Soviet Union; and the shortage of food and all resources managed by a comprehensive system of rationing. This was also a time of profound changes and hard struggles regarding Finland's international position and political regime. By the start of the 1950s, Finland's relationship to the Soviet Union was based on recognizing "legitimate" Soviet security interests and expecting that the Soviet Union would not try to push Finland towards the road of a "people's democracy."

In 1945, the Finnish People's Democratic League (i.e., Communists and left-wing Socialists), the Social Democratic Party, and the Agrarian Party—three parties with an almost equal electoral support—formed a coalition government. However, this collaboration, and the Communist participation in government, only lasted until 1948. Within the trade union movement, the Social Democrats won the battle for leadership by the end of the 1940s. Nevertheless, with a solid electoral base of around 20% of the electorate until the 1970s, their strong positions in many trade unions and their support from the Soviet Union, the Communists could be identified as a major challenge of national integration (Rainio-Niemi, 2008). After the parliamentary elections of 1966, resulting in a Socialist majority in parliament, the so-called popular front government was formed, consisting of Social Democrats, Communists, and the Center Party (the former Agrarian Party). The Communists became involved in reformist politics through the coalition governments with the Social Democrats and the Center Party as well as through cooperation with the social democratic majority in the trade union movement. The process resulted in political integration but also in an actual (although not formal) split within the Communist Party between the reformist majority and the minority, preserving its strong loyalty to the Soviet Union and proletarian internationalism.

The post-war return/progress to the old/new normalcy included a more or less shared national strategy of prosperity that was grounded in a high rate of investment and the hope and assumption that sacrifices in the form of more moderate growth of consumption would result in general prosperity in the future (Pohjola, 1994, p. 237). While the reparations required a significant extension of the metal industry (which also played a core role in later trade agreements with the Soviet Union), the wood processing business still preserved its position as the leading (and Western-oriented) export sector and its powerful role in defining the national economic interest.

As late as in 1940, about 60% of the Finnish population earned a living in agriculture and forestry. The expansion of the rural class of small farmers continued to be a major policy of national integration and was applied to the relocation of the Karelian population of the territories ceded to the Soviet Union. The number of small-size farms increased until the late 1950s. The livelihood of smallholders was dependent on the linkage between agriculture and wood processing through farmer-owned forests, and especially the seasonal demand for labor power in logging. As this linkage weakened through technological development and the diminished need for labor power in forestry, the change in socio-economic structures accelerated in the late 1950s and culminated in the 1960s. The Finnish welfare state was built up by efforts to manage this very rapid and profound structural shift and the simultaneous large-scale challenge of the very large baby boom cohorts entering schools and working life. Social policy reforms and the reforms of the education system were an integral part of creating an industrialized, urbanized wage work society.

At the same time, social policies were assessed from the perspective of the limits imposed by economic resources. In the dominant mode of thought, the increase in economic resources was seen to require internal austerity in responding to externally determined national necessities (Pekkarinen & Vartiainen, 1993). The state should play a vital role in ensuring a rational response, yet the social democratic idea of turning the state into an *instrument* of political will and planning never achieved in Finland the kind of hegemonic position as it did, especially, in Sweden. Arguably, in much of Finnish political thought, since the Hegelian philosophical framing of the nineteenth-century nation building, the planning was seen as an *inherent property* of the state itself, and good politics were supposed to put state agency into action. This implies the strong ideal of national consensus.

The ideal of consensus does not equal an absence of conflict. From the late nineteenth century until the late twentieth century, Finland's political history indicates that the demand for national unity may have generated difficult struggles about the right way and privilege of speaking in the name of the whole, "the people," and the national common good (Kettunen, 2004; see also Sect. 2.2). In Nordic comparison, deeper conflict—together with the stronger ideal of consensus—is a unique aspect of Finnish history. In the post-World War II era, the relatively strong support of the Communists was one of the political phenomena that made Finland exceptional in the Nordic context. In industrial relations, until the 1980s, "low-trust" elements were indicated by comparative strike statistics. The parliamentary system was unstable, and short-lived governments were typical until the early 1980s.

Admittedly, those arguing for social policy reforms—including the Fennoman leader Yrjö Koskinen in 1874 and later leaders of the Socialist labor movement—pointed out that such reforms were not just economic burdens but would also generate economic benefits. Nevertheless, a strong notion of novelty was expressed in the message of Pekka Kuusi, as in his book *60-luvun sosiaalipolitiikka* (Social Policy for the 1960s), published in 1961, he presented social policy as a precondition for economic growth (Kuusi, 1961).

Kuusi did not like the term "welfare state" but his book is, with good reason, seen as a design for the Finnish welfare state—"a plan for Finland" as the subtitle of the English edition (1964) states. A social scientist with social democratic sympathies and inspired by Gunnar Myrdal, Kuusi (1964, p. 34) wrote: "Democracy, social equalization, and economic growth seem to be fortunately interrelated in modern society. Social policy seems to spring from free and growth-oriented human nature." Promoting social equality through the redistribution of income, social security, and labor power policy would release people's productive capacities; the vicious cycle between poverty and passivity would be broken and turned into a growth-oriented virtuous circle. Rational planning would cover social policy as part of the broader "societal policy" (*yhteiskuntapolitiikka* in Finnish; *samhällspolitik* in Swedish) from which its objectives were to be derived.

A strong emphasis on national necessities was apparent in Kuusi's argumentation as well. For one thing, the book was motivated by the view that science-based planning was necessary to avoid the increase in social policy costs caused by political competition and uncoordinated compromises (Bergenheim, 2023). Even more, however, necessities were derived from Finland's place in the world of international competition between societies. Finland was situated between two highly dynamic and growth-oriented societies, Sweden and the Soviet Union. The mission Kuusi outlined was a matter of life and death: If we want to survive between these two societies, "we ourselves are doomed to grow" (Kuusi, 1964, p. 59).

Kuusi was not advocating for any third way between the societal systems of Sweden and the Soviet Union. However, his argument was also an example of the Finnish tendency to avoid any explicit association of social policy with the Cold War confrontation. In reality, this confrontation *was* a significant context for social policy considerations. The relatively strong support for Communism, in particular, promoted compliance with social policy reforms as a means of restraining protests and conflicts. Even for the political right, notably the National Coalition Party, an actively anti-social policy stance was not a viable alternative (Smolander, 2000). Nevertheless, while the Swedish Social Democrats had integrated their policy objectives into "democratic welfare politics" and contrasted it with capitalism and Communism (Edling, 2013), in Finland, the dominant orientation was rather to depoliticize social policies. Social policy reforms were often framed as steps along a path of general progress within the limits of economic resources, as necessary responses to emerging problems, or as issues of the pragmatic adjustment of conflicting interests in the name of the common national interest.

In Kuusi's book, the tone is different: The program for Finnish social policies was located in the context of nothing less than world history. However, in this way, it was located in a sphere above the Cold War confrontation between different societal systems, in a sphere of the evolution and growth of modern industrial society, with Sweden and the Soviet Union exemplifying such a society. This corresponded to the so-called convergence theories (Kettunen, 2013, pp. 224–225) and served to legitimize social policy as "our" joint national task.

2.7 Nordic Framework

Being a Nordic country was a taken-for-granted core element of the national self-understanding in Finland, but in the Cold War world, it also implied a proclamation that Finland did not belong to the Eastern Bloc (Majander, 2004). The limits to Nordic cooperation at the level of "high politics," notably security policies, did not hinder the broadening of practical communication between a wide spectrum of public authorities and voluntary organizations, nor between more or less institutionalized cooperation in international government and non-governmental organizations.

In 1952, a "hot" year in the Cold War, the freedom of Nordic citizens to cross intra-Nordic borders without passports was established, and 2 years later, the Nordic countries agreed on a common Nordic labor market. These were unique arrangements achieved between countries with diverging security political solutions: the North Atlantic Treaty Organization (NATO) members Denmark, Norway, and Iceland; and Sweden and Finland representing different variants of neutrality in relation to military alliances. Finland was part of this passport-free labor-market area even before it in 1955 became a member of the Nordic Council, founded in 1952 as a collaborative organization of Nordic parliaments and governments, and before the Soviet Union unexpectedly left the Porkkala military base close to Helsinki in 1956.

The common Nordic labor market was exceptional also as an economic and social arrangement. Common political objectives were formulated in the agreement, including the concerted maintenance of full employment. It promoted mutual recognition of national social security norms and a convergence of social security systems. However, the common labor market was actually turned into everyday reality most dramatically by national failures in the preservation of full employment. Asymmetrical relationships between the Nordic countries were revealed, in particular by those international comparisons of everyday life that led half a million Finns to permanently or temporarily emigrate to Sweden in the post-war decades, especially in the late 1960s, a time of rapid socio-economic and regional structural changes in Finland as well as high demand for labor power in Sweden.

Tough competition in the world market between the Nordic countries has served as an important backdrop for intra-Nordic comparisons and contacts. For example, the competition between the Finnish and Swedish wood processing sectors was a contributory factor in making the Swedish trade union movement willing to help the Finnish trade unions strengthen their influence in determining wage levels in the Finnish industry. The Finnish trade union movement was much weaker than the Swedish one before World War II and indeed right up until the 1970s, and it lacked the social democratic internal cohesion that was such a pronounced characteristic of the Swedish movement (Bergholm, 2012).

While Nordic cooperation included elements of transnational regional integration, it primarily provided a frame of reference for (re)shaping national identities and institutions. In the five Nordic countries, Nordic-ness was, in different ways, embedded in national identities and institutions (Sørensen & Stråth, 1997). Through the Nordic cooperation in the production of social knowledge, norms, and arguments—for example, by means of Nordic social statistics since 1946 (Petersen, 2006, p. 91)—the notion of a Nordic model of a national society was reinforced. In Finland, this concept came to represent a kind of normative standard and a code for the future, identified in everything that had "already" been achieved in Sweden.

The notion of Finland, the Nordic latecomer, served as the impetus for demanding that social reforms be implemented. However, influential conservative variants of comparison also existed. The "socialist" policies of Sweden's Social Democratic governments were referred to as warning signs, such as in the right-wing critique of the Finnish primary school reform in the late 1960s and early 1970s (Okkonen, 2017). A more moderate way of opposing social reforms was to argue that the Finns, at their lower stage of economic development, should wait and see how the reform in question would play out in Sweden. Nevertheless, lessons from the Swedish experience, including those associated with the mass emigration to Sweden, were a crucial ingredient of the politics that made the Finnish nation-state into a Nordic welfare state.

2.8 The Politics of Social Policies

In historical overviews of Finnish social policies, the late adoption of social insurance schemes has been presented as a major indicator of Finland being a latecomer. In the early 1950s, as Pekka Kosonen (1993, pp. 50–51) has stated,

"workers' accident insurance [since 1895] was almost the only legislative social insurance that fitted into the framework of the [Nordic] model. Child allowances were also introduced [in 1948]. A universal unemployment benefit was rejected on economic and moralistic grounds and the unemployed instead assigned to badly paid public work projects (the so-called spade line). The old-age insurance legislated in 1937 was not intended to become effective for a long time, and public sickness insurance plans were not adopted until the 1960s."

However, the history of social insurance schemes in Finland is not just a story of the country being a latecomer; it is also a history of long and contingent political processes preceding reforms. Ever since the 1880s, official commissions had made plans about social insurance. The vision of a comprehensive social insurance system was part of what was called post-war planning, but the pragmatic idea of proceeding step by step within the limits of economic possibilities was widely accepted (Kettunen, 2006b).

The Social Insurance Commission, appointed in 1945 by the coalition government of Communists, Social Democrats, and Agrarians was until 1954 active in planning schemes for different sectors of social security, making use of international, especially Nordic, comparisons and taking into account international norms like those included in the Social Security Convention of the ILO in 1952. Sickness insurance for wage workers was again the first priority of the Social Democrats, whereas the Agrarian Party, together with the Communists (who had wide support among small farmers and rural workers), preferred the reform of the old-age and disability pension schemes. This time too, as in the 1930s, the latter line was followed; it resulted in a greatly revised national pension scheme. The *National Pension Act of 1956* instituted unconditional flat-rate benefits combined with an income-tested assistance allowance. The Social Democrats' demands for income-related supplements to basic pensions were rejected.

However, the *Private Sector Supplementary Pension Act* was passed in 1961 on the basis of demands by both blue- and white-collar trade unions and negotiations between labor-market organizations. An important contributing factor was the gradual adoption of the term "wage earner" as the common label for blue- and white-collar workers and civil servants in the 1950s. The civil servants' old privilege of income-related pensions appeared more and more unacceptable, as did the various company-level private pension schemes for white-collar employees. A crucial point of departure for the creation of an income-related pension scheme was the discontent of the representatives of wage earners with the national pension scheme of 1956; this was seen as an income transfer that favored the agrarian population. However, in order to get the bill passed in 1961, it was necessary to reach a compromise that would make it possible for the Agrarian Party to also vote for it.

In any case, the Finnish pension system was constructed in the form of two separate schemes, each with its own administration (Hannikainen & Vauhkonen, 2012; Salminen, 1993). The difference from the united Swedish system—which only the Communists advocated for in Finland in 1961—was still more striking as the administration of the private sector supplementary pensions became a function of private insurance companies. This arrangement entailed an active contribution by Finnish employers to the new scheme and guaranteed their support for it, involving as it did the principle that firms could, on favorable terms, borrow back most of the funded portion of the contributions. Information and advice from Swedish employers, dissatisfied with their own system, played an influential role in shaping the policy of Finnish employers. Finally, the *Sickness Insurance Act* was passed in 1963, no longer as a Social Democrat project but by shaping the benefits, financing, and organization in accordance with the principles of the Agrarian Party (Kangas, 1992).

In the late 1950s, seasonal and structural unemployment—not least the smallholders dependent on seasonal wage work—was recognized as a major social problem (Kalela, 1989; Uljas, 2012). In addition to "spade-line" public works projects, unemployment insurance was established in 1960 through a compromise that extended and reinforced the system of voluntary trade-union-linked funds and completed it with a state-administered, flat-rate benefits system for those without access to the funds. This was a breakthrough reform, yet the level of compensation was low and the spade line was applied by the beginning of 1970s. In 1982, the reform of unemployment compensation created a comprehensive system combining the income-related benefits of the so-called Ghent model with basic unemployment allowances (Edling, 2006).

In general, in the 1970s and 1980s, the wage earner perspective—which was concerned with maintaining the income level and represented the common view of the traditional working class, the workers of the expanding service sector, and the so-called new middle class—was accentuated in reforms reshaping all parts of social security. At the same time, the principle of a minimum basic security containing flat-rate and means-tested benefits was established. In terms of the coverage and compensation levels of various forms of social insurance, in 1990, Finland did not differ from the other Nordic countries considerably more than the latter did from one another.

The appearance of Finnish industrial relations met "Nordic" criteria in the early 1970s, including a high rate of unionization and a centralized system of collective agreements, associated with the strong presence of trade unions at the workplace level as well (Kjellberg, 2001). Starting in 1968, national specificities appeared in the so-called income policy. Labor-market agreements were closely intertwined with political decisions on economic and social policies, and agricultural interests and their representatives were a significant part of income policy compromises (Bergholm, 2009). A regular part of the income policy agreements was the so-called social packages, which were a major form of expanding the Finnish welfare state in the 1970s and 1980s.

A comprehensive system of public services in care and education, a central characteristic of the Nordic welfare model, was built up in Finland in the 1970s through several reforms that transformed municipalities into the basic level of the welfare state. The Primary Health Care Act 1972 established a network of municipal health centers. The Child Day Care Act in 1973 obligated municipalities to implement policies that were meant to facilitate women's work outside the home. Due to its strong emphasis on social and regional equality, the *Primary Education Reform*, decided upon in 1968 and implemented in the 1970s, has achieved a chief role in the national narrative of the making of the Nordic welfare state in Finland.

The left-wing majority governments of 1966 to 1970 have remained in the history books as the ones who set the broad parameters of the welfare state in Finland into motion. Indeed, in the late 1960s, the willingness to compromise reached a point where it became possible to gain broad political support for major Nordic-type reforms in social and educational policies as well as in industrial relations.

However, important reforms of pension systems, sickness insurance, and unemployment policies had already been made from 1955 to 1965, a period of great parliamentary instability (Bergholm, 2009). All the social security reforms were achieved through political competition, conflicts of interest, and compromises within the limits of what was conceived of as national economic and political necessities, associated with experiences of profound socio-economic and regional change. Thus, the making of the Finnish welfare state was not such a consistent "project" as it is often retrospectively presented by those who currently defend it as a national achievement.

2.9 Interests, Work, and Gender

The history of the Finnish welfare state provides material for a critique of the "laborist bias" (Baldwin, 1990) in interpretations of the welfare state. The labor movement was a vital force in the agenda setting of social policy reforms, yet it would not be tenable to define the Finnish welfare state as a social democratic or working-class creation.

The farmers' interests and their representatives long played a significant role. Even the Finnish labor movement bore a strong rural stamp up until World War II; most of the Social Democrat voters still lived in the countryside. After the war, until the 1970s, the Communists and the Agrarian Party were strong rivals for the support of the small farmers in eastern and northern Finland. The Agrarian Party (since 1965, the Center Party) continued to be a more important player in the political system than corresponding parties in the other Nordic countries. Its strength in part came from its linkages to the foreign policy-based power of Urho Kekkonen, who was the president of Finland from 1956 until 1981. In any case, the party managed to remain a powerful voice of the provinces during the transformation, where the share of agriculture and forestry in the economically active population declined from 60% in 1940 to 35% in 1960, then to 13% in 1980 and 6% in 2000.

Historically, the prominence of farmers is certainly not a Finnish peculiarity. The political role of freeholder peasants and the cultural tradition of the "Lutheran peasant Enlightenment" (Sørensen & Stråth, 1997) have been emphasized in historical accounts of the Nordic welfare state. However, even for Sweden, one may question the narrative of a road from "the Lutheran peasant Enlightenment" to "the Social Democratic welfare state," and for Finland, this is still more the case. This account has an excess of egalitarian individualism in the rural community and too much social democracy in the welfare state (Kettunen, 1999).

Insofar as the Nordic welfare states can be interpreted as the products of secularized Lutheranism (Markkola, 2011; Nelson, 2017; Stenius, 1997; Thorgildsen, 1997), one of their main aims has been to make it everybody's right to follow the moral precept that everyone ought to work. Full employment became a shared programmatic objective in all the Nordic countries after World War II. However, the political commitment to this objective seems to have been stronger in Sweden and Norway than it was in Finland and Denmark (Kosonen, 1993; Therborn, 1986). In Finland, this did not mean that work was less important as a moral imperative than it was in Sweden and Norway. On the contrary, when the individual farmer's own work and will to work were appropriated to form the ideological core of the program for social peace and order, the principle of work as a *duty* was especially highlighted. Up until the 1960s, an institutional indicator of this work ethic was the dominance of the "work line" or "spade line" in dealing with unemployment (i.e., low-paid public works projects) (Kalela, 1989, pp. 159–192).

Generally, the histories of Nordic welfare states included an intertwining of three different ideological elements characteristic of the Nordic modernization processes: the idealized heritage of the free peasant, the spirit of capitalism, and the utopia of socialism. Arguably, this political and cultural context contributed to the parallel reinforcement and mutual adjustment of two principles (especially from the 1950s until the 1980s): the universalist idea of social rights based on citizenship and the normalcy of wage work. The combination of these two (far from self-evidently compatible) principles gained momentum at the same time as the political significance of the farmers declined and that of the new middle class increased. This combination is not covered by the concept of "decommodification" that was made popular by the Danish sociologist Gøsta Esping-Andersen (1985, 1990) and refers to liberating people from their dependencies on markets, especially on the uncertainties associated with the character of labor as a commodity.

The adjustment of wage work (i.e., commodified labor) and social citizenship can be found in the field of *social security*. The "work performance model," with its labor market-oriented and income-related benefits, was linked with the principle of the social rights inherent in citizenship. The right to a secured continuity of income came to be interpreted as an aspect of social citizenship. However, in the history of the Nordic welfare state, the most obvious mode in which the principles of wage work and social citizenship were simultaneously reinforced was the construction of extensive *public social services*. These services, defining and meeting the needs of health, care, and education, bore the character of universal social rights at the same time as they created the preconditions for generalizing wage work as the norm. A transformation of the gendered division of labor was crucial here, associated with redefining the relationship between the family and society (Lundqvist, 2017). A particular complex of the welfare state, the labor-market regime, and the gender system was formed. It includes, since the 1970s, a two-fold dependence of women on the welfare state: on the preconditions created for their work outside the home and on the jobs created within the welfare state, in strongly gender-segregated labor markets (Hirdman, 1990; Julkunen, 1990).

This description applies to the shape in which the Nordic welfare state was developed in Finland in the 1970s and 1980s. However, in light of the Finnish case, it would be especially questionable to claim that the concept of the working woman came into being only with the inception of the welfare state. In Finland, even more than in the other Nordic countries, the gendered division of labor—*before* being structured by the welfare state—did not meet the family ideals of middle-class educators. The hard labor of women in rural households included tasks that according to those ideals belonged to men. Neither was the industrial wage work of women in the late nineteenth and early twentieth centuries a marginal phenomenon. True, it was often a limited period in a woman's life before she got married and had her first child. Nevertheless, the number of married women working in factories and shops was remarkable, even before its expansion during World War II (Markkola, 1990; Suoranta, 2009).

Through the construction of the welfare state, the importance of wage work as both a norm and a source of individual autonomy were reinforced. The separate taxation of spouses was introduced in 1976 as part of the Nordic wave of similar reforms and as an aspect of what the Swedish historian Lars Trägårdh (1997) has called "statist individualism" in the making of the Nordic welfare state. Notwithstanding, while paid work was a source of independence, the dual-breadwinner practice was normalized as both a matter of equality and an economic necessity. Furthermore, the heritage from the rural community—where work was at the same time a necessity, a duty, and a source of dignity—still played a crucial role.

2.10 Challenged and Reshaped

National consensus was reinforced in Finland in the 1980s on the basis of a sense of pragmatism that was oriented towards an active adjustment to the requirements of national competitiveness. One indicator was the stabilization of the parliamentary system as it became a norm that the government could be built on any coalition including two of the largest parties (from 1987 to 1991, the Social Democratic Party and the National Coalition Party) and remain in power for the entire four-year period between elections. Another sign of consensus was a radical decrease in industrial actions at the turn of the 1980s and 1990s.

That said, the adjustment to what were experienced as new external necessities—including the globalized financial markets, the collapse of the Soviet Union together with the subsequent decline of the so-called Eastern trade, and the new phase of European integration—was far from unproblematic. A deep economic crisis with a dramatic rise in unemployment occurred in Finland in the early 1990s. In public discourse, the notion of politics as fulfilling national necessities was reinforced by this experience. It appeared not only in the justifications of cuts to welfare benefits and services, but also in the argumentation of those defending the welfare state and collective labor-market agreements. Trade unions and the Social Democratic Party attempted to prove that welfare state institutions were a necessary precondition for innovation-based national competitiveness (Blomberg et al., 2002).

The transformation called globalization questioned the assumption of a virtuous circle of the national economy, social policy, and democracy, which had provided an important part of the ideological underpinning of the Nordic welfare state. The premise for a symmetrical collective representation of employers and workers within a national society was weakened by a variety of developments: the multi- and transnational character of companies in the global economy; the network-type restructuring of production processes; the increase in the so-called atypical employment relationships; the growing fluidity of the boundary between wage work and entrepreneurship; and the rise of the ethos of entrepreneurship.

Applying the concepts of the American development economist Albert O. Hirschman (1970), the *exit* option (i.e., the option of leaving an unsatisfactory milieu) was now in a new way present to transnational companies and investors. Consequently, it was an effective structural means to exert a powerful *voice* for reshaping their (potential) operational contexts and defining the preconditions for their *loyalty* (i.e., for their commitment to the contexts' modes of functioning). Solidarity through shared national links was eroded. In Finland, the signs of breaches in the national consensus became evident in the conflict facing the wood processing industry in 2005, and later in the decision of business interest organizations to refuse to continue the practice of centralized income policy agreements.

In the Nordic tradition, some favorable preconditions existed for reorientation. Competitiveness was an integral part of the post-World War II ideology of virtuous circles. Thus, it was easy for trade unions to accept (at least in their programs) a value-added competition strategy based on innovation, training, and participation as an alternative to the cost-based strategies of social dumping and low-wage competition. Much of the ideological power of knowledge, education, and innovation in the Nordic countries stemmed from the promise that competitiveness and its preconditions in the global economy could—or even must—be seen from a wider perspective than that of neoliberalist deregulation.

However, tension seems to have emerged between what are presented as the institutional preconditions of competitiveness and the content of competitiveness itself. At the same time as egalitarian institutions and participatory practices can be defended as preconditions for knowledge-based competitiveness, true membership in a competitive community is a matter of individual competitiveness. This, in turn, consists of communicative and innovative skills and talent as well as the reflexive capabilities of monitoring oneself from the angle of competitiveness. Not only are there both winners and losers in this competition; there are people who cannot even participate in it.

The "social" aspect appears to have gotten a new Janus face. On the one hand, social policy is supposed to provide "social investments" that create "social capital" and "human capital", and support national competitiveness based on commitment, knowledge, and innovativeness. This task is associated with the intensified rivalry among territorial communities at different levels—at the national, regional, and local levels as well as at the level of the European Union (EU) and its global competitors—in offering attractive environments for competitive enterprises, investors, and people.

On the other hand, the "social" aspect exists in efforts to prevent and deal with social exclusion and to make possible peaceful co-existence between those inside and those outside the new economy. These efforts often take the form of the so-called activation policies. They also manifest historical continuities. In the formation of the Nordic welfare state, a widely shared regulative principle was that all people should have the right to fulfill their duty to work. From this point of departure, one obvious direction would be back to the pre-welfare state aims of social policy, associated with maintaining order and preventing idleness. The old emphasis on work as the basis of social order and disciplined citizenship is very much alive side by side with the marketing of the new concept of work as an unending demonstration of a person's individual innovative capacity.

In policies responding to cross-border mobility, it is easy to see a dualism of simultaneously increasing and decreasing "our" attractiveness. This dualism appears in the different policies concerning the mobility of capital and people yet also within migration policies, most strikingly in relation to "international talent" on the one hand and asylum seekers on the other. In Finland, most political actors have learned to recognize the need for migrant workers to meet the demographic challenge of a rapidly aging society, most urgently in healthcare and other kinds of care (Vaittinen et al., 2022). Moreover, opportunities to decrease labor costs using lower-paid migrants have proven attractive for some employers. At the same time, however, migration is thematized as a security problem — and for "us" rather than migrants (Palander & Pellander, 2019). In the shaping of national and European migration policies, support for bordering policies is greatest among far-right ethnonationalists, who tend to oppose any immigration (Tervonen, 2022).

In preventing the entry of unwanted people, in the return of those who are not allowed to stay and in the integration of those who are, the basic principles of the welfare state are reinterpreted. The differential inclusion of different non-citizen groups in the welfare state tends to reinforce the principles of hierarchy and conditionality in relation to social benefits at the expense of the tenet of universalism (Careja et al., 2015; Könönen, 2018).

While national responses to economic globalization and financialization place the competitiveness of the national "us" into the center of the political agenda, security has, in turn, strongly emerged as a national political objective in response to migration as well as to recent dramatic changes. These changes include the COVID-19 crisis and the "post-post-Cold War" rises of geopolitical and military confrontations, in particular, the Russian invasion of Ukraine. Finland's membership in the EU (since 1995) and NATO (since 2023) has been justified as necessary to strengthen the national agency responding to external challenges and threats. The concern about security has also influenced the views on and practices of Nordic cooperation.

In the history of the Finnish nation-state, security and competitiveness are far from new concerns. However, the intersecting perspectives of competitiveness and security have gained new impetus, even in the discourse on social problems, which are dealt with through social, employment, and educational policies. To describe the change facing the country, it is useful to think that nation-states such as the current Finnish one have many dimensions, and to conclude that the welfare-state aspect of the nation-state is, in new ways, affected by its competition-state and security-state dimensions. Welfare-state institutions are modified to serve competition-state and security-state functions. The steps taken in this direction have been, as a rule, justified by the idea of rescuing the welfare state. In Finland in the early 2020s, rescuing the welfare state is a popular argument for promoting a wide range of different policy objectives, including the cuttings of social benefits. The political rhetoric avoiding to question the welfare state itself indicates strong support for the welfare state among ordinary people. They experience it embedded in their daily life and involve social protection in their future expectations.

References

Alapuro, R. (1988). *State and revolution in Finland*. University of California Press.

Åmark, K. (2006). Women's labour force participation in the Nordic countries during the twentieth century. In N. F. Christiansen, K. Petersen, N. Edling, & P. Haave (Eds.), *The Nordic model of welfare—A historical reappraisal* (pp. 299–333). Museum Tusculanum Press.

Anderson, B. (1983). *Imagined communities. Reflections on the origin and spread of nationalism*. Verso.

Andersson, J. (2006). *Between growth and security: Swedish social democracy from a strong society to a third way*. Manchester University Press.

Aunesluoma, J. (2013). Two shadows over Finland: Hitler, Stalin and the Finns facing the Second World War as history 1944–2010. In J. Gilmour & J. Stephenson (Eds.), *Hitler's Scandinavian legacy* (pp. 199–220). Bloomsbury Academic.

Baldwin, P. (1990). *The politics of social solidarity: Class bases of the European welfare state 1875–1975*. Cambridge University Press.

Bergenheim, S. (2020). *Yhteiskunnan, kansakunnan ja kansan asialla: Järjestöt, yhteiskuntapolitiikka ja asiantuntijuus Suomessa 1930–60-luvuilla* [Diss.]. Faculty of Social Sciences, University of Helsinki.

Bergenheim, S. (2023). From survival mode to utopian dreams: Conceptions of society, social planning, and historical time in 1950s and 1960s Finland. In P. Haapala, M. Harjula, & H. Kokko (Eds.), *Experiencing society and the lived welfare state* (pp. 301–323). Palgrave Macmillan.

Bergholm, T. (2009). The making of the Finnish model: The qualitative change in Finnish corporatism in the early 1960s. *Scandinavian Journal of History, 34*(1), 29–48.

Bergholm, T. (2012). *Kohti tasa-arvoa. Tulopolitiikan aika I. Suomen Ammattiliittojen Keskusjärjestö 1969–1977*. Otava.

Blomberg, H., Hannikainen, M., & Kettunen, P. (2002). Lamafatalismin historiallinen ja vertaileva kritiikki. In H. Blomberg, M. Hannikainen, & P. Kettunen (Eds.), *Lamakirja. Näkökulmia 1990-luvun talouskriisiin ja sen historiallisiin konteksteihin* (pp. 7–13). Kirja-Aurora.

Careja, R., Emmenegger, P., & Kvist, J. (2015). An American dilemma in Europe? Welfare reform and immigration. In P. Kettunen, S. Michel, & K. Petersen (Eds.), *Race, ethnicity and welfare states: An American dilemma?* (pp. 128–149). Edward Elgar Publishing.

Castles, F. G. (1979). *The social democratic image of society: A study of the achievements and origins of Scandinavian social democracy in comparative perspective*. Routledge & Kegan Paul.

Christiansen, N. F., & Åmark, K. (2006). Conclusions. In N. F. Christiansen, K. Petersen, N. Edling, & P. Haave (Eds.), *The Nordic model of welfare—A historical reappraisal* (pp. 335–354). Museum Tusculanum Press.

Christiansen, N. F., & Markkola, P. (2006). Introduction. In N. F. Christiansen, K. Petersen, N. Edling, & P. Haave (Eds.), *The Nordic model of welfare—A historical reappraisal* (pp. 9–29). Museum Tusculanum Press.

Edling, N. (2006). Limited universalism: Unemployment insurance in Northern Europe 1900–2000. In N. F. Christiansen, K. Petersen, N. Edling, & P. Haave (Eds.), *The Nordic model of welfare—A historical reappraisal* (pp. 99–143). Museum Tusculanum Press.

Edling, N. (2013). The primacy of welfare politics: Notes on the language of the Swedish Social Democrats and their adversaries in the 1930s. In H. Haggrén, J. Rainio-Niemi, & J. Vauhkonen (Eds.), *Multilayered historicity of the present: Approaches to social science history* (pp. 125–150). University of Helsinki.

Esping-Andersen, G. (1985). *Politics against markets: The social democratic road to power*. Princeton University Press.

Esping-Andersen, G. (1990). *The three worlds of welfare capitalism*. Princeton University Press.

Fredrickson, G. M. (2000). *The comparative imagination: On the history of racism, nationalism, and social movements*. University of California Press.

Gerschenkron, A. (1962). *Economic backwardness in historical perspective: A book of essays*. The Belknap Press of Harvard University Press.

Gustafsson, B. (1993). Unemployment and fiscal policy in Sweden during the 1930s: Myths and reality. In W. R. Garside (Ed.), *Capitalism in crisis: International responses to the great depression*. Printer Publishers.
Häkkinen, A., & Forsberg, H. (2015). Finland's "famine years" of the 1860s: A nineteenth century perspective. In D. Curran, L. Luciuk, & A. G. Newby (Eds.), *Famines in European economic history: The last great European famines reconsidered* (pp. 99–123). Routledge.
Hannikainen, M., & Vauhkonen, J. (2012). *Ansioiden mukaan: Yksityisalojen työeläkkeiden historia*. Suomalaisen Kirjallisuuden Seura.
Hietala, M. (1987). *Services and urbanization at the turn of the century: The diffusion of innovations*. Finnish Historical Society.
Hietala, M. (1992). *Innovaatioiden ja kansainvälistymisen vuosikymmenet. Tietoa, taitoa, asiantuntemusta. Helsinki eurooppalaisessa kehityksessä 1875–1917 1. With an English summary: Know-how and professionalisation. Helsinki as part of European development 1875–1917*. Historiallinen Arkisto 99:1. Suomen Historiallinen Seura.
Hirdman, Y. (1990). Genussystemet. In *Demokrati och makt i Sverige. Maktutredningens vudrapport*. Statsrådsberedningen.
Hirdman, Y. (1997). Social planning under rational control: Social engineering in Sweden in the 1930s and 1940s. In P. Kettunen & H. Eskola (Eds.), *Models, modernity and the Myrdals* (pp. 55–80). The Renvall Institute for Area and Cultural Studies, University of Helsinki.
Hirschman, A. O. (1970). *Exit, voice, and loyalty: Responses to decline in firms, organizations, and states*. Harvard University Press.
Julkunen, R. (1990). Women in the welfare state. In M. Manninen & P. Setälä (Eds.), *The lady with the bow: The story of the Finnish women* (pp. 140–160). Otava.
Jussila, O. (1999). Finland as a grand duchy 1809–1917. In O. Jussila, S. Hentilä, & J. Nevakivi (Eds.), *From grand duchy to a modern state: A political history of Finland since 1809* (pp. 1–98). Hurst & Company.
Kalela, J. (1989). *Työttömyys 1900-luvun suomalaisessa yhteiskuntapolitiikassa*. Valtion painatuskeskus/Työvoimaministeriö.
Kangas, O. (1992). *The politics of social rights: Studies on the dimensions of sickness insurance in OECD countries*. Stockholms universitet.
Katzenstein, P. J. (1985). *Small states in world markets: Industrial policy in Europe*. Cornell University Press.
Kettunen, P. (1986). *Poliittinen liike ja sosiaalinen kollektiivisuus. Tutkimus sosialidemokratoiasta ja ammattiyhdistysliikkeestä Suomessa 1918–1930*. Suomen Historiallinen Seura.
Kettunen, P. (1990). Hur legitimerades arbetsgivarnas politik i 'första republikens' Finland? In D. Fleming (Ed.), *Industriell demokrati i Norden* (pp. 129–190). Arkiv förlag.
Kettunen, P. (1994). *Suojelu, suoritus, subjekti. Tutkimus työsuojelusta teollistuvan Suomen yhteiskunnallisissa ajattelu- ja toimintatavoissa. With an English summary: Protection, performance, and subject. Labour protection and the social modes of thought and action in Finland, c. 1880–1950*. Suomen Historiallinen Seura.
Kettunen, P. (1997). *Työjärjestys. Tutkielmia työn ja tiedon poliittisesta historiasta*. Tutkijaliitto.
Kettunen, P. (1999). A return to the figure of the free Nordic peasant. *Acta Sociologica, 42*(3), 259–269.
Kettunen, P. (2001). The Nordic welfare state in Finland. *Scandinavian Journal of History, 26*(3), 226–247.
Kettunen, P. (2004). The Nordic model and consensual competitiveness in Finland. In A.-M. Castrén, M. Lonkila, & M. Peltonen (Eds.), *Between sociology and history: Essays on microhistory, collective action, and nation-building* (pp. 289–309). Finnish Literature Society.
Kettunen, P. (2006a). Power of international comparison—A perspective on the making and challenging of the Nordic welfare state. In N. F. Christiansen, K. Petersen, N. Edling, & P. Haave (Eds.), *The Nordic model of welfare—A historical reappraisal* (pp. 31–65). Museum Tusculanum Press.

Kettunen, P. (2006b). The tension between the social and the economic—A historical perspective on a welfare state. In J. Ojala, J. Eloranta, & J. Jalava (Eds.), *The road to prosperity: An economic history of Finland* (pp. 285–312). Finnish Literature Society.

Kettunen, P. (2011). The transnational construction of national challenges: The ambiguous Nordic model of welfare and competitiveness. In P. Kettunen & K. Petersen (Eds.), *Beyond welfare state models—Transnational historical perspectives on social policy* (pp. 16–40). Edward Elgar.

Kettunen, P. (2013). The ILO as a forum for developing and demonstrating a Nordic model. In S. Kott & J. Droux (Eds.), *Globalizing social rights: The International Labour Organization and beyond* (pp. 210–230). Palgrave Macmillan.

Kettunen, P. (2018). Wars, nation and the welfare state in Finland. In H. Obinger, K. Petersen, & P. Starke (Eds.), *Warfare and welfare: Military conflict and welfare state development in western countries* (pp. 260–289). Oxford University Press.

Kettunen, P., Österberg, M., Petersen, K., & Lundberg, U. (2015). The Nordic model and the rise and fall of Nordic cooperation. In J. Strang (Ed.), *Nordic cooperation: A European region in transition* (pp. 69–92). Routledge.

Kivimäki, V. (2013). *Battled nerves—Finnish soldiers' war experience, trauma, and military psychiatry, 1941–44*. Åbo Academi University.

Kjellberg, A. (2001). *Fackliga organisationer och medlemmar i dagens Sverige. Andra utvidgade och reviderade upplagan*. Arkiv förlag.

Klinge, M. (1993). *The Finnish tradition: Essays on structures and identities in the north of Europe*. Finnish Historical Society.

Könönen, J. (2018). Differential inclusion of non-citizens in a universalistic welfare state. *Citizenship Studies, 22*(1), 53–69.

Koponen, J., & Saaritsa, S. (Eds.). (2019). *Nälkämaasta hyvinvointivaltioksi. Suomi kehityksen kiinniottajana*. Gaudeamus.

Koselleck, R. (1979). *Vergangene Zukunft: Zur Semantik geschichlichen Zeiten*. Suhrkamp.

Kosonen, P. (1993). The Finnish model and the welfare state in crisis. In P. Kosonen (Ed.), *The Nordic welfare state as a myth and as reality* (pp. 45–66). University of Helsinki.

Kurunmäki, J. (2011). "Nordic democracy" in 1935: On the Finnish and Swedish rhetoric of democracy. In J. Kurunmäki & J. Strang (Eds.), *Rhetorics of Nordic democracy* (pp. 37–82). Finnish Literature Society.

Kuusi, P. (1961). *60-luvun sosiaalipolitiikka*. WSOY.

Kuusi, P. (1964). *Social policy for the sixties—A plan for Finland*. Finnish Social Political Association.

Lindberg, V. (1934). *Utvecklingen av den allmänna inkomstskatten i Finlands statsskattesystem. Akademisk avhandling*. Helsingfors universitet.

Linnakangas, E. (2015). Tuloverotuksen synty ja kehtys. In *Verotus Suomessa 1865–2015* (pp. 7–18). Verohallinto.

Lundqvist, Å. (2017). *Transforming gender and family relations: How active labour market policies shaped the dual earner model*. Edward Elgar Publishing.

Majander, M. (2004). *Pohjoismaa vai kansandemokratia? Sosiaalidemokraatit, kommunistit ja Suomen kansainvälinen asema 1944–51*. SKS/Finnish Literature Society.

Markkola, P. (1990). Women in rural society in the 19th and 20th centuries. In M. Manninen & P. Setälä (Eds.), *The lady with the bow: The story of the Finnish women* (pp. 17–30). Otava.

Markkola, P. (2011). The Lutheran Nordic welfare states. In P. Kettunen & K. Petersen (Eds.), *Beyond welfare state models: Transnational historical perspectives to social policy* (pp. 102–118). Edward Elgar Publishing.

Mattila, M. (1999). *Kansamme parhaaksi. Rotuhygienia Suomessa vuoden 1935 sterilointilakiin asti. With an English summary: In our nation's best – Eugenics in Finland until the promulgation of the Sterilization Law of 1935*. Finnish Historical Society.

Möller, G. (1938). The unemployment policy. *The Annals of the American Academy of Political and Social Science, 197*, 47–71.

Nelson, R. H. (2017). *Lutheranism and the Nordic spirit of social democracy: A different Protestant ethic*. Aarhus University Press.
Ojala, J., Eloranta, J., & Jalava, J. (Eds.). (2006). *The road to prosperity: An economic history of Finland*. Finnish Literature Society.
Okkonen, V. (2017). *Peruskoulua vastaan – yksityisoppikoulut ja yhteiskuntajärjestys 1966–1975*. Turun yliopisto.
Palander, J., & Pellander, S. (2019). Mobility and the security paradigm: How immigration became securitized in Finnish law and policy. *Journal of Finnish Studies, 22*(1 and 2), 173–193.
Pekkarinen, J., & Vartiainen, J. (1993). *Suomen talouspolitiikan pitkä linja*. WSOY.
Petersen, K. (2006). Constructing Nordic welfare? Nordic social political cooperation 1919–1955. In N. F. Christiansen, K. Petersen, N. Edling, & P. Haave (Eds.), *The Nordic model of welfare—A historical reappraisal* (pp. 67–98). Museum Tusculanum Press.
Pohjola, M. (1994). Nordic corporatism and economic performance: Labour market equality at the expense of productive efficiency? In T. Kauppinen & V. Köykkä (Eds.), *Transformation of the Nordic industrial relations in the European context. IIRA 4th European Regional Congress, Helsinki, Finland*. The Finnish Labour Relations Association.
Pulkkinen, T. (1999). One language, one mind: The nationalist tradition in Finnish political culture. In T. M. S. Lehtonen (Ed.), *Europe's northern frontier: Perspectives on Finland's western identity*. PS-Kustannus.
Rainio-Niemi, J. (2008). *Small state cultures of consensus: State traditions and consensus-seeking in the neo-corporatist and neutrality policies in post-1945 Austria and Finland* [Doctoral dissertation]. Faculty of Social Sciences, University of Helsinki.
Salminen, K. (1993). *Pension schemes in the making. A comparative study of the Scandinavian countries*. The Central Pension Security Institute.
Satka, M. (1995). *Making social citizenship: Conceptual practices from the Finnish Poor Law to professional social work*. SoPhi.
Senghaas, D. (1985). *The European experience: A historical critique of development theory*. Berg Publishers.
Sluga, G. (2004). The nation and the comparative imagination. In D. Cohen & M. O'Connor (Eds.), *Comparison and history. Europe in cross-national perspective* (pp. 103–115). Routledge.
Smolander, J. (2000). *Suomalainen oikeisto ja "kansankoti." Kansallisen Kokoomuksen suhtautuminen pohjoismaiseen hyvinvointivaltiomalliin jälleenrakennuskaudelta konsensusajan alkuun. With an English summary: The Finnish right wing and "Folkhemmet" – Attitudes of the National Coalition Party toward the Nordic welfare model from the period of reconstruction to the beginning of consensus*. Finnish Literature Society.
Sørensen, Ø., & Stråth, B. (1997). Introduction: The cultural construction of Norden. In Ø. Sørensen & B. Stråth (Eds.), *The cultural construction of Norden*. Scandinavian University Press.
Stenius, H. (1997). The good life is a life of conformity: The impact of Lutheran tradition on Nordic political culture. In Ø. Sørensen & B. Stråth (Eds.), *The cultural construction of Norden* (pp. 161–171). Scandinavian University Press.
Suoranta, A. (2009). *Halvennettu työ. Pätkätyö ja sukupuoli sopimusyhteiskuntaa edeltävissä työmarkkinakäytännöissä*. Vastapaino.
Tervonen, M. (2022). Borders of welfare: Mobility control and the Nordic welfare states. In P. Kettunen, S. Pellander, & M. Tervonen (Eds.), *Nationalism and democracy in the welfare state* (pp. 150–165). Edward Elgar.
Therborn, G. (1986). *Why some peoples are more unemployed than others: The strange paradox of growth and unemployment*. Verso.
Thorgildsen, D. (1997). Religious identity and Nordic identity. In Ø. Sørensen & B. Stråth (Eds.), *The cultural construction of Norden* (pp. 138–160). Scandinavian University Press.
Trägårdh, L. (1997). Statist individualism: On the culturality of the Nordic welfare state. In Ø. Sørensen & B. Stråth (Eds.), *The cultural construction of Norden* (pp. 253–285). Scandinavian University Press.

Uljas, P. (2012). *Hyvinvointivaltion läpimurto. Pienviljelyshegemonian, kansalaisliikehdinnän ja poliittisen murroksen keskinäiset suhteet suomalaisessa yhteiskunnassa 1950-luvun loppuvuosina*. Into.

Upton, A. F. (1980). *The Finnish revolution 1917–1918*. University of Minnesota Press.

Urponen, K. (1994). Huoltoyhteiskunnasta hyvinvointivaltioon. In J. Jaakkola, P. Pulma, M. Satka, & K. Urponen (Eds.), *Armeliaisuus, yhteisöapu, sosiaaliturva: Suomalaisten sosiaalisen turvan historia*. Sosiaaliturvan Keskusliitto.

Vaittinen, T., Sakilayan-Latvala, M., & Vartianen, P. (2022). Filipino nurses as enablers of the future welfare state: The global commodity chains of producing racialized care labour for ageing Finland. In P. Kettunen, S. Pellander, & M. Tervonen (Eds.), *Nationalism and democracy in the welfare state* (pp. 184–208). Edward Elgar.

Waris, H. (1973). *Suomalaisen yhteiskunnan sosiaalipolitiikka. Viides painos*. WSOY.

Chapter 3
Agrarian Party and Kela: Evolutionary Development of Finnish Social Policy

Yuriko Shibayama

Abstract Kansaneläkelaitos (Kela) is a vital actor in the Finnish welfare state, established to administer the National Pension Act in 1937. The enactment of the Act was strongly influenced by the urban–rural social cleavage in Finnish politics. While the Social Democrats sought to protect the interests of wage workers, the Agrarian Party worked toward universal interests of all citizens. Through an interdependent relationship with the Agrarian Party, Kela expanded its operations to health insurance in the 1960s, and since the 1970s, various services have been transferred from the Ministry of Social Affairs and Health and municipalities to Kela, making the latter an institute of comprehensive basic security in Finland. However, the intentions of the Social Democrats have developed outside Kela, a genuine public scheme. Through conflicts and compromises, Finnish welfare systems such as pension and health insurance have been formed in a complex and unique way compared with other Nordic countries. This chapter will present the Finnish case of building the Nordic welfare state with the dominance of the Agrarian Party and Kela, which was founded under the influence of the party, and examine the nature of Finnish social policy through the perspective of those impacts.

Keywords Finland · Social policy · Social cleavages · Agrarian party · Kela · Party politics

Y. Shibayama (✉)
Department of Nordic Studies, School of Cultural and Social Studies, Tokai University, Hiratsuka, Kanagawa, Japan
e-mail: ys@tokai.ac.jp

N. Tokumaru et al. (eds.), *Creative Co-evolution of the Economies and Welfare States in the Nordic Countries*, Evolutionary Economics and Social Complexity Science 32, https://doi.org/10.1007/978-981-97-8569-8_3

3.1 Introduction

Finland, a small country in Northern Europe, has been internationally recognized for its high-level education policy, innovation policy—especially in the information and communications industry—and achievement of gender equality. Finland is positioned as a Nordic universalist welfare state, as represented by Esping-Andersen's (1990) study classifying Nordic countries as a "social democratic regime." However, Finland, which built a welfare state while facing various crises such as the path to achieving and maintaining independence and through relations with the Russian Empire or the Soviet Union, has a different political process from Sweden, an another neighboring country and pioneering builder of the Nordic welfare state. Then the question arises as to how Finland built a welfare state under various unfavorable circumstances. In Finland, social policy developed not through labor–capital conflict but through conflict between the Social Democratic Party, which represents wage laborers, and the Agrarian Party,[1] which represents farmers. In other words, a strong urban–rural cleavage was witnessed. It is also notable that the Agrarian Party became dominant as a result of external influences in addition to the social situation in Finland and when and how its political parties were "frozen" (Lipset & Rokkan, 1967).

To capture the uniqueness of Finnish social policy, this chapter focuses on the strength of the Agrarian Party in Finnish politics and its influence on social policy, especially Kansaneläkelaitos (Kela),[2] a major actor in Finnish social policy with strong ties to the party. Kela is an independent public institution directly under the Finnish parliament and is the managing body of social policy separate from the Ministry of Social Affairs and Health. The services it oversees are very broad, including national pensions, health insurance, public assistance, child allowances. Kela was founded in 1937 with the enactment of the National Pension Act. The establishment of this law reflected the Finnish politics of the time, namely the conflict of interests between the Social Democrats and the Agrarian League. The Social Democrats' health insurance proposal, mainly for wage earners, was replaced by a universal national pension plan for all citizens, led by the Agrarian League. Kela was established with the intention of managing this national pension plan. In the process of its establishment and the development of Finnish social policy, it is possible to point out Kela's close relationship with the Agrarian Party. Pesonen and Riihinen point out that Kela is an extremely political organization (Pesonen & Riihinen, 2002, p. 220) point out that Kela is an extremely political organization. This fact indicates the influence of the Agrarian Party in Finnish social policy and

[1] Maalaisliitto (Agrarian League) was established in 1906, and renamed "Keskusta" (the Centre Party) in 1965. In this chapter, "Agrarian League" refers to the earlier time, whereas "Centre Party" refers to the subsequent period. "Agrarian Party" refers to both the Agrarian League and the Centre Party time.

[2] Kansaneläkelaitos means "Institute of National Pension" in English; here it is called "Kela," the commonly shortened name.

suggests that the influence of the Social Democrats was rather limited compared with the case of Sweden. Thus, the driving force behind the construction of a "social democratic" welfare state in Finland was not necessarily the Social Democrats.

After World War II, the Agrarian Party and Kela continued to develop further under their mutual interdependence. In the Cold War structure, conservatives and Social Democrats were restrained, and the Agrarian League maintained a certain percentage of the vote; with the election of President Urho Kekkonen, the Agrarian League strengthened its power as a presidential party. The pension fund, as "the nation's wallet" (Haavikko, 1988, p. 18, Kekkonen, 1952), was inseparable from the economic policies and regional development led by President Kekkonen. The amendment of the National Pension Law in the 1950s from a flat-rate funded system to a pay-as-you-go system also reflected the wishes of the Agrarian League. The Conservative Party[3] and the Social Democratic Party, who were allergic to the Agrarian Party and Kela, tried to circumvent them and created a separate occupational pension system proportional to income.

Health insurance, which had been slow to progress, was introduced in the early 1960s in Finland, the last in Europe, and was intended to cover all citizens. Kela was put in charge of its operation, which led to an increase in Kela's role and functions. The size of the organization expanded nationwide. Here again, the interdependence between the Agrarian League and Kela can be observed, and it has been pointed out that the intention of Kela's management members played a strong role in the final decision to choose between voluntary insurance for wage earners and compulsory insurance for all citizens. As a result, compulsory system was chosen and Kela was appointed to be in charge of health insurance. The Social Democrats and Conservatives, once again dissatisfied with this decision, however later on they have worked together with Kela to develop a separate industrial health system.

From the 1980s, under the policy of rationalization, various social policy services were transferred from the Ministry of Social Affairs and Health and local governments to Kela. The functions of Kela became multilayered, and it became a vital actor as the institution responsible for basic social security in Finland. On the contrary, the Social Democratic Party, in conflict with the Agrarian Party, developed the pension and health insurance system through compromises outside of Kela or the pure public system. Sometimes it meant defeat that their wills did not come true, and sometimes it meant the alternative decision to intentionally avoid Kela or the Agrarian Party. In this way Finland's systems, such as pension and health insurance, developed in complex ways. Owing to the path dependency of the interdependence of the Agrarian Party and Kela embedded in social policy, the nature of the welfare state in Finland has a strong universalist nature that targets everyone through redistribution of income from cities to rural areas. This idea of "universalism" is a major pillar of Finnish social policy; the idea of Bismarckian insurance has been relatively weakly developed in Finland.

[3] The National Coalition Party (Kokoomus in Finnish) is a right wing, conservative party in Finnish politics.

In this chapter, while referring to comparative politics, especially the study of the welfare state of Finland in a comparative framework with Nordic welfare states from a neo-institutional perspective (Alestalo & Uusitalo, 1986; Kangas, 2007; Korpi, 1978; Smolander, 2000, etc.), the focus is on describing Finnish uniqueness, which is the dominance of the Agrarian Party and its impacts on social policy, and its symbol, Kela. Scholars have analyzed the political process of Finnish pension and health insurance and argued that it differs from that of Sweden (Haatanen & Kyösti 1992; Hannikainen & Vauhkonen 2012; Kangas, 1991, 1992, 1994, 2007; Keskimäki et al., 2019; Niemelä, 2014; Paavonen & Kangas, 2006; Smolander, 2000). In this chapter, the political process is analyzed based on the history of Finland's party politics (Arter, 1987; Jussila & Nevakivi, 2004; Knutsen, 2017; Mickelsson, 2015) and with reference to Kela's historical records (Haavikko, 1988; Häggman, 1997; Salmela, 1967). Examining the development of major social policies and politics in general, this study will clarify the impact of the Agrarian Party and Kela on the Finnish welfare state.

In the next section, Finland's position as a Nordic welfare state is presented, and the current structure of Kela, which supports Finland's basic security, is outlined. The third section clarifies the relationship between party politics and the Agrarian Party. In the fourth section, the development of social policy is examined from the perspective of the influence of the Agrarian Party, and subsequent to the establishment of the National Pension System, the relationship between the party and Kela. Finally, in the fifth section, the influence of the Agrarian Party and Kela on Finnish social policy, as quoting Pierson's words, "the Agrarian Party and Kela in Time" is examined (Pierson, 2004). This chapter will show that the Finnish welfare state, considered a "social democratic regime," was built through compromise and transformation. The strength of the Agrarian Party in social policy and the Kela system are unique among Nordic welfare states, and by examining Finnish social policy through Kela, Finland's evolutionary process as a Nordic welfare state can be observed.

3.2 Present Welfare System in Finland and Kela

Esping-Andersen (1990) categorized the Nordic countries into "social democratic" welfare state regime based on comparative welfare state research, and explained they have achieved the highest decommodification of welfare services, and providing comprehensive and higher standard of services which also require a commitment to work. He explained that Finland, which achieved the Nordic standard of welfare state in the 1970s–80s, was "social democratized" late (ibid.). However, the process of becoming a welfare state and the actors running it differ from those of other Nordic countries. This section delves into Kela's role in present Finnish society.

3.2.1 Kela's Service

Kela's role has been introduced as "providing basic security for everyone covered by the Finnish social security system at different stages of life, from maternity benefits to old-age pensions" (Kela, 2013, p. 2). The scope of its services is comprehensive, including security for families with children, income security for students, housing assistance, conscription benefits, unemployment compensation, health insurance, rehabilitation, pension security, benefits and services for people with disabilities, security for survivors, security for immigrants, and public assistance. It stated objectives are to (1) guarantee income, (2) promote health throughout Finland, and (3) support the ability of individual citizens to take care of themselves (ibid.).

Kela covers a wide range of social policy services in Finland. In 2023, Kela's total benefit expenditure came to about 17.2 billion EUR.[4] The largest expenditure categories were: health insurance (5591 million EUR), national pensions (2250 million EUR), unemployment benefits (1930 million EUR), reimbursements for medical expenses (1790 million EUR), general housing allowances (1680 million EUR), child benefits (1350 million EUR), basic social assistance (718 million EUR), student financial aid (690 million EUR), disability benefits (622 million EUR), and others (guarantee pension, child care allowance, child maintenance allowance, school transport subsidy, interpreter service for people with disabilities, survivors' pension, conscripts' allowance, maternity grant, front veterans' benefits and pension assistance).[5] According to Kela, 0.7 million people visit its customer service locations, 38.3 million people login to its online customer service, and 35.4 million login to its e-service called OmaKanta (for which 29.8 million electronic prescriptions have been issued).[6] These services are generally related to basic security, which accounts for approximately 20% of Finland's national budget.

Some services are provided only by Kela, and some are funded by other organizations, too. Regardless, Kela is responsible for most public sector benefits. For example, Kela conducted the 2-year basic income social experiment from 2017 to 2018. Regarding funding, nearly 70% is from the state, other insurance premiums, employers' and local government funds, and unemployment insurance from employees.[7] Kela has over 8000 employees working either in central or local offices, relatively high for an organization of its size in Finland. Kela operates throughout Finland.[8]

---

[4] Quoted from Kela's webpage, https://www.kela.fi/operations-funding-and-key-indicators

[5] Ibid.

[6] Ibid.

[7] See details on Kela's webpage, https://www.kela.fi/operations-funding-and-key-indicators

[8] ibid.

3.2.2 Legal Status of Kela

One of its most notable features is that Kela has had a special status as an institution directly under the parliament since its establishment in 1937—it is independent and not affiliated with any ministry. Another major actor of social policy is the Ministry of Social Affairs and Health. This means that Finland has a unique form of dual bureaucracy with Kela and the Ministry. An organization with similar status as Kela is the National Bank of Finland (Suomen Pankki). As with the Bank of Finland, Kela's activities are supervised by council members elected by the parliament in addition to their own management team. The Finnish Broadcasting Company and the Finnish alcohol retailing monopoly Alko also previously had a similar status. The parliamentary Act "Laki Kansaneläkelaitoksesta"[9] (hereinafter "the Kela Act") clearly states that Kela's status is that of "an independent institution under public law, the administration and management of which are supervised by a council elected by parliament" (Article 1 of the Kela Act). The right to social security is stated in Article 19 of the Constitution of Finland (Suomen perustuslaki), but Kela's duties include the implementation of social security and other related tasks (Article 2 of the Kela Act). In addition, each system in the field under Kela's jurisdiction, such as the national pension and social insurance, is regulated by its own law.

Article 3 of the Kela Act specifies that Kela's governing bodies are the council and the board of directors. The council is elected by the parliament from various political parties (Article 4 of the Kela Act), and the members of the board of directors are decided by the council. The members of the council and the board of directors are external to Kela. The council also elects Kela's director and up to five deputy directors, and the president appoints the director and deputy directors according to this proposal.

This system is significantly different from that in Sweden in that Kela has special powers directly under the parliament and is the main actor in the operation of the country, including in research and investigations into social policy. Services provided solely by Kela include national and guarantee pension, sickness and disability benefits, rehabilitation, parental and family benefits, housing benefits, and student financial benefits, provided on a residence-based basis. Social assistance and healthcare services are provided in collaboration with local governments, while local governments are responsible for social services and informal care allowance. Unemployment benefits are provided by Kela and unemployment funds. In addition, pension companies provide earnings-related pensions and benefits for accidents at work and occupational diseases, and, although rare, private insurance also exists.

[9] Finlex, https://www.finlex.fi/fi/laki/ajantasa/2001/20010731

3.3 Agrarian Party in Finnish Political System

This section presents an overview of party politics in Finland and its characteristics before looking at the political process of the launch of the national pension system and Kela and the subsequent development of social policy in Finland.

3.3.1 Nordic and Finnish Political Party System

The main points are as follows. The Nordic five-party system concept, developed by Lipset and Rokkan (1967), also applies to Finnish party politics. However, there are some differences. In Finland, the liberal Progressive Party disappeared after World War II, and the Swedish People's Party can be categorized as a liberal party, but it is small in size, mainly supported by Swedish-speaking residents—around 5% of the population. Furthermore, although the Social Democratic Party has been a major political party, it does not have much experience of stably running a government as in Sweden. The Agrarian Party, which is common in the Nordic countries, has a strong presence in Finland.

Finland achieved independence from the Russian Empire in 1917, but in 1906, when it was an autonomous Grand Duchy, a proportional representation unicameral parliament was established through parliamentary reform, and both men and women gained the right to vote and to be voted for. Among the traditional political parties, the Finns Party,[10] with its roots in the Fennoman movement, which aimed to improve the status of the Finnish language, and the Swedish Party, with its roots in the Svecoman movement, which sought to maintain the privilege of the Swedish language, gradually developed into political parties from the 1860s onward. Both were elite parties, and the Finns Party split into the conservative Old Finns Party, which advocated maintaining friendly relations with the Russian Empire, and the Young Finns Party, which sought independence. In 1899, the first mass political party, the Workers' Party, was born and was renamed the Social Democratic Party at the party conference in 1903. In the year of the parliamentary reform, a party organization that would form the roots of the Agrarian Party was born partly out of the Young Finns political movement. In Finland, industrialization progressed more slowly than in other Nordic countries, with <10% of the population employed in secondary industries in the 1900s and 1910s, and 70–80% working in agriculture. The pace of industrialization thereafter was also slow, and the country switched to an industrialized society only in the 1960s (Pernaa & Niemi, 2005, p. 169). After independence, Old Finns was officially established as the National Coalition Party and Young Finns as the Progressive Party, and after the civil war, the Social Democratic Party clearly split into the Social Democratic Party and the Communist Party of Finland.

[10] Finska partiet (later vanhasuomalaiset, the Old Finns).

In the first general parliamentary elections in 1907, the Social Democratic Party won 80 out of 200 seats, the Old Finns Party 59 seats, the Young Finns Party 26 seats, the Swedish People's Party 24 seats, the party that became the precursor of the Agrarian League nine seats, and other parties two seats, making the Finnish Social Democratic Party the largest socialist party in Europe (Häikiö, 1992; Mickelsson, 2015). However, owing to circumstances such as the civil war, the Agrarian Party's support grew and they gained seats gradually.

3.3.2 Nordic Five-Party System and the Agrarian Party

Lipset and Rokkan cite a five-party system consisting of the social democratic and communist parties in the left bloc, the agrarian party, the liberal parties, and the conservative parties in the bourgeois bloc as characteristics of party politics in Scandinavia (Knutsen, 2017, pp. 58–60; Lipset & Rokkan, 1967; Petersson, 1994). The existence of "agrarian parties" is a characteristic of the Scandinavian party system. In Nordic countries, the early stages of industrialization led to the era of large-scale democratization, and the interests of agricultural forces still played a major role both economically and politically, resulting in the red–green coalition (Manow, 2009). The urban upper class, labor force, and the peasant force, as well as the construction of the Nordic welfare state, was promoted through conflict and compromise among these three classes above (Pedersen & Kuhnle, 2017). Manow explains that proportional representation contributed to the formation of the welfare state system in the formation of political classes in Western democracies, and points out that in addition to the conflict between capital and labor, in Nordic countries there was a "red and green" coalition between social democratic and peasant parties, and in continental Europe there was a "red and black" coalition between social democratic and Christian democratic parties. He points out that while in continental Europe, the separation of state and church strengthened political parties that defended religion, in Nordic countries, where Protestantism was the mainstream, religious cleavage was weak, and the Lutheran state church did not feel threatened when the nation-state was formed.

In other European countries, the support of peasants was absorbed by conservative and Christian parties, but in Scandinavia, agrarian parties have existed independently. The reasons cited for this, common to all Nordic countries, are that (1) urban and industrial centers were relatively weak when universal suffrage was introduced, (2) the majority of the agricultural population was made up of independent family farmers, (3) there was a large cultural gap between rural and urban areas, which worked against the incorporation of the agrarian economy into the capitalist market in urban areas, and (4) the Catholic Church had no influence in these countries (Pedersen & Kuhnle, 2017; Petersson, 1994). Supporting Rokkan and Lipset's Nordic five-party system, from the explanations of Pedersen and Kuhnle, and Petersson, it can be said that owing to the delay in industrialization in the Nordic countries, at the time of the realization of universal suffrage, the cleavage between "cities" and "rural areas" as well as "elites" and "masses" had been cemented.

3.3.3 Rise of the Agrarian Party in Finland

Finland also had a slow industrialization process, and there was a large social cleavage between urban and rural areas. Finland clearly maintains an Agrarian Party, one of the characteristics of the Nordic five-party system. The Social Democrats won a landslide victory in the first election before independence, but the Agrarian League, founded a little later than the Social Democrats, grew significantly after that. The timing of the founding of the Agrarian Party in Finland coincided with the parliamentary reform in the country, making it the second Nordic country to be founded relatively early after Denmark.

In the Finnish party system, the Agrarian Party is a center-right party. It has been the largest party more times than any other, and has also participated in government as a coalition partner more times than any other while agrarian parties are in decline in many other European countries. They also have a stable number of seats in local councils.

In 1919, Finland has made a decision to be a "republic" and follows a presidential system. Of the 13 presidents till today, three have been from the Agrarian Party: the second president Lauri Relander (in office 1925–1931), the fourth president Kyösti Kallio (in office 1937–1940), and the eighth and longest-serving president Urho Kekkonen (in office 1956–1982). In the first parliamentary election, the newly established Agrarian League won nine seats as mentioned earlier, and in elections after independence increased its number of seats in the 1920s, winning more than 20% of the vote for a long time. At its peak, the party received around 30% of the vote, but now it is just over 10%. Agrarian Party has been the largest in the country more times than any other, led the government and coalition, and even if it they were not the biggest party, they have participated in many governments.

The establishment and expansion of the Agrarian Party in Finland has been supported by several factors, including their representation of rural areas, as in other Nordic countries, their involvement in the establishment of the republic, the high proportion of independent self-employed farmers, the division of the Left block, and their establishment as a presidential party. The large expansion of the "center" in the political space is one of the characteristics of Finnish politics.

Mickelsson (2015) points out that while the civil war intensified vigilance against the Left, the land reforms of the early 1920s produced many self-employed farmers, whose support the Agrarian Party absorbed. However, the sense of crisis over communism suppressed support for the Left, and the Social Democratic Party also split into the Communist Party and the Social Democratic Party, and organized a party to represent farmers, but it ended in failure (Mickelsson, 2015). More specifically, pointed out the following as reasons for the rise of the Agrarian Party in Finland before World War II: (1) the Finnish Agrarian Party played an important role in the nation-building period from 1917 to 1919, (2) in 1922, the Agrarian League led the implementation of the Land Reform Act (commonly known as the Kallio Act, or Lex Kallio), which also gained the support of far-Left forces, (3) the population of family farms increased owing to the resettlement of refugees from Karelia after World War II, (4) long-time president Urho Kekkonen contributed to maintaining good relations between the Agrarian Party and the Kremlin during the Cold War, and Kekkonen's foreign policy skills led to support for the Agrarian Party, and (5) the division and loss of power of the Social Democratic Party in the 1950s made it easier for the Agrarian Party to gain influence.

In the case of Finland, owing to various factors, the Social Democrats never became dominant, and the expansion of the Agrarian Party was noticeable. The red–green coalition exists as the red–land coalition in Finnish, but the role of the "land," or the Agrarian party, has been strong. The existence of the Agrarian Party is one of the characteristics of the Nordic five-party system. In the construction of the Nordic welfare states, the solidarity between social democratic parties and Agrarian Party contributed to significantly raising the level of income redistribution. Finland is the country where the Agrarian Party had the largest presence and role in solidarity.

3.4 Development of Social Policy in Finland and Kela

Kela is currently in charge of a wide range of social policy benefits and systems in Finland, as discussed in the second section. Kela's establishment and developments have been closely related with the Agrarian Party. Kela has been strongly influenced by Finnish politics, in a sense, and has been a political organization by itself.

In Sweden, the long-term government of the Social Democratic Party and its solidarity with other parties made it possible to mobilize power and advance the construction of a welfare state (Esping-Andersen, 1990). In Finland, the Social Democratic Party is the main rival of the Agrarian Party; the Agrarian Party's relative dominance in social policy developments meant the Social Democratic Party was often defeated. Finland's social policy developed mainly in the midst of the conflict between the Social Democrats and the Agrarian Party and was shaped by compromises and partial cooperation.

In this section, first the process of establishment of the national pension and Kela will be studied. Then, Kela's developments after World War II through when the National Pension was revised in the 1950s and health insurance was introduced in the 1960s will be analyzed. Furthermore, the expansion process of Kela to be basic security actor after the 1980s will be described.

3.4.1 From Social Insurance to National Pension Scheme: The Founding of Kela

The concept of social policy was brought to Finland in the late nineteenth century by Yrjö Sakari Yrjö-Koskinen, founder of the Finns' Party, before Finland became independent. He was influenced by German social policy, and social insurance, established by Otto von Bismarck, which became a topic of discussion in Finland as in other Nordic countries (Paavonen & Kangas, 2006, p. 253). Labor movements and socialism were also imported to Finland, and the Finnish Workers' Party (Social Democratic Party from 1903) was born, and in the first general election in 1907, gained wide support. The Social Democratic Party, which was gaining momentum, actively lobbied for the introduction of "social insurance" in the 1910s, but was unable to achieve this owing to Finland's political and financial situation. After that, the outbreak of the civil war and the defeat of the Red Army weakened the Social Democratic Party's power, while the increase in independent self-employed farmers owing to land reform also helped the Agrarian League expand its influence.

In March 1917, before Finland gained independence, a Social Democratic majority government was formed. Just before independence, the Old Finns Party, the Swedish People's Party, and the Agrarian League joined the majority government led by Young Finns (later the Progressive Party) in late November. The Agrarian League became the largest party for the first time in the 1922 election, and together with the National Coalition Party (the Conservatives) and the Progressive Party, an Agrarian minority government was formed. In 1927 and 1929, the Agrarian League also formed a sole government. In 1926, a Social Democratic government was formed for the first time in 10 years. The National Coalition Party, Progressive Party, and Agrarian League were the main ruling parties in the 1920s. Since the 1930s, the Swedish People's Party has also frequently joined the government. In the Liberal Party government in 1937, a coalition government of the Agrarian Party and the Social Democratic Party was formed for the first time, with the Progressive Party at the center. This was the first red–land government, that is, the red–green or center–left government in Finland. After that, the war against the Soviet Union broke out, and a grand coalition government continued from 1939 to 1945.

In 1925, the Ministry of Social Affairs presented a proposal for health insurance for salaried workers, estimated to cover 300,000 people, or 45% of the workforce. However, the plan did not cover independent farmers, self-employed people, or employees of companies with five or fewer employees, who made up the majority of agricultural workers; instead, it covered 220,000 industrial workers and 80,000 agricultural workers on large farms (Niemelä, 2014, pp. 56–57). Based on this proposal, the minority Social Democratic government, which came to power for the first time in 10 years in 1926, presented a bill for compulsory health insurance for workers to parliament in 1927, but it was rejected owing to opposition from the Agrarian League, as the target audience was mainly urban wage earners. From then, the debate over social insurance became a confrontational structure between "workers" and "farmers" and "urban" and "rural" areas. While the Social Democratic

Party aimed to establish health insurance, the Agrarian League prioritized the establishment of old-age and disability pensions. The minority Agrarian League government, which came to power in 1927, began considering a national pension law. The Progressive Party minority government, in coalition with the Agrarian League established in 1936, approved the bill, and the Agrarian League minority government, established in October 1936, submitted the bill to parliament; it was passed by a majority vote in the next Progressive Party majority government (Shibayama, 2020, p. 71). It is clear that the cooperation between the Agrarian League and the Progressive Party was important in the passage of this bill.

Häggman (1997, p. 31), in his study of Kela's history, points out that the name of the bill was changed from "National Insurance" to "National Pension." The introduction of a health insurance system was postponed until the 1960s, and the enactment of the National Pension Law was a victory for the Agrarian League.

Pension was operated as a funded system, with compulsory contributions from employers and all adults over 18, regardless of whether they had an income, to deal with the risk of old age and loss of ability to work. The pension age was 55, and the requirement to receive a pension was having made contributions for at least 10 years. Häggman (1997, p. 28) points out that the National Pension Act in 1937 was a mixture of old and new ideas; that is, it was based on the traditional selective, means-tested poverty relief system, but the payment of pensions was based on "citizenship" rather than "mercy," and the right to a pension was considered to be "one's earning ability." As it was aimed at citizens, not just wage earners, it became a system that covered the entire working population, including women. Finland did not introduce health insurance until the 1960s, and although the insurance system was adopted, it was the first large-scale social policy to introduce a system that covered all citizens. The Bismarckian insurance system, aimed purely at workers, was rejected, and the seeds of a social security system based on citizenship were seen here, moving from the Poor Law-style income guarantee system. It is also clear that the interests of the Agrarian League were given priority. Furthermore, Kela was established in December 1937 as a special institution directly under parliament to manage and administer the pension fund. While this organization played the role of the "the nation's wallet" by managing the pension fund (Haavikko, 1988, p. 18), it also maintained strong ties with the Agrarian Party and strengthened its role as a major actor in Finnish social policy. Kela was founded with the passage of the National Pension Act led by the Agrarian League, and Kela and the Agrarian Party mutually increased their political influence on social policy.

3.4.2 *Reform of the National Pension System and Introduction of Occupational Pension System: Path to the Dual Pension System*

The Agrarian League, which has consistently held around 25% of the seats in Finnish politics since the 1920s, has been strongly involved in the development of social policy by directing benefits to the party and its supporters, while at odds with the Social Democratic Party. The Act of National Pension in 1937 had several problems, including payment amounts and financial aspects. Even after the 1940s, the Ministry of Social Affairs and the Social Democratic Party continued to lead the review of "the Act of Health Insurance." A major point of contention was whether to adopt the flat-rate benefit system advocated by the Agrarian League or the income-proportional system advocated by the Social Democratic Party and the National Coalition Party. Meanwhile, from the 1950s, under the Cold War structure, both right- and left-wing parties were subject to restrictions from the Soviet Union and the Agrarian League grew stronger, and this tendency further increased when it became the presidential party.

In 1954, V. J. Sukselainen, a leading politician of the Agrarian League, became director of Kela (in position 1954–1971), and when he became prime minister in 1957, he enacted a new national pension system, changing from a funded system to a pay-as-you-go system, and establishing a flat-rate pension and an additional pension paid according to the spouse's income and the number of children under 16. The flat-rate pension system encourages income redistribution from urban to rural areas. The 1950s reform of the National Pension Act was passed under a coalition government consisting of the Agrarian League, Progressive Party, and Swedish People's Party. The Social Democrats were in opposition. The enactment of the National Pension Act in 1937 was a victory for the Agrarian League, and the party was victorious again in the pension reforms of the 1950s. The fact that Prime Minister Urho Kekkonen won the presidential election in 1956 and Sukselainen became Prime Minister continued as a director of Kela made the decision in favor of the Agrarian Party.

Meanwhile, while discussions on social insurance continued even after the war, the Ministry of Social Affairs and Health, not satisfied with the system of uniform benefits, sought to introduce a continental-style pension system rather than the Beveridge-style fixed pension model. In 1958, the Seamen's Pension Fund was launched, deviating from the conventional idea of equal uniform benefits. The Social Democratic Party's wishes were not completely rejected, and as the Agrarian League compromised, the Compulsory Employees' Pension Law was enacted in 1961, and the Law on Short-Term Employees' Pension was enacted the following year.

Kangas (2007) points out that the introduction of occupational pensions was motivated by the successful introduction of voluntary unemployment insurance in 1960. Unemployment insurance in many countries resulted from the Great Depression of the 1930s, and Finland also enacted the Unemployment Fund Act in

1934. However, it was largely ineffective, and unemployment remained a social problem even after the war. The Social Insurance Commission considered introducing unemployment insurance but concluded that it was premature. In the 1950s, discussions about compulsory unemployment insurance increased, and in 1955 the Kekkonen Agrarian League coalition government established an unemployment insurance committee; however, insurance not implemented, and a new committee was established. The Finnish People's Democratic League and the Agrarian League supported a new proposal in which insurance premiums would be borne by the national government, local governments, employers, and insured persons.

In response, the Ministry of Finance, the STK,[11] and the Conservative party supported a voluntary unemployment insurance system for wage earners only. After the 1960 elections, social democratic groups within the STK and SAK[12] began considering a voluntary unemployment insurance system based on the unemployment fund system (Yamada, 2006, pp. 113–116). This can be said to be an example of cooperative progress in labor–capital relations. The Social Democratic Party, which had held its position, decided that voluntary unemployment benefits would be more advantageous, and the Agrarian League agreed to voluntary unemployment insurance in exchange for local unemployment measures and avoiding a split in the ruling party (Kangas, 2007). In 1960, a fund-type unemployment insurance system was approved by the coalition government of the National Coalition Party, Social Democratic Party, and Agrarian League, according to which unemployment insurance would be paid to insured persons according to their income. This system can be described as a "red, blue, and land" alliance in which the Bismarckian model advocated by the National Coalition Party matched the wishes of the workers, and the Agrarian League also made compromises.

Kangas (2007, p. 266) also points out that the Conservatives and Social Democrats were skeptical of a public pension system, fearing that wage earners' pensions would somehow be "stolen" by agricultural workers. The Agrarian League minority government refused to introduce the bill, so it was eventually adopted as a private members' bill. Agrarian workers initially opposed the introduction of income-proportional occupational pensions, but their dissatisfaction was alleviated by the establishment of family pensions and pensions for agricultural workers and the self-employed. This pension scheme has been the result of conflicts and compromise, which is the case of the red–green (land) alliance in Finland. A comprehensive pension system was established by combining the national pension with occupational pensions covering a wide range of occupations. The introduction of occupational pensions had the effect of raising the social standard in Finland. By combining Beveridge- and Bismarck-type benefits, the country gradually approached the benefit levels of Nordic countries such as Sweden (Shibayama, 2022).

Other income-related pension laws were further developed thereafter; in 1964, the Local Government Employees' Pensions Act was enacted, targeting local

[11] STK, Confederation of Finnish Industries.

[12] SAK, The Central Organisation of Finnish Trade Unions.

government employees, and in 1967 the National Civil Service Employees' Pensions Act and the Evangelical Lutheran Church Act were enacted. In 1969, the Family Pensions Act institutionalized the payment of survivors' pensions, and in 1970 the Self-Employed Persons' Pensions Act and Agricultural Workers' Pensions Act were enacted. These were called occupational pensions and were income-related pension systems based on employment.

The two systems, along with the National Pension, which provided a minimum guarantee based on residence, were used in conjunction and were not unified. The conflict between the Agrarian Party and the Social Democratic Party can be seen as the background to the establishment of the two separate systems. The national pension is administered by Kela; the Pension Security Centre (Eläketurvakeskus), an agency under the Ministry of Social Affairs and Health, functions as the central coordinator for occupational pensions; and the compulsory earnings-related pensions are uniquely managed by private insurers under the control of public institutions. Kangas (2007, p. 269) characterizes this system as a "corporatist" and "semi-public" pension. The national pension is mainly funded by taxes, while occupational pensions are mainly funded by insurance premiums paid by employers and contract holders. Smolander (2000) argues that the Finnish pension system developed in a completely different way from Sweden. The pension system for all citizens advocated by the Swedish Social Democrats was advocated by the Agrarian League and the Finnish People's Democratic League, while the Social Democrats and the National Coalition Party presented an idea similar to the industry-based decentralized pension system advocated by the Swedish People's Party (Smolander, 2000). In Finland, the Agrarian League and the Finnish People's Democratic League represented the interests of the "rural areas" and emphasized social policies for "all citizens." The roles played by the Social Democratic Party in Sweden and Finland were also different, with the Agrarian Party functioning more strongly as a national party and pushing a "universal" social policy scheme.

3.4.3 Introduction of Health Insurance: The Expansion of Kela

As mentioned earlier, in the 1910s, 1920s, and 1930s, the social insurance system proposed by the Social Democrats was rejected by the Agrarian League. After the war, health insurance was gradually developed as a voluntary system, mainly by interest groups. In the 1940s, the grand committee was established to consider social insurance, led by bureaucrats. In 1949, the committee produced a report on compulsory health insurance for employees. However, this proposal was not realized owing to strong opposition from the Finnish Medical Association (Suomen Lääkäriliitto) and the Agrarian League (Niemelä, 2014, pp. 79–80). In 1953, the bureaucratic government proposed making health insurance a compulsory national-level scheme for all citizens. A similar health insurance proposal was approved in the same year in Sweden. Meanwhile, subsequent governments focused on reforming the National Pension Act, and in the 1950s, the introduction of a health insurance bill was postponed, despite continued discussions.

In the 1960s, the working population in the secondary industries finally exceeded the population in the primary industries, and at the same time, the service industry became the biggest group. Thus, Finland became an industrialized society. The demand for health insurance grew clearly, and with the pressure from President Kekkonen, the introduction of insurance became recognized as an urgent issue. The introduction itself became a self-evident goal, and the discussions shifted to the target population, waiting period, payment period, and management form. In 1962, the Soviet Union intervened in Finnish foreign policy, and President Kekkonen's re-election in the same year became certain. At the same time, the Agrarian League strengthened its political influence (Niemelä, 2014, pp. 95–96). In the parliamentary election held 3 weeks after the presidential election, the Agrarian League became the largest party, and a right-wing, bourgeois government was formed with the National Coalition Party and the Swedish People's Party. Meanwhile, the Social Democratic Party lost seats owing to internal divisions. The law was approved by parliament in 1963 and was implemented in 1964 and 1967 in stages.

It was the latest introduction of health insurance in Europe (Kuusi 1961). As a result, the proposal for a decentralized fund system was rejected, and a government-based health insurance system was adopted, with the centralized Kela as the insurer nationwide. As a result, Kela was able to handle social insurance nationwide, and the organization's presence in social policy was further strengthened. Niemelä (2014, pp. 95–96) points out that this decision was not an initiative of the Agrarian League parliamentarians but rather a strong push from Kela's upper management. The idea for Kela to manage the nationwide health insurance was justified on the grounds that the unified management of Kela, which already had human resources, organizations, and data, would allow its expertise to be effectively utilized and would be cheaper than the fund scheme. Kela rapidly expanded as a national organization, strengthening the agency's role in social policy. The adoption of the Kela system for health insurance is attributable to the intervention of President Kekkonen, the influence of the president's party, the Agrarian League, Kela itself, and the interdependence of the three actors.

The Act of Health Insurance supports medical insurance, as well as income security in the event of illness and during childbirth. The introduction of health insurance also boosted economic growth, and was of great significance in terms of building a truly universal welfare state. The initial plan sought a decentralized system that would utilize local government and occupational funds, as in other countries, but in the end it was decided to introduce a centralized system run by Kela, which was to oversee not only pension but also health insurance services. Here again the influence of the Agrarian League and the power of Kela can be seen. On the contrary, after the Health Insurance Act was enacted, the industrial health system, which had developed as voluntary insurance, was incorporated into the Kela system of reimbursement payments, leading to the dual development of public medical care and industrial health. The industrial health system was developed mainly by trade unions and employers' associations. In 1971, labor market organizations expanded workplace health management as part of income policy solutions, resulting in the enactment of the Occupational and Industrial Health Act in 1978 (Niemelä, 2014, p. 263). Finland, thus, came to have an eclectic system that combined equality and convenience (Shibayama, 2023).

Currently, Finnish health insurance is a unique system that combines a public medical model and an occupational health model, unlike the public medical model in other Nordic countries (Marttila, 2011, pp. 15–16). A similar pattern can be seen here as in the pension system. In other words, while the Agrarian League led the creation of a uniform system under Kela that covered all citizens, labor forces felt that this system was insufficient and created a separate income-proportional system.

3.4.4 Transfer of Other Services: Kela for Comprehensive Basic Security

The introduction of health insurance under its jurisdiction led to Kela's nationwide expansion. In 1969, Kela was also in charge of survivors' pension, and in 1971, it was in charge of front veterans' benefits. Subsequent major reforms included the introduction of unemployment benefits in 1985, disability benefits in 1989, and the transfer of a series of benefits in the 1990s, including child benefits, general housing allowance, and student financial aid. Most recently, basic social assistance was also transferred to Kela in 2017.

In the 1980s, a major reform of the social benefits tax system[13] was carried out and as part of this, the health insurance daily allowance was reformed and became taxable. This reform was linked to the increase in the allowance level and the elimination of the upper limit. This was in line with Kela's social insurance principles and strengthened the insurance nature of the allowance system (Häggman, 1997, p. 232). Based on this reform, the level of the limit of daily allowance of the unemployment insurance was also significantly increased, and it was made taxable income. There was a need to link national, health, and unemployment insurance, and it was thought that the application of the computer system that Kela was developing would be ideal. It was explored whether Kela could take over the reformed system. With the initiative of the new director of Kela, basic unemployment insurance was transferred from the employment service run across the Ministry of Social Affairs and Health and Department of Labour to the Kela regional office in 1982. The complex system was transferred to Kela, simplifying it. Since then unemployment allowance has been paid as an earnings-related allowance or a basic allowance. Basic unemployment allowance and labor market subsidy are administered by Kela, while unemployment funds administer the earnings-related unemployment allowance (Niemelä & Salminen, 2006, p. 31).

[13] Sosiaalietuuksien verotusuudistusta, the so-called SOVE reform.

The case of unemployment benefits has proved the "efficiency" of integration of services to Kela. An argument was made that there should be a single "one-stop place" where all services related to citizens' basic livelihood are accessible. This would serve citizens' interests, as providing the services out of a centralized location would make access to them easier and quicker as well as requiring less administrative input. These ideas were realized in the 1990s, after various services transferred to Kela. Thus, Kela has achieved the position of being responsible for basic and income security in Finland (Häggman, 1997, pp. 274–275).

Child home care and family allowances were transferred at the beginning of 1993, and general housing allowances, conscripts' allowances, maternity grants, and student financial aid in 1994. With these new functions, Kela became responsible for the entire aid system aimed at families with children. Considering that the basic unemployment protection and housing allowance schemes in the 1990s targeted young persons and families with children, it can be said that the new functions are in addition to the Kela's traditional role: mainly national pension and health insurance. Politically, the Centre government formed in 1991, clearly positioned the rationalization and concentration of basic security (ibid., pp. 252–253). Kela already has offices and staff all over the country and simplifying social welfare administration and improving service availability became a clear goal. Recently, public assistance was transferred to Kela in 2017.

3.5 Impact of the Agrarian Party and Kela on Finnish Social Policy

In this section, the characteristics of the long-term developments of Finland's social policy are summarized, based on the development history of the pension and health insurance systems mentioned above. Owing to the timing of the "frozen" Finnish party politics, the presence of the Soviet Union, and the presidential system and party politics influenced by it, Finnish social policy developed in a way that did not necessarily favor social democracy. As has been seen, the influence of the Agrarian Party was very large, and the party and Kela became the main actors in Finnish social policy. Not only did they achieve their goals, to the point of compromising other schemes, but they also had huge impacts to whole Finnish social policy. First, the nature of Finnish social policy from the introduction of the national pension, an early social policy will be analyzed, and then the process of how Kela's functions have become multilayered will be examined. At last, the impacts of the Agrarian Party and Kela on Finnish social policy as a whole are examined.

The first thing to note is that the idea of social policy itself was imported by the founder of the Conservative party, and the actual political movement to launch social insurance was initiated by the Social Democrats. The discussion on social insurance was transformed or refracted into a "national pension" by the Agrarian League. As the first major turning point toward adaptation to a welfare state, the national pension was enacted under the influence of the Agrarian League, and a strong sense of universalism was embedded in it. A proposal for social insurance based on occupation was rejected. Despite being influenced by Sweden and other countries, it differed in nature from the service providing a minimum standard of living under the initiative of the capitalist class when the working class was weak, or the service targeting only wage earners living mostly in urban areas. Although the system itself was immature, the starting point of Finnish social policy was characterized by targeting both urban and rural areas and all citizens regardless of livelihood or occupation. Universalism formed the foundation of Finland's social policy, and this continues even today. Subsequently, Kela was formed with a special status, directly run by the parliament.

Pension funds became important to the political power of the time, especially the Agrarian League. The foundation of Kela linked with the establishment of the national pension had a clear purpose, and in a sense it was occasional, not meant to run comprehensive basic income security in the end. After the war, Kela, a public institution independent from the ministries, became the main body for managing the Finnish welfare state. In addition to gaining control over pension funds and the interdependence with the Agrarian League that rose out of the internal "frozen" structure, external factors influenced the initiation of health insurance in the 1960s after long discussions. It became clear that Kela would be responsible for providing nationwide flat-benefits payments, especially cash-based services that had previously been operated separately by the Ministry of Social Affairs and Health, local governments, and other funds for efficiency. For nearly 90 years, Kela has reflected the needs of the times; as a result, it has become a decisive actor in Finnish social policy. The decommodification of welfare is managed by a dual bureaucratic social policy, with the Ministry of Social Affairs and Health focusing on in-kind benefits and Kela focusing on cash benefits, and its form is unique in Nordic countries. Even today, when the Agrarian Party is not as strong as before, Kela's presence is indispensable. Kela has expanded and concentrated its functions as a result of coexistence with the Agrarian Party. The fact that most Kela directors belong to the Agrarian Party also indicates the strong ties between these two actors (Junkkari, 2016).

The symbiotic relationship between Kela and the Agrarian Party had a major influence on Finnish social policy in general. The revisions to the National Pension Act and the introduction of Health Insurance strongly reflected the intentions of President Kekkonen, the Agrarian League, and the management of Kela linked with the party. As a result, income redistribution from urban to rural areas was strengthened further. Although the introduction of health insurance was delayed not only owing to financial problems but also because of opposition from the Agrarian League to a voluntary system, it resulted in compulsory insurance for all citizens.

On the contrary, Kela and the Agrarian Party's impact is not limited to the influence on the establishment of universal systems such as national pension and health insurance. Income-related occupational pensions, which were rejected by the Agrarian Party, were created under the initiative of the Social Democratic Party and Conservative and Liberal Parties. They avoided Kela for fear of confiscation of their funds. As a result, Finland's pension, health insurance, and unemployment benefits systems now have a public basic benefit system and a semi-public system that is proportional to income.

The Finnish pension system consists of national and occupational pension, both of which are pay-as-you-go. The national pension is administered by Kela and primarily funded by taxes. Occupational pensions are an insurance system coordinated by private insurers and the Finnish Center for Pensions, a subsidiary of the Ministry of Social Affairs and Health. Earnings-related pensions and health insurance were developed separately as a compromise, and their establishment was linked through a series of developments in other social policies, resulting in the Finnish system taking on a complex form.

Rather than being the result of solidarity, some compromises were made amid strong opposition, and systems were built up in a "patchwork" manner rather than the Swedish social engineering way. Baldwin (1990) explains that in the Nordic countries, ties between the Social Democratic Party, Agrarian Party, and Conservative Party have led to "social solidarity," embedding Beveridge-style universalism and Marshallese citizenship in Bismarck-style social insurance, resulting in relatively high standards. Through the case of Finland, other developments of this "merge" of a universalistic system and income-proportional system can be seen and this study describes the process and actors to achieve the Nordic model in Finland, which has similarities but also differences. In Finland's social policy, which developed as a rural–urban cleavage, the system of universal benefits was first strongly embedded, and this trend continued and was adapted in a uniquely Finnish form. As a result, the system combines strong universalism with an improved level of income proportionality, and has the characteristic of not becoming too Bismarckian.

3.6 Conclusion

This study closely observes the development of Finnish social policy from party politics and Kela. It can provide a background to explain how Finland has the same characteristics as the Nordic countries regarding some phenomena and different characteristics regarding others. Kela symbolizes the developmental history of Finnish social policy, and its influence on Finnish social policy has been enormous.

To summarize, Kela, born to reflect the interests of the Agrarian Party, (1) was strongly embedded with "universalism," representing the interests of all regions (interdependent relationship with the Party, (2) developed as a main player in Finnish social policy, (3) became a central actor in the universal system, and (4) became multilayered, while it also had a strong influence on other systems such as pension, health insurance, and unemployment insurance. As a result of adaptation, even as Finland developed into a Nordic welfare state, Kela made gradual changes and directly and indirectly influenced various systems, resulting in a unique and eclectic system (Thelen, 2004). The characteristics of Finland's social policy are shown based on the historical and political background.

Acknowledgments This research was supported by a KAKEN grant 19K20532 received in FY2019–2023 and 19H04368 in FY2019–2023. I would like to thank Prof. Taro Miyamoto and Prof. Takeshi Hieda for their meaningful comments at Japan Association for Comparative Politics in June 2023.

References

Alestalo, M., & Uusitalo, H. (1986). Finland. In P. Flora (Ed.), *Growth to limits: The western European welfare states since World War II*. Walter de Gruyter.

Arter, D. (1987). *Politics and policy-making in Finland*. St. Martin's Press.

Baldwin, P. (1990). *The politics of social solidarity, class bases of the European welfare state 1875–1975*. Cambridge University Press.

Esping-Andersen, G. (1990). *The three worlds of welfare capitalism*. Polity Press.

Haatanen, P., & Kyösti, S. (1992). *Suuriruhtinaskunnasta Hyvinvointivaltioon: Sosiaali- ja terveysministeriö 75 vuotta. Sosiaali- ja Terveysministeriö*. VAPK-kustannus.

Haavikko, P. (1988). *Kansaneläkelaitos 1937–1987*. Kansaneläkelaitos.

Häggman, K. (1997). *Suurten Muutosten Suomessa: Kansaneläkelaitos 1937–1997*. Gummerus.

Häikiö, M. (1992). *A brief history of modern Finland*. University of Helsinki.

Hannikainen, M., & Vauhkonen, J. (2012). *Ansioiden Mukaan: Yksityisalojen työeläkkeiden historia*. SKS.

Junkkari, M. (2016, August 4). *Pääkirjoitus: Miksi Kelan pääjohtaja on aina keskustalainen?* Helsingin Sanomat.

Jussila, O., Hentilä, S., & Nevakivi, J. (2004). *Suomen poliittinen historia 1809–2003*. WSOY.

Kangas, O. (1991). *The politics of social rights: Studies on the dimensions of sickness insurance in OECD countries*. Swedish Institute for Social Research.

Kangas, O. (1992). The politics of universalism: The case of Finnish sickness insurance. *Journal of Social Policy, 21*(1), 25–52.

Kangas, O. (1994). *The politics of social security: On regressions, qualitative comparisons, and cluster analysis*. Swedish Institute for Social Research.

Kangas, O. (2007). Finland: Labor markets against politics. In E. M. Immergut, K. M. Anderson, & I. Schulze (Eds.), *The handbook of west European pension politics* (pp. 248–296). Oxford University Press.

Kekkonen, U. (1952). *Onko maallamme malttia vaurastua?* Kustannusosakeyhtiö Otavan kirjapaino Helsinki.

Kela. (2013). *Kelan tilastollinen vuosikirja*. https://helda.helsinki.fi/items/c24ad2b1-a43f-4aa7-9b70-13ef44b6ef5c

Keskimäki, I., Tynkkynen, L.-K., Reissell, E., Koivusalo, M., Syrjä, V., Vuorenkoski, L., Rechel, B., & Karanikolos, M. (Eds.). (2019). *Finland: Health system review*. European Observatory on Health Systems and Policies.

Korpi, W. (1978). *The working class in welfare capitalism, work, unions and politics in Sweden*. Routledge & Kegan Paul.

Knutsen, O. (2017). *The Nordic Models in Political Science: Challenged, but still viable?* Fagbokforlaget.

Kuusi, P. (1961). *60-luvun Sosiaalipolitiikka*. WSOY.

Lipset, S. M., & Rokkan, S. (1967). *Party systems and voter alignments: Cross-national perspectives*. Free Press.

Manow, P. (2009). Electoral rules, class coalitions and welfare state regimes, or how to explain Esping-Andersen with stein Rokkan. *Socio-Economic Review, 7*(1), 101–121. https://doi.org/10.1093/ser/mwn022

Marttila, Y. (2011). *Suuria käännekohtia vai tasaista kehitystä? Tutkimus Suomen terveydenhuollon suuntaviivoista* (Sosiaali- ja terveysturvan tutkimuksia 116). Kela.
Mickelsson, R. (2015). *Suomen Puolueet*. Vastapaino.
Niemelä, H. (2014). *Yhteisvastuuta ja valinnanvapautta Sairausvakuutus 50 vuotta*. Kelan tutkimusosasto.
Niemelä, H., & Salminen, K. (2006). *Social security in Finland*. Finnish Center for Pensions.
Paavonen, T., & Kangas, O. (2006). *Eduskunta hyvinvointivaltion rakentajana*. EDITA.
Pedersen, A. W., & Kuhnle, S. (2017). The Nordic welfare state model. In O. Knudsen (Ed.), *The Nordic models in political science: Challenged, but still viable?* (pp. 219–238). Fagbokforlaget.
Pernaa, V., & Niemi, K. M. (Eds.). (2005). *Suomalaisen Yhteiskunnan Poliittinen Historia*. Kleio.
Pesonen, P., & Riihinen, O. (2002). *Dynamic Finland: The political system and the welfare state*. SKS.
Petersson, O. (1994). *The government and politics of the Nordic countries*. Fritzes.
Pierson, P. (2004). *Politics in time: History, institutions, and social analysis*. Princeton University Press.
Salmela, A. (1967). *Kansaneläkelaitos 1937–1967*. Kansaneläkelaitos.
Shibayama, Y. (2020). A study of Finnish social policy from the perspective of historical development of Kela (Kansaneläkelaitos) [In Japanese]. *Japanese Journal of Northern European Studies, 16*, 67–80.
Shibayama, Y. (2022). The politics of pensions in Finland. A study of the national pension reform and the introduction of occupational pension system in the 1950s and 1960s [In Japanese]. *Japanese Journal of Northern European Studies, 18*, 67–77.
Shibayama, Y. (2023). The political debate over health insurance implementation in Finland [In Japanese]. *Japanese Journal of Northern European Studies, 19*, 37–47.
Smolander, J. (2000). Suomalaisen hyvinvointivaltion poliittinen historia. In E. Railo & V. Laamanen (Eds.), *Suomi muuttuvassa maailmassa: Ulkosuhteiden ja kansallisen itseymmärryksen historiaa* (pp. 351–380). Kleio.
Thelen, K. (2004). *How institutions evolve: The political economy of skills in Germany, Britain, the United States and Japan*. Cambridge University Press.
Yamada, M. (2006). *Development of the Finnish welfare state: Social services and decentralization reforms* [In Japanese]. Bokutakusha.

Chapter 4
Family and thc Evolutionary Development of the Welfare States: A Comparison of the Discourse on Child and Family Policy in Finland and Japan

Chino Yabunaga

Abstract This chapter discussed Finnish and Japanese family policies from the perspective of situating institutions within a broader historical and evolutionary process, emphasising the 'context' in which they function, operate, and shape policy choices. The examination focused on how the two countries chose different family policies through processes of contingency and adaptation. Despite contrasting cultural norms regarding the family in the East and West, both countries have shared a history of dominant conservative rural values and an emphasis on women's maternal roles. In two countries, significant divergence in care policy occurred during the 1970s. While Finland reached compromised conclusions within the political power structures from the 1970s onwards, in Japan, one of the different arguments was reinforced or transformed by political power structures. Although familism and respect for family care were core values in both countries, differences existed in discourses regarding women's employment and gender equality. Rather than adopting a simplistic understanding of these typologies, this chapter examined how the development of welfare institutions in both countries was influenced by historical experience, religion and ideology, political regimes, industrial development, and precedents and advanced ideas from neighbouring countries as well as by core values.

Keywords Childcare policy · Finnish family policy · Japanese family policy · Political discourse · Cultural values

---

C. Yabunaga (✉)
Faculty of Global and Regional Studies, Toyo University, Bunkyo-ku, Tokyo, Japan
e-mail: yabunaga@toyo.jp

N. Tokumaru et al. (eds.), *Creative Co-evolution of the Economies and Welfare States in the Nordic Countries*, Evolutionary Economics and Social Complexity Science 32, https://doi.org/10.1007/978-981-97-8569-8_4

4.1 Introduction

This chapter examines Finnish and Japanese family (parenting) policies from the perspective of 'placing institutions in a broader historical and evolutionary context, with an emphasis on the "context" in which they function, operate and shape policy choices' (Steinmo, 2010, p. 243).

In welfare state studies, the typology of welfare regimes published by Esping-Andersen (1990) the most convincing starting point. However, this regime typology has been subject to a number of criticisms. Some point to the important missing elements that influence welfare state policies, claiming that the regime cannot always adequately explain every country. One of these concerns is regarding *care*—a fundamental element of welfare provision. The argument is that regime theory overlooks the role of the family in providing care for people in all situations, and for whom and how the welfare state provides the necessary care. Another major criticism is that typologies are ahistorical snapshots (Kettunen & Petersen, 2011) and neglect individuality, especially regarding the historical context of each country.

Pfau-Effinger (2005a) and Kremer (2007) argue that cultural differences tend to be ignored in welfare state studies aimed at explaining the differences between states. They insist that previous typologies of the welfare state considered economic rationality as the operating principle, though not always followed in practice. People actually behave according to their personal values and beliefs. While people's practice can be modified by policy, values, beliefs, and norms can also modify policy (Pfau-Effinger, 2005a). This is most evident in the choices of care. Parental ideals and gender norms regarding what care should look like influence parents' choices and behaviour. This is in accordance with the individuality of each country and cannot be explained by regime typology. On the other hand, the timing of economic development, industrial transformation, and other institutional constellations can create contingent welfare developments, with influential discourses on particular social policies, norms of the international community, and demographic trends specific to that period. Kremer (2007) describes the process of change in childcare in the Netherlands, noting that a combination of labour shortages, gender equality, political discourses, retirement of grandparents, and their availability to support with childcare, and so on, meant that the Netherlands, which was previously conservative in its approach to childcare, rapidly became a gender-equal work-sharing society.

These arguments are in line with critiques of the capitalism typology from the theory of varieties of capitalism (VoC; Hall & Soskice, 2001) and evolutionary theory (e.g. Hall & Thelen, 2008; Thelen, 2004). VoC theory argues that the market economy of each country is a combination of welfare state, political, fiscal and gender types. Therefore, the individual welfare state can be expressed as a combination of these elements. On the other hand, the evolutionary perspective considers changing institutional arrangements as a complex structure defined by actors' choices and interactions. Moreover, Hall and Thelen (2008) emphasise the individuality of the market economy. Furthermore, Steinmo (2010) highlights the 'contingency' and 'adaptation' captured by evolutionary theory and suggests that it be incorporated into historical institutional analysis.

Family and care are fundamental elements of the welfare state. With the development of industry and the economy, the welfare state has come to share the functions performed by the family and coordinated them with other actors in society; economic maintenance, care, and socialisation are its main functions. In addition, the welfare state has assumed greater responsibility for functions traditionally performed by the family owing to the increasing demand for support and care for the ageing population and for highly skilled human resources. Therefore, examining family functions and care policies is fundamental to understanding the welfare state. This chapter analyses family and care from an evolutionary perspective, focusing on turning points in policy in Finland and Japan.

4.2 Analytical Framework

4.2.1 Why Focus on Finland and Japan?

Finland and Japan appear to be welfare states with very different characteristics. In terms of the financial 'inputs' to the welfare state, Finland has the highest ratio of taxes and social security contributions to national income, whereas Japan has the lowest among developed countries. This input is calculated at the household level and contributes to the equalisation of disposable income through tax deductions, which reinforces economic interdependence within the family. The same is true of the 'output' ratio of public social spending to national income. This is particularly true of expenditure on benefits for children and the working-age population. Regarding 'outcomes', similar trends can be seen in the Gini coefficient, which measures the degree of equality in disposable income, and in the relative poverty rate, with Finland showing a high degree of income equality and Japan a high relative poverty rate. In particular, there are significant differences between households in terms of the number of children and gender. In other words, the government's income redistribution function is high in Finland, but remains low in Japan. In addition, the different levels of social services provision to support labour market participation—directly and indirectly enhancing the earning function of individuals— create differences not only in the equality of outcomes but also in opportunities for individuals. Nevertheless, there are some similarities between Finland and Japan. A universal pension and health insurance system, a system of basic services, low unemployment, and a high level of participation in higher education are features shared by both countries and other Nordic countries. Well-organised public administrations function at relatively the same level across these countries, and a commitment to full employment is the basis for universal welfare provision.

However, the social systems that support low unemployment and higher education completion rates differ significantly between Finland and Japan. For example, in Japan, a seniority-based wage system supports the burden of higher education tuition fees on families. Conversely, in Finland, higher education is largely financed by public expenditure. The principle of equal pay for work of equal value is shared as a substantive principle in Finland (see below), whereas in Japan, the dual structure of the labour market, which separates regular and non-regular employment, has enabled family members (mostly wives) to perform supplementary wage work in the male-breadwinner model society and absorb labour, which has recently created a serious underemployment problem.

The Nordic countries have developed distinctive welfare state models that are still thriving in the face of increasing Europeanisation and globalisation (e.g. Greve, 2007). However, Finland has characteristics that distinguish it from other Nordic countries. For example, there is a strong tendency towards government-led planning and administration, with a relatively small role for civil society (e.g. Kristensen & Lilja, 2011). Further, there is a high proportion of compensatory measures and a large gender pay gap. This indicates a relatively rigid labour market. These Finnish characteristics are similar to those of Japan.

4.2.2 Why Focus on Childcare and Family?

There are several reasons for focusing on care and family. As noted above, the functions and areas in which the welfare state is expected to operate are shifting as a result of the ever-changing demographic and industrial structures such as ageing and declining fertility, and the shift towards service industries and knowledge-based societies. A task of social policy research is to look ahead and examine policies to address these issues, which requires an understanding of changes in the welfare state. Among these challenges, the ageing demographic structure, which is the most significant and continuous pressure or constraint on the activities of the welfare state, is directly related to care. Therefore, positioning the family, which is responsible for the most care, is critical to understanding the welfare state.

However, the sustainability of the welfare state largely depends on the maintenance of economic activity. In the context of an ageing population, the welfare state not only responds to growing care needs but also seeks to ensure stable economic activity in an increasingly globalised environment and encourage more citizens to participate in the labour market to produce higher value-added goods. A policy objective from this perspective is social investment, which emerged as a new paradigm to replace both the dysfunctional Keynesian welfare state and neoliberal welfare reforms, and became one of the most important policy axes in Europe during the 2000s (Esping-Andersen, 2002; Morel et al., 2011). Social investment policies are based on Gunnar Myrdal's perspective in the 1930s that advocated a 'productive social policy' to increase economic growth and productivity not only through redistribution but also through active social policies, especially for children (Morel et al., 2011). In this approach, the state implements human capital investment policies, such as childcare, higher education, lifelong learning, vocational training, employment support for women, and other active labour market policies to increase competitiveness and create jobs.

4.2.3 Previous Studies

Numerous comparative studies have attempted to analyse the differences between welfare states from the perspective of family and care (e.g. Kremer, 2007). However, not many focus on the formation or historical background of childcare policies and include Finland or Japan in the comparison.

Pfau-Effinger has actively engaged in the international comparative analysis of welfare states and family (e.g. Pfau-Effinger, 1998, 1999, 2004, 2005a, 2005b). In her work on the process of establishing a full-time housewife culture in Europe, she highlights the model of the full-time housewife (male breadwinner), considered typical in the development of modern industrial societies, has never been established in Finland. She explains that until the mid-twentieth century, Finland had a free peasant culture and class base; the ideals of the 'domestic economy model' were dominant, and the sparse distribution of settlements did not encourage the formation of a separate culture for men and women. Consequently, the male-breadwinner model had unconsolidated, and women's integration into the labour market and the welfare state's assumption of care responsibilities took hold during the transformation to a service economy in the 1960s (Pfau-Effinger, 2004).

Meanwhile, Anttonen et al. (2003) conducted a comparative study of social care in five countries—Finland, Japan, Germany, the United Kingdom, and the United States. They reported that high welfare standards in Finland have not been achieved by communitarian or welfare advocate consensus, but rather been built up by opportunistic political coalitions. They attribute the high level of institutional care development to the relatively early entry of women into paid work. They also note that support for informal home care has been influenced by strategic coalitions of political parties (Anttonen et al., 2003). In addition, from a historical perspective, the development process of older adult care in the post-war period was incremental and selective, whereas childcare was dynamic and universalistic (Anttonen et al., 2003). On the other hand, Japan has a strong norm of family care provision and fulfilment, and ingrained stigma against social care (Anttonen et al., 2003).

Hiilamo (2002) compared the development of Finnish family and child policy in the 1990s with other European countries, especially Sweden, and pointed to the underlying 'Nordic tradition'. Finland and Sweden were slower than continental European countries in developing childcare facilities, and maternal and child benefits, but developed them rapidly in the 1960s and 1970s. In particular, child benefits were available to mothers in both countries, whereas in the rest of Europe, they were available only to male breadwinners. The switch to an individual taxation system led to a dramatic increase in women's participation in the labour market. Consequently, the development of childcare services in both countries differed significantly because of the rapid increase in the number of women in the labour force.

Finland consistently followed Sweden in introducing its policies. However, the home-based childcare allowance introduced in Finland was not accepted in Sweden at the time, illustrating the differences between Finnish and Swedish attitudes and practices towards care (Hiilamo, 2002). In other words, the socialisation of children through child day care and equal participation in the labour market were expected in Sweden, whereas in Finland, it was argued that child day care would integrate both parents into the labour market and separate them from their children; thus, a home care allowance was introduced.

Japan's welfare state characteristics remain controversial. Several studies have attempted to predict the future of East Asian countries. Among them, a type of familism unique to East Asia has been identified, which shares a Confucian cultural heritage and adopts filial piety as a pillar of family policy. (Choi, 2012; Lee & Baek, 2018; Peng & Chien, 2018).

4.2.4 The Present Study

This chapter focuses on the changes in childcare policy in both Japan and Finland. The analysis applies Pfau-Effinger's (2004) 'three levels of welfare culture' to explain the differences between these two welfare states by focusing on (1) the values and models underlying (child)care policy, (2) the dominant values and models among people regarding (child)care, and (3) the discourses used by actors to influence (child)care policy. As Pfau-Effinger (2005a) highlights, the analysis of welfare state differences must include individual values, beliefs, and norms that reflect culture. Therefore, this study's discussion is not based on a positivist approach, which requires an objective fact-based analysis, but on a constructivist approach, which focuses on people's subjective interpretations of the welfare state, its institutions and policies.

Pfau-Effinger's (2005b) analysis of the European welfare state shows that the arrangements for social security differ from those for family and gender. She argues that considering these two arrangements together creates contradictions and controversies in understanding the welfare state. Thus, the two aspects should be segregated as: (1) How family involvement is considered in care and how is gender reflected? and (2) How does the social security system position care needs and their fulfilment?

From the above background, the following case studies focus on (a) the overall cultural context in Japan and Finland that is thought to shape the welfare state; (b) the development of the welfare state with a focus on the social security system; (c) care and family policies with a focus on childcare; and (d) changes and transformation of childcare policies in both countries (generalisation/universalisation). After comparing these four phases in the two countries, the contingency and adaptation emphasised by evolutionary theory are analysed, focusing on the interaction between actors' discourses and the social environment.

4.3 Case Studies

4.3.1 Japan

4.3.1.1 General Background

Japan's early modernisation was characterised by the active accommodation of Western culture and knowledge and authoritarianism with a background of imperialism. Amidst the rapid westernisation of culture (civilisation and enlightenment) and growing power of the state (with the slogan, 'Enrich the Country, Strengthen the Armed Forces') accompanied by industrialisation, notions of the independent citizen and their citizenship have not fully penetrated in the society. During the feudal period, the samurai were separated from peasants and merchants by their privileged status. Bound by the principle of hereditary succession, samurai began to study Confucianism as an academic discipline. In the process of establishing a modern state, the samurai's ideals and Confucianism were reflected in the political system as authoritarianism. The westernisation of culture sprung modest democratic movements alongside the labour movement, and the right to universal suffrage was realised. However, gender equality and women's suffrage were not achieved until the new democratic constitution was established following World War II.

The defeat in the Second World War provided Japan with another opportunity to modernise. Under the Allied occupation mandate, the imperial government's authoritarian system was replaced by a democratic system under the leadership of the United States. In occupied Japan, the zaibatsu (the large Japanese conglomerate system) was dissolved, and basic human rights were enshrined as constitutional. The rural Liberal Democrats became the ruling party and assumed power in 1955 and remained until the 1990s. During the long-term hegemony of the Liberal Democrats (the 1955 regime), an iron triangle was created wherein members of the ruling party, industry associations and the government enjoyed stable, mutually beneficial cooperation and interdependence (Shinkawa, 2005).

Considering the norms regarding women in Japan, ideas emphasising the division of labour between male and female roles have been present since the early twentieth century. In the modernisation process, the idea of the 'good wife and wise mother' was imported into Japan along with European culture and thought. This idea argued that the mother's role in raising and educating children and the wife's role in managing the household and providing domestic help were 'essential' roles of women. Furthermore, women were seen as contributing not only at home but also to the state, by supporting men's activities such as work and military service, and by raising children, the next citizens. Thus, the role of women being in the home was reinforced by the addition of a national perspective (Koyama, 1991).

4.3.1.2 Development of the Welfare State

As part of the modernisation process, the imperial government introduced the Poor Relief Act at the end of the nineteenth century to help people living in poverty; however, it was not implemented until the late 1920s owing to successive wars. Meanwhile, the 1920s saw the rise of the labour movement and the partial development of workers' health insurance. In the 1930s, the workers' health insurance and pension system, the national health system and the maternal and child health system were successively developed, all aimed at ensuring a healthy population and raising funds for war in the context of the advance into mainland China.

However, comprehensive social security systems were not developed until after the Second World War. During the post-war occupation, a grand plan for the social security system was discussed and designed under the leadership of the Allied Forces. Influenced by the UK's Beveridge Report and others, the plan presented by the Council on Social Security Systems in 1951 was a systematic safety net covering all citizens, and each institution was legislated and implemented individually (Shinkawa, 2005).

Within the stable neo-corporatist system shaped by the hegemony of the Liberal Democratic Party (LDP), the social security system outlined in the Grand Design was individually designed by vertically structured administrative organisations and implemented nationwide through a centralised administrative structure. It was not until the LDP lost power in the 1990s that the social security system was fundamentally overhauled.

4.3.1.3 Family and Care for the Children in Japan as a Welfare State

The development of Japan's social security system after the Second World War was a milestone shaped by the long-term rule of the LDP. Consequently, the values of the LDP and its supporters—largely form rural areas—were strongly reflected in the system. Various social security and tax systems were designed considering the male-breadwinner household model. With the heightened economic growth of the 1960s, free medical care for older adults was introduced and pension levels increased, with a focus on improving their lives.

However, the oil shocks of the 1970s, the resultant changes in the international environment, and the temporary contraction of Japan's economic growth, all prompted the LDP government to change its policy. Ironically, this came just after the government had adopted the further expansion of welfare for older adults under the slogan, 'The Dawn of the Welfare State'. A new slogan of 'Japanese-style welfare society' was created by the LDP and declared in the Prime Minister's policy speech to the Diet in 1979:

> I am determined to work hard to build a fair and dignified Japanese-style welfare society by improving the family infrastructure… (25 January 1979, Prime Minister Ohira)

This statement was further explained in the government's 'New Seven-Year Economic and Social Plan', formulated in the same year:

> The future direction of Japan's economy and society, which has caught up with the advanced countries of Europe and the United States, is not to continue to seek the model of the advanced countries but to develop a society in which an efficient government provides adequate social welfare on the basis of individual self-help and solidarity with the family, neighbourhood and community, rather than on the model of the advanced countries. Thus, the plan must aim to realise a new welfare society, a Japanese-style welfare society, in which the creative vitality of the liberal economy is the driving force, and a path unique to Japan is chosen and created. (New Seven-Year Economic and Social Plan, 1979)

This 'Japanese-style welfare society' was further clarified in the LDP's educational material of the same year. The following concerns were also expressed:

> The tendency for women to work outside the home and to shift their emphasis to social activities rather than 'managing' the home is likely to continue, but this may undermine the family as a life-security system (LDP, 1979).

Subsequently, the idea of prioritising self-help efforts by individuals, communities, families, and enterprises; relegating public social security to a complementary position; and the conservative view of women and family were reflected in welfare and women's policies. Ochiai (2014) reports that the gender division of labour based on the male-breadwinner model, which was not traditional to Japanese society in the 1980s, is discussed as though it were a tradition rooted in Japanese culture *(traditionalisation of modernity*). For example, in 1984, Prime Minister Nakasone told the upper house budget committee, 'I may be called old-fashioned, but I still want women to be 100 per cent respectable as mothers first' (Ochiai & Johshita, 2014). As seen in this statement, the ideology was that married women should focus on unpaid domestic work, and their going out and working outside the home was perceived as 'cutting corners'. Even if they did work outside the home, they were to be limited to a combination of hobbies and practical gain, at most to earn extra income, and not neglect the family (Nishioka, 2021).

4.3.1.4 Generalisation of the Child Day-Care System

The day-care system in Japan began as charitable crèches to look after the children of single mothers. Later, they expanded to become statutory social work institutions for low-income families. After the war, the Child Welfare Law of 1947 was enacted, and day-care centres were established as facilities for the care of children, regardless of income. However, the supply could not keep up with the rapid increase in demand for childcare during the baby boom. In 1951, the supply of childcare was restricted by adding the condition of 'lack of childcare' owing to parents' special circumstances, such as low income, for admission to a day-care centre. Subsequently, urbanisation and the development of the nuclear family, combined with high economic growth, led to the emergence of full-time housewives. In the 1960s, the myth of the 3-year-old child was emphasised, according to which the child should be brought up at home until the age of three. Day care was seen as an exceptional option for families. Kindergartens then became the mainstream option in line with government policy, which was reluctant to respond to the shortage of childcare and increase in the number of full-time housewives. In the mid-1970s, when the number of full-time housewives was at its peak, alongside kindergarten enrolment, with approximately 2.5 million children attending. Kindergartens, with their short hours and long holidays, met the needs of housewives and the family norm, becoming a symbol of a healthy family.

With the end of the second baby boom and the budgetary constraints associated with the 'Japanese-style welfare society', the number of children enrolled in day-care centres declined through the 1980s. Although the Equal Employment Opportunity Law of 1985 and subsequent entry of women into the labour market meant an increase in the number of dual-earner families, day care was still considered a selective social welfare service provided by the local government, based on needs assessments.

This trend was changed by the '1.57 shock' caused by the record low birth rate of 1.57 in 1987. Since then, the term *shoshika*, referring to the decline in the number of births and children, has come into use and appears frequently in official government documents and mass media (e.g. White Paper on National Lifestyle, 1992). Simultaneously, the reconciliation of women's employment with childbirth and childrearing also began to be mentioned in government documents (e.g. White Paper on Health and Welfare, 1990). Nishioka (2021) analyses the discourse on the 'shoshika policy' and explains that the ministry bureaucrats succeeded in changing the selective childcare policy of the past by combining the issues of population decline and work-life balance and using them as magic words (Nishioka, 2021, pp. 225–267).

In 1993, the 1955 LDP regime collapsed and a non-LDP coalition government was formed. One of the new government's policies was to address the declining birth rate and ageing population. The Gold Plan, which targets the development of facilities for older adults, had already been initiated by the previous LDP government, and the Angel Plan, which targets the development of childcare facilities, was formulated by the new government as a top priority to combat the declining birth rate. In 1996, a registration system was introduced to replace the previous paternalistic system, in line with calls for the improvement of the childcare system by the left-wing coalition government, which had trade unions as its largest support base. Although the legal framework of the Child Welfare Act was not changed at this juncture, the capacity of childcare centres expanded rapidly thereafter, and in the 2000s, amendments removed the 'lack of childcare' clause and the system became the basis for universal childcare and an early childhood education system through the integration of functions with kindergartens and the formulation of the Child Care Support Act.

4.3.2 *Finland*

4.3.2.1 General Background

As a welfare state, Finland is characterised by strong communitarianism (Anttonen, 1998). This reflects the historical context, especially since the late nineteenth century. The rise of nationalism (the Fennoman movement) under Russian rule linked the bourgeois to the common people and, together with the mobilisation of women in popular movements, spread the idea of equality across class and gender in society. The radical parliamentary reform movements that emerged in the struggle against Russification in the early twentieth century strengthened national unity. In addition, the civil war immediately after independence led the socialist and worker organisations to lose power and the bourgeois to reintegrate the population. This process emphasised strict Lutheran Protestantism, with conservative peasant labour as the moral norm and central value (Alapuro, 2018; Anttonen, 1998). This was the background to Finland's reluctance to adopt the social goals of other Nordic countries and organise trade unions. The social engineering vision of economic and technological rationalisation, social and political integration, and the formation of self-regulatory bodies based on the protection of workers were adopted in other Nordic countries as a virtuous circle of social policy and economic prosperity in harmony. However, these reforms were not actively adopted in Finland until the Second World War. Moreover, in the post-war period, the strategy of depoliticising social policy was dominant in the context of the Cold War. Nevertheless, during the rise of nationalism in the late nineteenth century through parliamentary reforms, post-Civil War social integration and the Cold War, the concept of 'Nordic' was sometimes emphasised as a symbol and norm of modernity, freedom and democracy in bourgeois, conservative and social democratic discourses (Kettunen, 2006, 2021; Kettunen & Eskola, 1997; Kettunen & Petersen, 2011, 2021).

This historical background and the inter-party relations in the process of building the welfare state in the light of these discourses have, in the past, led to state-led social integration that emphasised 'the good citizenship of individuals who are responsible for productive activities required by the state' (Anttonen, 1994; Anttonen 1998). A reluctance to establish social citizenship in industrial working life also contributed to Finland's peculiarity as a welfare state among the Nordic countries.

4.3.2.2 Development of the Welfare State

Finland is considered a latecomer among the Nordic countries because of the late development of its social insurance system (Kosonen, 1993). Workers' accident insurance was introduced early (in 1895), but old-age and invalidity pensions, which were legislated in 1937, were not introduced until 1949. The system was extended to a universal national pension scheme only in 1956. Sickness insurance, which was developed earlier in many industrialised countries, was not introduced until 1963.

Kettunen (2001) explains this delay in the development of sickness insurance schemes as due to an 'uncertain political process'. After the war, until the late 1980s, the Centre Party (formerly the Agrarian Party) was almost exclusively in power, and continued to have a strong influence. On the other hand, the Social Democrats' stable participation in government only began after 1966 and, except for a short period, led a coalition government with the Centre Party until the 1980s. In the 1960s and 1970s, the influence of the Centre Party president increased, with diplomatic threats in the context of the Cold War (Häikiö, 1992; Kettunen, 2001).

Finland's vision of a comprehensive social insurance system also emerged after the war. The Social Insurance Commission, appointed in 1945 by the tripartite coalition government of the Social Democratic Party, Communist Party and Agrarian Party, remained active until 1954 and published several studies. However, amidst the conflicting interests of the three parties, priority was given to establishing a national pension system by the coalition of the Agrarian Party and Communist Party, which had substantial support from rural areas (Kettunen, 2001).

This process represents the strength of rural society and the rurally based agrarian party in Finland in the formation of the welfare state; Kettunen (2001) argues that the two fundamental principles of the Nordic welfare state—full employment and universal social rights based on citizenship—were established in Finland since the 1960s. The construction of the Nordic welfare state in Finland began with the income policy set out in the Liinamaa Agreement of 1968. Along with the modernisation of agriculture, the industrial structure had to be transformed, and the large influx of people from rural to urban areas created mass unemployment, and low wages, urban housing problems, and high immigration to Sweden were also major challenges. Securing the livelihoods of the growing number of urban workers was a pressing issue for the government. The government intervened in collective bargaining, where mutual 'low trust' made it difficult to reach a consensus. Central collective bargaining, led and coordinated by the state mediator Liinamaa and later intervened in by President Kekkonen, ended in the 1970s with state price adjustments, pension benefits, a minimum wage system, and an extended annual paid leave system, primarily in terms of income and workers' rights (Häikiö, 1992; Kettunen, 2006).

4.3.2.3 Families and Care for the Children in Finnish Welfare State

The Marriage Act of 1929 (Avioliittolaki, 234/1929) abolished man's guardianship over his wife and provided for equal relations between spouses. On the other hand, the Marriage Act stipulated that marriage was for the maintenance of the family and mutual support between husband and wife, and established the obligation to work and support the family. This gave women independent status. However, women did not have the right to enter into employment contracts until 1922, making it difficult for them to be economically independent; and thus, the Act continued to emphasise women's roles as mothers and caregivers of the family (Anttonen, 1998; Sulkunen, 1990; Manninen & Setälä, 1990).

Finland's early welfare state development was maternalistic (Anttonen et al., 1994). Maternity benefits were introduced in 1938 and are among the oldest financial benefits. The Child Benefit Act, introduced in 1948, paid 'mothers' for caring for their children. In addition, mother and child clinics began to operate voluntarily in the 1900s and became part of the public health service in 1944. In addition, the Sickness Insurance Act of 1963 introduced a mother's allowance (Anttonen, 1998).

Julkunen (1991, 1994) notes that in Finland, women were positioned as the 'mothers of society' (naisten yhteiskunnallinen äitiys; Rantalaiho, 1994) and active agents in achieving good education, health, and family life. Parliamentary reforms that provided equal suffrage for men and women in 1906 labelled women as enlightened agents of society, a term shared by society through practices in social movements, school education, and so on. Maternalistic discourse and familism were emphasised in the process of building the Finnish welfare state. The social policy of the 1960s (Kuusi, 1961), which was highly influential as the grand design of Finland's social policy programme, also reaffirmed this view of women and families.

4.3.2.4 Universalisation of the Child Day-Care System in Finland

The late 1960s and 1970s marked a turning point in the transition to a new family model and gender structure that positioned women as economically independent breadwinners. Influenced by the radical social movements Yhdistys 9 of the time that were mainly driven by academics and students, the Commission on the Status of Women, set up in Parliament at the suggestion of the Social Democratic Party's Women's Committee, made a number of social policy proposals and negotiated with the relevant government departments. The Commission's report stated that the 'conclusion' of the negotiations was women's reproductive rights, social activities, economic independence through paid work, in addition to a new role for men (Julkunen, 1991, 1994).

The Commission's report sought to achieve gender equality by (1) abolishing the obligation of spouses to support each other, even within the marriage system; (2) changing the basic gender structure of industrial society from male-dominated to gender-equal; (3) denying benefits for motherhood; (4) adequate employment opportunities and equal pay for work of equal value; and (5) a fair distribution of childcare and domestic work. For instance, the Committee's report states that:

> One of the most important conditions for gender equality is that there is no economic subordination between individuals and that each individual is economically independent. The crucial objective of social policy is that men and women should be equal in their ability to earn their own living. (Report of the Childcare Facilities Committee, KM 1970 quoted in Julkunen, 1994, p. 103).

However, the development of childcare systems faced strong criticism. The following issues were raised in the parliamentary debate on the Childcare Act:

> Children need love, which they can only get in the most precious place—at home, in the arms of their mother and father. (Alli Vaittinen-Kuikka, 1 Dec 1972)

Until the 1960s, childcare was divided into crèches (lastenseimi) for children under 3 years and kindergartens (lastentarha) for children over 3 years. Nurseries were staffed by nurses and kindergartens by teachers (Lastensuojelun Keskusliitto, 1970). The Day Care Centres Act of 1973 merged the two into the day-care system.

Yhdistys 9 raised questions about gender structures and the need for childcare to support women's paid work. The campaign for nurseries raised questions about the poor developmental conditions of children, mainly from disadvantaged families, at the time. The socialisation function of day-care centres for children was also emphasised. These arguments were made in the parliamentary committee for the Childcare Act. In the committee's report, some of the discussions were as follows:

> A surprisingly large number of children had little or no adult supervision at home, were left unregulated with unknown family members or were sent to other local institutions (Report of the Childcare Facilities Committee. KM 1967. B46).

> Day care is necessary because it provides stimulation for children and increases equality when educational conditions in the home differ (Report of the Childcare Facilities Committee. KM 1971. A 20).

These reports undermined the 'emotional and moral' (Julkunen, 1997) arguments in favour of housewives, which led to the Childcare Act of 1973 being passed with widespread support. Childcare capacity increased from 15,633 in 1969 to more than 130,000 in 1980. However, only one in four children under the age of 7 years actually had access to a municipal nursery (Hiilamo, 2002).

In rural areas, with no pressing need for out-of-home childcare, the Childcare Act was opposed because it focused on the urban wage-earning population. They demanded that home childcare be supported by income transfers to the rural population. The Social Democrats could not accept a wage for motherhood, as that would reverse the structure of gender equality. Nevertheless, childcare facilities were not installed in rural areas, and home childcare benefits were actually promoted at the local government level (Hiilamo, 2002; Yabunaga, 2009). Finally, to make progress on this issue, the Left changed its strategy of justifying government support for home childcare, whereas the Right emphasised women's right to choose between paid work and home childcare. The homecare allowance, as a national institution, was initiated in 1980 and enshrined in law in 1985. In addition, the right to parental leave up to the age of 3 years was secured in 1985. In 1990, a home childcare allowance was introduced for parents or guardians of all children under the age of 3 years who were not in out-of-home care; in 1996, childcare subsidies were made available for the use of private childcare facilities, completing the universal childcare support system with the subjective rights of parents.

4.4 Discussion

In this section, the Japanese and Finnish cases are analysed along three dimensions in line with the analytical framework: (1) the values and models underlying family and (child)care policies, (2) dominant values and models around family and (child) care, and (3) the discourses used by actors trying to influence policies. Thus, the process by which the two countries chose different family policies is examined from an evolutionary perspective, focusing on contingency and adaptation.

4.4.1 Values and Models Underlying Family Policies

In Japan, the values reflected those of the conservative LDP, which had been in power for nearly 40 years. In addition, the construction of the welfare state and policymaking was led by an authoritative centralised government, which formed a neo-corporatism with the employer side. Childcare was a selective social service provided to disadvantaged families. In Finland, the construction of the welfare state and policymaking tended to be state-led, and conservative rural values were initially dominant. In this context, family policy aimed to secure children's nurturing environment through maternity benefits, child allowances, and so on.

The turning point in the generalisation of childcare was the need to address Japan's declining birth rate. By identifying the lack of childcare support as an obstacle, the government was able to move from a selective childcare policy to universal provision. However, in Finland, 'Nordic' values have always been associated with the image of a welfare state with a virtuous circle between the economy and welfare. The positioning of women as economically independent breadwinners is the axis of the new equal family model and the basis for the universalisation of childcare facilities. The home care allowance was followed by the state guarantee of children's development and parents' right to choose. (In addition, the introduction of the private childcare allowance further strengthened the right to choose).

4.4.2 Dominant Values and Models Around Childcare, Care, and Gender

In Japan, a model was promoted wherein wives were to devote themselves to domestic work, including childcare, based on the reinforced idea of the 'good wife and wise mother'. At the time, dual-earner and single-parent families were exceptions, and a culture of housewives with children using kindergartens as a symbol of a healthy family spread. A competing culture (e.g. of working mothers) did not enter the mainstream. The generalisation of the childcare system developed with a focus on overcoming the declining birth rate, and gender equality and dual earning did not become dominant enough values to influence family policy.

In Finland, the discourse of the 'social mother' positioned women as enlightened in terms of education, health, and so on. However, this also meant that they were responsible for domestic work and care. In the 1960s, pioneering social movements for gender equality led to a revision of the entire welfare state system; however, it was heavily criticised. Typical of this was the belief that childcare would lead to a loss of loving care at home, and that children's healthy development could not be guaranteed.

4.4.3 *Discourses Used by Actors Seeking to Influence Policy*

In Japan, the ruling LDP and its supporting bureaucrats took the lead in formulating policy. The party, which was in power for much of the second half of the twentieth century, promoted childcare and welfare in the home. In Japan, 1973 was declared 'the dawn of the welfare state' and the expansion of social welfare was advocated. However, in 1979, in the face of global recession and neo-conservatism, the slogan 'Japanese Welfare Society' replaced this with a policy of self-help and state familism. The economic prosperity of the 1980s and the corporate society reinforced the male-breadwinner model, with the rhetoric of 'tradition' by LDP politicians. Bureaucrats led the generalisation of childcare as an affirmation of women's employment, which in turn was combined with the crisis of population decline to transform childcare policy.

In Finland, the state-led securing of the child's growth environment was promoted, initially using the discourse of the 'social mother'. The promotion of gender equality associated with the urban social movements that developed in the 1960s explicitly rejected the male-breadwinner model. Nevertheless, there were critics of institutional childcare who claimed that it hindered emotional development. In addition, rural parties and peasants opposed the introduction of the child day-care system, which benefited the urban workforce. Therefore, the Parliamentary Committee on the Status of Women and the Committee in charge of the Childcare System were persuaded to address the poor developmental environment of children from poor families. The child day-care system began as an eclectic system with the home care allowance.

4.5 Conclusion

This chapter discussed Finnish and Japanese family policies from the perspective of situating institutions within a broader historical and evolutionary process, emphasising the "context" in which they function, operate, and shape political choices. The examination focused on how the two countries chose different family policies through processes of contingency and adaptation. Despite contrasting cultural norms regarding family in the East and West, both countries have shared a history of dominant conservative rural values and an emphasis on women's maternal roles. This chapter traced the history of family policies in Finland and Japan, examining when and how they diverged, focusing on dominant discourses and political choices. Significant divergence in care policies occurred during the two turning points in the 1960s and 1970s. While Finland reached compromised conclusions within political power structures from the 1990s onwards, in Japan, one of the different arguments was reinforced or transformed by political power structures.

With a historical background of early modernisation influenced by Westernisation and authoritarianism rooted in imperialism and Confucianism, the Japanese welfare state developed through democratisation after World War II. The welfare state system is based on constitutional gender equality and the grand design of social security. The norm of the 'good wife and wise mother' has been reinforced by social and governmental discourse. The formation of the iron triangle of politics, government, and business under the long-term LDP regime since 1955 created characteristics of the Japanese welfare state, including dependence on corporate welfare, full employment, and limited public welfare provision. The economic prosperity of the 1980s and corporate-based society reinforced familism and the male-breadwinner model, along with selective social protection under the idea of the 'Japanese welfare society' using the rhetoric of 'traditionalizing the modern family' (Ochiai 2013). The public childcare system expanded since the 1990s as society faced a decline in the number of children and the government shifted to the left.

In Finland, strong communitarianism and egalitarianism, rooted in Lutheran Protestantism with conservative peasant labour as the moral norm, made Finnish welfare society slow to adopt a social engineering vision and firm in its maternalism. Post-World War II, the tense relationship with the Soviet Union and war experiences reinforced state-led social integration and reluctance to establish social citizenship in industrial working life. Political processes involving the Agrarian and Social Democratic parties led to modernisation of agriculture and industrial restructuring, causing significant population movements from rural to urban areas, unemployment, housing problems, and emigration. The women's movement, Yhdistys 9, demanded improved status for women and gender equality based on social engineering principles, envisioning a virtuous circle between economy and welfare, referencing Sweden. Deep-rooted familism and financial limitations in rural areas hindered the introduction of day-care systems, justified by protecting children's healthy development. Eventually, Finland's day-care system was introduced as a compromise, protecting rural benefits with the home care allowance.

Both countries' welfare states have conservative agrarian cultures at their roots and tend to be state-led in their construction. In childcare policy debates, both emphasised a good environment for children's development and the importance of motherhood in nurturing children at home. However, in Finland, radical social movements from the late 1960s led to universal childcare, necessary for women's economic independence and gender equality, moving closer to the Nordic model of harmonising social policy and economic prosperity. In contrast, Japan's rationale for universal childcare was not driven by the need for women's employment and economic independence but by the need to combat declining fertility in the 1990s.

While familism and respect for family care were core values in both countries, differences existed in discourses regarding women's employment and gender equality. This chapter did not adopt a simplistic understanding of these typologies but examined how the development of institutions in both countries is influenced by historical experience, religion and ideology, political regimes, industrial development, and precedents and advanced ideas from neighbouring countries. These factors are discarded or selected by discourses, influencing institutional choices in varying degrees. The analysis was based on the premise that understanding institutional change requires viewing it as an evolutionary process in a complex system, shaped by unattainable dynamics rather than as a planned one, resulting from interactions between actors that cannot be simplified or designed by a particular actor (Steinmo, 2010, p. 218).

Acknowledgments This research was supported by JSPS Grant-in-Aid for Scientific Research No. 19H04368.

References

Alapuro, R. (2018). *State and revolution in Finland*. Brill. https://doi.org/10.1163/9789004386174
Anttonen, A. (1998). Vocabularies of citizenship and gender: Finland. *Critical Social Policy, 18*(3), 355–374.
Anttonen, A., Baldock, J., & Sipilä, J. (Eds.). (2003). *The young, the old and the state: Social care systems in five industrial nations*. Edward Elgar.
Anttonen, A., Henriksson, L., & Nätkin, R. (Eds.). (1994). *Naisten hyvinvointivaltio* (1st ed.). Vastapaino.
Choi, Y. J. (2012). End of the era of productivist welfare capitalism? Diverging welfare regimes in East Asia. *Asian Journal of Social Science, 40*(3), 275–294. https://doi.org/10.1163/156853112X650827
Esping-Andersen, G. (1990). *The three worlds of welfare capitalism*. Princeton University Press.
Esping-Andersen, G. (Ed.). (2002). *Why we need a new welfare state*. Oxford University Press. https://doi.org/10.1093/0199256438.001.0001
Greve, B. (2007). What characterise the Nordic welfare state model. *Journal of Social Sciences, 3*(2), 43–51. https://doi.org/10.3844/jssp.2007.43.51
Häikiö, M. (1992). *A brief history of modern Finland*. University of Helsinki.
Hall, P., & Soskice, D. (Eds.). (2001). *Varieties of capitalism: Institutional foundation of comparative advantage*. Oxford University Press. https://doi.org/10.1093/0199247757.001.0001
Hall, P. A., & Thelen, K. (2008). Institutional change in varieties of capitalism. *Socio-Economic Review, 7*(1), 7–34. https://doi.org/10.1093/ser/mwn020
Hiilamo, H. (2002). *The rise and fall of Nordic family policy? Historical development and changes during the 1990s in Sweden and Finland*. STAKES.
Julkunen, R. (1991). Women in the welfare state. In M. Manninen & P. Setälä (Eds.), *The lady with the bow: The story of Finnish women*.
Julkunen, R. (1994). Suomalainen sukupuollimalli – 1960-luku käänteenä. In A. Anttonen, L. Henriksson, & R. Nätkin (Eds.), *Naisten hyvinvointivaltio* (pp. 179–202). Vastapaino.
Julkunen, R. (1997). *Työn jakaminen: moraali, talous, politiikka*. Vastapaino.

Kettunen, P. (2001). The Nordic welfare state in Finland. *Scandinavian Journal of History, 26*(3), 225–247. https://doi.org/10.1080/034687501750303864

Kettunen, P. (2006). The tension between the social and the economic – A historical perspective on a welfare state. In O. Ojala, J. Eloranta, & J. Jalava (Eds.), *The road to prosperity. An economic history of Finland*. Suomalaisen Kirjallisuuden Seura.

Kettunen, P. (2021, March 8–12). *The agent called society as a mediator between experiences and expectations* [Conference session]. HEX Conference 2021, Tampere University, Finland.

Kettunen, P., & Eskola, H. (Eds.). (1997). *Models, modernity and the myrdals*. The Renvall Institute for Area and Cultural Studies, University of Helsinki.

Kettunen, P., & Petersen, K. (2011). *Beyond welfare state models*. Edward Elgar.

Kettunen, P., & Petersen, K. (2021). Images of the Nordic welfare model: Historical layers and ambiguities. In H. Byrkjeflot, L. Mjøset, M. Mordhorst, & K. Petersen (Eds.), *The making and circulation of Nordic models, ideas and images* (pp. 13–33). Routledge.

Kosonen, P. (1993). *The Finnish model and the welfare state in crisis: The Nordic welfare state as an idea and as reality*. Renvall Institute Publications. https://helda.helsinki.fi/server/api/core/bitstreams/504a31ec-3ce3-4dd9-b28b-90911762d9cd/content

Koyama, S. (1991). *Ryosai Kenbo-toiu Kihan [The norm of the good wife and wise mother]*. Keiso publishing.

Kremer, M. (2007). *How welfare states care: Culture, gender and parenting in Europe*. Amsterdam University Press.

Kristensen, P. H., & Lilja, K. (Eds.). (2011). *Nordic capitalisms and globalization: New forms of economic organization and welfare institutions*. Oxford University Press.

Kuusi, P. (1961). *60-luvun sosiaalipolitiikka*. WSOY.

Lastensuojelun Keskusliitto. (1970). *Lasten päivähoito*. Lastensuojelun Keskusliitto.

Lee, S. S.-Y., & Baek, S.-H. (2018). The social investment approach in the productivist welfare regime: The unfolding of social investment in South Korea and Japan. In G. B. Eydal & T. Rostgaard (Eds.), *Handbook of family policy* (pp. 111–123). Edward Elgar Publishing. https://doi.org/10.4337/9781784719340.00017

Liberal Democratic Party. (1979). *Japanese-style welfare society' LDP's training material*. Liberal Democratic Party.

Manninen, M., & Setälä, P. (1990). *The lady with the bow: The story of Finnish women*. Otava.

Morel, N., Palier, B., Palme, J., & (Eds). (2011). *Towards a social investment welfare state? Ideas, policies and challenges*. Policy Press Scholarship Online. https://doi.org/10.1332/policypress/9781847429247.001.0001

Nishioka, S. (2021). *Nihongata Fukushi Kokka Saihen no gensetsu seiji to kanryosei – Kazokuseisaku no 'Shoshika taisaku' ka [Discourse politics and bureaucracy in the restructuring of the Japanese welfare state, The transformation of the family policy into the policy against the falling birth-rate]*. Nakanishiya Publishing.

Ochiai, E. (2013). The logic of global family change in transforming modernity: Focusing on Asia and Europe. *Japanese Sociological Review, 62*(4), 533–552. https://doi.org/10.4057/jsr.64.533

Ochiai, E., & Johshita, K. (2014). Prime Ministers' discourse in Japan's reforms since the 1980s: Traditionalization of modernity rather than Confucianism. In S. Sung & G. Pascall (Eds.), *Gender and welfare state in East Asia: Confucianism or equality?* (pp. 152–180). Palgrave Macmillan.

Peng, I., & Chien, Y.-C. (2018). Not all in the same family: Diverging approaches to family policy in East Asia. In G. B. Eydal & T. Rostgaard (Eds.), *Handbook of family policy* (pp. 236–248). Elgar. https://doi.org/10.4337/9781784719340.00027

Pfau-Effinger, B. (1998). Gender cultures and the gender arrangement—A theoretical framework for cross-national gender research. *Innovation: The European Journal of Social Science Research, 11*(2), 147–166. https://doi.org/10.1080/13511610.1998.9968559

Pfau-Effinger, B. (1999). The modernization of family and motherhood in Western Europe. In R. Crompton (Ed.), *Restructuring gender relations and employment: The decline of the male breadwinner* (pp. 60–79). https://doi.org/10.1093/oso/9780198294696.003.0004

Pfau-Effinger, B. (2004). Socio-historical paths of the male breadwinner model – An explanation of cross-national differences. *The British Journal of Sociology, 55*(3), 377–399. https://doi.org/10.1111/j.1468-4446.2004.00025.x

Pfau-Effinger, B. (2005a). Culture and welfare state policies: Reflections on a complex interrelation. *Journal of Social Policy, 34*(1), 3–20. https://doi.org/10.1017/S0047279404008232

Pfau-Effinger, B. (2005b). Welfare state policies and the development of care arrangements. *European Societies, 7*(2), 321–347. https://doi.org/10.1080/14616690500083592

Rantalaiho, L. (1994). Sukupuolisopimus ja Suomen malli. In A. Anttonen, L. Henriksson, & R. Nätkin (Eds.), *Naisten Hyvinvointivaltio* (pp. 9–31). Vastapaino.

Shinkawa, T. (2005). *Nihongata Fukushi rezimu no hatten to henyo [The development and transformation of Japanese welfare regime]*. Minerva Publishing.

Steinmo, S. (2010). *The evolution of modern states. Sweden, Japan, and the United States*. Cambridge University Press.

Sulkunen, I. (1990). The mobilisation of women and the birth of civil society. In M. Manninen & P. Setälä (Eds.), *The lady with the bow: The story of Finnish women*.

Thelen, K. (2004). *How institutions evolve. The political economy of skills in Germany, Britain, The United States, and Japan*. Cambridge University Press.

Yabunaga, C. (2009). Fukushikokka to Jisedai ikuseiseisaku: Finland ni okeru kodomo, katei heno seisakutaiou [Welfare state and policy for the next generation: A case study on the policy for families and children in Finland]. *Research Bulletin of the Faculty of Human Studies, Bunkyo Gakuin University, 11*(1), 27–47.

Part II
Industrial Transformation and the Welfare State

Chapter 5
Industrial Transformation, Innovation, and the Enabling Roles of the Nordic Welfare State

Norio Tokumaru

Abstract While it is necessary to improve the productivity of welfare services, transform industrial structure, and create new industries to make a welfare state economically sustainable, how the institutional features of the Nordic socio-economic model can contribute to this transformation process remains unclear. By examining the recent drastic industrial transformation in Finland, this chapter sheds new light on this important question. This study focuses on the case of industrial transformation in the Oulu region following Nokia's exit from the mobile phone business and the subsequent creation of the digital healthcare industry. This chapter aims to demonstrate two points. First, welfare state institutions and their reforms can promote the creation of new industries and innovation *by creating new demand* for innovative new industries. Second, local governments and intermediary organizations can play active roles as *catalysts* for stimulating and shaping innovation. Previous studies discussing the economic significance of the Nordic model, including the "social investment" thesis, have mainly focused on investments in education and training for individuals, emphasizing the implications of the Nordic model that effectively influence the *supply-side* of individual and collective capabilities. However, experience in advanced economies since the 2000s showed that the expectations of supply-side policies were too optimistic. By contrast, this chapter focuses on how the institutional features of the Nordic model affect the demand for these capabilities, shifting the emphasis to the potential for promoting industrial transformation and innovation from the *demand-side*.

Keywords Industrial transformation · Innovation · Catalyst · Enabling welfare state · Nordic model

N. Tokumaru (✉)
Faculty of Policy Studies, Kansai University, Osaka, Japan
e-mail: norio-t@kansai-u.ac.jp

N. Tokumaru et al. (eds.), *Creative Co-evolution of the Economies and Welfare States in the Nordic Countries*, Evolutionary Economics and Social Complexity Science 32, https://doi.org/10.1007/978-981-97-8569-8_5

5.1 Introduction

5.1.1 Institutional Foundations and the Policy for "Creative Destruction"

In capitalist economies, where private and decentralized investment and production must be adjusted *ex post*, intense metabolism within and between industries is inevitable. Schumpeter (2010, pp. 70–75) called this process "creative destruction." Indeed, the number of workers employed in primary and secondary industries is decreasing, whereas that in tertiary industries is increasing. This is a major trend in industrial transformation observed in developed countries. Absorbing the shocks of such a structural transformation and realizing a desirable industrial structure are important issues for every economy. There are at least the following reasons for this: First, developed countries are more or less characterized as welfare states. To secure adequate financial resources to maintain welfare services through income, value-added, and corporate income taxes, these countries must maintain high employment rates. Specifically, they must increase employment in some industries to compensate for declining employment in other industries. Furthermore, they must have a certain number of highly productive and profitable industries. Second, the industrial structures of advanced economies must become more differentiated from those of emerging economies as the industrial bases of emerging economies are strengthening and becoming more competitive than ever. Third, industrial transformation that increases the share of technologies and products with low environmental impact is essential.

Schumpeter describes creative destruction as a *natural* historical process based on dynamic competition, which involves the introduction of new innovations by entrepreneurs and natural selection through market competition. While it is indeed possible to agree with Schumpeter that the market is a primary mechanism for industrial transformation, the modern economy is largely coordinated by a variety of institutions other than the market, including employment and financial systems. In other words, the modern economy is a capitalist market economy embedded in institutional coordination. As we will see in Sect. 5.2, the economies of the Nordic countries are characterized by rapid industrial transformation. Which socio-economic institutions and policies make this possible? What are the characteristics of industrial restructuring and the subsequent creation of new industries in Nordic economies compared to Japan? The concept of the "entrepreneurial state," which convincingly demonstrates that governments play a role in creating markets by taking risks and making investments, provides an appropriate perspective from which to examine these questions (Mazzucato, 2013). However, it is also true that this argument has been criticized for overestimating the capacity of government. These criticisms strongly suggest that the dichotomous, "market or government" perspective is not relevant and that the institutional foundations of the entrepreneurial state need to be examined.

Is there a "Nordic model" of the entrepreneurial state? Clearly, this question requires multifaceted investigation. By focusing on the most recent, major industrial restructuring in Finland and examining its characteristics in detail, this chapter aims to provide clues on how the institutional characteristics of the "Nordic model" can contribute to industrial restructuring. The case in point is the industrial restructuring that took place after Nokia's exit from the mobile phone business and the subsequent creation of the digital health industry. Although industrial restructuring is always an ongoing, albeit slow, phenomenon, the impact of institutional characteristics is not readily apparent until a crisis occurs, which justifies the focus of our analysis on major crises. This case is also relevant for understanding the evolution of the welfare state because digital technology is considered critical for the sustainability of the welfare state, as it can contribute to raise the productivity of welfare services.

The remainder of this chapter is organized as follows. Section 5.2 quantitatively examines the characteristics of industrial transformation in some developed countries and highlights the characteristics in Nordic countries. Section 5.3 examines the characteristics of industrial transformation and adopted measures in the Oulu region in Finland, which was forced to undergo severe industrial transformation after the downturn in Nokia's mobile phone business, and illuminates the characteristics in comparison with the Japanese case. Section 5.4 examines how various policy measures contributed to the creation of the digital health industry, which flourished in the Oulu region after industrial restructuring. Finally, Section 5.5 summarizes the findings and discusses their implications.

5.1.2 Nordic Model, Industrial Transformation, and Innovation

Studies have repeatedly suggested that the institutional features of the Nordic socioeconomic model, as briefly described in Chap. 1 of this volume, can positively contribute to industrial restructuring and creation of new industries. First, the "enabling welfare state" (EWS) theses of Kristensen and Lilja (2011) and Miettinen (2012) argue that the Nordic universalist welfare state can facilitate the creation of new industries by making substantial social investments, including spending on education, training, and healthcare.

The second is the "Rehn-Meidner model" (Barth et al., 2014; Erixon, 2008, 2018; Iacono, 2018; Miyamoto, 1999; Perraton, 2018) encompassing the centralization of wage bargaining at the central level in the Nordic countries. This compresses wage differentials across industries and firms, resulting in high profits for high-productivity firms and allowing them to expand through reinvestment, whereas low-productivity firms are forced to lower their profits and are encouraged to exit.[1] Together, this promotes industrial transformation and both the compression of wage inequality and a strong increase in productivity in the economy can be achieved.

Third, if corporatism is understood in a broad sense as a mechanism for consensus-building through consultation among organizations with different interests, corporatism is also adopted to technology, innovation, and industrial policies in Nordic countries, allowing for rapid changes in the areas in which resources are invested. "Creative corporatism" (CC) thesis by Ornston (2012) argued that corporatism enables rapid changes in the industrial structure through the corporatist configuration.

However, these studies have several theoretical and empirical limitations. First, the EWS thesis does not examine *how new industries are created*. In other words, while it argues for how skilled human resources are *supplied*, it does not discuss how the *demand* for such resources is created. As we see in Sect. 5.2, the high unemployment rates in Finland and Sweden may point to a problem that cannot be solved by improving skills and promoting labor market flexibility alone, as the EWS thesis claims (Miyamoto, 2009, pp. 106–117).

Second, while the Rehn-Meidner model promotes the elimination of less efficient industries, they do not include the mechanism of *how new industries are created*, which depends on the entrepreneur's willingness to invest in high-productivity industries. Thus, we must understand how the institutional features of the Nordic model affect entrepreneurs' willingness to invest. Moreover, the stagnation of capital accumulation in Nordic countries despite rising profit rates since the 1990s (Perraton, 2018), suggests that the mechanism of industrial transformation by encouraging investment in high-productivity industries may have been at least partially undermined.

Third, the problem with the CC thesis is that it does not explain *why corporatism can be "creative"* in the sense that it can avoid agreements that reinforce path dependency and create new paths. In fact, there are many examples, including the recent innovation policy in Japan, where a policy developed as a result of consultations between organizations with different interests, even if it initially intended to create *new* pathways, reinforces the *existing* pathways due to the consultations (Tokumaru, 2020).

---

[1] Several sources confirm that the assumptions of the Rehn-Meidner model are not necessarily broken only in this sense, as wage compression still occurs in the Nordic countries compared to other advanced economies. For example, according to the *OECD Distribution of Earnings Database*, the gap between the top and bottom 10% of annual gross earnings of full-time workers in 2019 is 5.00 in the United States, 3.34 in the United Kingdom, 3.28 in Germany, and 2.78 in Japan, compared with 2.60 in Denmark, 2.56 in Finland, and 2.13 in Sweden. Consequently, annual salaries for ICT professionals were also relatively low: $75,741 in San Jose, $59,030 in Frankfurt, $52,920 in Stockholm, $47,952 in Helsinki, $42,624 in Oulu, $13,551 in Shanghai, and $13,200 in Bangalore (https://www.glassdoor.co.in/).

Considering these three observations, a critical issue is how a society can find new ways to allocate existing technology, knowledge, and human resources and how the institutional characteristics of the Nordic model contribute to this.

5.1.3 Analytical Framework

The analysis and discussion of this chapter are based on a framework developed from the evolutionary theory of the firm (Tokumaru, 2005). Goods are produced by combining both tangible and intangible *resources*. The resources possessed by individuals and organizations include routines, rules, knowledge (including technology), skills, know-how, and tangible resources. The resources are denoted as r_i ($1 \leq i \leq m$), where m is the number of resources. If there are m types of resources and n units of individuals and organizations, the overall resource endowment of society is represented by a matrix R with n rows and m columns, where each element is either zero or one. Because each technology can be used for different purposes, different functions can be extracted from a given resource. These functions are referred to as *services*. In other words, resources are useful to people and society only after the extraction of certain services (Penrose, 1995; Richardson, 1972). The services are denoted as s_j ($1 \leq j \leq k$), where k is the number of services. Given k services, the services provided to the society in question are represented by a k-dimensional vector S, where each element is either zero or one.

In many cases, new *services* are created by combining multiple *resources* in novel ways. For example, digital health combines information and communication technology (ICT) with knowledge and technology related to medicine and healthcare. New services are added to society by replacing old resources with new ones or combining multiple existing resources (Arthur, 2009; Frenken, 2017; Jacobs, 1969). Then, innovation processes are composed of the following three distinct logical steps:

1. Renewal of matrix R: Introducing new r_i and discarding old r_i.
2. Conversion $R \Rightarrow S$: Extract new services (S) by combining resources (R) in unknown ways, called "R-S transformation."
3. Orientation of new service extraction (S).

Logically, based on this framework, there are three possible policy measures for the creation of new industries and innovations: (1) the creation of new resources, (2) new combinations of resources, and (3) promoting and steering the search for new services. According to the aforementioned studies, while the Nordic model promotes (1), as the EWS thesis emphasizes, the implications of the Nordic model for (2) are unclear. Furthermore, while the Nordic model is considered favorable for (3), as the CC thesis suggests, the reason for this is unclear.

5.2 Industrial Transformation in Developed Countries

Before examining the case, this section provides a macroeconomic overview of industrial transformation in Finland and other developed economies. Changes in employment best illustrate industrial transformation. Tables 5.1 and 5.2 show the changes in and the share of employment in each industry in the five countries (1995 = 100). The following four observations were made: First, employment in the ICT sector has grown faster in Finland and Sweden than in other countries. As the top row of Table 5.1 shows, labor productivity in the ICT industry grew the fastest. Thus, these two Nordic countries are undergoing industrial restructuring which boosts economic growth as employment in the ICT industry increases along with rapid productivity growth. However, growth-enhancing industrial transformation in this direction has been slow in Japan and Germany, as shown in Tables 5.1 and 5.2, respectively. Table 5.3 shows the share of ICT specialists among the employed,

Table 5.1 Employment Change (2020: 1995 = 100)

	Manufacturing industry	Telecommunications industry	Distribution, food service, and transportation services	Professional, scientific and technical, administrative services
Labor productivity: EU (1995 = 100)	186.0	214.8	132.6	87.2
Germany (2019)	94.3	147.3	113.3	225.5
Finland	86.6	196.4	113.9	282.9
Sweden	77.1	185.3	119.0	207.0
United Kingdom	62.3	166.0	124.5	184.8
Japan (2019)	78.9	155.5	93.9	164.5

Source: Authors' calculations from OECD Stat

Note: Labor productivity is gross value added (expressed in fixed prices) divided by total hours worked

Table 5.2 Employment Composition (%) (2020)

	Manufacturing industry	Telecommunications industry	Distribution, food service, and transportation services	Professional, scientific and technical, administrative services
Germany (2019)	18.9	3.2	22.4	10.9
Finland	13.0	5.2	19.1	12.4
Sweden	9.9	5.3	18.5	13.3
United Kingdom	8.7	4.7	21.7	12.7
Japan (2019)	16.0	3.6	27.7	8.7

Source: Authors' calculations from OECD Stat

Table 5.3 Percentage of ICT Professionals Employed (% of total employment in 2019)

Sweden	7.0
Finland	6.8
United Kingdom	5.6
Germany	4.0

Source: Eurostat

where Sweden and Finland are at the top of the EU countries, suggesting that the two Nordic countries are ahead of other EU countries in terms of the digitalization of industries.

Second, Table 5.2 shows that the share of employment in professional, scientific, technical, and managerial services (hereafter, "professional services") increased more in Finland, Sweden, and the United Kingdom than in Germany and Japan. This sector largely comprises "knowledge-intensive business services" (KIBS), which often represent knowledge-based economies. Thus, Nordic countries and the United Kingdom are shifting their industrial structures towards a knowledge-based economy. In Germany, employment growth in this sector is remarkable (Table 5.1), but the employment share is not as high as in Nordic countries and the United Kingdom (Table 5.2). In Japan, employment in this sector has grown the least (see Table 5.1), and its share of employment is the lowest among the five countries (see Table 5.2).

Third, all five countries experienced a common decline in manufacturing employment but at different rates and proportions. The United Kingdom and Sweden experienced the largest declines in manufacturing employment. Indeed, their manufacturing employment shares are also low at 8.7% and 9.9%, respectively. Japan (78.9) and Finland (86.6) experienced the next largest decline in employment, but their employment shares were relatively high at 16.0% and 13.0%, respectively. Germany (94.3) experienced the smallest decline in manufacturing employment, with a high employment share of 18.9%.[2]

Fourth, the share of employment in community, social, and interpersonal services (hereafter, "community services") is high at approximately 30% in all countries. However, its employment growth is lower than that of ICT and other professional services. A typical example is long-term care services, which depend heavily on public social spending. The lack of employment growth in these industries may be a result of the increase in social spending, which is common in all countries.

In summary, while Germany and Japan have maintained relatively high levels of manufacturing employment and experienced relatively gradual industrial transformation, Sweden and Finland have experienced rapid structural changes in the form

[2] Although its ability to create jobs has declined, manufacturing remains important to these economies: in 2018, the share of manufacturing value added in total value added was 23.2% in Germany, 21.4% in Japan, 17.5% in Finland, 15.3% in Sweden, and 10.3% in the United Kingdom, exceeding its share of employment. The change in the value-added share of the manufacturing sector between 1995 and 2008 was positive in all countries (2.6% in Japan, 2.1% in Finland, 1.7% in Germany, and 0.0% in Sweden), except in the United Kingdom, where it was negative (−5.6%). Thus, the weight of manufacturing in total economic value added is increasing (calculated by the author from *OECD Stat*).

Table 5.4 Unemployment Rates (2019; % of labor force)

Germany	3.4
Finland	6.7
Sweden	6.8
United Kingdom	3.8
Japan	2.4

Source: OECD Stat

of increased employment in ICT and professional services. As Table 5.4 shows, the unemployment rates in the two Nordic countries are approximately twice as high as those in the other three countries, which means that the expansion of the ICT industry has not created enough jobs. Nevertheless, industrial transformation is taking place in the two Nordic countries, boosting economic growth because employment in the ICT industry, which has a high-productivity growth rate, is expanding rapidly.

5.3 Major Industrial Restructuring and Policy in the Aftermath of the "Nokia Shock": The Case of Oulu, Finland

Given the above dynamics at the national level, the industrial transformation in Oulu can be seen as a "microcosm" of the macro industrial transformation in Finland, as described below. It also suggests possible relevant policies for other regions to reduce their dependence on specific industries and diversify their industrial bases.

5.3.1 The "Nokia Shock" and Its Background

At its peak in the early 2000s, when Oulu was considered the world's largest research and development (R&D) center for wireless communication technologies, 14,000 people were employed in the high-tech industry in the region, an increase of 10,000 people per decade. Employment in the ICT industry accounts for 16% of employment in this region, far above the national average of 9% (Salo, 2014; Simonen et al., 2020). The development of Oulu's electronic technology began in the 1960s. One milestone was the establishment of the University of Oulu in 1958, which focused on science and engineering. The Department of Electrical Engineering was established in 1965. At the end of the 1960s, the focus of the university shifted from power engineering to radio engineering and electronics, which was strongly questioned by the central government at the time (Salo, 2014).

The University of Oulu has promoted industry-academia cooperation since its inception, and professors from the Department of Electronic Engineering began their own companies in the 1970s. *Polar Electro*, which developed the world's first heart rate monitor, is a prime example and was founded in 1982. Markku Mannerkoski, who served as a rector from 1968 to 1987, also helped establish *Technopolis* in 1982, the first incubator in Scandinavia (Kulju, 2002). Technopolis was jointly established by the City of Oulu, University of Oulu, National Development Fund, and 28 private companies to contribute to the development of diverse industries (e.g., pulp and paper, basic metals, construction, energy, infrastructure, and media), as evidenced by the wide range of companies that participated in its establishment. However, it soon became almost exclusively focused on wireless technology, even though Nokia was not initially involved (Salo, 2014; Simonen & Koivumäki, 2016). The Oulu branch of the Technical Research Centre of Finland (VTT) was established in 1974, which has been closely linked to the University of Oulu, thus creating a career path for university researchers to move to the private sector. For example, Matti Otala, a professor of electronic engineering, became a manager at VTT in 1975 and then moved to Nokia's R&D center in 1986 (Salo, 2014).

In 1973, Nokia began manufacturing mobile phones for the military in Oulu. In the mid-1980s, the company established a R&D center in Oulu to leverage the region's abundant technical talent. Nokia also developed a network of subcontractors in Oulu, employing several thousand people in total (Simonen et al., 2020). In fact, five of Nokia's top nine suppliers are located in Oulu (Salo, 2014). Consequently, Oulu's high-tech sector has built on its relationship with Nokia.

At the beginning of its expansion in Oulu, Nokia began a partnership with the University of Oulu to train engineers, which later expanded to include R&D and product development (Lindén, 2021). In 1987, the university established a customized training program for Nokia, whose relationship with Nokia deepened to the point that it became known as the "Nokia University." The share of mobile phones in Nokia's sales was only 10% in 1990, but by 2000 it was as high as 72% (Salo, 2014). In other words, as the economy of the Oulu region and institutions, such as the University of Oulu and VTT, became more dependent on Nokia, Nokia became more dependent on its mobile phone business.

The company's global share of the cell phone market fell from 40% in 2007 to 13% in 2013 owing to the emergence of smartphones. The number of employees in Nokia's mobile phone business in the Oulu region fell sharply, from 1200 in 2012 to 500 in 2013 (Salo, 2014). Table 5.5 presents a series of restructuring measures taken by Nokia and related companies. In 2009, the company made its first layoffs by inviting voluntary retirements, followed by a change in strategy to replace its Symbian operating system with that of Microsoft (MS) based on an agreement signed in February 2011, followed by the consolidation of offices and layoffs in the Oulu region. This restructuring affected not only Nokia's employees, but also those of subcontractors located in the Oulu region. Finally, in 2013, the mobile phone business was sold to MS, and Nokia decided to specialize in network equipment; however, MS and Broadcom, to which Nokia employees had been transferred, also ceased operations in Oulu, resulting in a large number of job losses (Simonen et al., 2020). Consequently, 3500 employees were laid off from Nokia and its subcontractors in the Oulu region in the 5 years following 2009 (Herala et al., 2017). By the

Table 5.5 Restructuring by Nokia and Related Companies

Year	Contents
2009	First layoffs: 200 R&D staff
2010	400 employees transferred to *Renesas Electronics*
2011	Large-scale layoffs and consolidation of offices in the Oulu area due to the change to the MS platform; 400 Symbian developers transferred to *Accenture*
2012	Hundreds of layoffs in the Oulu area: 700 people laid off at Nokia, mainly R&D staff; 135 transferred people laid off in *Accenture*; workforce reductions also at subcontractors
2013	Sale of cell phone division to MS: 4700 employees transferred to MS 1000+ laid off
	Renesas Electronics sold its operation in Oulu to Broadcom and transfers 500 employees
2014	Broadcom stops modem production in Oulu, 600 people lose their jobs.
	MS suspends operations in Oulu. A total of 1000 ICT professionals lost their jobs at both companies.
2016	Nokia cuts 1000 network equipment-related jobs nationwide, an estimated 250 of them are in the Oulu area.

end of 2014, more than 2000 high-tech engineers remained unemployed (Simonen et al., 2020).

Between 2009 and 2013, there was a significant outflow of jobs from the electronics industry, with approximately 1350 workers finding jobs in the high-tech services industry. Foreign companies have invested in Oulu to establish new operations that employ unemployed skilled workers (Simonen et al., 2020). However, the unemployment rate among highly skilled professionals has increased steadily (Herala et al., 2017). Each year, approximately 30% of those who were unemployed in the previous year were able to find a new job in the Oulu region, while 25–30% attend retraining courses. Even after 2 years, 60–80% of people are still unable to find a new job (Simonen et al., 2020). In addition, only 12% of those who re-entered the labor market saw their wages increase by more than EUR 500 per month, 46% suffered a wage decrease of up to EUR 500 per month, and 42% suffered a wage decrease of more than EUR 500 per month (Herala et al., 2017). Workers who lose their jobs also bear the costs of industrial restructuring. However, many did not leave the Oulu region and found new jobs there; in the 5 years since 2008, while 1700 people joined the electronics industry again in the Oulu region, 4100 people left, of whom many (1925) were re-employed in other industries in the Oulu region. Many others remained in the Oulu region, including those who were unemployed and attended retraining courses. Only a small number (132) become entrepreneurs (Herala et al., 2017).

5.3.2 *Industrial Transformation After the Nokia Shock*

While the restructuring of Nokia and its suppliers was drastic, the subsequent industrial restructuring in the Oulu region was also significant. Figure 5.1 shows the unemployment rate in the North Ostrobothnia region, including Oulu, which peaked in 1993 (23.2%) and 2015 (17.3%). The former was due to the great recession

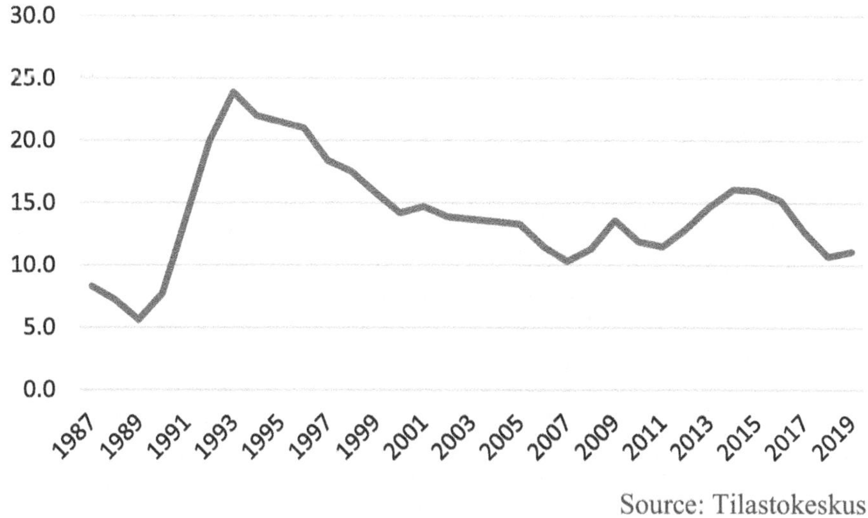

Fig. 5.1 Unemployment rate in Oulu and surrounding areas (%). Source: Tilastokeskus

Table 5.6 Composition (%) and change of employment by economic sector in Oulu region

	2007	2013	2018	Change in the number of employed persons (2007→18)
Manufacturing	17.7	13.6	13.6	−5745
ICT	2.9	2.8	3.3	814
Professional Services	5.0	5.5	5.5	1059
Health and social services	16.3	18.6	19.1	5567

Source: Authors' calculations from Tilastokeskus data

following the collapse of the former Soviet Union, and the latter, of course, to the Nokia shock. By 2019, the unemployment rate had been dropped to 11.7%, almost returning to the lowest level in the 2000s.

Table 5.6 shows the employment share by industry and the changes in the number of people employed in North Ostrobothnia between 2007 and 2018. Although employment in the manufacturing industry decreased by 5700 people because of restructuring, it increased by 5500 people in the health and social services industry, 800 people in the ICT industry, and 1000 people in the professional, scientific, and technical services industries, showing a major structural change. The number of persons employed per enterprise from 2013 to 2018, the only period for which data are available, increased from 14.9 to 16.1 in the manufacturing industry, 7.6 to 8.4 in the ICT industry, 4.7 to 4.7 in the professional, scientific, and technical services industry, and 17.8 to 17.7 in the health and social services industry. Thus, while the increase in employment in professional, scientific, and technical services and health and social services is solely due to an increase in the number of enterprises, the increase in employment in ICT is also due to growing size of enterprises.

Table 5.7 Composition of value-added by industry in Oulu and surrounding areas (%)

	2013	2014	2015	2016	2017	2018	2019
Manufacturing	31.9	28.3	30.0	28.2	27.2	23.5	23.3
ICT	2.3	5.0	5.2	5.8	6.2	6.5	6.5
Professional Services	7.3	7.5	7.9	6.6	6.5	7.3	7.4
Health and social services	4.9	5.0	4.8	5.3	5.1	5.8	6.0

Source: Authors' calculations from Tilastokeskus data

Table 5.8 Businesses opening and closing in Oulu city

	Quarterly average (2013 Q1–2021 Q1)			Annual average (2013–19)	
	Number of openings	Number of businesses closed	Ratio of business closures/ openings	Business opening rate (%)	Business closure rate (%)
Manufacturing	13.2	9.2	76.0	3.7	2.6
ICT	22.1	13.4	66.9	14.3	8.9
Professional Services	45.4	27.5	72.1	9.5	5.9

Source: Authors' calculations from Tilastokeskus data

Table 5.7 shows the changes in the composition of value added in the above four industries (2013–19). Although the manufacturing industry still accounts for a large share (23.3%), it has decreased by 8.5% since 2013. By contrast, the ICT industry accounted for 6.5%, an increase of 4.2% from 2013. However, for professional, scientific, technical, health, and social services, the change in value-added composition is rather small despite the large increase in employment. The change in value added per enterprise between 2013 and 2019 in the ICT industry increased by 3.0 times (from EUR 223,000 to EUR 668,000), but only by 1.2 times (from EUR 223,000 to EUR 259,000) in the professional, scientific, and technical services industry, and 1.4 times (from EUR 259,000 to EUR 253,000) in the health and social services industry. Thus, the increase in the composition of value-added of the ICT industry is due to the growth of enterprises. Considering that the number of persons employed per enterprise in the ICT industry increased only by 10% during the same period, we can also observe a rapid growth in labor productivity, as measured by the value added in the ICT industry.

Table 5.8 shows the average quarterly number of openings and closings, average closure/opening ratio (%), and average annual opening and closing rates (2013–19) for the manufacturing, ICT, professional, scientific, and technical service industries in Oulu.[3] The number of business openings exceeded the number of business closures in all these industries, indicating that the industries were entering a new phase. However, the intensity of this metabolism differs among industries. The ratio of closures to openings is 76.0% in manufacturing; 72.1% in professional, scientific, and technical services; and 66.9% in information and communications. Meanwhile, the opening and closing rates of the professional, scientific, and technical service industries were 9.5% and 5.9%, respectively, whereas those of the ICT industry were 14.3% and 8.9%, respectively. This indicates that the ICT industry has a more active metabolism than the other two industries.

5.3.3 Policy Responses for Industrial Transformation

One may question whether the industrial transformation described above is solely the result of entrepreneurship and market selection, as supposed by Schumpeter. We explore the contribution of policy responses to industrial restructuring in the Oulu region by examining various policy responses and outcomes, particularly those of local governments and private companies.

In September 2012, the Finnish government designated Oulu as an area of "sudden structural change" (*Äkillinen Rakennemuutos*: ÄRM). The ÄRM Fund was established by the Ministry of Employment and the Economy in 2006, which consists of government funds and those co-financed by the government and EU. The latter were obtained through applications to the *European Regional Development Fund* (ERDF) and *European Social Fund* (ESF). The ÄRM Fund provided EUR 30 million to the Oulu region which were allocated to each project by the North Ostrobothnia Region and the Center for Economic Development, Transport and Environment (*ELY Center*: Elinkeino-, liikenne- ja ympäristökeskukset), a government agency. Many projects were jointly managed by *Business Oulu*, an industrial development corporation owned by the City of Oulu, the University of Oulu, and the Oulu University of Applied Sciences (Herala et al., 2017, pp. 31, 59, 63).

In 2012, the Ministry of Employment and the Economy applied for the *European Globalization Adjustment Fund* (EGF), an EU fund that aims to support job creation and entrepreneurship in regions facing rapid employment adjustments due to

[3] The health and social services industry is excluded from this analysis because the number of openings and closings in this industry in each period is the same or lower than in the ICT industry. Since the number of firms by industry in Oulu is not available, the denominators of the opening and closing rates are those of North Ostrobothnia province. Since most enterprises in the Oulu region are located in the city of Oulu, the figures calculated here are considered acceptable as approximations.

globalization.[4] The EGF funds were allocated by the ELY Center and the Employment and Economic Development Office (*TE Office*: Työ- ja elinkeinotoimisto).

In addition, the ELY Center invested EUR 66 million of its own money in business and development support. The former Finnish Technology Agency (*Tekes*), a government agency that subsidized and financed innovation, invested EUR 490 million in North Ostrobothnia between 2010 and 2015, of which EUR 200 million supported the high-tech sector. In addition, *Finnvera*, a government-owned financial institution that provides loans and loan guarantees to internationalizing companies, provided EUR 16 million in loans to companies in the region from 2009 to 2011. Finally, the *Northern Start-up Fund*, which was established in 2012 with funding from the City of Oulu, the ERDF, and the private sector, invested in 22 companies in Oulu from 2013 to 2014 (Herala et al., 2017, pp. 74–77).

Next, we look at the measures for industrial restructuring.

5.3.3.1 Agreement on the Direction of the Transformation

Notably, attempts to foresee and anticipate a major structural change in the industry began as early as 2007, even before the first layoffs at Nokia, when the informal consultative, *Tar Group*, was established in Oulu. It was led by the ELY Center and included representatives from North Ostrobothnia Region, the City of Oulu, Business Oulu, the TE Office, the University of Oulu, the Oulu University of Applied Sciences, Finnvera, and the Oulu Chamber of Commerce and Industry. A free and informal discussion was held on the prospects of a possible Nokia crisis and responses. The focus was on finding ways to promote employment and entrepreneurship, and attract companies, with a view to using ÄRM funding from the Ministry of Employment and the Economy. Consequently, the stakeholders established the principle that the ÄRM funding should be used for completely *new* activities and not for *existing* ones with little future potential. This principle eventually led to the industrial restructuring. The same was true of the retraining policy discussed by the group, which was not to supplement the *existing* knowledge of the unemployed, but to provide training that would impart entirely *new* knowledge. A typical example is entrepreneurship training for engineers (Herala et al., 2017, p. 61; Simonen et al., 2020, p. 947).

In 2009, the *Oulu Innovation Alliance* (OIA) strengthened its cooperation in education and R&D in specific areas. The OIA agreed to focus its investments on five areas—the Internet, printed electronics, global business, water resources, and healthcare technology—and work on joint projects in education and research and development. As mentioned earlier, while the incubator Technopolis had been expected to play a role in industrial diversification in the region by handling various

---

[4] Specifically, it applies when there is unemployment or layoff of 500 or more workers per company, or when mass unemployment occurs in a specific industry in the same region.

technological and industrial fields when it was first established, it was no longer expected to be a driver of industrial diversification as it gradually became concentrated in ICT fields. Consequently, one may say that the OIA laid the foundation for regional industrial diversification (Herala et al., 2017, p. 61; Simonen et al., 2020, p. 945).

5.3.3.2 Projects Funded by Sudden Structural Change Fund

As mentioned above, the designation of the Oulu region as an area of sudden structural change (ÄRM) in September 2012 required close cooperation between government, industry, and research and education actors to develop a plan for creating new jobs. Therefore, the City of Oulu, the business community, the ELY Center, and North Ostrobothnia Region worked together to develop a plan for the necessary measures. The resulting ÄRM funding were not allocated to projects carried out by individual companies or organizations alone, but only to projects carried out jointly by several organizations. Among the agencies that allocated funds, North Ostrobothnia Region was responsible for developing new business environments and identifying and promoting new growth sectors. The ELY Center is responsible for implementing investment and development projects for small- and medium-sized enterprises. The TE office and ELY Center were jointly responsible for employment and training services at the individual level (Herala et al., 2017, p. 65).

The North Ostrobothnia Region allocated ÄRM funding to eight projects, all of which aimed either to develop business environments ("ecosystems") for specific industrial sectors, or support exports and overseas expansion of companies. Examples of the former include the "ONION" project, which aims to develop ICT infrastructure for healthcare, and the "Smart Cleantech Oulu 2020" project, which promotes environmentally friendly technology industries. An example of the latter is the "International Sales Promotion" project. EUR 5.95 million has been invested, of which EUR 3.77 million came from the EU (ERDF) and the government, EUR 1.62 million from local governments and other public institutions, and EUR 0.55 million from private companies. Although the projects have different objectives, they all have the ultimate goal of reemploying the unemployed. By 2015, 529 private companies had participated in these projects, creating 310 new jobs, 284 of which were in R&D (Pohjois-Pohjanmaan liitto, 2016).

In summary, the ÄRM funding was used to improve the business environment for the creation of industries who could be the recipients of new employment. In particular, the ÄRM funding were not just used for "customary" purposes, such as R&D, but also for projects intended to create demand for new industries. For instance, the ONION project aimed to create an "open and modular" information system and ecosystem for social services and was implemented from February 2013 to April 2015. The implementing agency was the Information Management Department of the City of Oulu with a budget of EUR 873,755. Finland has a declining birth rate and aging population. One of the pillars of the large-scale reform of social and healthcare services (*SOTE reform*: Sosiaali- ja terveydenhuollon uudistus) aimed at controlling cost increases is the digitization of services. This project was conducted to design the basic architecture of a new information system at the regional level considering the upcoming SOTE reform. Considering that this project was implemented as a project under the ÄRM funding rather than as part of a healthcare policy, this project explicitly intended to create demand for a new, digital healthcare industry, after the industrial transformation.

The ELY Center allocated ÄRM funds to SME projects. EUR 1.6 million were allocated to 11 projects, including projects related to vocational training and recruitment support for specific industries (e.g., gaming industry) and technologies. Of this amount, EUR 1.3 million came from the EU (ESF) and the government, EUR 200,000 from the local government, and EUR 90,000 from the private sector (Pohjois-Pohjanmaan liitto, 2016).

5.3.3.3 Promotion of Entrepreneurship and Retraining

The promotion of entrepreneurship among unemployed engineers is an important job-creation measure. Several measures have been implemented in the initiatives of public organizations and Nokia. An example of entrepreneurship support by public organizations is the *Oulun Yritystakomo* (Oulu Enterprise Forge), which was established in 2010 and is no longer active. It is an incubator that creates a community of unemployed engineers and helps them generate business ideas. Another is *Business Kitchen*, established in 2011 by Business Oulu and Oulu University of Applied Sciences with ERDF funding, which is a platform for high-growth companies. It is a free space that requires no commitment and is aimed mainly at SMEs and students interested in entrepreneurship. It hosts 200 events monthly. According to a 2014 survey, 38% of visitors were students, 33% were self-employed, 17% were employees of companies, and 13% were unemployed (Herala et al., 2017, p. 85).

Of particular note is the *Nokia Bridge Program* (2011–13), a re-employment and entrepreneurship support program implemented by Nokia itself, which had laid off a large number of employees. The program was open to employees who were laid off between 2011 and 2013. Five hundred people, or one-tenth of all employees laid off in the country, participated in the program. In Oulu, 161 people participated in the entrepreneurship support course. The main content of the course was support for preparing a business plan, financial support for starting a business, and loan guarantees with a maximum of EUR 25,000 per person. Of the 114 start-ups in Oulu, 85 remained in existence until 2016 (Herala et al., 2017, p. 84). A survey of the program participants showed that they highly valued the program's financial support and loan guarantees, commenting that they could not obtain loans without Nokia's loan guarantees. At the time of the survey, the companies that emerged from the program employed an average of 2.1 people, and 60% had no previous business relationship with Nokia (Autio et al., 2014).

Tekes has also invested money in creating an entrepreneurial environment. For example, *Innovation Mill*, launched in 2009 in collaboration with Nokia and Technopolis, was a program aimed at giving new companies access to unused technologies and ideas at Nokia. EUR 84 million was invested, half of which was subsidized by Tekes. Notably, the program reportedly created 1000 jobs (Herala et al., 2017, pp. 75–77).

Next, we consider retraining measures. The aforementioned EGF funding, which are EU funds for rapid employment adjustments, were invested in the Oulu region after three major restructuring projects: Nokia, Broadcom, and Microsoft. According to a survey conducted by the TE office on 854 Nokia project beneficiaries, the subsequent progress of 777 could be tracked, of which 312 were employees of Nokia's subcontractors and 542 were Nokia employees. Of these, 71% were re-employed, the unemployment rate had dropped to 10%, and those in training totaled 3%. The re-employment status of these EGF beneficiaries was better than the average unemployment in the ICT sector, suggesting that training in the EGF project was effective (Herala et al., 2017, p. 72). Small and Medium Enterprise Development Training (KEKO Training) has also been provided to facilitate the re-employment of project managers in SMEs (Herala et al., 2017, p. 74).

In addition to these EGF-funded programs, ELY centers, TE offices, training institutions, and ICT companies undergoing restructuring implemented 68 training programs in 2014. This training aims to increase employability and entrepreneurial skills. The training costs were borne by the TE office and employer, with the share varying according to training content. Note that the TE office was originally funded almost equally by the government and EGF (Herala et al., 2017, p. 91). Part of the retraining was "joint-procurement training," which was jointly funded by the employer and TE office. The majority of joint-procurement training was "change training," which is provided by the employer with the aim of increasing the re-employment chances of laid-off workers. The average training duration was 86 days and the employer paid, on average, 20% of the total cost. In particular, during the large Nokia layoffs that started in 2012, up to 23 change training sessions were organized in cooperation with Nokia's Bridge program (Herala et al., 2017, p. 92).

5.3.4 A Brief Comparison with the Japanese Case

In Japan, the decline in the business of dynamic random-access memory (DRAM) semiconductor devices in the 1990s was followed by a decline in liquid-crystal display (LCD). In this case, the companies that developed and manufactured these products merged to achieve economies of scale. *Japan Display Inc.* (JDI), established in November 2011 by Toshiba Mobile Display, Hitachi Displays, Sony Mobile Display, and the Innovation Network Corporation of Japan, a public-private fund, is a typical example. None of the three aforementioned examples has been able to survive as originally conceived (Nakata, 2019).

Although simple comparisons are difficult because of the differences in the product characteristics of mobile phones and electronic devices, a comparison of the measures taken by the two countries to deal with ailing industries reveals the following striking differences: The first notable difference is that, while in Finland, the basic principle was to dismantle existing companies that were in a slump and create new companies, in Japan, the basic principle was to keep existing companies alive by achieving a cost that was competitive with competitors in Korea, China, Taiwan, and so on, through economies of scale achieved through mergers. Finland's policy was to transform its industrial structure, whereas Japan's policy was to maintain it.

Second, while in the Finnish case, the injected public funding did not go to the ailing companies Nokia, Broadcom, and Microsoft but mostly to the North Ostrobothnia Region, in Japan public funds went to newly merged companies that were originally ailing.

The third difference lies in the entities that strategically decide the direction of industrial restructuring and implement the restructuring measures. In Japan, companies receiving public funds, the central government, and public-private funds are actors making strategic decisions and implementing measures. Meanwhile, in Finland, local governments, universities, chambers of commerce and industry, and other organizations at the regional-level consult with each other to determine strategic directions. Furthermore, regional organizations such as municipalities, universities, public research institutions, and public employment agencies worked together to implement these measures.

Thus, we not only see an easily discernible difference between the measures taken in the two countries in terms of whether they were aimed at industrial transformation but also the fact that the parties and systems responsible for designing and implementing the measures are very different. In Japan, the central government and relevant companies are the only players in policy development. Meanwhile, in the Finnish case, the main players were organizations at the local level[5] that existed between the central government and relevant companies, such as local governments, regional universities, and various intermediary organizations.

5.3.5 Summary

As mentioned at the beginning of this chapter, previous studies on the Nordic political economy have argued that the institutional factors that make up the Nordic model, such as wage compression through decentralized wage bargaining and active

[5] Myrdal (1960, pp. 92–102), looking at the development of the welfare state in Sweden at the time, noted that direct state intervention was declining and gradually being replaced by consultation between local governments and organizations. Even ignoring the fact that socio-economic conditions have changed dramatically since then, this case study suggests that his argument is still relevant in the context of industrial structural change and the creation of new industries.

labor market policies, promote industrial structural change in Nordic countries. Undoubtedly, these factors were also observed in the present case. However, corporatism at the regional level plays an important role in strategic decision-making, such as setting the direction of industrial structural transformation and determining the content of policies. In particular, compared with the Japanese case, the framework of corporatism at the regional level in Finland, especially the one that did not include existing ailing firms, was effective in envisioning industrial structural transformation without being influenced by the interests of declining firms and industries.

In addition, as regions are the most affected by industrial transformation, it is desirable to form a strategic consensus that reflects regional interests, unique circumstances, and visions to avoid exhausting the regional economy. Here, the EU and the central government are committed to providing financial support on the condition that the plans made by each region are "forward-looking" and "cooperative," which encourages consensus-building for positive structural transformation while publicly bearing its social costs. Although existing ailing companies, including Nokia, have taken measures to help their employees change jobs and start new businesses, these measures covered only a portion of the unemployed in the entire Oulu region, and their impact cannot be overestimated. If this is the case, the above example suggests that local governments and intermediary organizations with the ability to formulate, plan, and implement strategies play important and indispensable roles.

5.4 Digitalization of the Healthcare System in Oulu[6]

The key focus area of the industrial structural transformation discussed in Sect. 5.4 is the digital healthcare industry. Today, products and services that leverage the original strength of ICT in healthcare are becoming one of the core industries in Oulu. The City of Oulu's healthcare policy has also contributed to this industrial transformation and innovation. In Finland, similar to Japan, the declining birth rate, aging population, and depopulation of rural areas have created an urgent need to curb the rising costs of medical and health services. The Finnish government promoted the application of digital technology in healthcare to reduce costs and ensure quality. The City of Oulu can be viewed as a model that pioneered this approach.

[6] This section is based on the following interviews conducted by the author and on materials collected: Ministry of Social Affairs and Health, September 6, 2018; City of Oulu, November 7, 2019; Business Oulu, February 25 and 28, 2019; Oulu City Hospital, February 27, 2019; Fujitsu Finland Oy, September 18, 2019; 6Aika and Forum Virium Helsinki, September 23, 2019; Business Oulu, September 13, 2022; University of Oulu, September 22, 2023. Note that, as described in other chapters, the provision of social and healthcare services has been largely transferred from municipalities to counties after the SOTE reform came into effect on January 1, 2023. The City of Oulu is therefore no longer responsible for these services.

5.4.1 Development of the "Self-Care System"[7]

The City of Oulu launched the "Self-Care System" (*Oulun Omahoito*), a platform for digitalized health services, as early as 2010. Although residents of the city of Oulu and neighboring municipalities can choose whether to use this system, more than half of Oulu's residents do use the system. The system allows users to make appointments for hospital visits, communicate with specialists, perform self-checks of their health status, record and retrieve test results, and receive health advice via the internet. Nurses can also reduce unnecessary visits by determining whether a patient must visit a hospital. The system is designed to be flexible, so that new services can be added as subsystems. By introducing this system, it was expected that specialists would be able to focus on the most necessary tasks; for example, by replacing hospital visits with home-based measures and telephone calls, with as many online responses as possible. In fact, the City of Oulu estimates that the system saved approximately EUR 2.7 million over the 5-year period from 2012 to 2017.

The information system was developed and owned by a local IT company, and the city purchased its services. The history of this development is as follows. In 2004, the Deputy Mayor of the City of Oulu asked several local IT companies to propose how to digitalize the healthcare system. The city intended to not only enhance the efficiency of the healthcare system, but also promote a new industry by creating new demand. A team consisting of the City of Oulu, three local IT companies (Coronaria, Mawell (now CSAM), and ProWellness), the University of Oulu, the Oulu University of Applied Sciences, and the National Institute of Health and Welfare conducted system development and demonstration tests from 2005 to 2009.[8] Although these three companies had no business relationships, the development of a self-care system triggered their cooperation. The development of this system was a catalyst for the development of the healthcare industry in Oulu, as many healthcare products and services were developed through collaborations between several companies. This development was led by the city's Healthcare Department, which convinced the city's healthcare professionals (doctors, nurses, etc.) who were critical of digitalization and coordinated with Business Oulu, the city's industrial development corporation.

As mentioned above, this self-care system is an extensible platform to which new services can be added. Examples of these services include image chat systems and hearing testers for infants. The City of Oulu has created a new department in the healthcare system that leads to the development of new services. A typical role of this department is to invite companies to submit specific proposals for new services, hold a half-day meeting where several companies present their proposals, and then select companies from among them to form a partnership and develop a new

[7] This subsection is partially based on my previous work, Tokumaru (2024), with modifications.

[8] For the latter part of the project (2007–2009), which can be seen from the documents, development costs totaled EUR 1.85 million, of which 39% was covered by the National Institute of Health and Welfare, 43% by the Municipality of Oulu, and 18% by Tekes (Hirvasniemi & Kanto, 2010; Kanto, 2010).

service, as the following quote illustrates: This department also helps these companies by encouraging them to jointly develop a product to increase its impact.

> We [in Oulu] also take care of patients with diabetes and many technologies and solutions exist. We invited several companies to a half-day meeting to present their systems to diabetes specialists in our department. We found that there are systems that are very useful for self-care by patients themselves, and systems that are very useful for professionals involved in their care. We asked these companies to work together rather than compete to develop better systems. This helped companies, professionals, citizens, and patients. Often, one company's solution is only part of the whole, as is another company's solution. We [in the healthcare systems development department] help combine these partial solutions and make them better. (Interview with the City of Oulu, February 27, 2019).

Additionally, the department exchanges ideas with approximately 100 companies annually. In summary, the City plays a leading role in five important phases: creating a platform on which new products and services can be added; persuading doctors, nurses, and other professionals; developing concepts for new individual services; identifying, attracting, and ongoing dialogue with private companies; and forming partnerships between companies. The following quotes from interviews with a digital healthcare start-up appropriately describe the contributions of the Business Oulu and the City of Oulu from the start-up's perspective.

> Especially in the early stages, many events organized by them (Business Oulu and the City of Oulu) helped a lot. These were events in which startups, large established companies, and SMEs could meet, have dialogues, and network with people. They did not fund us but organized many events and gave us many good tips on who to meet. Gradually, they started to understand our products and services better and started to promote startups [like ours] to big companies in better ways (March 1, 2019).

5.4.2 Expanding the Infrastructure for Innovation: Oulu Health Lab as a Testbed

Although the self-care system is a platform that enables the development of applications, such as digital telemedicine, the *Oulu Health Lab* has also been created as a platform that enables the development of a wider range of digital healthcare devices and systems. This Lab is an environment in which new digital healthcare products and services can be tested in medical and healthcare settings. It is jointly operated by Business Oulu, Oulu University Hospital, Oulu City Hospital, University of Oulu, and City of Oulu. Business Oulu is the coordinator and the main link between hospitals, universities, cities, and private companies. It is also an opportunity for the City of Oulu, especially the Healthcare System Development Department, to meet companies that are developing applications for the aforementioned self-care system. An example of the collaboration results is the Internet-of-Things sensor developed by a company called *Kipuwex* for body data measurement. This is a tool for diagnosing and monitoring pain using digital data from sensors and is particularly useful for people who have difficulty communicating, which is expected to improve the efficiency of care.

Oulu Health Lab was funded by Tekes and the EU (ERDF and ESF). Funding for the latter was obtained through a joint application to the EU by the six largest cities in Finland (Helsinki, Espoo, Vantaa, Tampere, Turku, and Oulu). The *6Aika* project (2013–20), for which funds were used, aimed to create new industries, jobs, and know-how in the six major cities. The project has seven main themes (circular economy, smart cities, health and well-being, education and employment, learning, new knowledge and skills for SMEs, and mobility), and calls are issued annually. Cities, external organizations, universities, etc. apply, and private companies participate as partners. As of September 2019, 4100 companies had participated, 250 of which had developed new products and services. Each city will create 66 new "innovation platforms," where private companies can test and develop new products and services in real urban environments. Cooperation between cities, collaboration with companies, and networking among developers were considered the major achievements of the 6Aika Project (based on interviews conducted on September 23, 2019).

5.4.3 Summary

The EWS thesis argues that the Nordic welfare state is highly resilient to economic change, mainly by expanding the capabilities of each individual through active social investment and promoting labor market flexibility (Kristensen & Lilja, 2011). The CC thesis argues that the corporatist framework facilitates industrial transformation by redirecting resource allocation in a productive direction (Ornston, 2012). Although these mechanisms can also be assumed to be helpful in promoting the creation of new industries, this case shows that the welfare state can also do so *by creating qualitatively new demand.*

However, for public demand to lead to the creation of new industries, public demand must be for innovative, high-quality, and low-cost products and services, and not simply for existing products and services. The second implication of this case study is that active efforts by local governments and intermediary organizations are needed to identify and create such demand and encourage firms to supply it. These organizations play a more active role than what the concept "intermediation" implies, and their roles can be summarized as follows:

1. Challenging actors to plan more innovatively.
2. Creating linkages between actors.
3. Identifying the direction of actors' efforts through discussion.
4. Encouraging intensive consultation and dialogue among actors.
5. Providing technical advice.
6. Creating, maintaining, and developing an organizational basis for experimentation.

Actions (1) to (6) have one common aspect: they try to promote innovation by working with stakeholders to change their views, rules, and routines. We can refer to the role of local governments and intermediary organizations in the present case as a *catalytic action*, analogous to the case in which chemical reactions between substances become possible owing to the presence of catalytic substances (Tokumaru, 2022). Importantly, the space in which catalytic action takes place aims at dialogue between different groups with different values, views, and interests and does not explicitly aim at consensus-building, as in the case of corporatist negotiations.[9]

5.5 Discussion and Conclusion

In addition to the affinities between the institutional features of the Nordic model and industrial structural transformation that have been discussed repeatedly, this chapter suggests that, at least in the case of Oulu, the Nordic model contributes to industrial transformation and creation of new industries in the following three ways that have not attracted attention enough. First, the welfare state, especially the reform of the provision of welfare services, is expected to contribute to the creation of new industries by creating demand for innovative, high-quality, low-cost services, and new methods of service provision. Second, regional-level organizations can contribute to the creation of new industries by acting as active catalysts and influencing private sector innovation. Third, by constituting a system of corporatism at the local level, organizations are expected to play an important role in strategic decision-making, such as setting the direction of industrial structural transformation and determining detailed policy content.

Table 5.9 compares the present case with previous studies using the analytical framework described in Sect. 1.3. As reviewed in Sect. 1.2, while previous studies argue that the Nordic model contributes to industrial transformation and the creation of new industries by freeing up existing resources in the form of enabling labor mobility in productive ways and creating new resources, a new implication of this chapter is that the Nordic model can also contribute through two novel mechanisms: *encouraging the combination of resources in novel ways* and *encouraging and steering the search for new services*.

Table 5.9 Summary

	This case	Previous studies
Unbinding existing resources	✓	✓
Creating new resources	✓	✓
New combination of resources	✓	N/A
Promoting and steering the search for new services	✓	N/A

[9] Although there is not enough space for a full conceptual examination in this chapter, the concept of "negotiated economy," proposed to characterize the Danish socio-economic system, is worth mentioning. With this concept, Amin and Thomas (1996) try to capture a distributed public sphere in which strategy formation and needs identification are based on dialogue at both the *local* and *central* level among *various* actors, which is clearly different from the corporatism that seeks consultation, compromise, and consensus building among *certain* actors at the *central* level.

In this sense, the Nordic model, with a universalist welfare state and advanced decentralization at its core, may be more conducive to industrial structural transformation and the creation of new industries than previous studies have emphasized. Many argue that industrial structures in developed countries are changing and becoming "service-oriented" and "dematerialized" (Morotomi, 2020). In this process, personal services are considered to have become the potential engine of economic growth (Boyer, 2004). Since a large proportion of personal services are publicly provided in many advanced economies, public sector plays critical roles for the creation of new industries and innovation, which means that Nordic model can be compatible with this long-term historical transformation of capitalism due to its strong capacity to create new, welfare-critical service industries.

Recently, developed countries have pursued "mission-oriented innovation policies" (MOIP) aiming at promoting innovations that solve major societal problems (Mazzucato, 2018a, 2018b; Perez, 2016). While attempts to solve healthcare problems through the application of digital technologies can be interpreted as a typical case of MOIP, stimulating public demand alone is insufficient to drive the innovations required by MOIP. Rather, the institutional features of the Nordic model, such as a universalist welfare state, decentralization, and the existence of organizations with sufficient resources and competencies at the local level, help encourage innovations as required by MOIP (Tokumaru, 2017, 2018). Conversely, in Japan, as the case in this chapter shows, industrial restructuring has often been carried out primarily by the central government and firms concerned. This may be representative of the institutional characteristics of Japan, where public organizations, especially at the local level, lack sufficient financial resources, authority, and competence to act as intermediaries between the central government and concerned firms. The above discussion suggests that, although it may seem far-fetched, it is necessary to promote decentralization and provide financial resources and authority to various organizations at the local level to build their capacity for industrial restructuring and the implementation of MOIP.

A limitation of this study lies in the fact that it is impossible to overestimate the job-creation capacity of new ICT-intensive industries. As shown in Tables 5.1 and 5.2, the ICT industry, including the digital healthcare industry, does not have high job-creation potential, partly because labor productivity growth in this industry is high. Consequently, the healthcare and social services industries, which have a low labor productivity growth rate, may be forced to absorb more jobs. Since these sectors inevitably tend to have low profits, the private sector may find it difficult to provide them, forcing the public sector to provide them directly or indirectly. As discussed by Wren (2013, 2020), this will become a major constraint on public finances, which should be complemented by the expansion of highly profitable industries with well-paid jobs. Further investigation of this dilemma is a topic for future studies.

Acknowledgments The conception of this work was greatly aided by discussions with Osamu Eryu (Nagoya Institute of Technology) and Shinya Fujita (Nagoya University). Comments from Kari Lilja (Aalto University), Hiroo Hagino (Tohoku Fukushi University) and Taro Miyamoto (Chuo University), were also very helpful. The author is grateful to all the interviewees for sharing their information and views. The author is fully responsible for any errors. This research was supported by JSPS Grant-in-Aid for Scientific Research No. 19H04368.

References

Amin, A., & Thomas, D. (1996). The negotiated economy: State and civic institutions in Denmark. *Economy and Society, 25*(2), 255–281.
Arthur, B. (2009). *The nature of technology: What it is and how it evolves*. The Free Press.
Autio, E., Rannikko, H., Handelberg, J., & Kiuru, P. (2014). *Analyses on the Finnish high-growth entrepreneurship ecosystem*. Small Business Center, Small Business Center Aalto University.
Barth, E., Moene, K. O., & Willumsen, F. (2014). The Scandinavian model: An interpretation. *Journal of Public Economics, 117*, 60–72.
Boyer, R. (2004). *The future of economic growth: As new becomes old*. Edward Elgar.
Erixon, L. (2008). The Swedish third way: An assessment of the performance and validity of the Rehn-Meidner model. *Cambridge Journal of Economics, 32*, 367–393.
Erixon, L. (2018). Progressive supply-side economics: An explanation and update of the Rehn-Meidner model. *Cambridge Journal of Economics, 42*, 653–697.
Frenken, K. (2017). A complexity-theoretic perspective on innovation policy. *Complexity, Innovation and Policy, 3*(1), 35–47.
Herala, J., Karhinen, S., Orenius, S., Simonen, J., & Svento, R. (2017). *Luova tuho -Tie eteenpäin: Oulu akillisen rakennemuutoksen alueena [Creative destruction - The way forward: Oulu as an area of economic restructuring]*. Oulun Yliopiston Kauppakorkeakoulu.
Hirvasniemi, R., & Kanto, V. (2010). *Kansalaisten sähköiset itsehoitopalvelut-hanke (KASIO) 1.4.2007-30.11.2009 Oulun omahoito kehitysosio & teknologiaterveyskeskus loppuraportti*. Oulun Kaupunki ja Sosiaali-ja-Terveysministeri.
Iacono, R. (2018). The Nordic model of economic development and welfare: Recent developments and future prospects. *Intereconomics, 53*, 185–190.
Jacobs, J. (1969). *The economy of cities*. Random House.
Kanto, V. (2010). *Omahoito ja innovaatioympäristö terveydenhuoltopalveluille, toimintatavoille, tuotteille ja teknologiasovellutuksille 1.9. 2007-31.5.2009 Loppuraportti*. Oulun Kaupunki ja Tekes.
Kristensen, P. H., & Lilja, K. (Eds.). (2011). *Nordic capitalisms and globalization: New forms of economic organization and welfare institutions*. Oxford University Press.
Kulju, M. (2002). *Oulun ihmeen tekijät*. Gummerus.
Lindén, C.-G. (2021). *Kingdom of Nokia: How a nation served the needs of one company*. Helsinki University Press.
Mazzucato, M. (2013). *The entrepreneurial state: Debunking public vs. private sector myths*. Anthem Press.
Mazzucato, M. (2018a). The entrepreneurial state: Socializing both risks and rewards. *Real-World Economics Review, 84*(19), 201–217.
Mazzucato, M. (2018b). *Mission-oriented research & innovation in the European Union: A problem-solving approach to fuel innovation-led growth*. European Commission.
Miettinen, R. (2012). *Innovation, human capabilities, and democracy: Towards an enabling welfare state*. Oxford University Press.
Miyamoto, T. (1999). *The strategy of the welfare state: Political economy of the Swedish model* [In Japanese]. Horitsu Bunka Sha.
Miyamoto, T. (2009). *Social security* [In Japanese]. Iwanami Shoten.
Morotomi, T. (2020). *Capitalism in a new form* [In Japanese]. Iwanami Shoten.
Myrdal, G. (1960). *Beyond the welfare state: Economic planning and its international implications*. Yale University Press.
Nakata, Y. (2019). Can public-private funds promote innovation? - A case analysis of innovation network corporation of Japan, Sharp, JDI, and Renesas [In Japanese]. *Proceedings of the Annual Conference of the Japan Society for Research Policy and Innovation Management, 34*, 599–603.
Ornston, D. (2012). *When small states make big leaps: Institutional innovation and high-tech competition in Western Europe*. Cornell University Press.
Penrose, E. (1995). *The theory of the growth of the firm* (3rd ed.). Oxford University Press.

Perez, C. (2016). Capitalism, technology and a green global golden age: The role of history in helping to shape the future. In M. Jacobs & M. Mazzucato (Eds.), *Rethinking capitalism: Economics and policy for sustainable and inclusive growth*. M. Wiley-Blackwell.
Perraton, J. (2018). Social corporatism and capital accumulation: The fate of the Nordic model. *Intereconomics, 53*, 196–201.
Pohjois-Pohjanmaan liitto. (2016). *Liitteitä Oulun äkillisen rakennemuutoksen loppuraportiin*. Pohjois-Pohjanmaan liitto.
Richardson, G. B. (1972). The organisation of industry. *Economic Journal, 82*(327), 883–896.
Salo, M. (2014). High-tech centre in the periphery: The political, economic and cultural factors behind the emergence and development of the Oulu ICT phenomenon in Northern Finland. *Acta Borealia, 31*(1), 83–107.
Schumpeter, J. A. (2010). *Capitalism, socialism and democracy*. Routledge.
Simonen, J., Herala, J., & Svento, R. (2020). Creative destruction and creative resilience: Restructuring of the Nokia dominated high-tech sector in the Oulu region. *Regional Science Policy and Practice, 12*, 931–953.
Simonen, J., & Koivumäki, T. (2016). What happened to the growth?: The case of the ICT industry in Oulu, Finland. *International Journal of Entrepreneurship and Small Business, 29*(2), 287–308.
Tokumaru, N. (2005). Innovation and organization: Why should the analytical framework be dual-structured, evolutionary one? *NUCB Journal of Economics and Information Science, 49*(2), 13–26.
Tokumaru, N. (2017). New developments in innovation policy in the EU and Finland: The emergence of "evolutionary process governance" policy and its potential. In K. Yagi, K. Shimizu, & N. Tokumaru (Eds.), *European integration and socio-economic innovation: Evolution of region-based policy* [In Japanese] (pp. 399–434). Nihon Keizai Hyoronsha.
Tokumaru, N. (2018). New innovation policy and its organizational foundations in Finland: Thick layer of "mediating organizations" and their implications [In Japanese]. *Japanese Journal of Northern European Studies, 14*, 13–25.
Tokumaru, N. (2020). Thinking and policy making of two "mission-oriented innovation policies" [In Japanese]. *Trans/Actions, 5*, 133–166.
Tokumaru, N. (2022). Revealing and resolving bottlenecks by multiple intermediaries in public procurement of innovation. *Innovation: The European Journal of Social Science Research*. https://doi.org/10.1080/13511610.2022.2062305
Tokumaru, N. (2024). From national system of innovation to "public sphere for innovation": Mission-oriented innovation policy and the changing institutional configuration. In K. Yagi, Y. Shiozawa, Y. Aruka, M. Nishibe, & A. Isogai (Eds.), *Present and future of evolutionary economics: Japanese perspectives*. Springer.
Wren, A. (Ed.). (2013). *The political economy of the service transition*. Oxford University Press.
Wren, A. (2020). Strategies for growth and employment creation in a service-based economy: Skill formation, equality, and the welfare state. In A. Hassel & B. Palier (Eds.), *Growth and welfare in advanced capitalist economies: How have growth regimes evolved?* (pp. 255–288). Oxford University Press.

Chapter 6
The Potential of the Co-Creation Approach to Create Innovation to Better Meet the Needs of Communities

Kazue Haga

Abstract Who deals with social problems is changing. For example, in many European countries, including Finland, the church was traditionally the institution that provided support for poor people. Today, it is difficult for only one institution to deal with social problems because of their complexity and the financial burden. Collective approaches to cope with social challenges are increasingly understood as an effective alternative to the conventional assigned roles in which one particular institution is responsible for a social problem. Co-creation with various stakeholders, for example, residents in the community, municipal staff, academics, and companies, has the potential to create holistic and practical benefits for societies. In this chapter, challenges and potentials of co-creation as a collective approach to develop solutions to social challenges in communities are discussed referring to economic theories, mainly innovation theories. Because of the variety in the backgrounds of the participants, co-creation has the potential to develop creative knowledge and solutions embedded in the community. Interaction in depth between the participants is essential for success in co-creation. To overcome the difficulties arising from diversity in a team and to develop the project under high levels of uncertainty, "entrepreneurial" (in the broader sense of "change maker") participation is helpful.

Keywords Co-creation · Collective innovation creation · Bottom-up approaches · Living Lab

---

K. Haga (✉)
Waseda University, Tokyo, Japan
e-mail: khaga@aoni.waseda.jp

N. Tokumaru et al. (eds.), *Creative Co-evolution of the Economies and Welfare States in the Nordic Countries*, Evolutionary Economics and Social Complexity Science 32, https://doi.org/10.1007/978-981-97-8569-8_6

6.1 Introduction

This chapter sheds light on the roles of companies in society regarding social responsibility. Companies, as a component of society, exist in networks of that society, and their performance provides for more than one purpose of a certain social subsystem. Considering, for example, discussions about social entrepreneurship, companies have opportunities to provide social benefits for society beyond commercial value. Companies which realize social entrepreneurship have a function that integrates commercial approaches in solutions to social challenges. Companies are specialized as providers of material and immaterial goods in the market economy and also as the creators of innovation. They accumulate skills and experience which other actors of the society do not have to provide goods and services widely.

Conventionally, as taught in basic economics, social problems are not considered issues for commercial companies, but the government is considered to be responsible for handling social challenges such as unemployment and poverty. In many countries, church-related organizations such as Caritas are also considered responsible for such issues due to their philanthropic purpose. In the free market economy, not all desired goods are provided by the market. Only goods for which supply and demand meet in the market system are dealt with by the market. Even though some goods would help people who face social challenges, they are not provided by the market if companies cannot supply them at the low price desired by the users or if lower sales figures (demand in the market) than required to keep the business going are expected. Such goods therefore have to be provided to the people in need in a different way than via the market, for example, by government and church-related organizations. In any case, whoever supplies goods for the people experiencing these challenges, the question remains: whether the providers of the goods and services really do supply what is needed. Because they themselves do not face the challenges directly, they normally have the problem that they cannot fully understand what will help the people experiencing them. Support from such institutions, which want to solve social problems, may not meet the needs of the people who need help.

On the other hand, according to the subsidiarity principle (Kempen, 2016), people facing a social challenge have to try to solve the problem by themselves first. In Europe, the principle of subsidiarity is accepted and applied in practice. According to the principle of subsidiarity, the person who faces the challenge should try to solve the problem him- or herself as much as possible. Higher institutions should only be involved to handle issues which individuals cannot deal with. The subsidiarity principle is an important concept for the social market economy (German: soziale Marktwirtschaft) in Germany (Ottnad, 2000), and it was also adopted by the EU in 1992 in Article 5 (3) of the Treaty on European Union (Kempen, 2016, p. 9). The principle, which has a basis in the social teaching of the Catholic church,[1] respects citizens' rights and ensures that decisions for solutions for problems are

[1] "Quadragesimo anno" by Pope Pius XI on March 15, 1931 (Kempen, 2016, p. 10).

taken "at the closest possible level to the citizen" (European Union, n.d.), and the higher institutions support and get involved only when the citizen needs support.

The ideas outlined above represent the clear division of roles in social responsibility: a specific actor is responsible for acting to deal with a particular problem. Indeed, such questions about the advantages and disadvantages of big government and limited government and their respective features have been discussed intensively in research on welfare (Baumol, 2004; Soss, 1999). This discussion asks who should take the role as specialized providers able to produce a solution to a particular social challenge. However, considering the complexities of society and the limited abilities of individuals as assumed in economic theories, it is doubtful whether one actor really has the ability to solve social problems alone. In Scandinavian countries, limited government has been chosen and developed (Fujita, 2022). However, the limitations of the effectiveness of the conventional attitude of the government and its contributions have also been considered, and innovation is expected to contribute more to solving social challenges. More effective innovation policy will help to solve social challenges better. For this, the policy makers should be involved with a more entrepreneurial attitude to social challenges and participate intensively in innovation creation for a better society. This chapter takes a look at the community level on which concrete social challenges exist and have to be solved practically. This chapter sheds light on the possibilities of collective approaches to produce solutions to social problems. In particular, we consider the (potential) contributions of companies in collective approaches with other stakeholders for the creation of value for society. Relevant theories and research discussions are referred to.

6.2 Features of Challenges in Communities

Technical progress and innovation make work in many fields, such as industry and agriculture, easier and more efficient. They are also used to produce goods which make our lives more convenient. Nevertheless, this progress cannot completely compensate for social problems. Society still faces conventional and new challenges, such as regional disparities in the economy, difficulties in maintaining local communities and infrastructure due to the aging of residents, environmental problems, and natural disasters. Technical progress, i.e., innovation, has the potential to contribute more if it is applied more efficiently to produce solutions to social challenges, and innovation for such social purposes is also being developed as a program of innovation policy, for example, in "Horizon Europe" (2021–2027), a funding program based on the concept of mission-oriented innovation policies (European Commission, 2024; Interreg Europe, 2019) in the EU and the Japanese "Moonshot Research and Development Program" (Larrue, 2021). This chapter looks at possibilities for taking advantage of innovation to produce solutions to social challenges, appropriate approaches, and the value of doing so. For the discussion in this chapter, it is worth looking at features of regional social problems.

6.2.1 Embeddedness and Ill-Defined Problems as Features of Social Problems

One feature of social challenges in communities is embeddedness (Granovetter, 1985),[2] in other words, elements of communities, for example, the age structure of residents, affect social challenges, and therefore there are unique priorities in a particular challenge, for example, better support for families, in each community. Additionally, social challenges have characteristics of "ill-defined problems."[3] Ill-defined problems (Anzai & Shiose, 2020, p. 49) mean that there are multiple solution possibilities. Depending on the (subjective) definition of the social challenge for a community, the solutions created based on the definition have different focuses on the challenge (Anzai & Shiose, 2020).

As an example of an "ill-defined problem," it is observed in a community that a new assistive robot supported by AI for older people is not adopted as quickly and widely as expected. Such cases are seen, for example, in research by Kitajima (2021) and Brucksch and Schultz (2018), which examines typical difficulties in adopting robots and other high technologies for older people. Various interpretations of this phenomenon are possible. From direct observation, the problem may seem to be that the construction of the robot is not sufficiently developed. However, if one thinks more deeply and asks oneself why such a robot is needed, one may see this phenomenon from a different viewpoint: prevention of a decrease in musculature functions, i.e., keeping musculature functions working well longer, can overcome the need for assistive robots. Thinking in this way means that prevention has a higher priority than developing assistive robots. Besides physical exercise, prevention of decrease in musculature functions due to aging (frailty syndrome), which leads to the need for assistive robots for daily life, also includes psychosocial and cognitive aspects (Strawbridge et al., 1996; Woo et al., 2005). Increasing opportunities for older people to participate in social activities in the community (Saito et al., 2017; Shinkai et al., 2016) may be recognized as a more essential challenge in this community that should be dealt with first, rather than improving the construction of the assistive robot. Consequently, one may then try to develop communication strategies in daily life for older people rather than developing AI technology for assistive robots, and AI technology may be used in a different way than imagined at the start of work on this challenge. Among various possible solutions, fundamental solutions are more effective and useful than simply superficial and short-term solutions.

---

[2] Embeddedness has been first discussed in relation to the actions of individuals and companies influenced by social networks. However, this concept has since been adopted for discussions about actions by individuals in communities (Hagihara et al., 2011).

[3] There are also other expressions, for example, in design engineering, "wicked problem" (Rittel & Webber, 1973) is used.

6.2.2 Innovation and Solutions for Social Problems in Communities

Producing solutions to social challenges in communities is often considered social innovation. The definition of social innovation is not yet uniquely defined; in the "Stanford Social Innovation Review" (2003) social innovation was defined as "the process of inventing, securing support for, and implementing novel solutions to social needs and problems" (Phills Jr. et al., 2008), and in order to realize social innovation, "dissolving boundaries and brokering a dialogue between the public, private, and nonprofit sectors" (Phills Jr. et al., 2008) is required. Social innovation is therefore "[a] novel solution to a social problem that is more effective, efficient, sustainable, or just than existing solutions" (Phills Jr. et al., 2008) and creates values "primarily to society as a whole rather than private individuals" (Phills Jr. et al., 2008). The main motor for creation of social innovation is social entrepreneurship, which "combines the passion of a social mission with an image of business-like discipline, innovation, and determination commonly associated with, for instance, the high-tech pioneers of Silicon Valley" (Dees, 2001, p. 1).[4]

Social innovation gives less importance to using high technology than conventional innovation does. Bottom-up innovation (Lewis, 2021; Njøs & Fosse, 2018; Saari et al., 2015), which is developed mainly by the people who face the challenge directly or are close to those who do, is often undertaken by using human capital and social capital intensively, and it is also an innovation approach that has the advantage of using human and social capital in an efficient way. Research on social innovation often discusses non-profit organizations, but seldom the public sector and commercial companies. However, companies that provide new products with high technology also make contributions to social innovation. High technology contributes not only to increasing commercial or merely economic wealth, i.e., so that the company as provider of the new product with high technology obtains more profit or that a national economy can expect progress in its productivity or economic growth, but also to increasing social benefit. Contributions from high technology should not be underestimated. In relation to the contributions of companies and effects of high technology, Fig. 6.1, inspired by the view of Anzai and Shiose (2020, p. 18), shows the types of co-creation that distinguish questions about instruments/tools and questions about users' needs; the features of solutions are observed there referring to how broadly or selectively the challenge in a community is understood and interpreted (x-axis in Fig. 6.1) and which resource is mainly utilized to create the solution (y-axis in Fig. 6.1). The setting of the aims and objectives of problem solution affects the quality of its outcome (Anzai & Shiose, 2020, p. 17). If one starts with a discussion about a challenge in a community from the existing instruments or tools as a present solution, without consideration of users' needs, the determination of the question for the project is an easy task; however, the outcome of the

[4]This definition by Dees (2001) adopts the conventional definition of entrepreneurship based on Say, Schumpeter, and Drucker (Kraus et al., 2014, p. 278).

	Articulated needs / problems	Latent needs / problems
Unknown new approach	I New products and application in principle for present users	II New products and application for broader range of users
Existing approach (instruments, tools)	III Incremental improvement of present solution in principle for present users	IV Incremental improvement of present solution for present and new users
	Observed social problems	

Fig. 6.1 Outcomes depending on starting points of producing solutions to a challenge in a community and targets of solution. (Own illustration)

project often provides only a moderate effect in solving the problem (Field III in Fig. 6.1). Thinking about people's (latent) needs in order to determine the challenge in the community requires the imagination of the project members and is more difficult; however, it helps to understand what the fundamental challenge is there. Creative solutions are more likely to come from such kinds of questions, and new technology has different effects to respond to the challenge and can help to develop generalized solutions, not just for one specific community, but also for other communities that face similar challenges (Field II in Fig. 6.1).

For such cooperation, which acts in Field II (Fig. 6.1), networking and coordination of the stakeholders of the problem are critical and essential, because creative and open exchanges between project members are required to solve the question of the project as an ill-defined problem. Integration of approaches by commercial companies and public sectors into those for social innovation commonly made by non-profit organizations has the potential to use high technology better and to a greater extent for social innovation, i.e., solutions to social challenges in communities. It is therefore worth discussing possibilities for integration of commercial companies and/or the public sector in the process of the creation of solutions to social challenges in communities (Fig. 6.2. See also, for example, Inoue, 2019; Kania & Kramer, 2011; Tanimoto, 2009).

Co-creation between companies as producers of goods and services and (latent) users has also been discussed in design studies as well as in business management and business strategies. Concrete approaches for co-creation between producers and users such as "participatory design" has been developed in design studies, and this has strongly influenced the development of Living Labs as a co-creation approach to find solutions to social challenges in communities (see also Sect. 6.4).

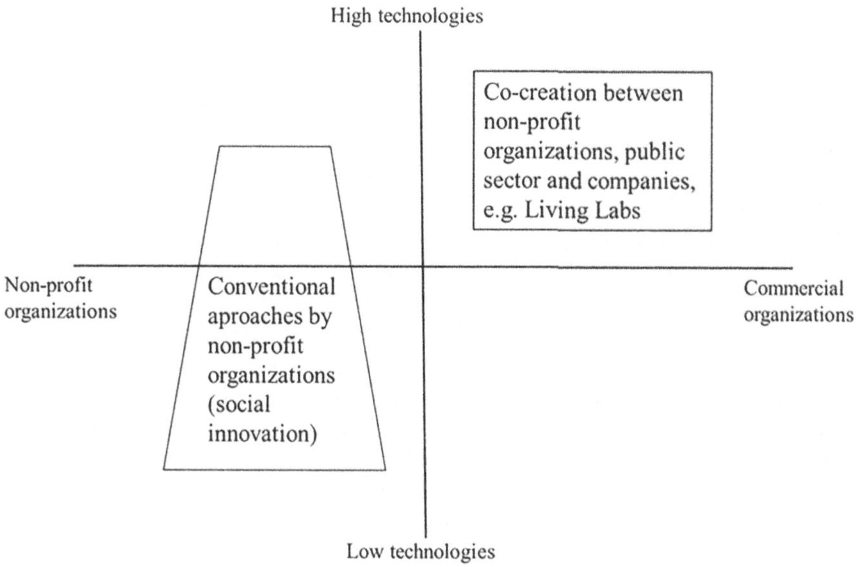

Fig. 6.2 Types of approaches based on variety in the solution teams. (Own illustration)

6.3 Approaches for Innovation Creation

6.3.1 Knowledge Creation for Innovation and Approaches for Innovation Creation

In line with the development of an economy accompanied by technical progress, the economic system is shifted to a knowledge-based economy, and the society is also changed into a knowledge-based society. Knowledge has been recognized as a decisive factor in production, for example, Marshall (1920) and Penrose (1959) focus on knowledge (Pyka, 2007, p. 461). In terms of innovation, new combinations of resources are a decisive mechanism for innovation creation (Röpke, 2002). Evolutionary economics adopted the knowledge-based approach and recognized the importance of knowledge for economic development (Pyka, 2007, p. 361). Neo-Schumpeterian economics considers knowledge in a wider sense than Schumpeter himself, who considered only "a certain type of knowledge that influences technical progress" (Helmstädter, 2007, p. 300). From the neo-Schumpeterian viewpoint, (new) knowledge is the key component of innovation (Helmstädter, 2007, p. 306; Iizuka, 2019, p. 282). New knowledge is generated through new combinations of knowledge (Helmstädter, 2007; Pyka, 2007). The observation of incomplete knowledge of individuals by neo-Schumpeterian researchers (Pyka, 2007, p. 366) and other researchers such as Nonaka and Konno (1998, p. 41) suggests the necessity of interaction with others for knowledge creation to compensate for gaps in the knowledge of individual participants.

Since Schumpeter (1912/2006), individuals who create innovation are considered to have entrepreneurship. Entrepreneurship is understood as the driving motor in the innovation creation process. This concept of entrepreneur (German: Unternehmer) as a specific charismatic function, an individual "entrepreneur," according to Schumpeter's early theory (Schumpeter, 1912/2006, "Mark I") is attractive to the general public and is thus also well-known (Pyka, 2007, p. 360; Röpke & Stiller, 2006, p. XXIX; Schumpeter, 1912/2006). However, beyond this image of an entrepreneur,[5] collective approaches for the creation of innovation began to be considered worthwhile in research as well as in practice. For example, neo-Schumpeterian economics considers networking and coordination as the central factors for innovation (Iizuka, 2019, p. 282; Pyka, 2007, p. 362). Since the 1980s, the perspective that innovation is created in interrelation between heterogeneous actors and knowledge fields has become dominant (Pyka, 2007, p. 360). Not only the shift from an individual to collective creators of innovation, but also interaction during the solution creation process has gained attention. The neo-Schumpeterian approach considers innovation as a systemic process and discusses innovation systems (Iizuka, 2019, p. 282; Lundvall, 2007, pp. 877–878). In research on organizational innovation too, collaborative efforts for the creation of innovation are stressed (DeCusatis, 2008, p. 155; Rill, 2016; Tortoriello et al., 2015, p. 423). From observation of the development of the co-creative approach in various academic fields, for example, from the viewpoint of design in a broader sense as a problem-solving process (Sanders & Stappers, 2008), one can see that the changes in the social structure since the 1960s have increased in complexity so that more intensive cooperation between social subsystems such as economics, academics, and politics has become necessary.

6.3.2 *Potential and Challenges of Collective Approaches*

In creating practical and effective solutions for societies, cooperation between various stakeholders has been considered beneficial in politics and academia and by individuals (Meissner et al., 2017). Along with this change of approach for innovation creation, various kinds of collective innovation creation have been proposed and implemented. As attempts to generate radical innovation by applying high technologies and knowledge from academia, intensive interaction between academia, industry, and politics is conceptualized as the "triple helix model" (Etzkowitz et al., 2000; Leydesdorff & Meyer, 2003). Academia, industry, and politics compensate for gaps in each other's knowledge. The "triple helix" model has been adopted practically and more intensively since the 1990s to cope with social challenges in a better way (Etzkowitz et al., 2000; Leydesdorff & Meyer, 2003; Meissner et al., 2017).

[5] Schumpeter himself also considered other actors, for example, big companies, as drivers of innovation ("Mark II").

This kind of collective approach is realized for example in the EU's Horizon Europe funding program (European Commission et al., 2018).

These collective approaches for innovation creation imply a typical problem of development of teams with members from different backgrounds. In general, teams of members with different backgrounds work less productively than those of homogeneous members. As Tuckman and Jensen (1977) already pointed out in the 1970s, diversity in a team often causes confusion in perspectives, roles, and aim-setting, and such teams are often less productive than homogeneous ones until they overcome their confused phase. Tuckman and Jensen (1977) categorized team development into five phases: forming, storming, norming, performing, and adjourning, and newly organized teams face chaotic conditions in the storming phase. Different members who are not integrated into a team confuse each other rather than contribute to high productivity and creativity. "(T)eams do not automatically benefit from the diverse knowledge provided by their members" (Tryba et al., 2022, p. 3). For example, a team formed for the creation of solutions to a social challenge in the community faces difficulties because the usual roles and expectations of the members vary. After their integration into a team and overcoming the storming phase, however, such a team can work more creatively than a monocultural team. Teams with different kinds of members have the potential to produce innovative outcomes. However, this benefit is not automatically provided: the team has first to be organized and has to manage conflicts between the members. Kania and Kramer (2011) summarize five features of a successful collective approach: (1) A vision for change that is shared by all participants, (2) Shared measurement systems, (3) A specific set of activities in the team that support and compensate the participants with different backgrounds and specializations to each other, (4) Continuous communication between the participants, and (5) Coordination by "staff with a very specific set of skills to serve as the backbone for the entire initiative" (Kania & Kramer, 2011). Diversity in teams per se does not necessarily stimulate a combination of diverse knowledge. This suggests that a function that stimulates interaction of knowledge is required. Related to this problem, the role of "catalyst" in the innovation creation process is gaining attention.

In some literature, the "catalyst" function is illustrated as if the person acting as "catalyst" knows the aim, i.e., what the team has to achieve (see, for example, Ansell & Gash, 2012). However, it is plausible that categorizing the catalyst function according to uncertainties linked to innovation creation is helpful for research on the catalyst function. It is likely that the catalyst function in innovation creation processes with fewer uncertainties is realized in a similar way to how the facilitator works. However, it is rather plausible that not everyone who acts as a "catalyst" is sure about the aim, in particular, in such cases as a consortium, for which members first meet on this occasion to create solutions for a challenge in the community. At first one knows very little about the other members, and it is difficult to determine the project aim with them. The quality of network, cooperation in the consortium, and the project and research outcomes of such a consortium are very uncertain, especially at the beginning, and the consortium members work in uncertainty to create new knowledge for the complex project object (a solution for a certain social problem). Or if the creation of solutions is characterized by high uncertainties (Field II in Fig. 6.1), no one can act as if he or she knows the outcome (innovation) exactly and also the routes to it exactly. It is actually to be asked whether one person can act as "catalyst." In this case, the "catalyst" acts in an innovation creation process under "true uncertainties." In an innovation process that treats ill-defined problems and/or acts under "true uncertainties," interaction in depth with other members is required instead of assigning roles according to the members' expertise. What a catalyst does in such conditions is first confuse the people involved (team members and non-team members) in terms of their common sense and value systems. For example, innovation is considered important in many disciplines, but the term's interpretation differs among the disciplines. The members first have to recognize the differences. Then they can start to think about and discuss how and to what extent the range of knowledge can be integrated or linked in a harmonious way. The "catalyst" function helps the team members to recognize the variety of knowledge and views among them and facilitates communication between team members.

6.4 Living Lab as Co-Creation Approach

In this section, Living Labs as one variation of a co-creation approach are illustrated and their potential and challenges are discussed.

6.4.1 Living Lab: Establishment and Evolution

Living Labs were proposed in the late 1990s by William J. Mitchell of MIT in the United States as a place for experiments in real living environments in the field of urban planning (Eriksson et al., 2006). Living Labs have gradually been understood more broadly, especially in Europe. The European Networks of Living Labs (n.d.) defines Living Labs as an open innovation ecosystem in real living environments through a repeated iterative feedback process for creating sustainable innovation.

One of the reasons why the concept of Living Labs developed more broadly in Europe is the shift in design studies there. In the 1960s and 1970s, the importance of understanding user needs was recognized in this field, and attempts to involve users in the development process began. An important change in the background of this shift is the increase in diversity in users' desires and in how goods and services are consumed. This trend was observed more clearly together with development of the knowledge society, where people have enough goods and having goods per se has become less meaningful than before (Yamamoto, 2016, p. 6). It became more difficult for producers of goods and services to understand the desires of users. They also recognized that consumers were not as satisfied with (new) products as they used to be. Regarding this problem, the idea of inviting users to participate in the development process in depth was suggested and discussed in design studies. This may help producers to understand better the (latent) desires of users and to develop new products that better meet users' needs. Actually, companies have already traditionally invited potential customers who are the target group to participate in product development. The significance of business and product development that involves consumers has been discussed in the field of business management (Prahalad & Ramaswamy, 2004; Thomke & von Hippel, 2002). However, a typical example was and is participation in testing prototypes of a new product. In this case, consumers participate in the product development process after the product specifications have already been decided. At this stage in the development process, it is hardly possible to add consumers' needs to the fundamental construction or functions of a new product. In the concept of co-creation and Living Lab, the producers try to work with potential users as partners in the product development intensively from the very beginning of the process. This type of development approach is called "participatory design"[6] in Europe and developed mainly in Scandinavia (Sanders & Stappers, 2008, p. 7). In Denmark and the Netherlands, participatory design is used not only as a method for product development but also as a method for creating solutions to social problems, which is called Living Labs. Living Labs are a variation of co-creation between researchers, citizens, companies, and governments and are considered to be an effective approach to bottom-up open innovation that creatively generates solutions to social issues.

6.4.2 Case Studies of Living Labs

Living Labs are conducted in various ways and thus have a huge variety in form. For Living Labs there is no unified method: the multi-method approach (Schuurman et al., 2016) is used. In other words, each Living Lab has its own unique features, and it is therefore best to apply the most suitable and effective method for each one.

In this chapter, three cases of Living Labs are used to illustrate this and are compared to each other. The following interviews were conducted for the case studies (see Table 6.1).

All three Living Labs have in common that they aim to solve challenges in the community through a bottom-up approach with diverse stakeholders related to the challenges that are embedded in the community. And each Living Lab has made progress gradually.

[6] In parallel, a similar concept called "user-centered design" has also been developed in the United States (Sanders & Stappers, 2008).

Table 6.1 Overview of the interviews about the Living Labs

Living Labs	Aims	Interviewees	Roles of interviewees in the Living Labs	Affiliations of interviewees	Dates of interviews
Komatsushima Living Lab	Revitalization of Komatsushima City	A	Coordinator of the Living Lab	University	January 12, 2024
Minna no Machizukuri Studio	Prevention of decrease in musculature functions of older people	B	Coordinators of the Living Lab	Urban Design Center Kashiwa-no-ha	February 14, 2024
		C		University	
Living Lab in Gundestrupgaard	Developing strategies for the economy in the region undergoing demographic change	D	Coordinator of the Living Lab	Västimaarlands Municipality	December 15, 2023

6.4.2.1 Komatsushima Living Lab, Komatsushima City, Tokushima Prefecture, Japan

Komatsushima City is located on the island of Shikoku, to the south of Tokushima City, the prefectural capital of Tokushima. It has a population of approximately 35,000 (Komatsushima City, 2024). Komatsushima previously had an important function as the "eastern gate of Shikoku" connecting the Kansai area on the main island of Honshu and Shikoku by sea traffic. In response to changes in the transportation network leading to a reduction in sea traffic, Komatsushima seeks different functions for the current era.

Komatsushima Living Lab has been run since 2018 by Tokushima University, Komatsushima City, and JA Higashi Tokushima (agricultural cooperative). It aims to make Komatsushima City more attractive and to revitalize the city. Komatsushima Living Lab arose from consultation between the three organizations: Komatsushima City and JA Higashi Tokushima wanted to realize the "sixth industry" approach for rural revitalization in Komatsushima and asked Tokushima University to cooperate with them. The "sixth industry" approach aims to create new added value in agricultural, forestry, and fishery products, as well as land, water, and other assets in farming, mountain, and fishing villages, by integrating production, processing, and distribution activities (Haga, 2015). Tokushima University proposed to conduct a Living Lab to revitalize the city, including the "sixth industry" approach. At that time, the concept of Living Lab developed in Northern Europe began to be introduced in Japan. Tokushima University was interested in the concept, but had no previous experience in implementing Living Labs.

Three stakeholder groups take the initiative in the Living Lab: the municipality (Komatsushima City), academia (mainly Tokushima University), and a local organization (JA Higashi Tokushima). Local residents in Komatsushima City and neighboring residents are the main participants.

Its activities are not limited to realization of the "sixth industry," which was the original intention of Komatsushima City and JA Higashi Tokushima. Adopting the suggestion of Tokushima University, it aims to understand the challenges and potential of Komatsushima City from the perspective of the local residents and to create solutions based on their ideas. For this reason, in this Living Lab providing opportunities for interaction between the diverse stakeholders who participate is emphasized. Workshops and lectures have been conducted. Experienced external facilitators were invited to the workshops in order to realize active communication among participants and to create prototypes based on the ideas proposed by them. Visualizing the ideas and resources that the citizens themselves possess through workshops has been effective in encouraging the participants, in particular, residents of Komatsushima, and in realizing their ideas. Through exchanges of ideas with others, individual ideas were developed concretely. From the Komatsushima Living Lab some ideas of residents have been realized, for example, creating a smart society by purifying the water quality of waterways, the development of local tourism content for cruise ship passengers, and the creation of farming experience guesthouses to encourage relocation (Komatsushima Living Lab, n.d.).

Interviewee A confirmed the effectiveness of the Living Lab as an open innovation system, but also mentioned difficulties. It is difficult to manage the Living Lab for the long run instead of as a one-time event. For example, people are interested in talks about success stories of other municipalities; however, it has been difficult to generate ideas or actions for Komatsushima City from the talks. Interviewee A realized also that the ideas of the Living Lab participants did not necessarily lead to revitalization of the city or to solving local challenges, even though these ideas per se were interesting. There was also a discrepancy in the expectations of the Living Lab between Komatsushima City, JA Higashi Tokushima, and Tokushima University. While Tokushima University wanted the Living Lab to work on issues that were not urgent but important in the long term, JA Higashi Tokushima and Komatsushima City placed value on realizing ideas for immediate regional revitalization in a short period of time. This difference made communication between the three organizations difficult. Interviewee A thinks that one reason for these difficulties was that Tokushima University was not able to spend enough time preparing for the implementation of the Living Lab before the project started. Currently, the Komatsushima Living Lab is not conducting any programs.

6.4.2.2 Urban Design Center Kashiwa-no-ha (UDCK) Minna no Machizukuri Studio (Minsuta) "AI for Prevention from Frailty: Services with AI to Extend Healthy Life Span," Kashiwa City, Chiba Prefecture, Japan

The Minna no Machizukuri Studio (Minsuta) is a town development project in the Kashiwa-no-ha area of Kashiwa City in Chiba Prefecture, which neighbors Tokyo. This area has been developed alongside the opening of the Tsukuba Express in 2005, a railway line that connects Tokyo and the northern suburbs, and has a population of approximately 13,300[7] (Kashiwa City, n.d.). Living Labs on various themes have been conducted there since 2020. "AI for prevention from frailty" is one of these and ran from November 2021 to July 2022. This Living Lab was run by UDCK, UDCK Town Management, and H-UTokyo Lab, a joint research project of Hitachi and the University of Tokyo. Private companies also participated in it. Public Intelligence Japan, the Japanese branch of a Danish consulting firm[8] specializing in solving problems in an aging society, participated in the planning and facilitation of the Living Lab as an advisor. Older people from the district, their families, and people working in nursing and caregiving participated as stakeholders in the issue "AI for prevention from frailty."

UDCK was established in November 2006 as a place for public-private-academic collaboration where many stakeholders with the expertise to drive Kashiwa-no-ha urban development gather. It is jointly operated by eight constituent organizations directly involved in Kashiwa-no-ha urban development, including Kashiwa City, Mitsui Fudosan (real estate developer), the University of Tokyo, and Chiba University. UDCK Town Management is an independent legal entity from UDCK for the management of urban development projects.

"AI for prevention from frailty" is considered an example of an approach that considers problem-solving using new tools. Ideas for the development of individual services for prevention from frailty were generated using big data technology developed by Hitachi-UTokyo Laboratory, and hypotheses were examined by creating prototypes. The product development and its introduction to the market is not included in the Living Lab, but is conducted as a post-Living Lab process (Igeta et al., 2023). In line with Public Intelligence Japan's "Living Lab Method," three workshops were held to form the vision and identify the issues for this Living Lab, and four workshops were held for ideation and prototyping (Igeta et al., 2023).

Interviewees B and C mentioned that they were impressed that the profile of stakeholders participating in the Living Lab was proposed clearly by Public Intelligence Japan, and that the Living Lab was strongly managed through the "Living Lab Method" by Public Intelligence Japan. The diversity of Living Lab participants was well planned and is considered a clear difference from the usual

[7] As of October 1, 2023. In comparison, the area had a population of just 625 in 2007 (Kashiwa City, n.d.)

[8] The parent firm, "Public Intelligence," is involved in the third case of Living Labs (see Sect. 6.4.2.3).

approach in Japan. In other Living Labs on "Minusta" (Living Labs not involved with Public Intelligence Japan), participation is largely left to the spontaneity of the participants and is not planned by the organizers.

Interviewees B and C also mentioned the motivations of companies to participate in the Living Lab. It is difficult for companies to have contact with potential consumers in a neutral environment without being influenced by the company. Living Lab provides them with opportunities to discuss and create ideas together with potential consumers. Living Labs are attractive for companies as a place where they can interact with potential consumers in an unbiased environment and on an equal level.

6.4.2.3 Gundestrupgaard, Västimaarlands Municipality, Denmark

Västimaarlands Municipality is located in the north of Denmark and has a population of about 36,000. The Gundestrupgaard Living Lab was launched in 2023 by Västimaarlands Municipality. It aims to create strategies for the economy in the region, which is undergoing social change, in particular, demographic change.

Västimaarlands Municipality is experiencing an aging population, and it is foreseen that there will be a shortage of staff in elderly care. The municipality felt that it was necessary to develop welfare technologies appropriate for the aging population, and that the administration should also take a more proactive role in technology development and introduction, rather than its traditional management-centered role. The Living Lab was chosen as an approach to actively engage with stakeholders, as it is difficult to commercialize welfare technologies that are acceptable to the elderly without the involvement of government officials with entrepreneurial spirit and active engagement with relevant stakeholders.

The Living Lab in Gundestrupgaard is currently in the launch phase (as of December 2023). It started in 2023, and the first business will be launched in 2024. The final plan is to complete the commercialization of the businesses launched from the Living Lab in 2027 and to establish an innovation park.

The agricultural facility Gundestrupgaard was purchased by Västimaarlands Municipality and used as the place for a Living Lab, where prototypes can also be tested in everyday life environments. The Living Lab is envisioned as a place where staff of the municipality, companies, and universities and research institutions can test new solutions focusing on welfare technologies and green transitions. Local residents will mainly participate in testing the developed technologies. Taking advantage of the location, which is close to a technical university and an international airport, it is expected that universities and research institutions will participate, as well as companies and other stakeholders from outside the region. According to interviewee D, the fact that the municipality is the organizer of the Living Lab makes it easier to encourage staff of the municipality to participate. It is also easy to build relationships with local companies. On the other hand, there is a difference in the innovation orientation between companies and the municipality. While the municipality wants to have successful effects of the Living Lab in a short time, companies have a desire to develop innovations over a certain (longer) amount of time.

Public Intelligence (the parent company of Public Intelligence Japan, mentioned in Sect. 6.4.2.2) is a consulting company involved in the Living Lab. The municipality has had a relationship with Public Intelligence for 15 years, and they are able to work well together. The approach to operating the Living Lab is based on Public Intelligence's "Living Lab Method" (Julius et al., 2023) with six steps: "creating a strategic framework," "user research survey," "understanding the issues," "ideation and prototyping," "prototype testing," and "testing in living environments."

6.4.3 *Discussion*

The three cases confirm the importance of participation of residents in the community. The feature of embeddedness of challenges in communities is dealt with in a process for creation of solutions to the challenges in this way. However, the roles of the residents vary in different Living Labs. Residents contribute as information providers about the social issues and local areas that are addressed in a specific Living Lab. The degree of involvement varies greatly, from a role similar to that of a prototype test subject (case 3, see Sect. 6.4.2.3) to an equal partner role in co-generating ideas. It seems that this depends partly on the degree of open innovation of the Living Lab (see Fig. 6.1).

The roles of universities, municipalities, and companies also vary. If the Living Lab intends to apply new technology intensively to produce solutions to the challenges in the community, they clearly invite producers of new technology, such as companies and researchers, as regular main participants. Compared to the deep involvement of companies in cases 2 (Sect. 6.4.2.2) and 3 (Sect. 6.4.2.3), the involvement of companies in Komatsushima Living Lab (Sect. 6.4.2.1) is weak. If Komatsushima Living Lab could use more of the know-how of companies, it is possible that more of its ideas could be commercialized in an efficient and effective way.

An important question from the cases is the variety among the members of Living Labs, in particular, to what extent the participants may and should be planned by the organizer of the Living Lab. Spontaneity in participation in a Living Lab seems to be in a trade-off relationship to its effectiveness. Interviewees B and C acknowledge that planning the profile of stakeholders who should participate by the management of the Living Lab is effective in setting its purpose efficiently and shortening the time required to run it. On the other hand, they also point out that doing so may limit ideas. If we can assume that diversity among participants who join the Living Lab spontaneously than that among participants who are invited according to a certain intention by the organizer is broader, the observation by interviewees B and C seems to confirm Tuckman's observation that heterogeneous teams are at the beginning less productive than homogeneous ones. However, this hypothesis cannot be confirmed before examining the relationship between the variety in the Living Lab and the recruitment methods of its participants. The question of variety among participants in a Living Lab is linked to the function of the "catalyst." As interviewees B and C confirmed, the "catalyst" function is more challenging if participants have more different backgrounds and expectations of the Living Lab.

6.5 Conclusion and Further Research

These three cases of Living Labs suggest they are an appropriate approach for developing open innovation. They suggest obviously the importance and usefulness of the participation of residents who face a social challenge in a community. These residents share their views, feelings, desires, and experiences with the challenge, and this helps the Living Lab members to develop a solution considering the features of the community and to meet the desires of the people who face the challenge.

There are some questions for further research. First, it is to be carefully examined what kinds of stakeholders for a social challenge to be solved through Living Lab are needed to be in the team. Besides Living Labs there are also other approaches for bottom-up cooperation. For example, cooperatives have existed for longer than Living Labs and some have adjusted successfully to the current situation. Agrokraft GmbH in Germany coordinates collective initiatives by local residents in the form of cooperatives to maintain the Rhön-Grabfeld district in Northern Bavaria (Haga, 2020). Some of these collectives have conducted projects with high technology, for example, to establish a bio gas plant. In contrast to Living Labs, local residents are members of cooperatives coordinated by Agrokraft, and other actors such as universities and companies work with them as external cooperation partners (Haga, 2020). In bottom-up approaches, contribution by companies is crucial; however, cooperation between residents and companies works well also in this structure. It is worth examining what advantages and disadvantages each structure has. Sarasvathy (2008) and Yoshida and Nakamura (2023), who research decision-making of entrepreneurs under "true uncertainties," point out the sunk cost calculated by the entrepreneurs as an important factor for them to decide whether to act or not. They take risks as much as they can, allowing an amount of investment that they cannot get back. This kind of calculation of the sunk cost may influence decision-making by companies in terms of whether and to what extent they are willing to be involved in Living Labs.

Furthermore, it is useful to examine more carefully the effectiveness of Living Labs for innovation creation. The Living Labs described in this chapter do not provide any clear answer. The Living Labs in Kashiwa City (case 2, Sect. 6.4.2.2) and in Gundestrupgarrd (case 3, Sect. 6.4.2.3) intend to make good use of high technologies to develop solutions; however, the degree of their success is uncertain. In case 2, the product development for prevention from decrease in musculature functions is conducted separately from the Living Lab. To what extent the outcome will be radically innovative (field II in Fig. 6.1) is still not able to be evaluated, and the contribution of the Living Lab cannot be evaluated either. Case 3 is still in its early phase and its outcome is still not able to be evaluated. The outcome from the Living

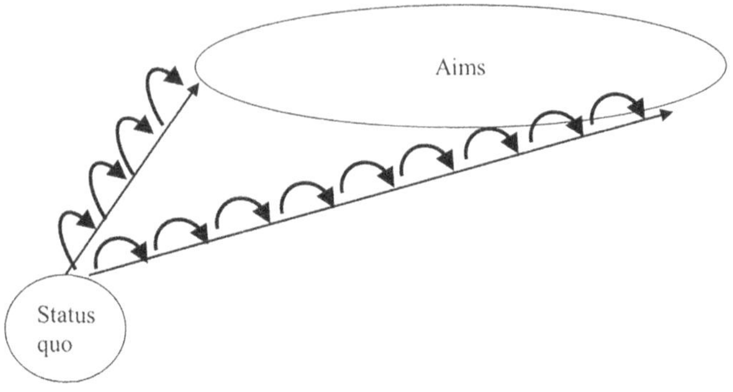

Individuals make progress in small steps. The aims are only roughly defined at the beginning, and there are various possibilities that may be realized, as the distance between the arrows shows. Which aim(s) will be realized will be determined through the steps.

Fig. 6.3 Innovation creation process inspired by Sarasvathy (2008). (Own illustration)

Lab in Komatsushima is many different projects. They may have potential for further development to more significant projects toward field II in Fig. 6.1. To achieve more innovative outcomes, a strongly functioning catalyst seems to be an important condition. In relation to the potential for their further development, the effectuation approach developed by Sarasvathy (2008) seems to provide an insight: projects under high uncertainties make incremental progress (Fig. 6.3).

Individuals typically achieve a small positive outcome at any one time because they cannot plan strategies due to uncertainties in order to achieve their aim at once. Such small progress is accumulated until they achieve their aim. Creating radical innovation is therefore time-consuming. Considering this aspect, some meaningful questions are: how long a Living Lab should run; whether it should run continuously without time limit; and whether it is possible to develop a project based on former outcomes of the Living Lab achieved by (partly) other participants. In summary, for this chapter Living Labs are an interesting experiment as an open innovation approach in which the participants become aware of their own blind spots and compensate for each other's.

References

Ansell, C., & Gash, A. (2012). Stewards, mediators, and catalysts: Toward a model of collaborative leadership. *The Innovation Journal, 17*(1), 1–21.

Anzai, Y., & Shiose, T. (2020). *Toi no Dezain Sōzō-teki Taiwa no Fashiritēshon [The design of questions. Facilitation of creative dialogue]*. Gakugeishuppansha.

Baumol, W. J. (2004). Welfare economics and the theory of the state. In C. K. Rowley & F. Schneider (Eds.), *The encyclopedia of public choice*. Springer. https://doi.org/10.1007/978-0-306-47828-4_214

Brucksch, S., & Schultz, F. (2018). Ageing in Japan. Domestic healthcare technologies. A qualitative interview study on care robots, monitoring sensor systems, and ICT-based telehealth systems. *Deutsches Institut für Japanstudien*. Retrieved July 18, 2024, from https://leidenasia-centre.nl/wp-content/uploads/2018/09/Final_Report-30.08.2018.pdf

DeCusatis, C. (2008). Creating, growing and sustaining efficient innovation teams. *Creativity and Innovation Management, 17*(2), 155–164.

Dees, J. G. (2001). *The meaning of 'social entrepreneurship'*. Retrieved July 22, 2024, from https://centers.fuqua.duke.edu/case/wp-content/uploads/sites/7/2015/03/Article_Dees_MeaningofSocialEntrepreneurship_2001.pdf

Eriksson, M., Niitamo, V.-P., Kulkki, S., & Hribernik, K. A. (2006). Living labs as a multi-contextual R&D methodology. In *2006 IEEE International Technology Management Conference (ICE)* (pp. 1–8). IEEE.

Etzkowitz, H., Webster, A., Gebhardt, C., & Terra, B. R. C. (2000). The future of the university and the university of the future: Evolution of ivory tower to entrepreneurial paradigm. *Research Policy, 29*(2), 313–330.

European Commission. (2024). *Horizon Europe strategic plan 2025–2027*. Retrieved July 19, 2024, from https://op.europa.eu/en/publication-detail/-/publication/6abcc8e7-e685-11ee-8b2b-01aa75ed71a1/language-en/format-PDF/source-334580874

European Commission, Directorate-General for Research and Innovation, Türk, A., Arrilucea, E., & Skov Kristensen, F. (2018). *Mission-oriented research and innovation: Inventory and characterisation of initiatives: Final report*. Retrieved from https://data.europa.eu/doi/10.2777/697082

European Union. (n.d.). *Principle of subsidiarity*. EUR-Lex. Retrieved June 24, 2024, from https://eurlex.europa.eu/EN/legal-content/glossary/principle-of-subsidiarity.html

Fujita, N. (2022). *Shakai o tsukutta keizaigakusha-tachi [Economists who made societies]*. Nagoya Daigaku Shuppankai.

Granovetter, M. (1985). Economic action and social structure: The problem of embeddedness. *American Journal of Sociology, 91*(3), 481–510.

Haga, K. (2015). Innovation and entrepreneurship in aging societies: Theoretical reflection and a case study from Kamikatsu. Japan. *Journal of Innovation Economics & Management, 18*, 119–141.

Haga, K. (2020). "New Combinations" as an approach for efficient participation of local residents in regional enterprises in rural areas: A case from Germany. *Sophia Journal of European Studies, 12*, 135–148.

Hagihara, K., Hoshino, S., Hashimoto, S., & Kuki, Y. (2011). "Umekomoi" gainen ni motozuku jūmin jichisoshiki no ruikeika: shakai nettowāku bunseki ni okeru burokku moderingu no tekiyō o tsūjite [Classification on the social network structure in the local community organization by application of social embedded concept – Through the application of the block modeling in social network analysis]. *Journal of Rural Planning Association, 30*, 357–362.

Helmstädter, E. (2007). The role of knowledge in the Schumpeterian economy. In H. Hanusch & A. Pyka (Eds.), *Elgar companion to Neo-Schumpeterian economics* (pp. 296–315). Edward Elgar Publishing.

Igeta, Y., Sasao, T., Kitamura, H., Tai, M., Kurita, T., & Deguchi, A. (2023). Methodology for functionalization of "living lab" under concept of smart cities. In N. A. Streitz & S. Konomi (Eds.), *Distributed, ambient and pervasive interactions. HCII 2023* (Lecture notes in computer science) (Vol. 14037). Springer. https://doi.org/10.1007/978-3-031-34609-5_1

Iizuka, M. (2019). Neo Shunpetarian to Inobēshon [Neo-Schumpeterian and innovation]. In T. Okamoto & Y. Koike (Eds.), *Keizaigaku no parareru wārudo [Parallel worlds of economics]* (pp. 275–302). Shinhyoron.

Inoue, H. (2019, January 21). Korekutibu inpakuto jissenron. Kigyō to shakai no reiki wa itchisuru [Practical theory of collective impact. The interests of companies and society can be harmonized]. *Harvard Business Review*. Retrieved from https://dhbr.diamond.jp/articles/-/5677

Interreg Europe. (2019). *Grand challenges: The new mission-oriented innovation frontier.* Retrieved July 19, 2024, from https://www.interregeurope.eu/policy-learning-platform/news/grand-challenges-the-new-mission-oriented-innovation-frontier

Julius, P., Hannibal, M., & Klostergaard, A. W. (2023). Living labs are the silver lining for creating sustainable health and care for the future. In N. A. Streitz & S. Konomi (Eds.), *Distributed, ambient and pervasive interactions. HCII 2023* (Lecture notes in computer science) (Vol. 14036). Springer. https://doi.org/10.1007/978-3-031-34668-2_4

Kania, J., & Kramer, M. (2011). Collective impact. *Stanford Social Innovation Review, 9*(1), 36–41. https://doi.org/10.48558/5900-KN19

Kashiwa City. (n.d.). *Hokubu machizukuri jigyō no shinchoku jōkyō [Progress report of the development of the northern part of the city].* Retrieved July 18, 2024, from https://www.city.kashiwa.lg.jp/hokubuseibi/shiseijoho/keikaku/machizukuri/hokubu/shinchoku.html

Kempen, O. E. (2016). Das Subsidiaritätsprinzip – europäische Zauberformel oder demokratische Herausforderung für die EU-Bürger? [The subsidiarity principle – European magic formula or democratic challenge for EU citizens?]. In O. E. Kempen & G. Ulshöfer (Eds.), *Subsidiarität in Europa. Bürgernähe, Partizipation und effiziente Steuerung* (pp. 9–21). Springer VS.

Kitajima, M. (2021). Nihon ni okeru kaigo robotto no fukyū kadai. Bijinesu ekoshisutemu no shiten ni motozuite [Challenges for adoption of nursing care robots in Japan from the viewpoint of the business ecosystem]. *Annals of the Society for Industrial Studies, 36*, 21–37. https://doi.org/10.11444/sisj.2021.21

Komatsushima City. (2024). *Shi no jinkō [Population of the city].* Retrieved July 18, 2024, from https://www.city.komatsushima.lg.jp/docs/14256.html

Komatsushima Living Lab. (n.d.). *Kore made no katsudō purojekuto [Previous projects].* Retrieved July 18, 2024, from https://kll.itlab.org/project2018/

Kraus, S., Filser, M., O'Dwyer, M., & Shaw, E. (2014). Social entrepreneurship: An exploratory citation analysis. *Review of Managerial Science, 8*(2), 275–292.

Larrue, P. (2021). Mission-oriented innovation policy in Japan: Challenges, opportunities and future options, OECD Science, Technology and Industry Policy Papers, No. 106. OECD Publishing. https://doi.org/10.1787/a93ac4d4-en

Lewis, P. (2021). The innovation systems approach: an Austrian and Ostromian perspective. *The Review of Austrian Economics, 34*, 97–114. https://doi.org/10.1007/s11138-020-00507-8

Leydesdorff, L., & Meyer, M. (2003). The triple helix of university–industry–government relations. *Scientometrics, 58*(2), 191–203.

Lundvall, B.-Å. (2007). National innovation systems: From list to freeman. In H. Hanusch & A. Pyka (Eds.), *Elgar companion to Neo-Schumpeterian economics* (pp. 872–881). Edward Elgar Publishing.

Marshall, A. (1920). *The principles of economics.* Macmillan Press.

Meissner, D., Polt, W., & Vonortas, N. S. (2017). Towards a broad understanding of innovation and its importance for innovation policy. *Journal of Technology Transfer, 42*, 1184–1211. https://doi.org/10.1007/s10961-016-9485-4

Njøs, R., & Fosse, J. K. (2018). Linking the bottom-up and top-down evolution of regional innovation systems to policy: Organizations, support structures and learning processes. *Industry and Innovation, 26*(4), 419–438. https://doi.org/10.1080/13662716.2018.1438248

Nonaka, I., & Konno, N. (1998). The concept of "Ba": Building a foundation for knowledge creation. *California Management Review, 40*(3), 40–54.

Ottnad, A. (2000). Die Rolle der Freien Wohlfahrtspflege in der Sozialen Marktwirtschaft [The role of social care in the social market economy]. *Sozialer Fortschritt, 49*(11/12), 270–278.

Penrose, E. (1959). *The theory of the growth of the firm.* Basil Blackwell.

Phills, J. A., Jr., Deiglmeier, K., & Miller, D. T. (2008). Rediscovering social innovation. *Stanford Social Innovation Review, Fall 2008.* https://ssir.org/articles/entry/rediscovering_social_innovation

Prahalad, C. K., & Ramaswamy, V. (2004). Co-creation experiences: The next practice in value creation. *Journal of Interactive Marketing, 18*(3), 5–14.

Pyka, A. (2007). Innovation networks. In H. Hanusch & A. Pyka (Eds.), *Elgar companion to Neo-Schumpeterian economics* (pp. 360–376). Edward Elgar Publishing.

Rill, B. (2016). Resonant co-creation as an approach to strategic innovation. *Journal of Organizational Change Management, 29*(7), 1135–1152.

Rittel, H. W. J., & Webber, M. M. (1973). Dilemmas in a general theory of planning. *Policy Sciences, 4*, 155–169. https://doi.org/10.1007/BF01405730

Röpke, J. (2002). *Der Lernende Unternehmer [Learning entrepreneurs]*. BOD.

Röpke, J., & Stiller, O. (2006). Einführung zum Nachdruck der 1. Auflage Joseph A. Schumpeters "Theorie der Wirtschaftlichen Entwicklung" [Introduction to the reprint of the first edition of "the theory of economic development" by Joseph A. Schumpeter]. In J. Schumpeter (Ed.), *Theorie der wirtschaftlichen Entwicklung. Nachdruck der 1. Auflage von 1912* (pp. V–XLIII). Duncker & Humblot.

Saari, E., Lehtonen, M., & Toivonen, M. (2015). Making bottom-up and top-down processes meet in public innovation. *The Service Industries Journal, 35*(6), 325–344. https://doi.org/10.1080/02642069.2015.1003369

Saito, M., Kondo, N., Aida, J., Kawachi, I., Koyama, S., Ojima, T., & Kondo, K. (2017). Development of an instrument for community-level health related social capital among Japanese older people: The JAGES Project. *Journal of Epidemiology, 27*(5), 221–227. https://doi.org/10.1016/j.je.2016.06.005

Sanders, E. B.-N., & Stappers, P. J. (2008). Co-creation and the new landscapes of design. *Co-design, 4*(1), 5–18.

Sarasvathy, S. D. (2008). *Effectuation*. Edward Elgar Publishing.

Schumpeter, J. A. (1912/2006). *Theorie der Wirtschaftlichen Entwicklung [The theory of economic development]* (1st ed.). Duncker & Humblot.

Schuurman, D., De Marez, L., & Ballon, P. (2016). The impact of living lab methodology on open innovation contributions and outcomes. *Technology Innovation Management Review, 6*(1), 7–16. https://doi.org/10.22215/timreview/956

Shinkai, S., Yoshida, H., Taniguchi, Y., Murayama, H., Nishi, M., Amano, H., et al. (2016). Public health approach to preventing frailty in the community and its effect on healthy aging in Japan. *Geriatrics & Gerontology International, 16*, 87–97.

Soss, J. (1999). Lessons of welfare: Policy design, political learning, and political action. *The American Political Science Review, 93*(2), 363–380. https://doi.org/10.2307/2585401

Strawbridge, W. J., Cohen, R. D., Shema, S. J., & Kaplan, G. A. (1996). Successful aging: Predictors and associated activities. *American Journal of Epidemiology, 144*(2), 135–141. https://doi.org/10.1093/oxfordjournals.aje.a008900

Tanimoto, K. (2009). Sōsharu bijinesu to sōsharu inobēshon [Social business and social innovation]. *Hitotsubashi Business Review, 57*(1), 26–41.

The European Networks of Living Labs. (n.d.). *What are Living Labs*? Retrieved March 16, 2024, from https://enoll.org/about-us/whatare-living-labs/

Thomke, S., & von Hippel, E. (2002). Customers as innovators: A new way to create value. *Harvard Business Review*. https://hbr.org/2002/04/customers-as-innovators-a-new-way-to-create-value

Tortoriello, M., McEvily, B., & Krackhardt, D. (2015). Being a catalyst of innovation: The role of knowledge diversity and network closure. *Organization Science, 26*(2), 423–438.

Tryba, A., Patzelt, H., & Breugst, N. (2022). Knowledge diversity and venture growth: The contingent effects of early planning and experimentation. *British Journal of Management, 34*, 343–362. https://doi.org/10.1111/1467-8551.12600

Tuckman, B. W., & Jensen, M. A. C. (1977). Stages of small-group development revisited. *Group & Organization Studies, 2*(4), 419–427. https://doi.org/10.1177/105960117700200404

Woo, J., Goggins, W., Sham, A., & Ho, S. C. (2005). Social determinants of frailty. *Gerontology, 51*(6), 402–408.

Yamamoto, T. (2016). *Ninchi shihonshugi [Cognitive capitalism]*. Nakanishiya Shuppan.

Yoshida, M., & Nakamura, R. (2023). *Efekkuchuēshon. Sugureta kigyōka ga jissensuru itsutsu no gensoku [Effectuation. Five principles which excellent entrepreneurs put into practice]*. Diamond.

Chapter 7
Understanding the Change of the Finnish Digital Health and Welfare Ecosystems

Marika Iivari, Minna Pikkarainen, Julius F. Gomes, Jouni Kaartinen, and Parisa Gazerani

Abstract Digital transformation, enabled via the evolution of technology and the use of data, has been considered to create new opportunities and benefits for the healthcare industry. Digital transformation is supposed to enable resilient and adaptive approaches to the long-term development of healthcare services and the response to abrupt crises. Based on an empirical study of digital health experts in Finland, this chapter explores the concept of digital health through the lens of complex adaptive systems. It identifies several key capabilities that are essential to advancing digital health. The need to access useful information promptly was recognised as a critical factor. At a national level, policymakers need to pay more attention to data-driven decision-making and invest in interoperability between different

---

M. Iivari (✉) · J. F. Gomes
Martti Ahtisaari Institute, Oulu Business School, University of Oulu, Oulu, Finland
e-mail: marika.iivari@oulu.fi; Julius.francisgomes@oulu.fi

M. Pikkarainen
Martti Ahtisaari Institute, Oulu Business School, University of Oulu, Oulu, Finland

Department of Rehabilitation and Health Technology, Oslo Metropolitan University, Oslo, Norway

Department of Product Design, Oslo Metropolitan University, Oslo, Norway
e-mail: minna.pikkarainen@oslomet.no

J. Kaartinen
Human Sensing, VTT, Technical Research Centre of Finland, Espoo, Finland
e-mail: jouni.kaartinen@vtt.fi

P. Gazerani
Department of Life Sciences and Health, Faculty of Health Sciences, Oslo Metropolitan University, Oslo, Norway

Centre for Intelligent Musculoskeletal Health (CIM), Faculty of Health Sciences, Oslo Metropolitan University, Oslo, Norway

Department of Health Science and Technology, Faculty of Medicine, Aalborg University, Aalborg Øst, Denmark
e-mail: parisaga@oslomet.no

N. Tokumaru et al. (eds.), *Creative Co-evolution of the Economies and Welfare States in the Nordic Countries*, Evolutionary Economics and Social Complexity Science 32, https://doi.org/10.1007/978-981-97-8569-8_7

systems to utilise better future AI-based digital services and the increasing numbers of health data. There is also a need to utilise non-medical and heterogeneous data to support better treatments and clinical decision-making. At an organisational level, leadership capabilities are needed in healthcare providers and technology companies to support healthcare professionals and policymakers. For these changes to happen, a deeper collaboration is needed in all sectors of the economy that are directly linked with healthcare. Hence, an innovative ecosystem-driven approach is central to advancing digital health in Finland.

Keywords Digital Health · Digital transformation · CAS theory · Complex adaptive systems

7.1 Introduction

Due to increasing care requirements, our health and welfare systems face high demands and challenges. These requirements are caused by the general trend of ageing populations and the increase in non-communicable diseases (Gomes et al., 2022). World Health Organization (WHO, 2023) states that among six WHO regions, the European region has the highest number of patients affected by the main types of non-communicable diseases, i.e. cardiovascular diseases, cancer and chronic respiratory diseases, diabetes, and Alzheimer's disease. Controlling healthcare expenses is one of the most critical challenges, but they must be handled along with other long-term societal needs (Dias & Escoval, 2012). The challenge is not, however, only about balancing resources and managing costs. Investments in healthcare should improve performance so that health systems also demonstrate *good value* in terms of improved health, equity, access, and responsiveness (Dias & Escoval, 2012; Hyrkäs et al., 2020). A future-oriented, proactive approach to healthcare further highlights the need to consider general well-being rather than reactive treatment (Hood et al., 2012; Pikkarainen et al., 2017). The digitalisation of the healthcare sector has been seen as a response to match the demographic changes and cost increases (Marques & Ferreira, 2020). As defined by Vial (2019), the transformation brought by digital technologies implies a process intending to improve an entity by triggering significant changes to its properties through combinations of information, computing, communication, and connectivity technologies (Kraus et al., 2021). Finland has ambitious goals to pioneer the digitalisation of healthcare by reforming processes and digitalising services (Koivuluoma et al., 2022). The integration and utilisation of different health information systems and databases, as well as the engagement of citizens with the use of electronic services, have been identified as two main goals in Finland.

The overall steady pace of digitalisation in the healthcare sector was abruptly disturbed by the COVID-19 pandemic. The pandemic caused an unforeseeable pressure on the healthcare systems globally (Inkster et al., 2020). Previous research (see, e.g. Kaiser et al., 2021; Haldane et al., 2021) has reported that during pandemics, regular service provisioning processes in medical care are disrupted as a consequence of a need to handle the care for regular healthcare issues and simultaneously manage the immense pressure caused by the health crisis on the healthcare system. In this context, digital technologies can enable creative and innovative responses (e.g. maintaining quality while reducing the increase in resources). Digital health is expected to provide better and faster solutions and opportunities to handle the increasing need for health services during crises. At the same time, the ongoing digitalisation of healthcare as a systemic phenomenon will continue to progress beyond the crises (Kaiser et al., 2021).

Therefore, change in the healthcare sector should be seen as an adaptive process. Then, changes can be better understood as evolutionary processes (whether slow and systemic or abrupt), which highlights the digital transformation process of the health and welfare sector as an ecosystemic phenomenon. The ecosystem perspective enables us to understand better external, rapidly changing economic, social, political, and technological determinants that impact digital health (Pikkarainen et al., 2017). The literature on digital health information systems is limited in explaining what is needed in the changing ecosystems of digital health and the impact of health crises on those capabilities. However, academic research has the power to offer such holistic frameworks for identifying critical and more uniform capabilities for digital health interventions at a systemic level (Iivari et al., 2019).

We argue that to address this escalating need in digital healthcare, a particular focus must be on enabling efficient digital care solutions that not only help minimise healthcare demands for chronic diseases but also offer an immense capability for handling health crises. This argument stems from the current evidence showing that digital platforms can transform care processes to overcome the challenges of the increasing number of patients, where patient-centred healthcare is also proliferating (Islind et al., 2019). On closer inspection, we also argue that crises such as pandemics and natural crises can speed up the progress of digitalisation towards the ecosystem perspective for data-driven/digital personalised services and professional decision support systems with the newest, most powerful technologies.

Besides the technological requirements, changes in health systems and the generation of a digital health ecosystem are highly complex, and it seems necessary to address healthcare transformation from a complexity perspective. To do so, we use complex adaptive systems theory to explore and provide an integrated and more comprehensive understanding of relevant change processes in digital health. The theoretical examination using the complexity theory and conceptual constructs of digital health, based on different theoretical contributions, is necessary to understand digital health and its rapid change in the health systems. To increase understanding and contribute to research on digital transformation in healthcare in the context of Nordic welfare states, this chapter explores and presents the findings of an empirical study conducted on Finland's digital health ecosystem. We start by reviewing the concept of digital health ecosystems and then discuss the theoretical considerations from a complexity perspective. We then present our empirical study and discuss the implications of our findings on the future of digital health in Finland.

7.2 Digital Health and Healthcare Digitalisation

Finland and other Nordic countries have traditionally been ranked high in international quality-of-life and well-being-related studies (Kokko et al., 2018). In 2024, Finland was named the Happiest Country in the World for the seventh consecutive year, with all other Nordic countries in the top ten since before COVID-19 (Helliwell et al., 2024). The Nordic welfare system has been argued to be one of the key factors behind this success. However, there is no clear consensus on the reasons behind this success. According to Kokko et al. (2018, p. 3), it is both demanding and complex "to study relationships between the welfare state and health outcomes, and results are therefore inconsistent… Regardless of this, it is argued that the Nordic welfare model and health promotion have parallel or even mutual key principles that have led to comprehensive implementation of health promotion through public policy action in the Nordic countries".

The concept of value-based care and the so-called Triple Aim framework for a simultaneous improvement of population health, patient experience, and the costs of care have been embraced at both national health policy and organisational levels, especially in publicly financed health systems, such as the Nordic countries (Kokko & Kork, 2021). Value-based care is "part of a transformation from traditional public administration to new public governance, which emphasises value-creation for citizens, customer responsiveness and cost-effective service models" (Kokko & Kork, 2021, p. 3). Kokko and Kork (2021) explored how value-based care was manifested in the Nordic welfare state context and found that patient experience and population health have been identified as the main policy objectives in Finland. The authors highlight that improving individual patient experience and the healthcare system's ability to provide high-quality care are essential goals. Patients increasingly demand more individual choices and care. Not only the growth of individualism in the 2000s in the Nordic countries may explain the transformation towards personalised care (Fatehi et al., 2020), but this trend may also have been caused by digitalisation and knowledge management. They have equipped patients with knowledge about treatment alternatives and quality requirements. Such a secure, value-based, human-centric approach to healthcare data channelling between various stakeholders has been coined, for instance, in the MyData principle, which is a Nordic Model for human-centred personal data management and processing (Pikkarainen et al., 2020; Poikola et al., 2020).

The current societal challenges are speeding up the healthcare sector to become more digital than ever before. Technological evolution has been considered to create new opportunities and benefits for healthcare (Hyrkäs et al., 2020), such as access to care outside hospitals via connected and e-Health solutions (Chouvarda et al., 2015; Gjellbæk et al., 2020). Also, increasing interest in artificial intelligence (AI)-driven innovations is considered increasingly crucial for healthcare organisations in bridging the gap between future possibilities of digital health and healthcare delivery (Gomes et al., 2022).

Technology is an enabler for developing digital health services that support healthcare providers (e.g. health practitioners in public and private hospitals and municipalities) and individuals (e.g. healthy or sick people) to move towards personalised, proactive, and predictive healthcare systems (Jayaraman et al., 2020; Pikkarainen et al., 2017). In this vein, digital health can be defined as a field of knowledge and practice associated with developing and using digital technologies to improve health (Fatehi et al., 2020; Värri et al., 2020). This refers to how healthcare provision is conceived and delivered by healthcare providers using information and communication technologies to monitor and improve patients' well-being and health and empower them to manage their health and that of their families (Ilyawa et al., 2016). Digital health connects and empowers people and populations to manage health and wellness, augmented by accessible and supportive provider teams working within flexible, integrated, interoperable, and digitally enabled care environments that strategically leverage digital tools, technologies, and services to transform care delivery (Snowdon, 2022).

Digital health connects e-Health, digital consumers, smart devices, and connected equipment. Technologies and themes such as AI, big data, Internet of Things (IoT), blockchain, health data, telemedicine, health information systems, interoperability, and infodemic are commonly understood to belong to digital health. The digital health services offered to healthcare providers and individuals are, for example, multiple cutting-edge digital technologies such as IoT, including wearables, mobile smartphones, social networks (e.g. Facebook and X (previously Twitter), electronic health record systems that health practitioners use to manage data and the traditional EMRs that are used to collect medical imaging data in multiple situations (Jayaraman et al., 2020). Most of these devices, for example, smartphones, wearable sensors, medical health records, or EMR systems, can generate an enormous amount of data powered by platforms, algorithms, and AI technologies, providing a baseline for new digital care that allows an ability to make information systems that can either make or support users (health practitioners, individuals) to make informed decisions (see, e.g. Häikiö et al., 2020). Thus, the goal of AI in digital health, for example, is to make a new type of complex information system that assists healthcare practitioners in making clinical decisions and provides individuals with more efficient personalised services (for the prevention and management of chronic diseases) that will improve the efficiency of the healthcare systems by reducing costs as well as the prevention, treatments, and care models (Jayaraman et al., 2020).

The COVID-19 crisis also gave a surge to healthcare digitalisation. Tremendous leaps were taken during the pandemic. Enabling virtual visits, telemedicine, remote care, and the need to process vast numbers of reports in a short period are a few examples of the role of technology during the pandemic (Baudier et al., 2023; Haldane et al., 2021). The WHO also recognised the health and economic consequences of COVID-19, and the critical role that digital transformation of the health sector can play in mitigating the risks from such health emergencies (WHO, 2022).

However, providers' roles cannot be neglected in the healthcare context. Healthcare professionals need to be able to implement emerging technologies, potentially being creative and more proactive regarding severe non-communicable health conditions (Gomes et al., 2022). In addition, digital health innovators need to understand specific needs in crises and be able to create and develop solutions. In connection with this system, the support and roles of policymakers also seem critical (Iivari et al., 2019). A recent study by Haldane et al. (2021) has emphasised the importance of healthcare resilience in this context. They define healthcare resilience as institutions' and health actors' capacities to prepare for, recover from and absorb shocks while maintaining core functions and serving their communities' ongoing and acute care needs. In their study of 28 countries' responses to COVID-19, access and use of digital technologies were found to be factors in health service delivery and adapting health system capacity, which calls for careful observation of ethical and privacy concerns (Haldane et al., 2021). The concept of digital health must, therefore, be considered in two dimensions: acute (crisis) and long-term (chronic) changes in global health. Moreover, it should be coupled with resilience, as efforts should focus not only on absorbing unforeseen shocks precipitated by emerging health needs but also on ensuring continuity in health improvement, sustaining gains in systems functioning, and fostering people-centredness while delivering high-quality care (Haldane et al., 2021).

This sub-chapter presents insights into why developing digital health services in changing health ecosystems is complex, especially when challenged with abrupt emergencies, such as COVID-19. We will continue exploring the context in more detail in the next sub-chapter.

7.3 Digital Health Ecosystems from a Complexity Perspective

We define a healthcare ecosystem as an innovation system that includes universities and research organisations, start-ups and private companies, public and private healthcare system operators, hospitals and well-being services counties, and citizens. An ecosystem perspective on digital health (Ilyawa et al., 2016) enables, for instance, the combination of technology expertise with life sciences for smart ICT solutions for delivering advanced, personalised, and connected health service solutions, as realised within the OuluHealth ecosystem vision (Jansson et al., 2014). However, according to Lehto and Malkamäki (2023), healthcare in Finland is based mainly on the capacity of the public sector, "which is why the resourcing of public sector actors is particularly important for the sector's ecosystem" (Lehto & Malkamäki, 2023). Healthcare as a system differs quite distinctively from other sectors. Public state health systems often represent primary, complicated, and fragmented types of customers (Iivari et al., 2019). Health systems as main customers are also different from the actual users, i.e. people. Innovations in healthcare relate not only to novel technologies, such as AI, as discussed in the introduction, nor are they limited to medical or pharmaceutical innovations alone (Ciani et al., 2016). Today, the complexity of healthcare is further increased by the fact that many new approaches to preventing illnesses and promoting the well-being of people (Gabriel et al., 2017) are increasingly dependent on sensitive, personal health data (Pikkarainen et al., 2020). The recent Digital Health in the WHO European Region 2023 report also addressed data's role in digital health transformation.

The complexity in healthcare comes from the problem being solved, i.e. the systemic challenges, and the area of constructing the solution, i.e. digital transformation. The development of digital health systems is compounded due to the complex technological issues and organisational factors, which are often beyond the control of the health technology providers. A well-functioning ecosystem refers to the system's capacity to renew itself and strengthen and is better equipped to respond to complex challenges (Lehto & Malkamäki, 2023). Park and Mithas (2020) have referred to organised complexity, which in healthcare often relates to the sector relying on the power of domain experts (compared to the power of authority) "because it employs physicians who are 'experts', and who are more driven by altruistic, status, and legalistic values than economic values" (Park & Mithas, 2020, p. 100). In the case of digital health, the complexity is multiplied due to the need to combine different technological solutions, ethical and safety issues, and work over organisational boundaries. In global companies, it is also between the different changing health systems (Vayena et al., 2018).

The COVID-19 pandemic also contributed to the development of the European Health Data Space (EHDS) proposal by the European Commission in 2022. This is to foster a genuine single market for digital health services and products, the importance of which was demonstrated in the health area during the pandemic. With this development, the European Commission sought to address the complexity of rules, structures, and processes across EU member states, as these have made it difficult to access and share health data securely and safely, especially cross-border. Safety and security concerns are becoming increasingly important due to cyber-attacks and cybercrime.

The European Health Data Space plays a central role in how healthcare will be provided in the European Union. Alongside the Nordic MyData principles, the EHDS is envisioned empowering individuals to control and utilise their personal health data while ensuring full compliance with the EU's data protection standards and regulations, such as the General Data Protection Regulation (GDPR). The EHDS offers a trustworthy, efficient, consistent framework for research, innovation, policy-making, and regulatory activities. In this way, it supports the use of health data for better healthcare delivery but also enables the EU to facilitate a safe and secure exchange, use, and reuse of health data (European Commission, 2022).

As a health-specific ecosystem, the EHDS builds on common foundations of standards, rules, practices, governance frameworks, and infrastructures. When realised, the EHDS will empower individuals through increased digital access to and control of electronic personal health data and the free movement of this data at the national and EU levels. Hence, it can foster a genuine single market for electronic health record systems, medical devices, and AI systems. A joint action towards the EHDS was coordinated by the Finnish Innovation Fund Sitra, involving

25 partners during 2021–2023, with a focus on the secondary use of health data (Kalliola et al., 2023).

The systemic changes experienced by our health systems have resulted in an increasing interest in strengthening cooperation between healthcare, the information communication technology sector, and life sciences (Hyrkäs et al., 2020; Kraus et al., 2021). Furthermore, the multi-stakeholder ecosystem perspective allows us to explore how ecosystem stakeholders exploit digital technologies (Kraus et al., 2021). Therefore, these aspects must also be examined for digital health in the framework of a changing environment. In this line, having perspectives from healthcare users and providers is essential, reflecting on the interrelations within a complex digital health ecosystem, as healthcare providers "need to rely on complex interactions with various stakeholders, yet they also need to make decisions in a highly dynamic and unpredictable environment" (Häikiö et al., 2020). Therefore, a better understanding of the change is needed to guide future studies towards more homogenous efforts, which will, in turn, advance the global health agenda.

Sturmberg (2021) has presented a new frame of understanding health and disease as a dynamic complex-adaptive system, considering all of the features in affected patients, such as somatic, psychological, social, and cognitive needs. In such a model, the consequences of the disease will be tailored to the person as a whole, and health service delivery will, therefore, need to provide integrated care to change from disease to health (Sturmberg, 2021). To prevent and manage chronic conditions and associated comorbidities, digital health approaches can view the patient's health and well-being holistically and provide interactive tools, connecting users with healthcare personnel and offering educational choices for access to care in the form and amount needed. This will, in turn, empower patients and provide a dynamic possibility that can adapt quickly to a crisis should it occur. This will lead to a sustainable solution that can last longer and be adaptive.

In this book chapter, we decided to apply Complex Adaptive Systems (CAS) theory as a lens to explore and build an understanding of the change of a rapidly changing healthcare ecosystem in Finland. The key concepts in CAS theory are agents, interactions, environment, and capabilities. Figure 7.1 describes these concepts and how they apply to digital health. According to CAS theory, agents are individual actors or basic entities of actions in a complex adaptive system (Ellis & Herbert, 2011; Nan, 2011). In digital health, agents can represent various entities such as individuals, health professionals, technology or health organisations, future digital health concepts, or future AI-based decision support systems acting with the others in the system. In the CAS theory, there is a set of input/output statements linking an agent's perception of the world around it (Holland, 2006). According to the CAS theory, the agents inspect the structures of the environment and behaviours with the other agents. The behaviour is executed using information collected from the first step as input, which may preserve or change the focal agent's actions (Nan, 2011). Agents require different attributes and capabilities to perform the necessary actions. Information analytics capability, for instance, describes the quality of management practices (Park & Mithas, 2020). In digital health, this would mean how

KEY CONCEPT	DESCRIPTION IN CAS THEORY	IMPLICATION TO DIGITAL HEALTH
Agents	Individuals or organisation units, including people, objects, concepts and attributes needed for interaction	Individuals, health professionals, technology providers, health organisations, digital health concepts, or decision support systems
Interaction	Mutually adaptive behaviour, connection, and flow of resources among agents	Connections and actions between people, but also medical devices, sensors and data that flow from one agent to another
Environment	The internal and external environment (e.g. structures, social context, populations) the agents interact with	The health system in which the agents, i.e. health technology companies and healthcare provider organisations, operate to provide better health services for individuals
Capabilities	To engage in behaviour, an agent must be capable of doing so. Capability is the effort required to overcome knowledge hurdles associated with the action, such as 1) capabilities in information analytics, 2) installing desired behaviours and values, 3) leadership and 4) developing appropriate information management processes	1) Practices for integrating digital health solutions into operational and managerial processes at hospitals or other organisations, 2) e.g., proactiveness needed to impact and change the behaviour of individuals to decrease risks for chronic diseases, 3) capabilities required to orchestrate and leverage necessary resources to advance digitalisation and 4) Utilising data-analytics in sense-making, collection, organisation, and dissemination of information

Fig. 7.1 Digital health from the lens of CAS theory

digital health solutions are integrated into the operational and managerial processes at hospitals or other organisations.

Flows in CAS theory refer to the movements of resources through the agents and connections (Holland, 2006). Resources can be physical objects such as goods or virtual factors such as information and knowledge. In the case of digital health, the resources can be medical devices and sensors, as well as the data flowing from one agent to another. Mobile apps, sensors, and devices continuously generate data that can be stored in the platforms and used by agents through different platforms, decision support systems, and data visualisations. If the data from heterogeneous sources can be utilised, there is a possibility of making more advanced decision support systems that use agent interaction (Benbya & McKelvey, 2006).

The environment is where the agents interact. According to CAS theory, there is a mutual–influence relationship between the environment and agents (Nan, 2011). In digital health, the environment is the health system in which the agents, i.e. health technology companies and healthcare provider organisations, operate to provide better health services for individuals. Digital health services are offered through the healthcare systems that include all organisations, people, and activities needed to provide well-being and healthcare for the people (national health systems throughout the world). Healthcare systems have experienced rapid changes during the past decade. As discussed earlier in this chapter, current health systems, particularly in Europe, are increasingly considering preventive, digital, and social care. This highlights the need to consider health and well-being beyond the healthcare sector to include the concept of welfare. The demographic changes with the increase in non-communicable diseases have implications for the funding of the welfare state, the adequacy of social and health services, democracy, and the acceptance of novel technologies (Dufva & Rekola, 2023). This means that we should take an ecosystem perspective to ensure complementarity and avoid fragmentation of digital technologies between different organisations (Plekhanov et al., 2022), as they also support the flow of resources and connections between agents and thus help to overcome organised complexity (Park & Mithas, 2020) of healthcare organisations. Still, we also need to acknowledge the systemic complexity. What are the critical capabilities required for the context of digital health? This is explored in our empirical study in the following sub-chapter.

7.4 Empirical Study Design

Existing studies and public reports conclude that data and the data science that drive digital health innovations should be essential to future healthcare innovation policies and decision-making (see, e.g. Iivari et al., 2019). Addressing data provenance is crucial to avoid unintended consequences that could appear from predictions, diagnoses, risk scores, and decisions about where or to whom finite resources and care should be prioritised (Bayram et al., 2020). Using CAS theory as a lens to observe digital health raised several questions. Firstly, how to utilise and integrate data and devices for advanced decision-making support systems. Second, how do different ecosystem stakeholders interact with their environment, for example, existing health systems, to ensure coherent digital health services? Pre-existing capacities of healthcare systems are central when there is a need to respond to both structural and long-term changes at a societal level and in crises. Thirdly, we also need to consider how digital health solutions are integrated into operational and managerial processes at hospitals and other organisations operating in the healthcare sector. What capabilities are necessary for the digitalisation of healthcare has remained an ambiguous challenge, which we seek to address in this sub-chapter. A qualitative, explorative study is, therefore, the best approach to understanding the change and complexity of digital health transformation, as it allows us to explore and identify interlinked (eco)systemic change factors from the perspective of working professionals, companies, and researchers in the environment they operate in.

7.4.1 Data Collection

Empirical data for this study was acquired through purposive sampling during 2020–2021. Since this explorative study aimed to understand the change in the digital health ecosystem and its future directions in Finland from different perspectives, we involved 34 people with varying areas of expertise in our study, i.e. medical experts, industrial experts, and researchers. The participants included 12 professors, senior researchers, and medical experts who were mainly working on research related to the new digital health technologies and technology innovations. We also interviewed eight company directors responsible for digital health technology-related R&D activities and 14 directors of universities and research centres working with digital health and digital health-related research agendas as a part of their daily activities. The involved directors in the universities and research organisations worked in a more diverse area of digital health. Most of the interviewed experts from companies and research institutes were working in the domain of health systems and health data. However, some experts were more specialised, for example, in rehabilitation, surgical care, e-Health, brain health, and preventive healthcare. Because of the diverse and experienced interviewees' backgrounds, we believe that the selected sample in the study is highly representative of experts who are key players involved in directing the future of digital healthcare in Finland.

The interview questions were prepared and validated with the research team. The questions related to defining digital health, the future of digital health, who benefits from it, and how they benefit from it. Ethical permission was not required for this type of study. However, specific informed-research-consent forms were prepared and signed by the study participants to ensure consent for data usage in the conducted research. The semi-structured interviews allowed interviewees to steer the conversation based on their roles, duties, and interests. Each interview was between 60 and 90 min, and the language used was English. All the interviews were recorded and transcribed. To increase the value of our research, we performed additional supplementary data collection after the worst peak of COVID-19, with four additional interviews.

7.4.2 Data Analysis

Research on ecosystems would benefit from adopting better-founded theorising behind the core methodological choices. Phillips and Ritala (2019) have suggested that complex adaptive systems (CAS) would be a helpful approach when addressing ecosystem-related topics. In our analysis, we used the CAS theory and inductive method for data sense-making as described by Glaser (2002). The capabilities described by Park and Mithas (2020) were used as a starting point for the analysis. This is because their study seems to be the most comprehensive contribution to the discussion on capabilities when they looked through the CAS theory in the digital world. The analysis identified new capabilities and linked them to the emerging categories (Charmaz, 2008), agents, and their interactions.

Based on the coding, we obtained 153 codes from the data. The capabilities were identified in the analysis through questions of CAS theory. Describing the capabilities was relevant when categorising the research results. In particular, we explored (1) What new capabilities are needed in digital health, especially considering actions between individuals, health professionals, technology and health organisations, digital health concepts, and decision support systems in health ecosystems; (2) What capabilities are needed for mutually adaptive behaviour, as well as the connection and flow of resources between agents; (3) What capabilities are needed when different agents, for example, individuals, health professionals, technology or health organisations, or different elements such as digital health concepts or decision support systems interact with the environment; and (4) How do the different ecosystem partners interact with their environment, for example, existing health systems to assure coherency and interaction of the digital health services.

7.5 Towards Digital Health of the Future

Qualitative research data is mapped according to the theoretical framework of complex adaptive systems theory. We used the agent, interaction, and environment constructs of CAS theory. Our analysis focused on the capabilities needed to improve digital health between the agents (healthcare professionals, companies, and people) in a changing health ecosystem. This means that the capabilities are the key variable in our analysis (Venkatesh & Brown, 2001). The key findings of our empirical data lead us to different data and organisational perspectives that need to be considered in the change of digital health and wellness ecosystems. However, as digital health is largely linked to the digitalisation of the public domain as well, the *policy* perspective was also a central finding in our study. We will discuss our findings in more detail below.

7.5.1 Policy-Level Change Factors

The analysis revealed that in a crisis, there is an increasing need to understand and manage healthcare-related legislation (6/34 interviews). From the perspective of the changing environment, we must increase public and private organisations' understanding of managing legislation to ensure safe data collection and usage. This is important for different ecosystem actors, such as policymakers, public organisations, and companies. 15/34 respondents also mentioned that in crises, it is imperative for the government to use and share money wisely between the different agents to support digitalisation activities. This also concerns the long-term benefits of the decisions about different health outcomes.

Another policy-level change factor that emerged from our analysis (14/34 answers) was the policy-level capability to move from the management of chronic illnesses to preventive healthcare. It was revealed in 9/34 interviews that the emphasis on Finland's digital health and welfare system should be put on chronic illness risk prevention and pre- and post-stages of the care pathways. This is because these home care stages are the ones that bring the most return on investments related to future digital health.

It was mentioned in interviews (17/34) that ecosystems need to create more personalised, human-centric solutions for chronic disease prevention and monitoring that support self-care, especially in crisis situations. This, however, requires that the policymakers provide easier access to health services, for example, in remote areas (6/34). Additionally, 9/34 respondents mentioned a specific need to understand and manage health systems in crisis situations. This was divided into the following categories: the need to see and manage care processes across organisation borders, involvement of ecosystem actors in system-level solution development, and understanding the links between social and policy systems.

7.5.2 Organisational Level Change Factors

In 16/34 interviews, it was mentioned that in crises, when innovations are urgently needed, healthcare providers need to engage critical experts in innovation activities to enable more meaningful innovation development. The results related to this hypothesis were divided into categories describing the need to convince medical experts about the benefits of innovation work (2/34), involving medical experts in discussing solution needs and building mutual trust between healthcare providers and companies (2/34).

In the case of crisis, there is a need for different ecosystem players to orchestrate ecosystem-level innovation development for chronic disease prevention and support (16/34 interviews). This includes activities such as setting business models, (2) setting common goals, (3) sharing ideas, (4) understanding other stakeholder perspectives, (5) understanding process complexity, and (6) using resources at the ecosystem level. The need for national-level interoperability between the organisations in crisis situations was also mentioned in 10/34 interviews. It was stated, for instance, that the crisis is increasing the need to manage the connectivity between different regional systems, manage the information flow between different systems, and use national platforms to support system interoperability.

7.5.3 Data-Related Change Factors

Among the data-related factors, the participants (12/34) frequently viewed that in the rapidly changing digital health ecosystems, there is a need to use non-medical data together with other heterogeneous data as a way to support better treatments and clinical decision-making for people at risk of chronic diseases or people with chronic diseases. The data generated by the different actors in the care processes need to be analysed using machine learning techniques. This is an enabler for improved treatments and decision-making among different ecosystem actors in the case of a pandemic or other crisis.

Data access need was revealed in 17/34 interviews. It was divided into the ability to gain data access from electronic health record systems and gain data access through technological solutions, i.e. specific algorithms, AI, and automation. Data access was seen as necessary in pandemics or other crises to offer more personalised digital solutions, disease-specific services, and specialised treatments.

From a preventive healthcare perspective, there was a need (revealed in 6/34 interviews) to integrate genomic/biobank data with the behavioural/sensor/wearable data that people generate daily better to understand the situation of risk or chronically ill patients and to create better personalised digital health services.

7.6 Discussion and Conclusion

In this study, we explored the required capabilities for digital health from two dimensions discussed in the literature: acute (crisis) and long-term (chronic) changes in the context of change in healthcare ecosystems. We used CAS theory as a theoretical lens to identify and analyse our empirical findings regarding the new capabilities essential for healthcare in digital health ecosystems. Our data collection occurred before and during a health crisis (the COVID-19 pandemic and beyond); hence, we could add novel information about a sudden change (Kaiser et al., 2021) in health services.

Focus on self-care, preventive healthcare, use of non-medical and heterogeneous data to support better treatments, and clinical decisions were among the key elements that we identified in our study. We also discovered that innovative processes and actions are essential in digital health. The digitalisation of healthcare contributes significantly to reducing the costs of providing care and offers an improved user experience and quality of care (Kokko & Kork, 2021; Marques & Ferreira, 2020). The COVID-19 pandemic has also highlighted the role of digital innovations, such as telemedicine and virtual care for remote treatment (Baudier et al., 2023; Bokolo Anthony, 2020) and, in fact, advanced digitalisation of healthcare in Finland overall (Koivuluoma et al., 2022). The most critical aspect of managing digital health in crises in Finland's digital health and welfare system was found from a data perspective to provide the most useful information in a timely fashion. In a crisis, good communication strategies help manage people's fears and increase the likelihood that they will adhere to the measures imposed on them (Fagherazzi et al., 2020).

The ability of Finland to respond to abrupt changes is not a question of technology. However, deeper collaboration is needed in all sectors of the economy that are directly linked with healthcare. At the national level, policymakers need to pay more attention to data-driven decision-making and invest in interoperability between different health sectors and systems. This will also allow better data access for future AI-based digital services and research. Leadership capabilities are needed in healthcare provider organisation agents and companies developing future technologies to support professionals and policymakers during the decision-making process, as pointed out in previous research (Gomes et al., 2022; Iivari et al., 2019). Companies should be aware of and follow specific laws and regulations for accountability when designing AI-based health systems at the EU level. For example, developing AI for specific health-related tasks is essential to ensure that AI-driven outcomes will not cause harm to patients or society (Trocin et al., 2021). In this context, the privacy and security challenges need careful and proper handling between these agents (healthcare provider organisations and companies), where overlapping areas ranging from AI, the Internet of Things, electronic health, telehealth, and big data are mainly involved and play essential roles in healthcare service delivery (Gomes et al., 2022; Kaiser et al., 2021). However, the impact of the use and implications of these different technologies also require a more systematic approach, which we found in our study.

When examining the interactions between the different actors in digital health ecosystems, it can be argued that the capabilities to orchestrate research and innovation actions in digital health is often a challenge for different ecosystem actors (see also Pikkarainen et al., 2017). There is room for improvement, primarily related to the shared values, aligned targets, and understanding of the legislation and the perspectives of different actors and cultures in digital health ecosystems. Kemppainen et al. also noted some of these elements earlier (Kemppainen et al., 2019). One future goal of digital ecosystem implementation includes improving the efficiency of communication. In practice, each player in an ecosystem has data, information, and knowledge that could be better used and analysed in novel and innovative ways (Benis et al., 2021). In this sense, our findings align with Benis et al. (2021), who indicate a need for managing, collecting, storing, archiving, and analysing data related to information processing. For example, data access, data safety, and data integration between wearables, medical devices, and genomic data are important areas for future improvement in digital health and integrated data for better practical usage.

From an organisational perspective, the areas that appeared commonly in the study were related to data-driven decision support systems and resource management issues, especially in healthcare organisations. The need for further or better capabilities was particularly associated with using non-medical and heterogeneous data to support better treatments and clinical decision-making. Addressing these issues requires a new and innovative ecosystem-driven approach and novel technologies that reinforce the ability of traditional systems to prevent and control chronic diseases (Benis et al., 2021).

In practice, personalised health services need to be built by considering an individual's variability in terms of family history, living and working environment, digital health literacy, choices and preferences, and overall lifestyle. Finland is currently undergoing its most extensive social and healthcare reform (Sote), which became fully active on the 1st of January, 2023. The reform was initiated with the idea that public administration would be organised at three levels: the state, counties, and municipalities. Municipalities and counties will be jointly responsible for promoting public health, and rescue services will be organised alongside healthcare and social welfare services. Along with the principles of value-based care, this reform aims to homogenise the delivery of services within countries and create seamless service chains and well-functioning collaboration between different sectors and both public and private service providers within the sectors (Kangas &

Kalliomaa-Puha, 2022). However, challenges in executing this reform naturally exist, such as the balance and ability of public health centres to diagnose and treat patients, especially concerning specialist services. As the occupational healthcare system is accessed by those in employment, health centres are biased towards treating patients with higher healthcare and social care needs, not only children and elderly but also people from lower socioeconomic or educational levels (Tynkkynen et al., 2023). As patient waiting times have increased tremendously, digital care and e-Health solutions could perhaps aid in ensuring equal and timely access to care for all.

The use of CAS theory allows us to view the change in the Finnish healthcare system, both supported and boosted by digital transformation, as indeed something that expands the concept of reactive health and care to proactive health and well-being in a resilient, sustainable manner. The increasing political tensions have also brought to focus the growing numbers of cyber-attacks, hybrid warfare, and the role of data security and safety, which may also have implications for digital health systems. Digital health has the potential to provide solutions and opportunities to manage and bring flexibility and resilience under regular conditions but also in health crises such as pandemics, natural disasters or crises caused solely by humans, but only if we build systems that are sustainable, resilient, and responsible. Our discussion can guide the research agenda for future studies and the required capabilities to build upon sustainable, fair, resilient, and safe digital health in the future.

References

Baudier, P., Kondrateva, G., Ammi, C., Chang, V., & Schiavone, F. (2023). Digital transformation of healthcare during the COVID-19 pandemic: Patients' teleconsultation acceptance and trusting beliefs. *Technovation, 120*, 102547. https://doi.org/10.1016/j.technovation.2022.102547

Bayram, M., Springer, S., Garvey, C. K., & Özdemir, V. (2020). COVID-19 digital health innovation policy: A portal to alternative futures in the making. *OMICS, 24*(8), 460–469. https://doi.org/10.1089/omi.2020.0089

Benbya, H., & McKelvey, B. (2006). Toward a complexity theory of information systems development. *Information Technology & People, 19*(1), 12–34. https://doi.org/10.1108/09593840610649952

Benis, A., Tamburis, O., Chronaki, C., & Moen, A. (2021). One digital health: A unified framework for future health ecosystems. *Journal of Medical Internet Research, 23*(2), e22189. https://doi.org/10.2196/22189

Bokolo Anthony, J. (2020). Use of telemedicine and virtual care for remote treatment in response to COVID-19 pandemic. *Journal of Medical Systems, 44*(7), 132. https://doi.org/10.1007/s10916-020-01596-5

Charmaz, K. (2008). The legacy of Anselm Strauss in constructivist grounded theory. In N. K. Denzin, J. Salvo, & M. Washington (Eds.), *Studies in symbolic interaction* (Vol. 32, pp. 127–141). Emerald Group Publishing Limited. https://doi.org/10.1016/S0163-2396(08)32010-9

Chouvarda, I. G., Goulis, D. G., Lambrinoudaki, I., & Maglaveras, N. (2015). Connected health and integrated care: Toward new models for chronic disease management. *Maturitas, 82*(1), 22–27.

Ciani, O., Armeni, P., Boscolo, P. R., Cavazza, M., Jommi, C., & Tarricone, R. (2016). De innovatione: The concept of innovation for medical technologies and its implications for healthcare policy-making. *Health Policy and Technology, 5*(1), 47–64.

Dias, C., & Escoval, A. (2012). The open nature of innovation in the hospital sector: The role of external collaboration networks. *Health Policy and Technology, 1*(4), 181–186. https://doi.org/10.1016/j.hlpt.2012.10.002

Dufva, M., & Rekola, S. (2023). *Megatrends 2023 - Understanding an era of surprises* (p. 225). SITRA Studies.

Ellis, B., & Herbert, S. I. (2011). Complex adaptive systems (CAS): An overview of key elements, characteristics and application to management theory. *Informatics in Primary Care, 19*(1), 33–37. https://doi.org/10.14236/jhi.v19i1.791

European Commission. (2022). *Proposal for a regulation of the European Parliament and of the Council on the European Health Data Space* EUR-Lex. https://eur-lex.europa.eu/legal-content/EN/TXT/?uri=CELEX:52022PC0197.

European Observatory on Health Systems and Policies, Tynkkynen, L.K., Keskimäki, I., Karanikolos, M., & Litvinova, Y. (2023). *Finland: Health system summary, 2023*. World Health Organization. Regional Office for Europe. Retrieved May 9, 2024, from https://iris.who.int/handle/10665/366710

Fagherazzi, G., Goetzinger, C., Rashid, M. A., Aguayo, G. A., & Huiart, L. (2020). Digital health strategies to fight COVID-19 worldwide: Challenges, recommendations, and a call for papers. *Journal of Medical Internet Research, 22*(6), e19284. https://doi.org/10.2196/19284

Fatehi, F., Samadbeik, M., & Kazemi, A. (2020). What is digital health? Review of definitions. In A. Värri et al. (Eds.), *Integrated citizen centered digital health and social care: Citizens as data producers and service co-creators*. IOS Press.

Gabriel, M., Stanley, I., & Saunders, T. (2017). *Open innovation in health: A guide to transforming healthcare through collaboration*. Nesta.

Gjellbæk, C., Svensson, A., Bjørkquist, C., Fladeby, N., & Grundén, K. (2020). Management challenges for future digitalization of healthcare services. *Futures, 124*, 102636. https://doi.org/10.1016/j.futures.2020.102636

Glaser, B. G. (2002). Conceptualization: On theory and theorizing using grounded theory. *International Journal of Qualitative Methods, 1*(2), 23–38. https://doi.org/10.1177/160940690200100203

Gomes, J. F., Iivari, M., Koivumäki, T., Immonen, M., Jansson, M., Pikkarainen, M., et al. (2022). Care pathway as the basis for collaborative business model innovation in healthcare. In L. M. Camarinha-Matos, A. Ortiz, X. Boucher, & A. L. Osório (Eds.), *Collaborative networks in digitalization and Society 5.0. PRO-VE 2022. IFIP advances in information and communication technology* (Vol. 662). Springer. https://doi.org/10.1007/978-3-031-14844-6_27

Häikiö, J., Yli-Kauhaluoma, S., Pikkarainen, M., Iivari, M., & Koivumäki, T. (2020). Expectations to data: Perspectives of service providers and users of future health and wellness services. *Health and Technology, 10*(3), 621–636. https://doi.org/10.1007/s12553-020-00410-z

Haldane, V., De Foo, C., Abdalla, S. M., Jung, A.-S., Tan, M., Wu, S., et al. (2021). Health systems resilience in managing the COVID-19 pandemic: Lessons from 28 countries. *Nature Medicine, 27*(6), 964–980. https://doi.org/10.1038/s41591-021-01381-y

Helliwell, J. F., Layard, R., Sachs, J. D., De Neve, J.-E., Aknin, L. B., & Wang, S. (Eds.). (2024). *World happiness report 2024*. University of Oxford: Wellbeing Research Centre.

Holland, J. H. (2006). Studying complex adaptive systems. *Journal of Systems Science and Complexity, 19*(1), 1–8. https://doi.org/10.1007/s11424-006-0001-z

Hood, L., Balling, R., & Auffray, C. (2012). Revolutionizing medicine in the 21st century through systems approaches. *Biotechnology Journal, 7*, 997–1001. https://doi.org/10.1002/biot.201100306

Hyrkäs, P., Haukipuro, L., Väinämö, S., Iivari, M., Sachinopoulou, A., & Majava, J. (2020). Collaborative innovation in healthcare: A case study of hospitals as innovation platforms. *International Journal of Value Chain Management, 11*, 24. https://doi.org/10.1504/IJVCM.2020.105475

Iivari, M., Pikkarainen, M., Gomes, J. F., Ranta, J., & Ylén, P. (2019). Toward open innovation and data-driven health policy making. In A.-L. Mention (Ed.), *Digital innovation: Harnessing the value of open data* (pp. 199–225). World Scientific.

Ilyawa, G. E., Herselman, M., & Botha, A. (2016). Digital health innovation ecosystems: From systematic literature review to conceptual framework. *Procedia Computer Science, 100*, 244–252. https://doi.org/10.1016/j.procs.2016.09.149

Inkster, B., O'Brien, R., Selby, E., Joshi, S., Subramanian, V., Kadaba, M., et al. (2020). Digital health management during and beyond the COVID-19 pandemic: Opportunities, barriers, and recommendations. *JMIR Mental Health, 7*(7), e19246.

Islind, A. S., Lindroth, T., Lundin, J., & Steineck, G. (2019). Shift in translations: Data work with patient-generated health data in clinical practice. *Health Informatics Journal, 25*(3), 577–586. https://doi.org/10.1177/1460458219833097

Jansson, N., Ahokangas, P., Iivari, M., Perälä-Heape, M., & Salo, S. (2014). The competitive advantage of an ecosystemic business model: The case of OuluHealth. *Interdisciplinary Studies Journal 3*(4), 282–295. http://urn.fi/URN:NBN:fi:amk-201905037535

Jayaraman, P. P., Forkan, A. R. M., Morshed, A., Haghighi, P. D., & Kang, Y.-B. (2020). Healthcare 4.0: A review of frontiers in digital health. *WIREs Data Mining and Knowledge Discovery, 10*(2), e1350. https://doi.org/10.1002/widm.1350

Kaiser, F. K., Wiens, M., & Schultmann, F. (2021). Use of digital healthcare solutions for care delivery during a pandemic-chances and (cyber) risks referring to the example of the COVID-19 pandemic. *Health and Technology (Berlin), 11*(5), 1125–1137. https://doi.org/10.1007/s12553-021-00541-x

Kalliola, M., Drakvik, E., & Nurmi, M. (Eds.). (2023). *Advancing data sharing to improve health for all in Europe: Main findings of joint action towards the European Health Data Space 2021–2023* (p. 236). SITRA Studies.

Kangas, O., & Kalliomaa-Puha, L. (2022). *Finland finalises its largest-ever social and health-care reform*. ESPN Flash Report 2022/39. European Social Policy Network (ESPN), Brussels: European Commission. Retrieved from https://urn.fi/URN:NBN:fi-fe2022091258782

Kemppainen, L., Pikkarainen, M., Hurmelinna, P., & Reponen, J. (2019). Data access in connected health innovation: Managerial orchestration challenges and solutions. *Technology Innovation Management Review, 9*, 43–55. https://doi.org/10.22215/timreview/1291

Koivuluoma, M., Haverinen, J., & Reponen, J. (2022). Digital health services as part of care processes. *Finnish Journal of EHealth and EWelfare, 14*(3), 284–298. https://doi.org/10.23996/fjhw.111788

Kokko, P., & Kork, A.-A. (2021). Value-based healthcare logics and their implications for Nordic health policies. *Health Services Management Research, 34*(1), 3–12.

Kokko, S., Liveng, A., & Torp, S. (2018). 20 years of health promotion research in the Nordic countries: Health, wellbeing and physical activity. *Scandinavian Journal of Public Health, 46*(20), 3–6.

Kraus, S., Schiavone, F., Pluzhnikova, A., & Invernizzi, A. C. (2021). Digital transformation in healthcare: Analyzing the current state-of-research. *Journal of Business Research, 123*, 557–567. https://doi.org/10.1016/j.jbusres.2020.10.030

Lehto, P., & Malkamäki, S. (2023, June 8). *The Finnish health sector growth and competitiveness vision 2030*. Working paper. Sitra. Retrieved May 10, 2024.

Marques, I. C. P., & Ferreira, J. J. M. (2020). Digital transformation in the area of health: Systematic review of 45 years of evolution. *Health and Technology, 10*(3), 575–586. https://doi.org/10.1007/s12553-019-00402-8

Nan, N. (2011). Capturing bottom-up information technology use processes: A complex adaptive systems model. *MIS Quarterly, 35*(2), 505–532.

Park, Y., & Mithas, S. (2020). Organized complexity of digital business strategy: A configurational perspective. *MIS Quarterly, 44*(1), 85–127.

Phillips, M. A., & Ritala, P. (2019). A complex adaptive systems agenda for ecosystem research methodology. *Technological Forecasting and Social Change, 148*, 119739. https://doi.org/10.1016/j.techfore.2019.119739

Pikkarainen, M., Ervasti, M., Hurmelinna, P., & Nätti, S. (2017). Orchestration roles to facilitate networked innovation in a healthcare ecosystem. *Technology Innovation Management Review, 7*, 30–43. https://doi.org/10.22215/timreview/1104

Pikkarainen, M., Koivumäki, T., & Iivari, M. (2020). Seizing the business opportunities of MyData service delivery network: Transforming the business models for health insurance companies. *Journal of Business Models, 8*(2), 39–56.

Plekhanov, D., Franke, H., & Netland, T. (2022). Digital transformation: A review and research agenda. *European Management Journal., 41*, 821–844. https://doi.org/10.1016/j.emj.2022.09.007

Poikola, A., Kuikkaniemi, K., Kuittinen, O., Honko, H., Knuutila, A., & Lähteenoja, V. (2020). *MyData - An introduction to human-centric use of personal data*. 3rd, revised version. White paper. Ministry of Transport and Communications. Retrieved May 10, 2024.

Snowdon, A. (2022). *Digital health: A framework for healthcare transformation*. HIMSS.

Sturmberg, J. P. (2021). Health and disease are dynamic complex-adaptive states implications for practice and research. *Frontiers in Psychiatry, 12*, 595124. https://doi.org/10.3389/fpsyt.2021.595124

Trocin, C., Hovland, I. V., Mikalef, P., & Dremel, C. (2021). How artificial intelligence affords digital innovation: A cross-case analysis of Scandinavian companies. *Technological Forecasting and Social Change, 173*, 121081. https://doi.org/10.1016/j.techfore.2021.121081

Värri, A., Delgado, J., Gallos, P., Hägglund, M., Häyrinen, K., Kinnunen, U.-M., et al. (Eds.). (2020). *Integrated citizen centered digital health and social care: Citizens as data producers and service co-creators*. IOS Press.

Vayena, E., Haeusermann, T., Adjekum, A., & Blasimme, A. (2018). Digital health: Meeting the ethical and policy challenges. *Swiss Medical Weekly, 148*, w14571. https://doi.org/10.4414/smw.2018.14571

Venkatesh, V., & Brown, S. A. (2001). A longitudinal investigation of personal computers in homes: Adoption determinants and emerging challenges. *MIS Quarterly, 25*(1), 71–102. https://doi.org/10.2307/3250959

Vial, G. (2019). Understanding digital transformation: A review and a research agenda. *The Journal of Strategic Information Systems, 28*, 118–144. https://doi.org/10.1016/j.jsis.2019.01.003

World Health Organization, Regional Office for Europe, Data and Digital Health. (2022). *Resolution: Leveraging digital transformation for better health in Europe: Regional digital health action plan for the WHO European Region 2023–2030 (RC72)*.

World Health Organization. (2023, September 16). *Non-communicable diseases*. Retrieved November 28, 2023, from https://www.who.int/news-room/fact-sheets/detail/noncommunicable-diseases

Chapter 8
Innovation and Social Capital in Nordic Welfare States: The Advantages of Nordic Societies in a Modern Economy

Mayuko Kitai and Tatsushi Waragai

Abstract The importance of creating innovations for modern welfare states in knowledge-based economies continues to increase. This chapter investigates the impact of social capital on innovation by considering the varying natures of social capital and the type thereof supporting innovation systems in Nordic countries. By classifying countries into four clusters of social capital types according to generalized and particularized trust, we illustrate the effects of each social capital category on innovation. The results show that social capital characterized by high generalized trust and high particularized trust has the greatest positive impact on innovation. Another important finding is that Nordic countries have a hybrid type of social capital with both high generalized and particularized trust. Finally, our findings confirm that the function of innovation systems in Nordic countries is supported by the hybrid type of social capital. This study provides new evidence that each type of social capital has a significantly different effect on innovative performances.

Keywords Innovation · Social capital · RIS approach · Generalized trust · Nordic countries

8.1 Introduction

The environment of welfare states is changing dramatically alongside structural changes in economics and societies, such as globalization, digitalization, and declining birth rates. Specifically, the emergence of knowledge-based economies

M. Kitai (✉)
Matsuyama University, Matsuyama, Japan
e-mail: m.kitai@g.matsuyama-u.ac.jp

T. Waragai
Osaka Sangyo University, Daito, Japan
e-mail: waratts-2@ge.osaka-sandai.ac.jp

N. Tokumaru et al. (eds.), *Creative Co-evolution of the Economies and Welfare States in the Nordic Countries*, Evolutionary Economics and Social Complexity Science 32, https://doi.org/10.1007/978-981-97-8569-8_8

has increased the significance of innovation in modern welfare states. Here, the success of innovation is a crucial aspect of providing welfare services financially because innovation capacity is a key determinant of the economic performance of firms, regions, and nations.

In this regard, Nordic countries have put great efforts into promoting innovative activities through policies. Accordingly, the European Innovation Scoreboard 2023 categorizes Sweden, Finland, and Denmark as "innovation leaders." Sweden and Finland are characterized as "strong innovators." Stiglitz and Greenwald (2015, p. 146) claim that "the Nordic model consists of exactly the kind of policies that one would expect to see in a leader." Economically, innovation capability is an important factor for understanding why Nordic welfare states can survive in knowledge-based economies while maintaining universal welfare services.

Nordic welfare states are well known as societies that comparatively succeed in achieving high economic performance and help prevent the further widening of inequalities in the modern world. The success of Nordic countries has attracted the attention of researchers and policymakers in other countries. Most foreign studies have concentrated on the classic policies in Nordic countries, such as active labor policies, generous family policies, and triple helix. However, several domestic researchers have argued that the function of the Nordic model is essentially supported by the informal aspects of societies, which are referred to as social capital (Bertilsson & Hjorth-Andersen, 2009; Rothstein, 2002; Trägårdh, 2007). Nordic countries have distinctly high levels of social trust, high institutional trust, equalitarianism, and individualism (Rothstein, 2009; Kumlin & Rothstein, 2005; Holmberg & Rothstein, 2020). In particular, the Nordic Council of Ministers, the official body for intergovernmental cooperation, explains the exceptionally high level of social trust as one of the main reasons for the success of these countries (Andreasson, 2017).

Recently, such social factors have gained increasing attention for understanding the differences in innovation capacity between countries and regions, alongside the sophistication of innovation. The complexity of social challenges, diversification of demands, and advancement of technology urge us to overstep traditional boundaries to exchange information and ideas, as well as collaborate between actors in the process of innovation. Social capital is one of the frameworks used to analyze the impact of social factors on innovation regarding the interaction between actors. There has long been interest in why innovation activities are unevenly distributed across spaces. Social capital could contribute to the distribution of innovative activities and the function of innovation policies implemented in Nordic countries.

This chapter investigates the relationship between social capital in Nordic countries and innovation. Furthermore, using the social capital theory, this study aims to demonstrate the advantages of Nordic societies in terms of innovation. In this chapter, we not only focus on Finland but also stress the differences between Nordic countries and the rest of the world.

8.2 The Innovation System Approach and Role of Social Capital

8.2.1 The Innovation System Approach

Nordic countries have applied the innovation system approach (Serger & Palmberg, 2022). This approach emerged as the second framing of science, technology, and innovation (STI) policies in the form of a "national system of innovation" around the 1980s (Asheim et al., 2020; Lundvall, 1992; Schot & Steinmueller, 2018).[1] The approach differed from the first framing of STI policies following four modifications represented by R&D: "First, rather than a global public good, it was recognized that scientific and technological knowledge often contained important tacit elements. Knowledge did not freely travel over geographical and cultural distances, but instead was 'sticky.' Second, the ability to absorb knowledge from the worldwide network of research and researchers depends on absorptive capabilities which require prior experience in related research and application. Third, 'absorptive capacities' were found to be social capabilities that stemmed not only from the level of education but also its qualities and the social capability of entrepreneurship. Fourth, the character of technological change was recognized as being cumulative and path-dependent" (Schot & Steinmueller, 2018, p. 1558). These modifications suggest that important international differences might exist in the capacity to innovate and highlight the processes of learning and relationships between different organizations in society (Schot & Steinmueller, 2018).

In other words, the innovation system approach is a framework for explaining the uneven geographical distribution of innovation in the international space and for designing policies that aim to stimulate innovation capability concerning the interactive process of innovation. Specifically, the approach emphasizes the interactive learning processes that occur between multiple actors and organizations (entrepreneurs, firms, universities, public agencies, government, and civil society). Nordic countries, especially Sweden and Finland, push hard to construct innovation systems by implementing a triple helix. Thus, the triple helix is a representative model of this innovation policy approach.

Although the innovation system approach emerged from the discussion on "the national system of innovation" (Lundvall, 1992), it has also been applied at the regional level. This is because differences in heterogeneous landscapes generated the need for a more place-based, differentiated regional innovation policy in Europe (Asheim et al., 2019). The regional innovation system (RIS) approach is another outcome of the second framing, which became dominant in the 1990s in the EU (Asheim et al., 2020). A key argument of the RIS approach is that innovation should be understood as the outcome of interactive learning and collaboration in localized

---

[1] The third framing, "transformative change," which deals with how to solve grand societal challenges (Schot & Steinmueller, 2018; Asheim et al., 2020), has been increasing in importance since 2010. Mission-oriented innovation policies (MOIPs) are included in the third framing, except where related discussions stress the role of government (Mazzucato, 2019, 2021).

innovation networks embedded in specific sociocultural settings (Asheim et al., 2019; Asheim & Coenen, 2005). Networks and other linkages are pivotal for innovation because they support the exchange of knowledge and other resources among RIS actors. Nordic countries are categorized into the ideal type of RIS, which is the regionally networked innovation system (Asheim & Coenen, 2005). In this type of RIS, firms and organizations are intentionally embedded in a specific region and characterized by localized and interactive learning through an institutional infrastructure.

This focus on collaboration between actors and the exchange of knowledge over organizational and sectoral boundaries in the innovation process is also mentioned in the discussion on "open innovation.[2]" Research has shown that the adoption of open innovation improves business performance and the radicalness of innovation, notably in R&D-intensive industries (Chesbrough, 2017; Cammarano et al., 2019). Access to external knowledge allows firms to generate inventions of higher originality and novelty. Internal development is more suitable to reinforce existing technologies (Cammarano et al., 2019). In other words, firms rely heavily on the exchange of knowledge with external parties, such as suppliers, customers, universities, other key individuals, and sometimes even competitors, as they create innovations (Laursen et al., 2014). Figure 8.1 illustrates the direction of open

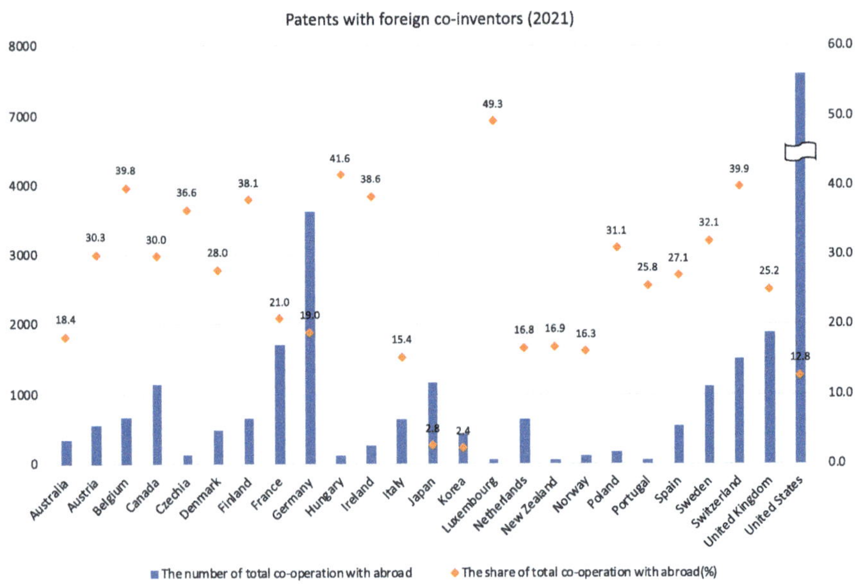

Source: OECD stat.

Fig. 8.1 Number and share of patents with foreign co-investors. Source: OECD stat

[2] "Open innovation is a distributed innovation process that relies on purposively managed knowledge flows across organizational boundaries, using pecuniary and nonpecuniary mechanisms in line with the organization's business model to guide and motivate knowledge sharing" (Chesbrough & Bogers, 2014, p. 3).

innovation in relatively small European countries in terms of international collaboration. Among the Nordic countries, Finland has the highest share of patents with foreign co-investors. Interaction and collaboration between actors have become increasingly important for producing knowledge and innovation.

However, the extent and efficiency of collaborations are strongly associated with informal institutions, as argued in the RIS approach. The RIS approach also underlines the informal institutional context (i.e., norms, trust, and routines) in which such interactive learning takes place (Cooke, 1998). Moreover, "knowledge is created through learning—and learning is a social activity, one that depends on trust, communication and reciprocity" (Anderson, 2007, p. 9). Therefore, the informal institutional context must be investigated as an important determinant of innovation capacity. Furthermore, many studies argue that these social factors (trust, communication, and reciprocity) are abundant in Nordic countries (Steinmo, 2010; Statistics Finland, 2006; Rothstein, 2002, 2008, 2009; Kumlin & Rothstein, 2005; Andreasson, 2017; Kääriäinen & Lehtonen, 2006). These social factors must be attributed to the success of innovation and function of RIS as informal institutions in these countries. However, only a relatively small body of literature focuses on this context. Thus, in the next section, we assess the significance of social factors in innovation and contribute to the understanding of the role of social factors in the innovation system based on social capital theory.

8.2.2 Social Capital in the Process of Innovation

Previous studies applied social capital theory as an analytical framework to examine the role of informal institutional settings in stimulating innovative activities. Furthermore, the importance of social capital as an antecedent to innovation has received considerable theoretical attention (De Dominics et al., 2013; Echebarria & Barrutia, 2013; Kristensen & Dubois, 2021; Laursen et al., 2014; Nahapiet & Ghoshal, 1998; Westlund et al., 2014). Social capital theory was formulated by sociologists (Bourdieu, 1986; Coleman, 1998) and spread through Putnam's (1993) study. His definition, "social capital refers to features of social organization, such as trust, norms, and networks that can improve the efficiency of society by facilitating coordinated actions," is well known among researchers (Putnam, 1993, p. 167).

However, definitions of social capital are diverse and not unified. While Putnam (1993, 2001), Fukuyama (1995, 2001), and Ostrom and Ahn (2009) understand social capital as a resource for achieving and facilitating cooperation, Bourdieu (1986) and Lin (2001) consider it an aggregate of the actual or potential resources embedded in or drawn from social networks. Lin (2001) emphasizes that social networks are not a component of social capital. However, there is much debate within social capital theories regarding its components and subordinate concepts, such as categories. In this chapter, similar to the former group of theorists, we understand social capital as a resource inherent in social relations that improves the efficiency of society by achieving cooperation among individuals.[3] In terms of economics, the outcome of social capital is considered to be a reduction in transaction costs. Moreover, we are convinced that social capital is composed of norms, trust, and networks and gives rise to positive and negative externalities depending on how cooperation is achieved (Fukuyama, 2001; Kitai, 2018; Yamagishi, 1998).[4]

For example, when people in a society are disposed to treat others equally or inclusively, regardless of organizational boundaries, the radius of trust tends to be extensive, increasing the latent possibility of cooperation. Thus, generalized trust and bridging (or inclusive) networks are relatively easy to form in such societies. These characteristics are understood as social capital with positive externalities. However, when ties in a community are strengthened by excluding heterogeneous individuals and maintaining cooperation in a particular relationship, the connections in the community or organization become dense and solid. However, these types of social relations negatively affect larger societies, resulting in decreased tolerance, increased distrust, and increased transaction costs with outsiders. In other words, generalized trust and bridging networks rarely accumulate in society. This is referred to as social capital with negative externalities. As social capital with negative externalities accumulates in society, it is more likely to be characterized as having particularized trust and a bonding network.[5]

Regarding innovation, social capital is a useful perspective from which to analyze the interaction and collaboration between actors in the innovation process. As explained earlier, knowledge production comprises social and interactive activities, and the process of innovation becomes more open. In this context, social capital is considered a determinant for generating extensive collaboration and facilitating the exchange of knowledge, including tacit knowledge. Furthermore, social capital can serve as a channel through which firms or entrepreneurs can improve their capacity to understand the demand.

---

[3] By following Laursen et al.'s (2014) approach, we avoid a situation in which observed social capital could be nothing more than a reflection of a local firm's ability to establish functioning external relations, as per Putnam (1993).

[4] Researchers are divided on understanding whether trust is a strict historical norm or rational choice based on information (Svendsen & Svendsen, 2009). From an economics perspective, trusting is considered the reflection of trustworthiness, and trustworthiness is confirmed by the other's self-interest. In other words, people believe that other people are trustworthy when acting credibly benefits others and themselves (Yamagishi, 1998). According to Yamagishi (1998), many studies regarding social capital theories ignore the distinction between trusting and trustworthiness. Theoretically, this subjective belief or disposition can be independent of objective conditions regarding trustworthiness (Ostrom & Ahn, 2009; Yamagishi, 1998; Yamagishi & Yamagishi, 1994). Therefore, our definition of social capital focuses on the aspect of trusting, not on that of trustworthiness.

[5] Our category of social capital is based on Putnam (2001) and Fukuyama (2001). Although there are other subordinate categories of social capital, the distinction of bridging and bonding social capital is an essential and universal framework through which to understand the characteristics of the concept.

Although most studies recognized the significant positive effect of social capital on innovative activities, their arguments are divided into two hypotheses: Burt's structural hole hypothesis and the density hypothesis (Burt, 2001; Hemphälä & Magnusson, 2012, p. 3). The former builds on arguments that open networks eliminate information redundancy by involving cooperative relationships that encompass diverse entities and by promoting innovation based on Burt's structural holes and Granovetter's weak ties (Burt, 2001; Granovetter, 1973). Fukuyama (2001) further proposes that social capital with negative externalities resulted in the loss of opportunities for new ideas and information by excluding heterodox individuals at the periphery of the social network. On the other hand, the latter builds on arguments for closed network structures for innovation. Dense closed networks with frequent social interactions reinforce reciprocity and facilitate the combination of tacit knowledge by matching absorptive capabilities through routine accumulation. Nahapiet and Ghoshal (1998) contribute to the research on creating knowledge by proposing a comprehensive framework of the effects of social capital on innovation in intrafirm closed relations based on absorptive capabilities.

Moreover, some research has adopted the hypothesis that a society or an organization receives benefits from both open and closed networks in parallel, even though the condition of coexistence among different types of social capital has not been specified. In other words, some societies or organizations do not embrace both open and closed networks because social capital with excessive negative externalities creates an environment that hampers the formulation of generalized trust and bridging networks (Svendsen & Svendsen, 2009). This paradox is caused by an emphasis on the results of social capital, and a lack of perspective on its characteristics. Most studies on the impact of social capital on innovation have not systematically distinguished between social capital with positive and negative externalities. Thus, to solve this paradox and illustrate the kind of social capital that stimulates innovative activities, we consider the type of social capital with categories of trust as an analytical framework, namely generalized and particularized trust.

Considering the aforementioned trends in innovation, the process is not completed within a single firm or industry in terms of open innovation. Creating innovation depends on collaborations with external actors to acquire and combine knowledge, information, and technologies, regardless of geographical, organizational, or sector differences. Therefore, we propose that innovation is more active in countries where social capital has positive externalities, especially those characterized by generalized trust, because this type of social capital is more effective in lowering both transaction and search costs in accessing new knowledge, thereby promoting innovation. In addition, we assume that the informal institutional setting that supports the functional innovation system, in which both external and internal firms effectively use locally embedded resources in Nordic countries, is also characterized as social capital with positive externalities, that is, generalized trust.

8.3 Empirical Analysis

This section examines the relationship between innovation and social capital quantitatively. First, we measure and demonstrate the characteristics of social capital in Nordic countries according to trust categories. Second, we explain the types of social capital that have a significant positive effect on innovation.

8.3.1 *Measurement of Social Capital*

To determine the characteristics of social capital in each country, we used the joint European Values Survey/World Values Survey (EVS/WVS) 2017–2021 dataset. We used the following questions: Do you trust people from your family (v32), people in your neighborhood (v33), people you know personally (v34), people you meet for the first time (v35), people of another religion (v36), and people of another nationality (v37)? The response options were: 1 = trust completely, 2 = trust somewhat, 3 = do not trust very much, and 4 = do not trust at all.

Using this, we conducted principal component analysis and k-means clustering to measure and classify social capital in these countries. First, we conducted principal component analysis to reduce the dimensions of the data vector. The two largest eigenvalues were extracted. Table 8.1 shows eigenvectors for each eigenvalue.[6] The first principal component (PC1) was interpreted as an aggregated indicator to illustrate interpersonal trust in society because all entries of the eigenvector were positive. The second principal component was used as an indicator to explain two categories of trust: generalized and particularized. A high score for the second principal component indicates that the country has social capital with generalized trust since your family (v32), people in your neighborhood (v33), and people you know personally (v34) are negative, whereas people you meet for the first time (v36), people of another religion (v37), and people of another nationality are positive. Thus, when both types of trust are balanced in a country, the score of the second principal component is zero. We then calculated the mean of each principal

Table 8.1 The eigenvectors for each principal component

	1st Principal component	2nd Principal component
Trust in your family	0.20	−0.73
Trust in people in your neighborhood	0.39	−0.39
Trust in people you know personally	0.42	−0.23
Trust in people you meet for the first time	0.44	0.17
Trust in people of another religion	0.46	0.34
Trust in people of another nationality	0.47	0.34

[6] Each element of the first principal component was inverted for ease of interpretation.

component score individually by country to describe the aspect of social capital in an aggregated country.

Next, we apply k-means clustering to classify the social capital of the 89 countries into four groups. Because we must specify the number of clusters in advance, we assume that they should be four according to the Bayesian information criterion (see Fig. 8.4 in Appendix). The results are shown in Fig. 8.2. The vertical axis represents comprehensive trust, and the horizontal axis represents the type of trust. Group 1 had the highest interpersonal trust, followed by Groups 3, 2, and 4. Furthermore, Group 1 is roughly positioned at the center of the horizontal axis, indicating that both generalized and particularized trust are high and balanced. Interestingly, all Nordic countries were clustered into Group 1. The overall tendency of Group 3 was toward generalized trust and embracing a mid-level of aggregated interpersonal trust. In contrast, Group 2, which includes a relatively large

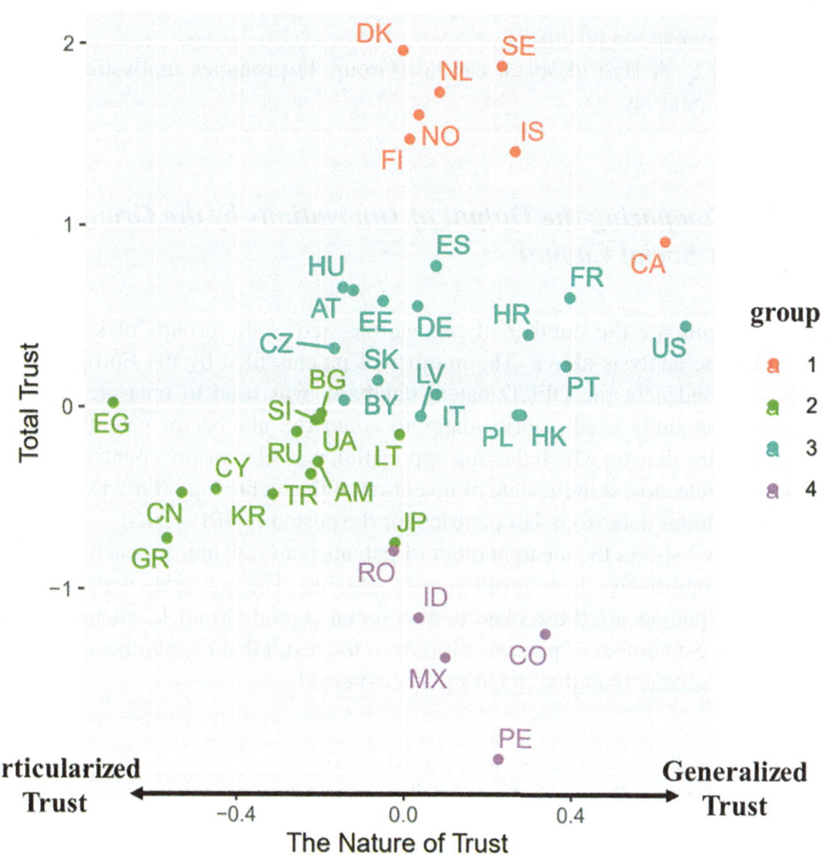

Fig. 8.2 Four groups of social capital. There are only countries included in our regression dataset. The countries included in our dataset are listed in Table 8.6 in Appendix

number of Asian countries, has a strong tendency toward particularized trust. Group 4 had the lowest trust.

Based on the theoretical classification of social capital, we distinguish Groups 1 and 3 as having social capital with positive externalities because these two groups have adequate generalized trust. This result partially supports our hypothesis that Nordic countries have social capital with positive externalities. However, Group 1, which includes the Nordic countries, was an exception. Figure 8.2 indicates that the coexistence of generalized and particularized trust is found in limited cases. Note that this group is characterized by a hybrid type of social capital that distinguishes it from other types of social capital with positive externalities, as demonstrated in Group 3. Furthermore, we assume that only Group 1 can benefit from an effective network that combines closed density and openness (Reagans & Zuckerman, 2001). Thus, the following hypothesis was developed for the regression analysis:

Hypothesis 1: Social capital with positive externalities (Group 1 and Group 3) affects innovation positively.

Hypothesis 2: A Hybrid social capital (Group 1) promotes innovation the most among countries.

8.3.2 Comparing the Output of Innovations by the Group of Social Capital

We now compare the number of innovations across the groups of social capital given by the analysis above. The number of patents filed by the European Patent Office, included in the OECD patent database, was used to measure innovation output. This study used priority dates to count the number of patents. This was defined as the date on which the first application was filed in any country worldwide and is the date closest to the date of invention of the technology (OECD, 2001). Our dataset includes data from 41 countries for the period of 2017–2020.

Figure 8.3 shows the mean number of patents per GDP unit for each social capital group. Intuitively, these results are reasonable. The countries with the highest number of patents are those classified as social capital Group 1, whereas Group 4 has the lowest number of patents. Moreover, the result that the number of patents in Group 1 is greater than that in Group 3 is expected.

8.3.3 Ceteris Paribus Approach

Here, we approach the relationship discussed in the previous section, ceteris paribus. In general, the production of new knowledge (innovation) is described based on Romer's (1990) knowledge production function, partly following previous empirical

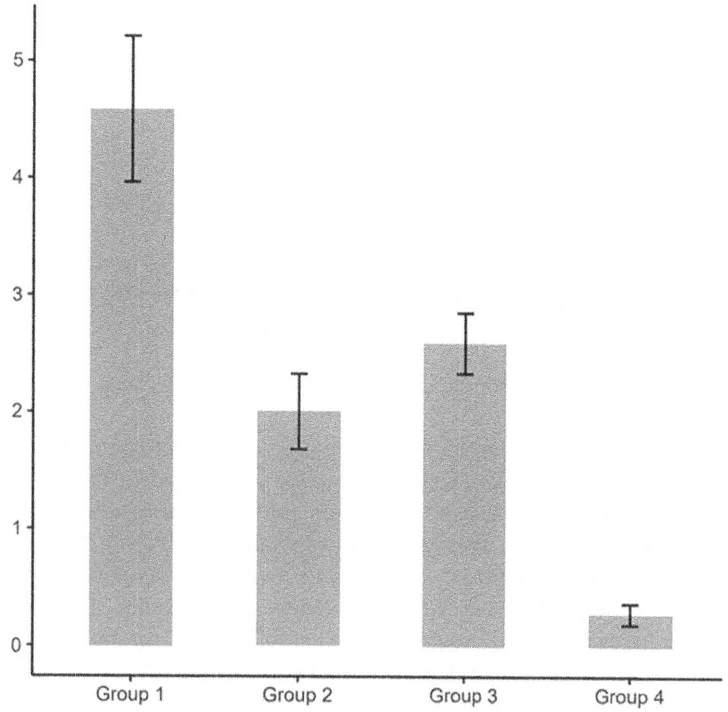

Fig. 8.3 Mean patents per GDP (unit: 10^{-10}). *Note*: The bar charts show the mean number of patents per GDP unit for each social capital group. Error bars indicate 95% confidence intervals

research (e.g., De Dominics et al., 2013[7]). The control variables are selected based on this function, and the specifications are as follows:

$$\ln \dot{A}_{cjt} = \alpha_0 + \alpha_1 \ln A_{cjt} + \alpha_2 \ln R_{ct} + \beta_1 \ln I_c + \gamma_1 SC1_c + \gamma_2 SC2_c + \gamma_3 SC3_c + \theta_{cj} + \tau_t + \varepsilon_{cjt}$$

where $\dot{A}$ is the number of patents, A is the stock of patents, R is the real R&D expenditure, and I is institutional trust. $SC1$, $SC2$, and $SC3$ are social capital group dummies. θ_{cj} is the fixed effect of countries × technology fields, and τ_t is the time fixed effect. Finally, c and j represent the country and technological fields, respectively.

Our empirical model captures the effects of balanced social capital on new knowledge creation. However, it is unclear whether innovation favors social capital with a relative bias toward generalized or particularized trust or whether social capital balances both types of trust. Therefore, we considered not only the effect of social capital that is comparatively biased toward one side, such as in the United

[7] De Dominics et al. (2013) develop the regional model to investigate the impacts of geographical proximity and social capital on innovations following Stern et al. (2000) and Riddel and Schwer (2003).

Table 8.2 Means of the raw scores by country

	Your family	People in your neighbor	People you know personally	People you meet for the first time	People of another religion	People of another nationality
China	3.85	2.99	3.01	1.95	1.98	1.93
Finland	3.88	3.38	3.51	2.65	2.94	2.95
Mexico	3.64	2.49	2.37	1.60	2.03	1.82
United States	3.54	2.76	3.20	2.23	2.78	2.78
Mean of 90 countries	3.77	2.87	3.02	2.06	2.38	2.32

Note: We defined the response scores as follows: 4 = trust completely, 3 = trust somewhat, 2 = do not trust very much, and 1 = do not trust at all. In addition, the gray color indicates a value higher than the mean of the 90 countries

States and China, but also that which is balanced and high, as seen in Finland (see Table 8.2).

We constructed a panel dataset for 41 countries, 8 technology fields of patents, and 4 years (2017–2020). The technology fields correspond to the International Patent Classification. Our balanced panel data consists of 1068 observations. The number and stock of patents were obtained from the OECD Patent Database.[8] Real R&D expenditure was calculated from R&D expenditure (% of GDP) and GDP (constant 2015 US$) from the World Development Indicators. To discriminate between the effects of interpersonal trust and confidence in formal institutions on innovation, we considered the following question in the joint EVS/WVS 2017–2021 dataset indicative of institutional trust: How much confidence do you have in the education system (v117)?[9]

The results of our model are presented in Table 8.3. We provide only the results that include R&D expenditure as a control variable and where both are included because the single correlation between R&D expenditure and patent stock is high at 0.87 (see Table 8.4 in Appendix). In Column (2), countries clustered in Group 1 have a high tendency to produce many innovations, as indicated by the largest coefficient of social capital in Group 1. This result is consistent with our second hypothesis. Column (4) of Table 8.3 shows that the effect of each social capital category on innovation is robust to the addition of patent stock. In other words, the effect does not change fundamentally, either quantitatively or qualitatively.

[8] We calculate a patent stock as follows:

$$A_{cjt} = \dot{A}_{cjt} + (1-\delta)\dot{A}_{cj,t-1} + (1-\delta)^2 \dot{A}_{cj,t-2} + \cdots\cdots + (1-\delta)^k \dot{A}_{cj,t-k}$$

where δ is depreciation of knowledge stock. Our assumption is $\delta = 0.13$, in accordance with Han (2007).

[9] Because of the availability of data, confidence in public institutions other than the education system could not be considered.

Table 8.3 OLS estimation using patent data by country and technical fields

	(1)	(2)	(3)	(4)
R&D Expenditure	1.46*** (0.34)	1.46*** (0.34)	0.66** (0.33)	0.66** (0.33)
Patent Stock			2.82*** (0.34)	2.82*** (0.34)
Social Capital (group 1)		21.49*** (6.65)		28.43*** (6.70)
Social Capital (group 2)		10.02*** (3.79)		19.93*** (4.04)
Social Capital (group 3)		5.33*** (0.91)		−0.24 (1.06)
Institutional Trust		111.09*** (39.31)		196.81*** (16.04)
Country—Technology Dummy	Yes	Yes	Yes	Yes
Year Dummy	Yes	Yes	Yes	Yes
R-squared	0.97	0.97	0.98	0.98
Number of Unique Countries	41	41	41	41
Number of Unique Technology Fields	8	8	8	8
Number of observations	1068	1068	1068	1068

Standard errors in parentheses are robust
* Represents statistical significance: ***$p < 0.01$, **$p < 0.05$, and *$p < 0.1$

8.4 Discussion and Conclusion

This study examines the strength of societies in Nordic countries in terms of the relationship between informal institutional settings and innovation by applying the social capital theory. This study addresses the relationship between social capital and innovation outcomes, as well as the type of social capital in Nordic countries. Evidence from this study shows that countries with hybrid social capital (Group 1) are the most innovative. In addition, it was shown that Nordic countries are characterized by social capital with positive externalities, exceptionally high generalized trust, and particularized trust. These results partially supported our hypotheses.

However, a significantly positive impact on innovation was found for Group 2, which was characterized by particularized trust. A possible explanation for this may be the difference in innovation processes between European and Asian countries. Figure 8.1 shows that European countries have a relatively higher share of patents owned by foreign co-investors than Japan and Korea. Differences in the innovation process affect the type of innovation (product/process innovation or radical/incremental innovation). As previously mentioned, open innovation is suitable for radical innovation. Since this study focused only on the number of innovations per se, it is not possible to distinguish between the quality of innovation outcomes (product innovation, process innovation, etc.). The lack of the type of innovation is the most important limitation of this research. According to Hemphälä and Magnusson

(2012), dense networks are better at supporting incremental innovation, whereas open networks are better at facilitating radical innovation. Therefore, each category may positively affect different types of innovation. Further analysis is needed to examine the relationship between the categories of social capital and the type of innovation.

On the other hand, the most noteworthy finding of this study is that social capital in Nordic countries is characterized by both high generalized and particularized trust. The function of the innovation ecosystem in Nordic countries is characterized by frequent and broad collaboration between multiple actors deeply associated with the hybrid type of social capital. Another question raised by this result is the different nature of particularized trust, which constitutes social capital with negative externalities, from that constituting the hybrid type of social capital. More research is required to account for the coexistence of these two types of trust. Previous research indicates that universal welfare states foster social capital, especially generalized trust (Kumlin & Rothstein, 2005; Levi, 1996; Rothstein, 2002, 2008, 2009; Trägårdh, 2007). Thus, the characteristics of universal welfare states may create an environment that enables the generation of social capital with highly generalized and particularized trust.

In conclusion, this study finds that Nordic societies' strength in innovation is a hybrid type of social capital. As mentioned in Sect. 8.2, little was found in the literature on the relationship between the quality of informal institutions and innovation. Hence, this study contributes to understanding the differences in innovation capacities between countries in terms of informal institutions. Social capital is useful for capturing informal institutions in innovation systems and systematically explaining their effects on innovation. However, previous studies have not quantitatively determined the effect of each social capital category on innovation. Thus, the empirical results strengthen the notion that social capital is an important determinant of innovation.

Acknowledgments This work was supported by a Special Research Grant from Matsuyama University received in FY2023.

Appendix (Fig. 8.4, Tables 8.4, 8.5, and 8.6)

References

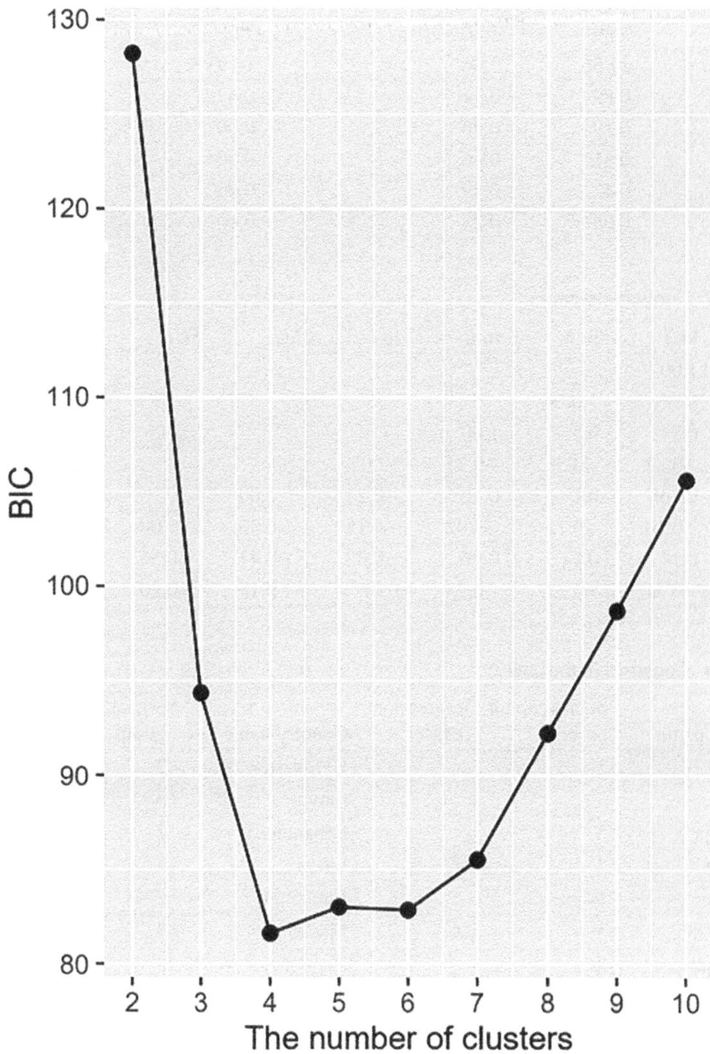

Fig. 8.4 The Bayesian information criterion (BIC) for any k-means clustering

Table 8.4 Summary statistics

Variable	Mean	Standard deviation	Minimum	Maximum
$\ln \dot{A}$	3.88	2.35	−3.40	9.22
$\ln A$	5.89	2.30	1.08	11.13
$\ln R$	22.56	2.06	16.93	27.23
$\ln I$	0.89	0.11	0.62	1.24
$SC1$	0.19	0.40	0.00	1.00
$SC2$	0.31	0.46	0.00	1.00
$SC3$	0.42	0.49	0.00	1.00
$SC4$	0.08	0.28	0.00	1.00

Table 8.5 Correlation matrix

	$\ln \dot{A}$	$\ln A$	$\ln R$	$\ln I$	$SC1$	$SC2$	$SC3$	$SC4$
$\ln \dot{A}$	1.00							
$\ln A$	0.98	1.00						
$\ln R$	0.84	0.87	1.00					
$\ln I$	−0.37	−0.35	−0.35	1.00				
$SC1$	0.16	0.19	0.12	−0.23	1.00			
$SC2$	−0.10	−0.12	−0.02	−0.15	−0.33	1.00		
$SC3$	0.14	0.14	0.06	−0.02	−0.41	−0.56	1.00	
$SC4$	−0.31	−0.31	−0.23	0.61	−0.15	−0.20	−0.25	1.00

Table 8.6 Countries in the dataset

Country name	Social capital group	Regression dataset	Country name	Social capital group	Regression dataset
Albania	2		Kyrgyzstan	2	
Andorra	3		Latvia	3	✓
Argentina	3		Lebanon	2	
Armenia	2	✓	Libya	2	
Australia	1		Lithuania	2	✓
Austria	3	✓	Macao	3	
Azerbaijan	2		Republic of North Macedonia	3	
Bangladesh	2		Malaysia	2	
Belarus	3	✓	Maldives	2	
Plurinational State of Bolivia	4		Mexico	4	✓
Bosnia and Herzegovina	3		Mongolia	2	
Brazil	4		Montenegro	3	
Bulgaria	2	✓	Morocco	4	
Canada	1	✓	Myanmar	2	
Chile	2		Netherlands	1	✓
China	2	✓	New Zealand	1	

(continued)

Table 8.6 (continued)

Country name	Social capital group	Regression dataset	Country name	Social capital group	Regression dataset
Colombia	4	✓	Nicaragua	4	
Croatia	3	✓	Nigeria	4	
Cyprus	2	✓	Norway	1	✓
Czech Republic	3	✓	Pakistan	2	
Denmark	1	✓	Peru	4	✓
Ecuador	4		Philippines	2	
Egypt	2	✓	Poland	3	✓
Estonia	3	✓	Portugal	3	✓
Ethiopia	2		Puerto Rico	3	
Finland	1	✓	Romania	4	✓
France	3	✓	Russian Federation	2	✓
Georgia	2		Serbia	2	
Germany	3	✓	Singapore	3	
Greece	2	✓	Slovakia	3	✓
Guatemala	4		Slovenia	2	✓
Hong Kong	3	✓	Spain	3	✓
Hungary	3	✓	Sweden	1	✓
Iceland	1	✓	Switzerland	1	
Indonesia	4	✓	Taiwan	3	
Islamic Republic of Iran	2		Tajikistan	2	
Iraq	2		Thailand	2	
Italy	3	✓	Tunisia	2	
Japan	2	✓	Turkey	2	✓
Jordan	3		Ukraine	2	✓
Kazakhstan	2		United Kingdom	1	
Kenya	2		United States	3	✓
Republic of Korea	2	✓	Uruguay	2	
Kyrgyzstan	2		Bolivarian Republic of Venezuela	4	
Kenya	2		Viet Nam	2	
Republic of Korea	2	✓	Zimbabwe	2	

Anderson, J. (2007). *Socializing capital, capitalizing the social: Contemporary social democracy and the knowledge economy* [Working Paper Series, #145]. Center for European Studies.

Andreasson, U. (2017). *Trust - The Nordic gold*. Nordic Council of Ministers.

Asheim, B. T., & Coenen, L. (2005). Knowledge bases and regional innovation systems: Comparing Nordic clusters. *Research Policy, 34*(8), 1173–1190.

Asheim, B. T., Isaksen, A., & Trippl, M. (2019). *Advanced introduction to regional innovation systems*. Edward Elgar Publishing Limited.

Asheim, B. T., Isaksen, A., & Trippl, M. (2020). The role of the regional innovation system approach in contemporary regional policy: Is it still relevant in a globalised world? In M. González-López & B. T. Asheim (Eds.), *Regions and innovation policies in Europe: Learning from the margins* (pp. 12–29). Edger Elgar Publishing Limited.

Bertilsson, T. M., & Hjorth-Andersen, C. (2009). The Nordic welfare state. In G. T. Svendsen & G. L. H. Svendsen (Eds.), *Handbook of social capital: The troika of Sociology, political science and economics* (pp. 212–227). Edward Elgar Publishing.

Bourdieu, P. (1986). The forms of capital. In J. G. Richardson (Ed.), *Handbook of theory and research for the sociology of education* (pp. 241–258). Greenwood Press.

Burt, R. S. (2001). Structural holes versus network closure as social capital. In N. Lin, K. Cook, & R. S. Burt (Eds.), *Social capital: Theory and research* (pp. 31–56). Aldine de Gruyter.

Cammarano, A., Michelino, F., & Caputo, M. (2019). Open innovation practices for knowldge acquision and their effects on innovation output. *Technology Analysis & Strategic Management, 31*(11), 1297–1313.

Chesbrough, H. (2017). The future of open innovation. *Research-Technology Management, 60*(1), 35–38.

Chesbrough, H., & Bogers, M. (2014). Explicating open innovation: Clarifying an emerging paradigm for understanding innovation. In H. Chesbrough (Ed.), *New frontiers in open Innovation* (pp. 3–28). Oxford University Press.

Coleman, J. S. (1998). Social capital in the creation of human capital. *American Journal of Sociology, 94*, S95–S120.

Cooke, P. (1998). Introduction: Origins of the concept. In P. Cooke, M. Heidenreich, & H. J. Braczyk (Eds.), *Regional innovation systems* (2nd ed., pp. 1–18). Routledge.

De Dominics, L., Florax, R. J. G. M., de Groot, L. F., & H. (2013). Regional clusters of innovative activity in Europe: Are social capital and geographical proximity key determinants? *Applied Economics, 45*(17), 2325–2335.

Echebarria, C., & Barrutia, J. M. (2013). Limits of social capital as a driver of innovation: An empirical analysis in the context of European regions. *Regional Studies, 47*(7), 1001–1017.

Fukuyama, F. (1995). Social capital and the global economy. *Foreign Affairs, 74*(5), 89–103.

Fukuyama, F. (2001). Social capital, civil society and development. *Third World Quarterly, 22*(1), 7–20.

Granovetter, M. S. (1973). The strength of weak ties. *American Journal of Sociology, 78*, 1360–1380.

Holmberg, S., & Rothstein, B. (2020). *Social trust-The Nordic gold? QOG, Working Paper Series, 1*, 1–25.

Han, Y. J. (2007). Measuring industrial knowledge stocks with patents and papers. *Journal of Informetrics, 1*, 269–276.

Hemphälä, J., & Magnusson, M. (2012). Networks for innovation – but what networks and what innovation? *Creativity and Innovation Management, 21*(1), 3–16.

Kääriäinen, J., & Lehtonen, H. (2006). The variety of social capital in welfare state regimes - A comparative study of 21 countries. *European Societies, 8*(1), 27–57.

Kitai, M. (2018). Discussion on the relationship between the generosity of welfare state and the category of social capital. *Social Policy and Labor Studies, 10*(3), 108–118.

Kristensen, I., & Dubois, A. (2021). Social constructing of a rural bioeconomy cluster: The case of the Processum biorefinery complex in northern Sweden. *Journal of Rural Studies, 86*, 87–96.

Kumlin, S., & Rothstein, B. (2005). Making and breaking social capital the impact of welfare state institutions. *Comparative Political Studies, 38*(4), 339–365.

Laursen, K., Masciarelli, F., & Prencipe, A. (2014). Regions matter: How localized social capital affects innovation and external knowledge acquisition. *Organization Science, 23*(1), 177–193.

Levi, M. (1996). Social and unsocial capital: A review essay of Robert Putnam's making democracy work. *Politics and Society, 24*(1), 45–55.

Lin, N. (2001). *Social capital a theory of social structure and action*. Cambridge University Press.

Lundvall, B. Å. (1992). *National systems of innovation: Towards a theory of innovation and interactive learning*. Pinter Publisher.

Mazzucato, M. (2019). *Governing Missions in the European Union*, European Commission, Luxembourg.

Mazzucato, M. (2021). *Mission economy- A moonshot guide to changing capitalism*, Penguin UK.

Nahapiet, J., & Ghoshal, S. (1998). Social capital, intellectual capital, and the organizational advantage. *Academy of Management Review, 23*(2), 242–266.

OECD. (2001). Using patent counts for cross-country comparisons of technology output. *STI Review, 27*, 129–146.

Ostrom, E., & Ahn, T. K. (2009). The meaning of social capital and its link to collective action. In G. T. Svendsen & G. L. H. Svendsen (Eds.), *Handbook of social capital: The troika of Sociology, political science and economics* (pp. 17–35). Edward Elgar Publishing.

Putnam, R. D. (1993). *Making democracy work: Civic traditions in modern Italy*. Princeton University Press.

Putnam, R. D. (2001). *Bowling alone: The collapse and revival of American community*. Simon and Schuster.

Reagans, R., & Zuckerman, E. (2001). Networks, diversity, and productivity: The social capital of corporate R&D Teams. *Organization Science, 12*, 502–517.

Riddel, M., & Schwer, R. K. (2003). Regional innovative capacity with endogenous employment: Empirical evidence from the US. *The Review of Regional Studies, 33*, 73–84.

Romer, P. M. (1990). Endogenous technological change. *Journal of Political Economy, 98*(5), 71–102.

Rothstein, B. (2002). Social capital in the social democratic state. In R. D. Putnam (Ed.), *Democracies in flux: The evolution of social capital in contemporary society* (pp. 289–332). Oxford University Press.

Rothstein, B. (2008). The state and social capital: An institutional theory of generalized trust. *Comparative Politics, 40*(4), 441–459.

Rothstein, B. (2009). The universal welfare state. In G. T. Svendsen & G. L. H. Svendsen (Eds.), *Handbook of social capital: The troika of Sociology, political science and economics* (pp. 197–211). Edward Elgar Publishing.

Schot, J., & Steinmueller, W. E. (2018). Three frames for innovation policy: R&D, systems of innovation and transformative change. *Research Policy, 47*(9), 1554–1567.

Serger, S. S., & Palmberg, C. (2022). Towards transformative policy in Finland and Sweden: Some viewpoints from practice. In M. Benner, G. Marklund, & S. S. Serger (Eds.), *Smart policies for societies in transition the innovation challenge of inclustion, resilience and sustainability* (pp. 143–188). Edward Elgar Publishing.

Steinmo, S. (2010). *The evolution of modern states: Sweden, Japan, and the United States*. Cambridge University Press.

Statistics Finland. (2006). *Social capital in Finland-Statistical review*. Statistics Finland. Social Statistics.

Stern, S., Porter, M. E., & Furman, J. L. (2000). *The determinants of national innovative capacity* [Working Paper, No. 7876]. National Bureau of Economic Research.

Stiglitz, J. E., & Greenwald, B. C. (2015). *Creating a learning society: A new approach to growth, development, and social progress*. Columbia University Press.

Svendsen, G. T., & Svendsen, G. L. H. (2009). The troika of sociology, political science and economics. In G. T. Svendsen & G. L. H. Svendsen (Eds.), *Handbook of social capital: The troika of Sociology, political science and economics* (pp. 1–13). Edward Elgar Publishing.

Trägårdh, L. (2007). The "civil society" debate in Sweden: The welfare state challenged. In L. Trägårdh (Ed.), *State and civil society in Northern Europe: The Swedish model reconsidered* (pp. 254–270). Berghahn books.

Westlund, H., Larsson, J. P., & Olsson, A. R. (2014). Start-ups and local entrepreneurial social capital in the municipalities of Sweden. *Regional Studies, 48*(6), 974–994.

Yamagishi, T. (1998). *The structure of trust – The evolutionary games of mind and society*. University of Tokyo Press.

Yamagishi, T., & Yamagishi, M. (1994). Trust and commitment in the United States and Japan. *Motivation and Emotion, 18*(2), 129–166.

Part III
The Evolution of the Welfare State and New Welfare Governance

Chapter 9
Creative Evolution of Finnish Regional Governance

Pekka Valkama and Lasse Oulasvirta

Abstract This study identifies the kinds of public policy reforms that have shaped Finnish regional governance to discern the main developmental phases it has undergone. The idea is to deepen the understanding concerning the problematic features of the latitude of regional public affairs and role of regional policymaking in constructing, shaping, and consolidating the Finnish welfare state. Our study is based on a literature review and analyses of law drafting materials and ministerial and other governmental reviews and white papers. The main historical phases of regional governance include four distinct eras. During the first, locally developed reform initiatives generated frail systems of regional public services. The second era entailed the expansion and consolidation of regional public services based on inter-municipal collaboration (IMC). The third aimed to improve efficiency through further regionalisation and amalgamations. At the beginning of 2023, the latest era started with the foundation of new welfare regions. The creative evolution of regional governance has been flexible and evolving, enabled some regional variations, and improved economies of scale. In addition, it has been unpredictable and progressed without a stable consensus concerning the societal functions of the regional public authorities. Above all, it has supported undemocratic regional structures.

Keywords Regional public services · Inter-municipal collaboration · Wellbeing services counties

P. Valkama (✉)
Turku School of Economics, University of Turku, Turku, Finland

City of Helsinki, Finland
e-mail: pekka.valkama@tuni.fi

L. Oulasvirta
Tampere University, Tampere, Finland
e-mail: lasse.oulasvirta@tuni.fi

N. Tokumaru et al. (eds.), *Creative Co-evolution of the Economies and Welfare States in the Nordic Countries*, Evolutionary Economics and Social Complexity Science 32, https://doi.org/10.1007/978-981-97-8569-8_9

9.1 Introduction

Regional governance is a distinct type of ruling system that aims to manage the public affairs of regions, which are geographical areas situated between local governments and a nation state. In its purest form, regional governance is realised by the regional authorities pursuing the regions' collective interests. These regional authorities have their own public bodies, but they also engage and guide various stakeholders in pursuing regional public welfare (Anttiroiko et al., 2011; Bevir, 2010; Hooghe et al., 2010; Widuto, 2018).

Many previous studies have contended that Western European countries need to develop and refine their regional governance systems. Hulst (2005) has argued that well-planned regional governance would enhance the functionality of democracy and improve the accountability of public policymaking. Hudson (2005) has claimed that as regional issues vary in different regions, national legislatures face growing challenges devising nationally unified solutions, ultimately requiring the delegation of some public duties to regional bodies. Nevertheless, European countries have tackled the challenges of regional governance in various ways, reflecting national administrative traditions or newly adopted reformist ideologies (Tavares & Feiock, 2018).

In this book chapter, we analyse the creative evolution of regional governance in Finland, focusing on both the regional public authorities and services. The aim is to identify the kinds of public policy reforms that have shaped Finnish regional governance to discern the main developmental phases it has undergone. Our idea is to deepen understanding of the scope and latitude of regional public affairs and the role of regional policymaking in constructing, shaping, and consolidating the Finnish welfare state.

We focus on the direct and indirect democratic governance of regional public affairs and services while excluding the state's regional agents and provincial administration from our analyses. On the one hand, the study is based on an extensive literature review systematising and summarising perspectives reported in the research literature. On the other hand, the study relies on the analyses of law drafting materials and ministerial and other governmental reviews and white papers recognising principal policy arguments and specifying some details of the public policy reforms.

9.2 Analytical Framework

9.2.1 Regionalisation as a Precondition of Regional Governance

Regionalisation can be understood as the creation of a new intermediary administrative level or strengthening the existing regional authorities and other institutions acting between the state and local governments (Anttiroiko & Valkama, 2017;

CDLR, 1998; Hörnström, 2013; Le Gales & Lequesne, 1998). The process of regionalisation progresses through the decentralisation of national responsibilities or the centralisation (i.e. aggregation) of local functions (Anttiroiko & Valkama, 2017; Blomqvist & Bergman, 2010; CDLR, 1998; Schrijver, 2005). Since the late 1980s, a prevailing global trend of central-regional-local relationships has been political decentralisation, as state governments have sought to transfer some decision-making powers to lower levels of public administration (Loughlin, 2009). However, Sharpe (1993) has demonstrated that unitary states have encountered more challenges than federal states in establishing functional administrative systems for regional governance (cf. Hulst, 2005).

Three alternative theorems have been developed to explain the progress of regional governance in the context of small European unitary states (Olsson & Åström, 2003). According to the first, the strengthening of regions can be understood as a result of Europeanisation, which has emphasised the ideology of 'the regions of Europe' in the policies of the European Union (EU). This doctrine highlights the need for regional economic cohesion within and between countries (cf. Antunes & Loughlin, 2020; Sjöblom, 2020). The Europeanisation of Finland's national economy and legal system was realised through Finland's memberships of pan-European organisations and its access to the European Single Market (ESM). For example, Finland gained full membership of the Council of Europe in 1989 and updated some of its human rights legislation, committing to the European Charter of Local Self-Government (ECLSG, 1985). Even more remarkable steps were Finland's membership of the European Economic Area (EEA) in 1994 and its EU membership 1 year later.

The second theorem challenges the first by asserting that the role of Europeanisation has been interpreted too simplistically. It argues that regionalisation processes and reforms of regional governance possess national and country-specific characteristics shaped or controlled primarily by domestic policy traditions and a nation state holding the highest authority (Hörnström, 2013; Kettunen & Kungla, 2005; Olsson & Åström, 2003).

The third theorem explains that regionalisation represents the forces of regional mobilisation driven by defensive, competitive, or separatist rationales. Regions develop their own initiatives either to protect themselves from external forces and negative changes, position themselves more competitively in the globalising world, or to emphasise or support their linguistic or ethnic qualities (Tomblin, 2007).

The arguments regarding the potential benefits and drawbacks of regional governance between the state and local governments have focused on the issues of efficiency, spillovers, and equity (Hall et al., 2018). It has been suggested that the regional delivery of public services, which would otherwise be performed by municipalities, could enhance economic efficiency by realising economies of scale and scope in service production. The regional service systems would also internalise negative and positive spillover effects caused by local investments and operations (Verhoest, 2013). Proponents of regionalisation also contend that the regionalised services will promote equity among citizens of different communities by consolidating locally dispersed service structures (Hall et al., 2018).

From the perspective of public choice theorists, powerful regional governance is viewed as problematic or detrimental, as it diminishes or eliminates competition between municipalities. They argue that economic efficiency is predominantly improved through decentralised government structures in which numerous small municipalities are compelled to compete for mobile citizens and enterprises by offering suitable combinations of local taxes and services (Boyne, 1997). Advocates of municipal governance argue that spillover issues can be mitigated by financial compensation schemes or state grants, maintaining decentralised structures while strengthening local autonomy. They also posit that regional governance cannot guarantee enhanced regional equity, and equity can be supported through alternative means such as national public policies delivering redistributive programmes (Coaffee, 2005; Hall et al., 2018).

9.2.2 Regional Governments vs. Inter-Municipal Collaboration

Fundamentally, regionalisation may progress either through the creation of regional governments or developing the systems of inter-municipal collaboration (IMC) (Hulst, 2005; Tavares & Feiock, 2018). Regional governments are formal public law bodies designed to perform long-term duties. Genuine regional governments are also democratic institutions and normally have general competence and taxation rights, even though their real features and administrative capacities are country-specific. The classic argument for regional governments is that they secure the public interest in a democratic society by promoting pluralism, participation, and public choice (the 3Ps). In this conceptual 3P scheme, pluralism refers to the capacity of the public body to accommodate alternative political views to avoid a tendency of centralised autocracy. The key idea of participation is to provide the opportunity for people to play an active role in society, acquiring the habits and skills which underpin democratic foundations. A regional government may also serve as a platform of public choices by providing services in accordance with regional needs and preferences, rather than in accordance with uniform national standards (Bailey, 2008; Young, 1988).

According to some other arguments, regional governments are needed to perform regional planning to coordinate local authorities' polices, govern negative and positive externalities originating in local communities, and fix the failures of state planning. A more practical argument has been that regional governments would provide better access to European funding. Nevertheless, it is important to pay attention to contextual factors when evaluating these arguments. For example, if a country has geographically large and populous local authorities covering their residents' coherent working areas, the need for regional governments is smaller than in the case of very many small municipalities with overlapping commuting areas (Hulst, 2005).

Regionalisation without regional governments through inter-municipal joint efforts is a case of horizontal collaboration and represents a territorially varying administrative ideology. Municipalities may collaborate by creating joint municipal organisations (JMOs) or by signing mutual contracts. By abstract terms, the concept of collaboration refers to joint working or a process of working by shared contributions to promote the achievement of common goals (Rayle & Zegras, 2013). By working together, municipalities aim to achieve something impossible for a local authority acting alone (Sorrentino & Simonetta, 2013).

Both Metze and Levelt (2012) and Hulst (2005) have emphasised potentially negative impacts of IMC. Hulst argues that while municipalities may have some common interests, they also have incompatible interests, making IMC risky. He claims that IMC causes efficiency losses and democratic deficiency because inter-municipal organisations (IMOs) are not governed by citizen-elected representatives. Metze and Levelt (2012) state that many differences in local cultures and interests and weak administrative skills may hinder and prevent the applicability and functionality of collaborative initiatives in the municipal sector. The theory of collaborative advantage, which has been developed by analysing collaborative relationships in the context of public services, points out that although delivering some benefits, collaborative arrangements may suffer or even fail due to collaborative inertia, which arises as opposing interests interfere, or as mistrust replaces trust (Huxham, 2003).

However, IMC may be a flexible alternative for juridically strictly regulated and territorially fixed regional governments able to scale up or scale down regional activities more easily. IMC enables diversified bodies and structures in different parts of a region or a state. As municipalities may also collaborate through private law entities, municipalities can be flexible and make decisions quickly, limiting the financial risk of collaboration to the share capital they have invested.

9.2.3 Key Dimensions of Regional Public Authorities

In this study, a regional public authority is understood as a joint public body of local governments or a proper regional government with democratic institutions. The regional public authority has single, continuous, and non-intersecting boundaries, including a large area that covers multiple jurisdictions of the local authorities (Hooghe et al., 2010). According to Hooghe et al. (2010), the regional public authority must have some capacity for authoritative decision-making and exercising power over those who live or run a business on its territory. Table 9.1 presents an applied set of questions for evaluating the political foundations and capacity of the regional public authorities.

Regional authorities may be defined and protected by a constitution, or they are created and empowered by lower norms like ordinary laws or statutory orders. The institutional depth of the regional authorities is a complex issue from the perspective of autonomy, but it can be approached by the fundamental questions concerning 'freedom to' and 'freedom from'. The policy scope of the regional authorities is extensive if they have general competence. In opposite cases, the regional

Table 9.1 Key dimensions of regional authorities (adapted from Marks et al., 2008; Hooghe et al., 2010)

	The authority exercised by a regional public authority over those who live, own properties, and engage in a trade on its territory
Constitutional position	The position and protection given by a constitution to a regional public authority
Institutional depth	The extent to which a regional government is autonomous rather than deconcentrated
Policy scope	The range of public policies for which a regional government is responsible
Fiscal autonomy	The extent to which a regional government can independently tax its residents and enterprises
Representation	The extent to which regional residents govern and control a regional government

authorities are allowed to operate only in one field of public service industry or a corresponding one. When fiscal autonomy is evaluated, the focus is often on income and expenditure autonomy (Oulasvirta & Turala, 2009). Regional elections and participation systems are the key elements of the representative characters of the regional authorities.

9.3 The Context of Finnish Regional Governance

Finland used to be understood as a decentralised unitary state with a two-tier system of government, including the national central (i.e. state) government and local governments. Finland is also an institutional welfare state, practising detailed welfare state policies in the framework of the Nordic welfare ideology, which emphasises the realisation of the civil and basic rights of citizens. In this welfare state model, the role of the state government is strong, as it has sole legislative powers and multiple sources of tax revenues. The state government takes care of foreign policy and security, including the army and police, the legal system, legislation, the funding of higher education, and social security, while local governments are responsible for important and extensive community and welfare services, supporting citizens' everyday life (Salminen, 2008).

Stoker et al. (1996) classifies European countries by whether they are federal, classic unitary, devolving, or regionalised states. In Table 9.2, they present Finland in two categories—the primary category of the classic unitary state without brackets, and the secondary category of a devolving unitary state in brackets—for a special reason. Finland is in the category of devolving unitary states, as it lacks elected regional authorities, only having joint municipal authorities (JMAs), except for the special arrangement of the Region of Åland. It was therefore more appropriate to classify Finland without brackets as a classic unitary state.

Table 9.2 Two typologies of European states (Bailey, 2008; Stoker et al., 1996)

Stoker et al. (1996)	*Federal*	*Classic Unitary*	*Devolving Unitary*	*Regionalised*
	Austria Belgium Germany	Denmark **Finland** Greece Ireland Luxembourg Sweden UK	France the Netherlands Portugal **(Finland)**	(Belgium) Italy Spain
Bailey (2008)	*Regional governments established within formally federal structures*	*Autonomous regions founded within the constitutions of member states but not part of a federal structure and not covering the nation as a whole*	*Regions located within local government systems*	
	Austria Belgium Germany	**Finland** Italy Portugal Spain UK	France the Netherlands Denmark Norway Sweden	

A JMA is a regional or sub-regional public law body and juridically independent organisation with its own legal capacities and internal governance bodies. Two or more Finnish local governments can establish this kind of joint municipal authority. JMAs lack general competence, as their sphere of authority is limited to performing tasks in a specific field of public services defined in their basic agreements signed by owner municipalities. JMAs are allowed to own real and movable properties, sign contracts, and contract debts without authorisation from their owners. However, their member municipalities bear financial risks since they have the juridical responsibility for their JMAs' commitments (Valkama et al., 2016).

In Table 9.2, Bailey (2008) categorises European countries in three categories from the perspective of regional governance. According to his evaluation, Finland has some similarities with Italy, Portugal, Spain, and the UK because these countries are not based on federated structures but have autonomous regions not covering the nation as a whole.

As a sovereign country, Finland gained its independence in 1917, and the country's constitution was confirmed in 1919. Municipalities as democratic governance institutions were included in the constitution, which also confirmed that municipalities had local self-government. However, the regions did not receive the same constitutional position because the self-government of the regions was defined as a matter of ordinary legislation. This constitutional premise created an administrative framework that maintained the weak relevance of the regions (Sjöblom, 2020) for a long period: it took more than a 100 years before the Finnish parliament could establish modified versions of regional governments with limited self-government.

9.4 Evolution of Regional Governance Through Inter-Municipal Collaboration

9.4.1 Regionalisation Before the Second World War

Historically, Finnish municipalities have been too small to make independent efforts to build up the modern institutions of a welfare state. For example, at the beginning of the twentieth century, Finland had as many as 510 municipalities, making their average size very small given that the entire population of the country was only 2,655,900. Some municipalities had already begun to develop sub-regional services based on municipal–municipal collaboration in the 1860s (Hietalahti, 2016). The first joint municipal mental hospital was established in Harjavalta in 1903; the second was established during the First World War. The first joint municipal tuberculosis sanatorium, established by 21 municipalities, was opened in Oulainen in 1914 (Manninen, 2010; Mykkänen, 2012).

Regionalisation was accelerated in 1929 by a new law giving state grants to municipalities if they operated mental hospitals and tuberculosis sanatoriums. The law partly integrated the state finances into local public services and promoted the construction of new joint municipal health services in the 1930s (Manninen, 2010).

The first mental hospitals and the tuberculosis sanatoriums were often governed by joint meetings of the representatives of municipalities regulated by the Municipal Act. However, some were limited companies regulated by company law. Because the joint meetings' operation models were difficult to standardise, the new Municipal Act in 1932 introduced a union of municipalities *(kuntainliitto)* as a new organisational public law form to be voluntarily used in IMC (Manninen, 2010).

The state government owned and funded Finnish hospitals, while the municipalities took care of basic healthcare services based on the work of municipal general practitioners and the operations of municipal hospitals and sick rooms. Some municipalities began to demonstrate a greater interest in being involved in the special healthcare governance system because the state had difficulties in funding medical services and repairing hospital buildings. The Turku region's municipalities were the first ones to take responsibility for a regional state hospital. This transfer of the state hospital was a prime mover of a new phase, which gradually resulted in the full municipalisation of the state hospitals by JMAs (Saarivirta et al., 2010).

A special region of Åland (*Ahvenanmaa*) was also established soon after Finland's independence and the First World War. The Åland Islands lie between Finland and Sweden. Åland is an example of regional mobilisation because as Swedish speakers, the islands' residents wished to become citizens of Sweden after Finland gained its independence. The Finnish parliament reacted to these demands by giving autonomy to the region in issuing a special law in 1920. However, Finland and Sweden disputed the islands' position, resulting in the League of Nations was asked to intervene and find a solution. The League of Nations resolved the conflicting territorial claims by confirming that Åland belonged to Finland, with the condition that its cultural customs, linguistic foundations, local customs, and self-governing administrative system must be preserved. The Finnish Constitution in force guarantees that Åland has legal powers to enact laws in specified public policy areas (Arter, 2022).

9.4.2 Reforms of Regional Governance Between the 1940s and the Late 1980s

In 1943, a new law obliged municipalities to fund 50% of the costs of special healthcare hospitals, referring to the former state regional hospitals now called central hospitals (Saarivirta et al., 2010). The state ownership of these central hospitals was transferred to the special healthcare JMAs (called the unions of municipalities until the early 1990s) after the Second World War.

Statutory JMAs were introduced in 1948, when all municipalities were required to be members of a JMA taking care of tuberculosis sanatoriums. The compulsory regionalisation was accelerated in 1952 by the new law on mental hospitals and in 1956 by the new law on general hospitals. In 1958, the new law on vocational education did not formally introduce compulsory JMAs, but as it required municipalities to book student places in the vocational schools, it contributed in practice to the founding of novel regional schools taken care of by educational JMAs. These were the key reforms expanding and standardising regional governance through statutory JMAs as organisational tools to advance the aims of the Finnish welfare state. Furthermore, the municipalities continued their bottom-up efforts to improve the supply of municipal services by establishing fresh voluntary JMAs. In the 1950s, JMAs' expenditure grew more than twice as rapidly as the expenditure of municipalities (Manninen, 2010).

The first and bottom-up regional land-use plan was published in Satakunta Region in 1942, drafted by the famous architect Alvar Aalto. Regional land-use planning was regularised from 1959, when the legislature made the regional land-use plans compulsory. Municipalities began to establish compulsory JMAs as new regional planning authorities (*seutukaavaliitto*). The representation of the Finnish regions and the preservation of local and regional heritage were not then priorities, as these operations were taken care of by regional associations (*maakuntaliitot*). Municipalities funded and were the members of these associations, which were private law bodies operating on a non-profit basis.

The expansion of the public welfare services through regional authorities owned by municipalities was enabled by the country's economic growth after the war. Manufacturing industries could expand and renew their production lines and hire new workers. Cities also started to grow more quickly than before by welcoming new residents, while workers were liberated from traditional occupations based on agriculture and forestry. The public sector took its share of the economic growth by enjoying growing tax revenues, introducing new taxes, and increasing the rates of existing taxes, enabling them to allocate more state funds to public service systems at the national, regional, and local levels.

The municipal health services were upgraded and standardised in 1972 when the National Health Act (*kansanterveyslaki*) came into effect. Municipalities had to replace municipal general practitioners, who were often individuals carrying on a trade, by establishing municipal health centres (*terveyskeskus*), which hired various medical and healthcare personnel as municipal sector employees. As it was impractical and too expensive to build health centres for small local governments, such municipalities created sub-regional entities and established voluntary JMAs for public health work (Ihatsu, 2014; Niemelä & Saarinen, 2015). Some local authorities also developed selected inter-municipal health services through contractual arrangements without establishing a separate legal entity.

Mandatory requirements to perform IMC in healthcare through JMAs expanded from special healthcare to the care of the disabled. The Act on Special Care for People with Intellectual Disabilities (*laki kehitysvammaisten erityishuollosta*) was enacted in 1977, requiring all municipalities to be a member of a JMA as a district for the special care of the intellectually disabled (*erityishuoltopiiri*). At first, municipalities organised 14 statutory JMA districts. Later, the number of JMAs decreased, as some JMAs were amalgamated with JMAs responsible for special healthcare (Hakoma & Niemelä, 2018).

The central government advanced the development of regional service systems through two essential means. The most important was to decree such legislation which introduced the statutory JMAs to special healthcare, regional planning and development, and the care of the disabled. The state grant system also played an important role because the state grants were earmarked and cost-based contributions given directly to JMAs and supported their financial independency from their member local governments even though they were fully owned by the member municipalities (Niemelä & Saarinen, 2015).

9.4.3 Reforms of Regional Governance from the Late 1980s to 2022

The Europeanisation of the economy and Finland's legal system also created some changes in regional governance and promoted the further regionalisation of municipalities' local services. The organisation and role of regional planning and development were reconsidered in the early 1990s because of Finland's EEA membership. Regional councils (*maakuntien liitot*) were created by amalgamating the regional planning authorities and regional associations based on the Act on Regional Development in 1994. The reform was needed to redesign regional governance structures to meet certain terms regulating the national regional policy stipulated by the EEA agreement and to fulfil the EU's accession requirements (HE, 1993a; Kull, 2009). The regional councils were created as statutory JMAs responsible for regional development and planning and the management and allocation of EU structural funds (Anttiroiko & Valkama, 2017; HE, 1993a; Kull, 2009). There were 18 of these kinds of JMAs on Finland's mainland in 2024.

After a long period of economic growth, Finland's national economy drifted into a recession in the early 1990s because of the strong difficulties of a carelessly liberated banking sector and losses in foreign trade. Until the 1980s, the regionalisation was mostly based on the expansion aims of municipal welfare services, but the main motivational factors to the regionalisation subsequently changed. The state government then began to prefer reform policies designed to increase efficiency, productivity, and effectiveness (cf. HE, 1988; HE, 2006). As Table 9.3 illustrates, some new reforms clearly reduced the number of JMAs through their amalgamations.

Municipal waste management used to be a local and in-house function of local authorities, but the EU's environmental and waste directives forced Finland to update its waste legislation and begin to upgrade the methods of waste treatment in use. According to the new targets of waste policies, landfilling of waste should be decreased radically by increasing recycling and the reuse of waste materials and the energy recovery of waste. The central government concluded that nearly all municipalities must collaborate to enable these targets to be achieved. Municipalities had to begin to close their local landfills and build new and modern waste treatment facilities. The central government strongly insisted on the regionalisation of municipal waste management, as it considered single municipalities were too small to introduce such radical changes. A new waste management law came into force in 1993 that stipulated that municipalities must regionalise the organisation and finances of their waste management services primarily on a voluntary basis. If municipalities would not make voluntary arrangements, the central government

Table 9.3 Development of the number of municipalities, average population size of municipalities, number of municipal employees and civil servants, and number of joint municipal authorities between 1972 and 2021 (adapted from Valkama & Oulasvirta, 2021)

Year	Number of municipalities	Average population size of municipalities	Number of municipal employees and civil servants	Number of joint municipal authorities (JMAs)
1972	512	9089	209,000	321
1976	475	9960	273,000	384
1980	464	10,318	317,000	403
1984	461	10,616	384,000	381
1988	461	10,747	430,000	422
1992	460	10,989	412,000	286
1996	455	11,280	409,000	250
2000	452	11,463	416,000	231
2004	444	11,794	431,000	217
2008	415	12,834	437,000	164
2012	336	16,151	437,000	130
2017	311	17,727	419,000	118
2021	309	17,955	434,000	121

made it clear that it might introduce stricter collaborative requirements. This was a turning point in the governance of municipal waste management because municipalities began to establish JMOs throughout the country, and the state did not need to introduce any more severe legislative measures. Nowadays, about 93% of local authorities now run their waste management services through JMOs. Most of the inter-municipal waste management organisations are joint municipally owned corporations (JMOCs), but some local authorities still prefer to use JMAs (HE, 1993b; Valkama, 2013; Valkama et al., 2022).

The reform of fire and rescue services illustrates a nationally led regionalisation of local services that aimed to improve economies of scale and risk governance. Lawmakers enacted a new law in 2001 that closed down the local governance of the fire and rescue services and regionalised them based on 22 rescue regions. Municipalities had the opportunity to choose whether they wished to collaborate by signing inter-municipal contracts or operating the services via JMAs. Regional governance through contracting enabled a flexible arrangement through joint committees, without establishing a separate legal entity. The joint committees were shared governance bodies hosted by a single local government, called a host municipality by the Municipal Act in force. The host municipality model of the joint committee based on contracting proved popular, as only two new rescue areas (Lapland and Päijät-Häme) decided to organise their service via JMAs (Haiko, 2014; Kallio & Tolppi, 2012).

The system of Finnish polytechnics (i.e. universities of applied sciences) was created in the early 1990s. First, the state transferred the ownership of its secondary schools to municipalities. Second, the former state secondary schools and selected municipal secondary schools were upgraded by making them polytechnics. Several new municipal polytechnics were in-house entities owned by single municipalities; others were jointly owned by many local authorities operating as JMAs and JMOCs. When the new Polytechnics Act (*ammattikorkeakoululaki*) came into effect in 2015, it introduced the compulsory corporatisation of all polytechnics, discontinuing the use of JMAs (Linna, 2016).

The municipal and service structures were reformed by top-down measures between 2007 and 2012 by the 'Paras' reform (*paras* means 'the best' in English). The aim of the reform was to increase efficiency and productivity in municipal services and create such organisational structures which would have a sufficient structural and financial basis for their provision of services. The ultimate goal of the 'Paras' reform regarding basic health and social care was to guarantee a minimum population base of 20,000 for the organisations responsible for such services. A minimum population requirement for vocational education was 50,000 residents. In practice, to achieve these targets municipalities had to make municipal mergers or establish new regional governance institutions. However, some special circumstances enabled municipalities to overlook the requirements concerning the population bases. The central government let municipalities decide whether they create the new regions of these services through JMOs or contracting based on the host municipal model (Anttiroiko & Valkama, 2017; Satka & Hämeenaho, 2015; Valkama & Oulasvirta, 2021). Local governments welcomed the reform with controversial attitudes, but it produced significant organisational changes. The number of municipalities fell by 95 from 2006 to 2011 due to voluntary municipal mergers implemented with the support of special state amalgamation grants (see Table 9.3). In all, 230 municipalities regionalised their services through 63 new collaboration regions (Valkama & Oulasvirta, 2021).

The reformist 'Paras' programme managed by the state government also included efforts to regionalise some duties of municipalities in the capital (i.e. Helsinki) region. The idea was to create a new metropolitan body to take care of land-use planning and housing, public transport, and some other public policies, but these plans failed (Antikainen et al., 2015).

9.5 New Welfare Regions Established in 2023

After multiyear and subtle political and juridical preparations made by several central governments, the parliament finally accepted the big-bang reform of regional governance. Dozens of JMAs were shut down, and numerous contract-based inter-municipal service arrangements were cancelled at the end of 2022. At the beginning of 2023, the country was divided into 21 welfare regions (formally *wellbeing services counties*) with the full responsibilities of the core welfare services including all former municipal and inter-municipal social services, basic and special healthcare, and fire and rescue services (see Table 9.4). The capital city of Helsinki and Åland were omitted from the reform (cf. Pekkola et al., 2023).

The welfare regions represent a historical change, as they are democratic regional public authorities. The highest body of a welfare region is a regional council, which

Table 9.4 Key characteristics of the new welfare regions (WR) established in 2023

	The authority exercised by a regional public authority over those who live on its territory
Constitutional position	WRs are not named in the Finnish constitution like municipalities; they were created by an ordinary legislation authorised by the constitution.
Institutional depth	In principle, WRs have self-governance in non-financial issues like human resource and property management, but their autonomy is limited in revenue issues (including incurring of a debt) and capital investments in particular.
Policy scope	WRs lack general competence authority, as their activities are limited to statutory duties, which include social care and healthcare, and fire and rescue services. Furthermore, they are allowed to conduct low-risk businesses if such activities support the implementation of their statutory tasks.
Fiscal autonomy	WRs lack taxation rights, making them nearly completely dependent on grant allocations from the state budget. However, WRs can collect small customer fees within legal limits.
Representation	WR are legitimated democratic entities, as their councils are directly elected by regional citizens every fourth year (Jesse et al., 2023, p. 19). WRs also provide participatory opportunities to citizens to influence regional public affairs.

regional citizens elect through general and equal voting rights every fourth year. However, the functional capabilities of the democratic welfare regions are more limited than the municipalities', and what has been agreed in ECLSG (1985). Finland therefore had to notify the European Council that the welfare regions did not fulfil the terms of the ECLSG concerning the rights of taxation and service charges, general competence, and the right to contract debts.

The reform did not grant taxation rights to the welfare regions, leaving them without their own revenue. They were almost completely funded by state grants from the state budget coordinated by the Ministry of Finance. The Parliamentary Committee on County Tax (2021) highlighted that the introduction of a new regional tax could be argued based on the aspect of regional self-government, financial incentives, and possibilities of funding regional investments. However, the regional tax has been strongly opposed because its use is considered to grow the general tax burden on employment and carrying on a trade.

The welfare regions were not given general competence, meaning they have to limit their activities within the mandatory duties the legislation gives them. This solution was argued by referring to the need to safeguard the basic social rights of citizens provided by the constitution and the funding system of the regions, forcing them to operate without taxation rights. However, the welfare regions are allowed to collect small service charges from their customers. In addition, the welfare regions are allowed to conduct low-risk business if it supports the implementation of their statutory tasks (HE, 2020).

The welfare regions lack the autonomy to borrow money. Only the central government can grant rights annually to them to contract a debt with the purpose of using it for investment. Success in receiving the authority to take out a loan depends on what the calculatory debt service capacity of a region is, and whether their investment plan has been approved by a relevant ministry.

Table 9.5 compares how the delivery of the Finnish social care and healthcare services are organised compared with the Scandinavian countries. The Finnish welfare regions most resemble the Danish regions, which are democratic institutions

Table 9.5 Main responsibilities of the delivery of social services and healthcare services in the Scandinavian countries and Finland (Agerholm et al., 2024; Kettunen et al., 2016; Willberg & Valtonen, 2007)

	Social services	Basic healthcare services	Special healthcare services
Denmark	Municipalities	Regions are responsible for basic and hospital care. Municipalities take care of preventive healthcare, rehabilitation, and home nursing	Regions
Finland	Regions (wellbeing services counties)[a]	Regions (wellbeing services counties)[a]	Regions (wellbeing services counties)[a]
Norway	Municipalities	Municipalities (through public procurements)	State government (through four hospital companies)
Sweden	Municipalities	Regions (counties)	Regions (counties)

[a]Promoting wellbeing and health is organised jointly by regions and municipalities

responsible for most health services. The Danish regions also operate without tax revenue and are mostly co-funded by the state and by local governments to a lesser extent.

Table 9.5 demonstrates that Scandinavian countries prefer social services to be organised locally based on municipal duties. In this respect, the Finnish big-bang regional governance reform is radical, as it transferred municipal social work and care to the new regional authorities.

9.6 Discussion and Conclusion

The creative evolution of Finnish regional governance can be summarised by dividing it into the four main eras presented in Table 9.6. The administrative vacuum between the local and state governments began to get some random regional and, in particular, sub-regional service structures when municipalities began to develop their IMC systems during the first era of regional governance. During the second era, IMC was established as a substitute for democratic regional governments through the expansion of statutory and voluntary JMAs. The third era emphasised reappraisal policies and introduced reforms amalgamating JMAs, jointly corporatising inter-municipal services, and promoting efficiency improvements through inter-municipal contracts. The fourth and newest era began with the closing down of

Table 9.6 The main eras of Finnish regional governance

	I era	II era	III era	IV era
Period	1860s–WWII	WWII–late 1980s	late 1980s–2022	2023–
Regionalisation through	Municipal bottom-up initiatives	Top-down legal reforms and bottom-up initiatives	Top-down national reforms and bottom-up initiatives	Top-down and big-bang reforms so far
Impetus	To gradually create new inter-municipal services while responding to the problem of the small average size of municipalities	To expand and strengthen inter-municipal services while avoiding the creation of regional governments	To improve the efficiency and productivity of the municipal and inter-municipal services, coping with the Europeanisation of some service sectors	To decrease the differences in public welfare and health, improve accessibility of services, limit the growth of service expenditures
Key regional public law authorities	Joint meetings of the representatives of municipalities	Statutory and voluntary JMAs the total number of which was highest in the late 1980s	Statutory and voluntary JMAs	Welfare regions and statutory and voluntary JMAs

(continued)

Table 9.6 (continued)

	I era	II era	III era	IV era
Legal governance for the most part by	Voluntary actions and contracts of municipalities	Municipal Act, developing sectoral legislation	Municipal Act, Municipal and Service Structure Reform Act, sectoral legislation	Welfare Services Counties Act, Funding of Welfare Services Counties Act, Municipal Act, and sectoral legislation
Other prominent institutions	Unestablished institutions	Inter-municipal collaborative contracts	Joint committees (i.e. host municipality arrangements) and JMOCs	Inter-welfare region collaboration, developing collaborative arrangements between the welfare regions and municipalities, JMAs, JMOCs, inter-municipal collaborative contracts
Distinctive feature of regional funding	Municipal contributions	Statutory JMAs were funded by direct state grants and municipal contributions	JMAs were funded by municipal performance-based payments	Nearly full state funding of welfare regions
Illustrative examples or distinctive features	Joint municipal mental hospitals and tuberculosis sanatoriums were prominent achievements	Establishment of joint municipal central and regional hospitals and vocational schools	Amalgamations of central and regional hospitals, joint corporatisation of municipal waste management and polytechnics	National employment services will be municipalised and regionalised, or sub-regionalised in some areas, in 2025

many JMAs, transferring social, health, and fire and rescue services from municipalities and giving them to new welfare regions with democratic decision-making bodies, but without their own revenues.

Municipalities' regional governance has provided some obvious benefits but has also entailed some deficiencies and problematic features. For the most part, the evolution of Finnish regional governance has been creative in the sense that it has enabled opportunities to flexibly establish and expand inter-municipal welfare services that would be too expensive or otherwise too demanding for small local authorities. As the creative evolution has included both nationally organised reforms and municipal bottom-up arrangements, it has enabled regional variations in IMOs and inter-municipal contracts. Through the IMC systems, municipalities have been able to avoid some overlapping investments, improve economies of scale, and share risks associated with the ownership of modern service institutions such as hospitals and educational institutions. The regional governance based on IMC has also unified some political aims of municipalities, reduced mutual competition, and coordinated their local actions.

However, the evolution of regional governance has been unpredictable and sporadic, as it has progressed without the long-term vision of how to agree and define the optimal division of labour between local communities and regions. The ultimate purpose and societal functions of the regional public law authorities have been to some extent unstable, while the role of regional public policymaking has developed through contradictions which have sustained fragmentary regional structures. The sectorised system of regional governance has enabled sub-optimisation by scattered JMOs or limited the opportunities to improve economies of scope. More importantly, the prominent problem of regional governance by municipalities has been the democratic deficit (Valkama et al., 2022). The highest JMA decision-makers have not been elected by regional citizens, and the composition of the highest decision-making bodies has not been based on the aggregated results of the local elections. JMAs as semi-autonomous bodies are distant from their municipal owners, creating communication and coordination challenges.

For the most part, regional governance has evolved based on domestic public and welfare policies and as a response to the challenges of the municipalities' small average size. The impact of the Europeanisation of Finland's legal system and economy has remained minor, being limited mostly to regionalisation of municipal waste management services and the foundation of the regional councils by amalgamating the regional planning authorities and regional associations. Linguistic and geographical special characteristics explain the special position of the autonomous region of Åland.

Since the historic reform, which established 21 new welfare regions, the country now has a unified system of regional governance of social, health, and fire and rescue services, providing a rare opportunity to improve the integration of social care and basic and special healthcare services. However, the welfare regions are only half-finished regional governments without some classic features of self-government. Regions lack their own taxation rights, and the division of their own income sources therefore does not follow the division of their tasks, which is against the economics of fiscal federalism (Musgrave & Musgrave, 1989). Because the ultimate financing relies on the central government, and the law concerning regions stipulate that if financing is inadequate for financing their obligatory service obligations, the central government must add financing correspondingly. The incentives to economise and rationalise their own service production are not optimal because they lack classic financial responsibilities. The policy regarding the income and expenditure autonomy of the welfare regions is not arranged consistently (Oulasvirta & Turala, 2009).

The transition of social care and healthcare and rescue services was followed by a complex plan on how to redirect tax incomes and state grants from municipalities to the regions. This plan incentivised municipalities to spare their social care and healthcare service expenditures in 2021–2022 because the transition of state grants to the regions could be minimised accordingly. This was one reason the welfare regions had to introduce budgets for their first fiscal year having significant deficits. It remains to be seen how the welfare regions' severe funding problems will be resolved: how much funding the state can add to the regions, whether some regions will be forced to merge to be economically more viable, and how well the regions can improve efficiency and productivity.

The creative evolution of regional governance produced the present welfare regions, JMAs, JMOCs, and inter-municipal contracts. These regional structures have a twofold nature. The welfare regions represent more rigid and classic public governance, operating under the generic guidance of the state government; the other elements of regional governance are more adaptable, have more regional and sub-regional variation, and are more strongly associated with local policymaking. The functionality and appropriateness of these elements are not a given because of the endless demographic, financial, ideological, and other societal changes that are likely to call for the continuity of the regional reforms.

References

Agerholm, J., Pulkki, J., Jensen, N. K., Keskimäki, I., Andersen, I., Burström, B., et al. (2024). The organisation and responsibility for care for older people in Denmark, Finland and Sweden: outline and comparison of care systems. *Scandinavian Journal of Public Health, 52*(2), 119–122. https://doi.org/10.1177/14034948221137128

Antikainen, J., Hämäläinen, T., Holstila, E., Jalasto, P., Tolonen, S., & Vartiainen, P. (2015). *Tahdommeko kehittää metropolia? Metropolipolitiikan kehittämistarpeet.* Ympäristöministeriön raportteja 12/2015. Ympäristöministeriö.

Anttiroiko, A.-V., Bailey, S. J., & Valkama, P. (2011). Innovations in public governance in the western world. In A.-V. Anttiroiko, S. J. Bailey, & P. Valkama (Eds.), *Innovations in Public Governance* (pp. 1–22). IOS Press.

Anttiroiko, A.-V., & Valkama, P. (2017). The role of localism in the development of regional structures in post-war Finland. *Public Policy and Administration, 32*(2), 152–172. https://doi.org/10.1177/0952076716665879

Antunes, S., & Loughlin, J. (2020). The European Union, subnational mobilization and state rescaling in small unitary states: A comparative analysis. *Regional & Federal Studies, 30*(2), 121–136. https://doi.org/10.1080/13597566.2018.1512974

Arter, D. (2022). Personal representation or party representation? Elections in the autonomous Åland Islands. *Regional & Federal Studies, 32*(4), 511–524. https://doi.org/10.1080/13597566.2022.2047940

Bailey, S. J. (2008). The rationale for regional government within the EU: Function, form and finance. In S. Setnikar-Cankar & Z. Sevic (Eds.), *Decentralisation and regionalisation: The Slovenian experience in an international perspective* (pp. 109–127). Greenwich University Press.

Bevir, M. (2010). *Democratic governance.* Princeton University Press.

Blomqvist, P., & Bergman, P. (2010). Regionalisation Nordic style: Will regions in Sweden threaten local democracy? *Local Government Studies, 36*(1), 43–74. https://doi.org/10.1080/03003930903435740

Boyne, G. A. (1997). Public choice theory and local government structure: An evaluation of reorganisation in Scotland and Wales. *Local Government Studies, 23*(3), 56–72. https://doi.org/10.1080/03003939708433876

CDLR. (1998). *Regionalisation and its effects on local self-government.* Report by the Steering Committee on Local and Regional authorities (CDLR) prepared with the collaboration of

Professor Gérard Marcou. Local and regional authorities in Europe, No. 64. Council of Europe Publishing.
Coaffee, J. (2005). New localism and the management of regeneration. *International Journal of Public Sector Management, 18*(2), 108–113. https://doi.org/10.1108/09513550510584937
ECLSG. (1985, October 15). *European charter of local self government* [European Treaty Series – No. 122]. Strasbourg.
Haiko, M. (2014). *Selvitys alueellisen pelastustoimen synnystä.* Pelastuslaitosten kumppanuusverkoston julkaisu 3/2014.
Hakoma, R., & Niemelä, M. (2018). *Erityishuoltopiirit poistuvat, työ ja palvelut jatkuvat. Selvityshenkilöraportti erityishuoltopiirien asemasta soteuudistuksessa.* Sosiaali- ja terveysministeriön raportteja ja muistioita 42/2018. Sosiaali- ja terveysministeriö.
Hall, J. C., Matti, J., & Zhou, Y. (2018). Regionalization and consolidation of municipal taxes and services. *The Review of Regional Studies, 48*(2), 245–262. https://doi.org/10.52324/001c.8001
HE. (1988). *Hallituksen esitys eduskunnalle Erikoissairaanhoitolaiksi ja laiksi erikoissairaanhoitolain voimaanpanosta.* 1988 vp. – HE n:o 94.
HE. (1993a). *Hallituksen esitys Eduskunnalle laeiksi alueiden kehittämisestä ja saariston kehityksen edistämisestä annetun lain muuttamisesta.* 1993 vp – HE 99.
HE. (1993b). *Hallituksen esitys Eduskunnalle jätelaiksi ja laiksi ympäristölupamenettelylain muuttamisesta.* 1993 vp – HE 77.
HE. (2006). *Hallituksen esitys Eduskunnalle laiksi kunta- ja palvelurakenneuudistuksesta sekä laeiksi kuntajakolain muuttamisesta ja varainsiirtoverolain muuttamisesta.* HE 155/2006 vp.
HE. (2020). *Hallituksen esitys eduskunnalle hyvinvointialueiden perustamista ja sosiaali- ja terveydenhuollon sekä pelastustoimen järjestämisen uudistusta koskevaksi lainsäädännöksi sekä Euroopan paikallisen itsehallinnon peruskirjan 12 ja 13 artiklan mukaisen ilmoituksen antamiseksi.* HE 241/2020 vp.
Hietalahti, J. (2016). *Ajatus yhteisestä lainasta. Kuntien varainhankinnan historiaa 1909–1996.* Kuntien takauskeskus.
Hooghe, L., Marks, G., & Schakel, A. H. (2010). Measuring regional authority. In L. Hooghe, G. Marks, & A. Schakel (Eds.), *The rise of regional authority: A comparative study of 42 democracies*. Routledge.
Hörnström, L. (2013). Strong regions within the unitary state: The Nordic experience of regionalization. *Regional & Federal Studies, 23*(4), 427–443. https://doi.org/10.1080/13597566.2013.765867
Hudson, C. (2005). Regional development partnerships in Sweden: Putting the government back in governance? *Regional & Federal Studies, 15*(3), 311–327. https://doi.org/10.1080/13597560500223297
Hulst, R. (2005). Regional governance in unitary states: Lessons from the Netherlands in comparative perspective. *Local Government Studies, 31*(1), 99–120. https://doi.org/10.1080/0300393042000332882
Huxham, C. (2003). Theorizing collaboration practice. *Public Management Review, 5*(3), 401–423. https://doi.org/10.1080/1471903032000146964
Ihatsu, S. (2014). *Terveyttä kaikille – terveyskeskukset 1970-luvulta 1990-luvulle.* CasaCo Studio Oy.
Jesse, M., Jeurissen, P., Figueras, J., Simon, F., Stoltenberg, C., Leichsenring, K., et al. (2023). *Audit of the Finnish Institute for Health and Welfare (THL) by an international panel.* Reports and memorandums of the Ministry of Social Affairs and Health 2023:28. Helsinki: Ministry of Social Affairs and Health.
Kallio, O., & Tolppi, R. (2012). *Alueellinen pelastustoimi seitsemän toimintavuoden jälkeen – Muutoksia ja kokemuksia aluepelastuksesta 2004–2010. Seurantatutkimuksen 3. vaiheen loppuraportti.* Suomen Kuntaliitto.
Kettunen, P., & Kungla, T. (2005). Europeanization of sub-national governance in unitary states: Estonia and Finland. *Regional & Federal Studies, 15*(3), 353–378. https://doi.org/10.1080/13597560500223321

Kettunen, P., Sandberg, S., & Fredriksson, C. (2016). *Eurooppalaiset hallintojärjestelmät vertailussa*. Valtioneuvoston selvitys- ja tutkimustoiminnan julkaisusarja 37/2016.

Kull, M. (2009). Local and regional governance in Finland: A study on institutionalisation, transformation and Europeanization. *Halduskultuur, 10*, 22–39.

Le Gales, P., & Lequesne, C. (Eds.). (1998). *Regions in Europe: The paradox of power*. Routledge.

Linna, J. (2016). *Yhtiöstä opettaja?: Systeemiteoreettinen tulkinta ammattikorkeakoulujen yhtiöittämisestä*. Helsingin yliopisto.

Loughlin, J. (2009). Reconfiguring the state: Trends in territorial governance in European states. *Regional & Federal Studies, 17*(4), 385–403. https://doi.org/10.1080/13597560701691912

Manninen, A. (2010). *Palveluja vai byrokratiaa? Suomen kunnallishallinto sotien jälkeen. Kunnallisalan kehittämissäätiö*. Edita.

Marks, G., Hooghe, L., & Schakel, A. H. (2008). Measuring regional authority. *Regional & Federal Studies, 18*(2–3), 111–121. https://doi.org/10.1080/13597560801979464

Metze, T., & Levelt, M. (2012). Barriers to credible innovation: Collaborative regional governance in The Netherlands. *The Innovation Journal: The Public Sector Innovation Journal, 17*(1), 2–15.

Musgrave, R. A., & Musgrave, P. B. (1989). *Public finance in theory and practice* (5th ed.). McGraw-Hill Book Co.

Mykkänen, A. (2012). Kuntayhtymä – sylkykuppi, himmeli vai pelastaja? In A. Mykkänen (Ed.), *Kuntayhtymä pelastaa?* (pp. 12–19). Kunnallisalan kehittämissäätiö.

Niemelä, M., & Saarinen, A. (2015). Terveydenhuoltopolitiikan muutokset. In M. Niemelä, L. Kokkinen, J. Pulkki, A. Saarinen, & L.-K. Tynkkynen (Eds.), *Terveydenhuollon muutokset. Politiikka, järjestelmä ja seuraukset* (pp. 13–26). Tampere University Press.

Olsson, J., & Åström, J. (2003). Why regionalism in Sweden? *Regional & Federal Studies, 13*(3), 66–89. https://doi.org/10.1080/13597560308559435

Oulasvirta, L., & Turala, M. (2009). Financial autonomy and consistency of central government policy towards local governments. *International Review of Administrative Sciences, 75*(2), 311–332. https://doi.org/10.1177/0020852309104178

The Parliamentary Committee on County Tax. (2021). *Report of the parliamentary committee on county tax*. Publications of the Finnish Government 2021:15. Helsinki: Finnish Government.

Pekkola, E., Johanson, J.-E., Kujala, E.-N., & Mykkänen, M. (2023). The structures of the Finnish public administration. In E. Pekkola, J.-E. Johanson, & M. Mykkänen (Eds.), *Finnish public administration. Governance and public management* (pp. 57–75). Palgrave Macmillan. https://doi-org.proxy.uwasa.fi/10.1007/978-3-031-34862-4_4

Rayle, L., & Zegras, C. (2013). The emergence of inter-municipal collaboration: Evidence from metropolitan planning in Portugal. *European Planning Studies, 21*(6), 867–889. https://doi.org/10.1080/09654313.2012.722932

Saarivirta, T., Consoli, D., & Dhondt, P. (2010). Suomen terveydenhuoltojärjestelmän ja sairaaloiden kehittyminen. Vaatimattomista oloista modernin terveydenhuollon eturintamaan. *Kasvatus & Aika, 3*(4), 25–41.

Salminen, A. (2008). Evaluating the new governance of the welfare state in Finland. *International Journal of Public Administration, 31*(10–11), 1242–1258. https://doi.org/10.1080/01900690801973352

Satka, M., & Hämeenaho, P. (2015). Finnish eldercare services in crisis: The viewpoint of rural home care workers. *Nordic Social Work Research, 5*(1), 81–94. https://doi.org/10.1080/2156857X.2014.943265

Schrijver, F. (2005). Regionalism in Galicia after regionalisation. *Tijdschrift voor Economische en Sociale Geografie, 96*(3), 275–286. https://doi.org/10.1111/j.1467-9663.2005.00459.x

Sharpe, L. J. (1993). The United Kingdom: Disjointed meso. In L. J. Sharpe (Ed.), *The rise of meso government in Europe* (pp. 247–295). Sage Publications.

Sjöblom, S. (2020). Finnish regional governance structures in flux: Reform processes between European and domestic influences. *Regional & Federal Studies, 30*(2), 155–174. https://doi.org/10.1080/13597566.2018.1541891

Sorrentino, M., & Simonetta, M. (2013). Incentivising inter-municipal collaboration: The Lombard experience. *Journal of Management Governance, 17*(4), 887–906. https://doi.org/10.1007/s10997-011-9204-3

Stoker, G., Hogwood, B., Bullman, U., Osei, P., & Cairney, P. (1996). *Regionalism*. Local Government Management Board.

Tavares, A. F., & Feiock, R. C. (2018). Applying an institutional collective action framework to investigate intermunicipal cooperation in Europe. *Perspectives on Public Management and Governance, 1*(4), 299–316. https://doi.org/10.1093/ppmgov/gvx014

Tomblin, S. G. (2007). Effecting change and transformation through regionalization: Theory versus practice. *Canadian Public Administration, 50*(1), 1–20. https://doi.org/10.1111/j.1754-7121.2007.tb02000.x

Valkama, P. (Ed.). (2013). *Markkinainnovaatiot yhdyskuntajätehuollossa: Tutkimus jätehuoltopalvelujen markkinoiden evoluutiosta, sovelluksista ja jännitteistä kunnallisen ja yksityisen sektorin rajapinnassa*. Johtamiskorkeakoulu, Tampereen yliopisto.

Valkama, P., Asenova, D., & Bailey, S. J. (2016). Risk management challenges of shared public services: A comparative analysis of Scotland and Finland. *Public Money and Management, 36*(1), 31–38. https://doi.org/10.1080/09540962.2016.1103415

Valkama, P., & Oulasvirta, L. (2021). How Finland copes with an ageing population: Adjusting structures and equalising the financial capabilities of local governments. *Local Government Studies, 47*(3), 429–452. https://doi.org/10.1080/03003930.2021.1877664

Valkama, P., Torsteinsen, H., & Kettunen, P. (2022). Impacts of joint municipal agencification on the democratic governance of waste management. *International Journal of Public Sector Management, 35*(5), 533–548. https://doi.org/10.1108/IJPSM-05-2021-0114

Verhoest, K. (2013). Agencification processes and agency governance: Organizational innovation at a global scale? In P. Valkama, S. J. Bailey, & A.-V. Anttiroiko (Eds.), *Organizational innovation in public services: Forms and governance* (pp. 49–71). Palgrave Macmillan. https://doi.org/10.1057/9781137011848_4

Widuto, A. (2018). *Regional governance in the EU*. Belgium: European Parliamentary Research Service (EPRS). Retrieved March 21, 2023, from https://policycommons.net/artifacts/1335678/regional-governance-in-the-eu/1942343/

Willberg, M., & Valtonen, H. (2007). *Pohjoismaiden terveydenhuollon rahoitus- ja palvelujärjestelmien vertailu*. Sosiaali- ja terveysministeriön selvityksiä 2007:36. Helsinki: Sosiaali- ja terveysministeriö.

Young, K. (1988). Local government in Britain: Rationale, structure and finance. In S. J. Bailey & R. Paddison (Eds.), *The reform of local government finance in Britain*. Routledge.

Chapter 10
The Evolution of Finnish Welfare State and Its Structural Reforms of Welfare Provision

Chino Yabunaga

Abstract This chapter examines the structural reforms of Finnish welfare provision, focusing on changes in the local government system and intergovernmental relations. The Finnish welfare state and its welfare provision are characterized by a complex interplay between central and local government. Since the 1990s, Finland has undertaken numerous reforms to make its welfare provision more flexible and responsive to changing societal needs. These reforms have been driven by factors such as globalization, demographic changes, technological advances, and Finland's integration into the European Union. The analysis highlights the role of local governments in welfare provision and their ability to innovate and adapt to new challenges with initiatives and support from central government. Case studies illustrate how Finnish local and central governments have implemented reforms, sometimes initiated by central government and sometimes driven by local needs. The chapter concludes that the Finnish approach to welfare provision is dynamic and evolving, influenced by both external pressures and internal innovation. Reforms are seen as part of an adaptive process by local governments to create new initiatives and ensure the sustainability of welfare provision with the support of central government although initiated by both top-down and bottom-up processes.

Keywords Welfare provision · SOTE reform · Social and healthcare services

C. Yabunaga (✉)
Faculty of Global and Regional Studies, Toyo University, Bunkyo-ku, Tokyo, Japan
e-mail: yabunaga@toyo.jp

N. Tokumaru et al. (eds.), *Creative Co-evolution of the Economies and Welfare States in the Nordic Countries*, Evolutionary Economics and Social Complexity Science 32, https://doi.org/10.1007/978-981-97-8569-8_10

10.1 Introduction

10.1.1 Background and Purpose

Nordic welfare states have traditionally aimed to achieve a harmonious balance between the economy and welfare, and focus on social and welfare policies that contribute to the economy. These states have strongly responded to various labor and welfare-related challenges of the twenty-first century, such as transitioning from an industrial to information-based and service economy society, globalized products, labor, and financial markets, as well as maturing populations and fluid family structures (Taylor-Gooby, 2004; Armingeon & Bonoli, 2006; Bonoli & Natali, 2012; Hemerijck, 2013). This can be attributed to various factors, including the traditional productive social policy line centering on Sweden, based on which active labor market policies (activation) and flexicurity are formed, including measures to promote labor market participation; social investment approach, which seeks to maximize the use of labor by investing in human capital; and defamilization, which aims to reduce the burden of family care and advance gender equality. Research on welfare states considers Nordic-style welfare states as systems that aim to maximize the association between the commodification of labor and expansion of taxpayers by simplifying the entry of individuals into the labor market through generous welfare benefits in kind, simultaneously increasing indirect employment, such as those engaged in care and training work (Esping-Andersen, 1989, 1999), and the mechanisms and basic structures of support for welfare states.

Considering the welfare provision structure of Nordic welfare states, central and local governments developed as two halves in the process of building a welfare state. Based on a degree of central government control to ensure a universal provision of services, local governments are responsible for a wide range of administrative tasks, having acquired discretionary powers to monitor the expanding provision of services (Heikkila et al., 1999; Rose & Ståhlberg, 2005). Furthermore, local governments in mature Nordic welfare states have implemented wide-reaching reforms in their respective countries to effectively and sustainably provide services.

With regard to the development of Nordic welfare states, Finland distinguishes itself in several aspects. A complex situation of overcrowding interests and financial resources also emerges under the two-tier structure of the center and basic regional governments, with administrative associations with diverse frameworks and members forming in different administrative fields as Chap. 9 illustrated. In this backdrop, intermittent reforms of the welfare provision structure of Finnish welfare state since the 1990s have made it flexible and easy to change, making it one of the foundations for the creation of new industries.

This chapter highlights various examples of structural reforms of welfare provision in Finland's local and regional governance system, arguing that change is being generated through diverse and innovative initiatives and that the regional system is shifting toward facilitating the generation of new initiatives.

10.1.2 Analytical Perspectives

Research on welfare states has used various approaches, such as power resource theory, which emphasizes support for the welfare state and mobilization of political resources to support it, or historical institutionalism, focusing on path dependency and other factors behind the stalemate surrounding the welfare state crisis (Myles & Quadagno, 2002). Since the 2000s, researchers have used discourse and political theory to discuss the reorganization of the welfare state in the post-industrial era of globalization (Nishioka, 2021).

The reform of multiple welfare provision structures in Finland, discussed in this chapter, is a relatively recent effort, specifically, since the 2000s. Finland's accession to the European Union (EU) in 1995 transformed its national system, making its power structure complex. The inflow and outflow of labor has become complex and frequent, and resources allocated by the EU have been invested directly in the sub-national unit. Populist parties have also expanded their influence amid globalization. The transformation of the industrial structure in a post-industrial society also changed the state of labor and employment and the structure of interest groups. In the wake of advancements in science and technology such as computerization, the services that welfare states provide have changed and diversified.

To understand the process of change in the welfare state in these circumstances, it could be useful to employ an evolutionary theory perspective, which analyzes change as a process by which the subject of analysis adapts to the new environment in a complex situation (Steinmo, 2010). From this perspective, this chapter focuses on individual changes (reform movements) as a continuous process, emphasizing their political and historical contexts and underlining the contingencies driven by the complex interactions between interdependent variables.

10.2 Context of Regional Governance System Reform in Finland

10.2.1 Welfare State and Local Governments

Local governments are important actors in the development of welfare states. As providers of welfare services, they have been involved in the procurement, coordination, and allocation of resources, mainly welfare services. Intergovernmental relations of the welfare state and the nature of local government affect the functioning of the welfare state (e.g., Kitayama, 2011; Sellers & Lidström, 2007). The capacity of local governments to provide welfare depends on the volume and quality of welfare available to residents; they also have the potential to optimize welfare supply according to the geographical, economic, and social characteristics of a region. Furthermore, they discovered new needs and developed benefits, systems, and services, thus making a nationwide impact (e.g., Ota et al., 1986; Komamura & Tanaka, 2019).

However, for local governments to actively provide welfare and innovate for efficient and effective operation, they must have the required capacity. Kitayama's (2011) analysis of the historical development of Japan's national health insurance system reveals that local governments have the capacity as an infrastructure framework for the provision of welfare services, and the central government utilizes the capacity of the local government and further invests in them. This demonstrates how local governments develop in an interactive process of expanding their policies. Thelen (2004, pp. 37–45) analyzed the development of welfare states from the perspective of evolution, and it raises institutional layering and diversion as specific mechanisms that reshape institutions in subtle, but important ways. Institutional layering refers to the addition of new elements to a stable system that produces development that was not intended originally.

10.2.2 Local Governments and Provision of Welfare in Finland

The Finnish welfare state, compared to other Nordic countries, was affected by the late start of industrialization and the relatively major influence of rural society for a duration after the war. The Social Democratic Party (SDP) and peasant parties formed coalitions and substantially influenced policy-making, affecting the implementation of the pension system, and delaying the introduction of the health insurance system (Petersen et al., 2017, pp. 88–114).

The regional system comprises a two-tier structure, which includes the central and local governments. The number of municipalities exceeded 600 during the peak period in the 1970s; however after their subsequent merger, the number fell below 500 until decentralization reform was performed in the 2000s. Municipalities have varying populations and areas; the population is concentrated in the south, while the north, east, and island areas are mainly underpopulated, with populations under 1000. Ensuring service provision capacity in these municipalities has been a longstanding challenge. Therefore, the 1948 law on self-government (Kunnallislaki 642/1948) introduced the joint municipal association system, under which several municipalities conducted their administrative tasks jointly. For tasks such as waste disposal and public transport, which seemed difficult for a single regional government to carry out independently, administrative associations were established to manage them. Furthermore, administrative associations established health and medical care under a different framework. The 1943 law on central hospitals divided the country into about 20 districts, and established medical systems responsible for hospital care, including central hospitals in each district. In 1989, five areas were established centered on university hospitals for providing specialized medical care. (The hospital districts were abolished with the establishment of new regional governments, which will be discussed below). Other bodies were also being set up for regional development. In 1994, in response to EU membership, maakunta, responsible for regional planning, were established as statutory regional administrative areas for approximately 20 historically cohesive "regions" (Laki alueiden kehittämisestä 1135/1993). Additionally, an association of maakunta, a federation of municipalities in the region, was established as a mandatory organization. Municipalities could also establish public corporations either individually or jointly and operate projects requiring economies of scale (See Chap. 9 for more detailed information).

10.2.3 Development and Decentralization of the Local Autonomy System

The basic function of local governments was to provide service, developed from the 1960s to the early 1990s, based on individual subsidies that accounted for financial disparities among local governments. The Valtava reform of disbursement from the state treasury was implemented in 1984, as part of efforts to realize universal social welfare services by strengthening local governments and increasing financial transfers from the central government to them by eliminating financial disparities through general subsidies, and integrating national subsidies by project (Yamada, 2006). However, the reforms required local governments to submit social welfare and healthcare plans as well as detailed reports on the projects and use of national subsidies to the central governments every 5 years, so that the central government could provide comprehensive guidance and supervision to social and healthcare services that local governments provided (Yamada, 2006, p. 206).

This strong direction of control from the state underwent a major transformation with the introduction of a comprehensive subsidy system in 1993. Under this system, calculations were carried out in the fields of education, healthcare, and welfare, while ear-marked, project-specific subsidies were shifted to comprehensive subsidies. Furthermore, financially vulnerable municipalities were provided support through tax revenue equalization subsidies to reduce the revenue gap (Yamada, 2006). The facility construction subsidy and fiscal power index were abolished in 1995, which left only tax equalization subsidies to adjust for tax revenue disparities (Yokoyama, 2019).

Meanwhile, the amendment of the Local Government Act of 1995 reduced the scale of fiscal transfers and enabled flexible administrative management through greater discretion in the method of service provision (Yabunaga, 2008). In 2008, the central government's jurisdiction over local administration and regional development was transferred from the Ministry of the Interior to the Ministry of Finance, with the central government's oversight function shifting from ensuring the quality and quantity of services by enhancing, strengthening, and controlling the service provision functions of the local government to supervising local government fiscal

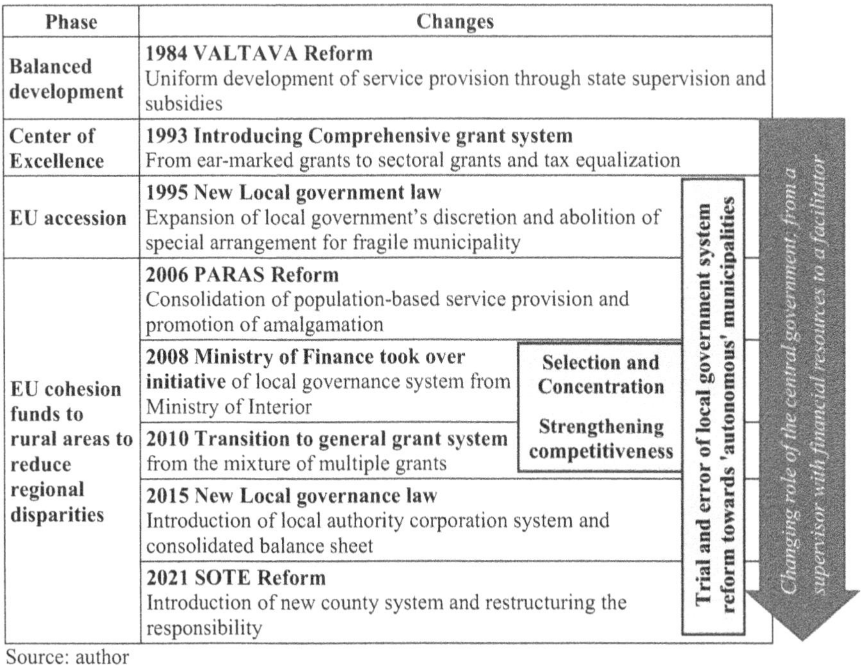

Fig. 10.1 Major local institutional reforms and changes in central-local relations in Finland since the 1980s. Source: author

discipline. The amendment of the Local Government Act in 2015 tightened the fiscal discipline of regional governments, also applying the European Fiscal Compact, which made revenues and expenditures of the regional governments subject to the control of consolidated revenues and expenditures of the related group of organizations, the local authority corporation, kunta konserni. Meanwhile, the choices of regional governments were extended with regard to their organization and decision-making mechanisms such as the standing committee model, and their opportunities to make independent decisions.

The central government changed its relationship with local governments, beginning in the 1990s, deliberately shifting the responsibility of development initiatives to the local/regional level. The central government's role shifted from investing and coordinating to improving the service provision environment in the region; promoting and balancing local development to reducing legal systems and financial constraints; and supporting the development of the region through the development of all-in bases and other means (Valtiovarainministeriö, 2015, p. 6). Essentially, it created an environment in which municipalities could make their own choices and operate autonomously (See Fig. 10.1).

The next section discusses the reforms and initiatives that led to the establishment of a regional government in Finland and analyzes the process of regionalization amid this changing environment.

10.3 Examples of Reforms

10.3.1 Establishment of a Regional Government in the Kainuu Administration Experiment

The Kainuu region is located in central Finland, on the eastern side of the Russian border, and forms a broad administrative area, comprising a population of about 71,000. Households had the lowest national per capita and disposable income in the country, and unemployment rates as of 2000, before the administrative experiment proposal, was about 20%. The region registered a rapid population decline as the aging population rose. The search for sustainable regional development continued, but following a petition to the Prime Minister, the Kainuu Administrative Experiment Act (343/2003) was implemented in 2003.

The reform aimed to achieve sustainable regional development by (1) making the supply of public services sustainable through the reorganization of municipal administrative work, formulation of an overall strategy, and reducing costs, and (2) creating a business environment that is a prerequisite for regional development, creating employment, and curbing population outflows. A regional government with a directly elected assembly was established in 2005 to oversee health and welfare services (except childcare) and the operation of high schools and vocational schools, as well as general development policies. However, the experiment ended in 2012 following opposition from the participating municipalities.

Young people from the Kainuu region began migrating, leaving behind an aging population. However, the employment–industry policy was under the jurisdiction of the central government, which was unable to address issues such as employment mismatches. Therefore, it was decided to combine the budget of the employment and industry sectors managed by the central government with the regional development and planning budgets of the Kainuu region, as part of efforts to expand development, matching the actual conditions of the region. Meanwhile, although joint municipal authorities based on individual agreements between municipalities have been established to provide basic services such as social welfare, healthcare, and education, the supreme decision-making body for joint undertakings, including budget execution, is a consultative body comprising members elected by the participating municipal councils, which is not a central decision-making body for each municipality. Therefore, establishing a council comprising directly elected members was expected to prioritize the common interests of the region and make bold reforms taking advantage of the economies of scale. The reforms were aimed at strategic transformation and development tailored to regional needs by eliminating the misspend caused by double administration. They also provide clear decision-making channels by consolidating administrative tasks dispersed between the central government, municipalities as well as joint municipal authorities.

In enacting the special law for the administrative experiment, its frameworks were deliberated and written by an Investigator, selvitysmies, appointed by the central government. The Investigator had been involved in regional administration since long and had extensive experience in local administration as well as the central government. During the implementation stage, a highly specialized senior staff member was appointed as the executive director of the preparatory organization for the implementation of the administrative experiment. The executive director had served in the same position for 15 years in the Kainuu Hospital District and had a PhD in public health. He became the executive director of the preparatory organization, and later the Kainuu regional government. The preparatory organization practiced a participatory development method when specifically designing this system, involving a wide range of staff and stakeholders. More than 70% of interviewee comments after the experiment reported the facilitation method, in which staff participated actively in discussions during the preparatory process, as a success factor.

The finances of the participating municipalities improved during the implementation period of the experiment. Smaller municipalities located in the periphery had increased resident satisfaction in terms of services owing to the increase the variety of services as well as improved access to advanced services, despite deterioration in the frequency of supply and close access to general services owing to service expansion.

However, the main obstacle to reform was the institutional impossibility of half of the overall reform strategy owing to central government resistance, and lack of commitment from politicians who were involved in the decision-making mechanism. The stalemate in overall strategy can be attributed to the central government's resistance. The initial proposal from Kainuu was to transfer the employment industry and other policies from the central government to the regional government, which could not be implemented because of opposition from relevant ministries and agencies. They opposed the dismantling of existing services and organizations amid concerns of weakening positions and loss of fairness between regions, and distrust of the capabilities of municipal officers. Meanwhile, local politicians expressed reluctance because they would have to make decisions such as service cuts directly. The experiment as originally conceived was only partially realized and concluded after 8 years primarily because of the relationship between the relevant ministries and cooperation among the participating municipalities, both of which were critical to the success or failure of the administrative experiment. The transfer of industrial policies to the regional government failed amid resistance from the then Ministry of International Trade and Industry, which prevented the overall development of the Kainuu region. The administrative experiment ended because one of the eight participating municipalities opposed its continuation (Yabunaga, 2008, 2021).

10.3.2 South Karelia Social Welfare and the Eksote Healthcare District Reform

The South Karelia region, located along the Russian border in southeast Finland, is a long north–south strip, comprising a population of about 130,000 and nine municipalities. Before the establishment of the South Karelia Social Welfare and Eksote

Healthcare District, there was a division between medical care provided by the hospital district and primary care at health centers provided by the municipalities, which resulted in overcrowding and a lack of proper follow-up care. Rising costs were also considered an issue in the backdrop of population aging. Following the PARAS reforms (described in Sect. 10.3.4) of 2007, which sought a certain scale of provision units for social welfare and healthcare services, in 2009, municipalities decided to review the provision units of primary care and social welfare services provided by each municipality, and integrate them into the South Karelia Healthcare District responsible for hospital care, resulting in the establishment of the municipal federation (joint authority) Eksote. With the support of the Finnish Innovation Fund Sitra, the project has evolved since 2014 as a social welfare and healthcare service provision system for all residents in the target region, and a social welfare and healthcare information management system was introduced that integrates residents' health and service use. It has also developed new services such as an on-call emergency system and 24-h online services. In addition, it introduced a personal budget system for people with disabilities and products developed by start-ups. Before the introduction of Eksote, spending had continuously increased by 6.1% to 9.5% every year, but since its introduction, spending has been limited to an increase of 1.4–5.8%. It has simultaneously reduced expenditure, while enhancing the value of services, prompting other regions to adopt the model.

One of the characteristics of Eksote is the implementation of reforms based on business management methods, in collaboration with various actors. The roadmap for implementing the initial development strategy was developed in 2 months using the Group Decision Support System (GDSS) through meetings between 13 people that included the Director of Eksote, Director of Planning and Development, managers of each service department, and the chief physician. This process applied knowledge developed at the then Lappeenranta Institute of Technology. For example, the development strategy was formulated using the decision support room, GDSS, and software for this purpose. After formulating it, the effect of GDSS on the group's collaborative process was measured based on interviews with project participants (Korpela et al., 2012).

Owing to its long and narrow shape, the South Karelia area is unfavorable to the provision of efficient services, so it was necessary to promote the transition to home care and form a network to build a continuous care process between the hospital, institutional, and home care. However, the conflicting interests of individual municipalities prevented drastic reforms, making it necessary to develop an operating model afresh to prevent it from being bound by the old territorial frameworks of the municipalities and the region, entirely replacing traditional management methods. This required a reform of organizational culture and the understanding and capacity of the staff. Therefore, integration of services was envisioned through networking with three-stage developmental tactics with strategic steps. The first stage concerned pre-integration where individual municipalities are responsible for the supply of primary care and social welfare services, while hospital care provision of the hospital district functions separately. The second stage involved the creation of economies of scale through by integrating nine municipalities and hospital districts. In the third stage, each of the integrated organizations defined and shared functions and built a network. This network responded to the needs of clients in an assigned manner. It worked in cooperation with external parties such as the central government and private organizations (Korpela et al., 2012).

In the process of implementing the development strategy, external funding was actively used to secure development funds. For example, the development of an on-call emergency system was funded by the EU regional development subsidy and subsidies from the Ministry of Employment and Industry, while the Digituki project to strengthen citizen skills in using digital services used subsidies from the Ministry of Finance. The development of the SOTE information management system integrating resident health and service use received financial support from The Finnish Innovation Fund Sitra. The project also collaborated with various research institutions, including the University of Eastern Finland and Saimaa University of Applied Sciences. Management and leadership development of the project were clearly established and knowledge management was strengthened to improve the service delivery system. Personnel in charge of management received professional management education, mentoring, and testing. A unique proprietary business development process called Paja, which incorporates a lean model and allows employees to proactively review operations, was also developed and became a reference case for good practice in the EU. As of 2019, of the total staff of 4954, 40 R&D staff and 350 management staff have been deployed in strategic support services.

10.3.3 Child and Family Services Reform LAPE

The Child and Family Services Reform Program (Lapsi-ja perhepalveluiden muutosohjelma, referred to as LAPE) was implemented in Finland between 2016 and 2019, aimed at strengthening the wellbeing and resources of children, adolescents, and families. It also promoted the coordination of work among professionals in the fields of welfare, healthcare, and education forming networks in each region to provide public social services for children, by shifting the management entity from the municipality to the regional level. It was also an initiative that aimed at structurally transforming the traditional system of providing public child-related services and the relationships between different professions, even changing the philosophy or culture shared by child welfare service workers. It was successfully implemented by the then Juha Sipilä government (Center Party, 2015–2019) and is regarded as the only successfully implemented welfare-related reform and policy program concerning children in Finland during this period (Sosiaali- ja terveysministeriö, 2019; Owalgroup, 2019).

The LAPE reform commenced when the Sipilä administration (Center Party), after being elected in 2015, placed social welfare and healthcare as one of its priorities. Of the 26 priority projects with the strategic goal of improving the welfare of future generations, five were in the social welfare and healthcare sectors, and LAPE was one of them. School health surveys had shown widening disparities and differences in academic ability and physical and mental health of some children, leading to child protection, while parents who were facing problems in their lives, failed to receive support before protection. Although more than half the cases resulting in out-of-home protection can be attributed to parental fatigue, insufficient parenting skills, discord between family members and deteriorating relationships, etc., 70% of the cases had never made use of services before, and more than 30% of the cases were driven by shifts in family relationships such as divorce, unemployment of the mother, or long-term illness.

In 2005, Finland formulated the action plan "A Finland Fit for Children," based on the call document adopted at the United Nations Special Session on Children in 2002 and set up a children's ombudsman and council that would focus on the best interests of children; however, it was unable to focus on child welfare as a policy area. Subsequent government initiatives triggered by the investigation of cases of girls' deaths and other deaths in 2008 led to preventive efforts to change the organizational culture led by the Ministry of Education and Culture, such as the establishment of a three-tier model of support, enactment of the School Student Welfare Act, promotion of the participation of elementary, junior, and senior students, support for coordination between teachers and medical professionals in the education field, and child protection system reforms (Functional child welfare, Toimiva lastensuojelu 2014), as well as the accumulation of policy changes and advanced cases surrounding children's welfare, including examples of advanced child welfare initiatives in basic municipalities and hospital districts in the National Development Program for Social Welfare and Health Care I, II (KASTE I, II) implemented over two phases between 2008 and 2015. However, although individual efforts in the field progressed, they remained within the field, which was also a challenge for LAPE. This led to cases where problems were exacerbated without access to services owing to the long gap between appointment dates as actual services for children or families were handed off to accommodate professionals' schedules.

After LAPE was specified in the administration's program in May 2015, the Minister of Family Affairs and Social Services was assigned to implement it, and the government's welfare and health group was in charge of managing the implementation process. Concrete preparation began on October 1st. Maria Kaisa Aula, a member of the Center Party who served two terms as Finland's first ombudsman for children, was appointed Program Director. Aula established and chaired the Steering Committee, which set policy from formulating the plan for implementation to evaluation. The Steering Committee comprised heads of municipalities responsible for providing services and representatives from the municipal federation, representatives from the Ministry of Social Affairs and Health, Ministry of Justice, and Ministry of Education and Culture, as well as representatives and practitioners from private and non-profit organizations and federations engaged in various services related to children and families. The Project Committee responsible for implementation included representatives from each ministry. Steering Committee meetings to formulate the concept and subsequent regular committee meetings held substantive discussions based on the opinions of professionals familiar with the actual practices in the field, creating a strong foundation for the reforms. At the beginning of 2016, without waiting for a formal decision on the basic concept, Aula began to describe LAPE at the association of municipalities to which municipalities across Finland belonged. Dedicated staff was assigned in March 2016, the concept was announced in April, and briefings in the area began.

The decision to implement LAPE was made by a regional administrative region based on maakunta (a broad regional administrative unit that comprised several municipalities forming an administrative federation), which as a regional federation was already responsible for development planning, and would be the unit for the delivery of financial resources for the reform. LAPE Committees were established in broad administrative areas and change agents were appointed for coordination and facilitation between municipalities and professionals for the management and implementation of the committees, who also served as bridges between the central government and the respective regions.

Although the central government took the initiative of setting up the philosophy, purpose, framework of the development projects, and planning structure of LAPE, in order to respect the autonomy of each region, specific details of implementation and provision methods were left to the discretion of regions. It was mandatory to implement at least one of the four development projects in a region; while some implemented all four, others implemented only one. In addition, since the reform budget was subsidized on a regional basis, reforms could be implemented on a certain scale, which also enhanced the ability of regions to implement them. LAPE Committees were required in each region, and they had to include representatives from healthcare, welfare, education, and youth programs, service providers including both public and private sectors, parish and youth representatives, and related parties, who were entrusted with leading both the planning and implementation of projects within the LAPE region. This also allowed for the formulation and implementation of plans that corresponded to the local situation in each region. Meanwhile, as mentioned above, the aim of LAPE was to reorganize services related to children and family welfare from different administrative levels at the regional level although it was not implemented directly by the regions. However, individual regions were responsible for organizing the network of services and providing services for children and families; the method of supply within each region was left to the discretion of individual regions.

In addition to support from the administration, the smooth implementation of LAPE was possible because of Aula's professional and political experience in public administration and children's policies. They included managerial approaches such as the ability to clearly define and share goals in the implementation process, the discretionary system that encouraged initiatives by implementers, introduction of change agents to facilitate reform, and the establishment of Committees to systematically take in a wide range of opinions, including those of professionals in the field (Yabunaga, 2020).

10.3.4 SOTE Reform: Establishment of Wellbeing Area (Alue)

As mentioned in Sect. 10.2, the gradual decentralization of the relationship between the central and local governments had been progressing since the 1990s, leading to repeated discussions on the restructuring of regional systems. Finland had a two-tiered governance structure with the central government and local municipalities. There is a large variation between the population sizes of different municipalities, which averages about 17,000, lower than Denmark and Sweden. Therefore, the focus was on securing the scale required to ensure stable social welfare, healthcare, and welfare services. With Finland's accession to the EU in the late 1990s, its experience with prolonged recession, and an increasing aging population, it was imperative that the government provides guidelines for the operation of a sustainable welfare state.

Therefore, the two-term Vanhanen government (Center Party, 2003–2007, 2007–2010) implemented PARAS for restructuring local government and services to ensure stable social and health and welfare services, and a certain population size was required for basic service provision units. Smaller municipalities were forced to choose between merging and cooperating with other municipalities, purchasing services from other municipalities and private enterprises, or utilizing public enterprises. In parallel with these reforms, large-scale municipal mergers were promoted using subsidies (Kettunen & Yabunaga, 2013).

The subsequent Katainen and Stubb government (National Coalition Party, 2011–2015) proposed the expansion of municipal services that had been provided through inter-municipal cooperation, as well as the creation of five municipal unions and catchment areas responsible for social welfare and healthcare. However, the proposals were rejected without an agreement on the delimitation of districts. After they were rejected, Prime Minister Katainen announced a metropolis policy to strengthen large cities. Before his resignation, he organized an expert meeting and released a report "Municipalities in Crisis," suggesting the possibility of voluntarily abandoning the existence of municipalities that were unable to maintain functions and transferring the functions to the central government (Valtiovarainministeriö, 2014, p. 16).

In 2015, the Sipilä government (Center Party, 2015–2019) assumed office and pledged SOTE reforms, planning to establish a state in 2017 and hold elections for a new organization in 2019. However, they could not proceed owing to their inability to reform the healthcare system, introduce competitive principles in the healthcare fields, and a lack of consensus regarding the establishment of regions. There was also a delay in planning the SOTE reforms during the late stages of their administration, and the lack of inter-party agreement for implementation eventually led to the resignation of the cabinet.

After the Sipilä government, the government shifted from the Center Party to SDP. When Sanna Marin became Prime Minister in December 2019, a proposal for SOTE reform was again submitted to the Parliament in December the following year. The reform proposal was passed on June 23, 2021, and went into effect on July 1st. The Sanna Marin government (SDP, 2019–2023) finally implemented the sub-national system reform that Vanhanen, Kaitanen, and Sipilä had all worked on until that point. The Marin government's proposed reforms narrowed the area of restructuring from the entire region system, which had previously been the aim, to the areas of social welfare, healthcare, and emergency rescue.

The SOTE reforms (healthcare, social welfare, and rescue services) were introduced as a means to realize one of the eight policy goals of the Sanna Marin's administration to achieve "Inclusive and Competent Finland" (Valtioneuvosto, 2019). It was aimed at minimizing regional disparities in services, ensuring equal access to services, and improving accessibility. The government clearly identified regional disparities and narrowed down the areas to make the Ministry of Social Affairs and Health a competent authority, setting it apart from previous administrations that aimed to achieve comprehensive regional system reform.

The SOTE reforms established 23 regional authorities or wellbeing county (Hyvinvointialue "alue") across Finland, based on the broader maakunta established as regional planning units with a capital area exception. A SOTE Center was established in each alue as a center of implementation, and the alue organization became a legal autonomous entity separate from basic local and central governments, as well as the primary provider of social welfare, healthcare, and emergency and rescue services, which are statutory. Meanwhile, it can carry out related projects to the extent that it does not interfere with statutory operation and can also serve as a maakunta. It may also outsource or purchase services for specific municipalities by agreement (Valtioneuvosto, 2020c).

Alue requires sufficient technical level, capacity, and structure to provide health and welfare services required to residents under all circumstances, including emergency and exceptional conditions. It is required to freely use professional social and medical staff and other personnel necessary to carry out tasks, to have facilities, equipment, and other necessary conditions, and to provide staff benefits and other amenities to fulfill organizational responsibilities (Valtioneuvosto, 2020a, 2020b). An alue need not be the producer of service, but it is responsible for securing and providing services in its region, that is, provide welfare.

The government explained the benefits of establishing the alue as follows (Valtioneuvosto, 2020a, 2020b, 2020d). Establishing alue makes decision-making easier and allows supply entities to centrally manage more human resources and other materials. It therefore makes it possible not just to introduce a variety of professionals and advanced equipment, but is expected to expedite client response. Furthermore, it allows further promotion of the digitization of remote services. In conjunction with the promotion of digitalization, the centralization of records for medical and welfare services facilitates information sharing across levels and disciplines. Specifically, the ability to comprehensively understand information about clients including "low-threshold services," strengthening the development of early detection and preventions. Digitization of information on each individual's use of social welfare, healthcare, and services also promotes self-care by making it accessible for individuals. Essentially, the goal of establishing alue is not limited to improving the efficiency of conventional delivery of services. Enabling the provision of cross-sectional and cross-level services allows the system to provide comprehensive services, as well as the strengthening of early response and preventive service development. It also accounts for self-care, allowing clients to proactively enhance their wellbeing, as an important factor, and aims at reforming social welfare and healthcare services.

Behind this explanation is the fact that functioning through alue was practical. A form similar to the current system was already in place for some alue, where each hospital district was responsible for its own health and medical services. As seen already in the case of Eksote introduced above, a variety of professionals and advanced equipment were introduced based on the centralized management of human resources, information, and other resources, which alue appear to have successfully achieved, leading to expeditious service for clients, digitization of remote services, enhancement of early detection and preventions, and promotion of self-care (Eksote, 2017; Yabunaga, 2021).

10.4 Discussion

10.4.1 Reform Cases in Context

While positioning the four cases above in their political and historical contexts as described in Sect. 10.2, they have been analyzed as adaptations to environmental changes, focusing on the actors involved.

The Kainuu administrative experiment became a pioneering case of regionalization as a choice for the survival of local governments exposed to competition in the wake of integration with EU markets. Finland had completed the process of developing a welfare state by the 1980s and joined the EU in the 1990s amid deep recession. It had already completed the development of a centralized welfare state by the 1980s, and by decentralizing through subsidy reform in the 1990s, it sought to stabilize its financial base for small municipalities in vulnerable rural areas, where the population was aging or migrating, by moving away from individual subsidies to economies of scale through mergers and other measures. The establishment of regional governments was also in line with the direction of the SDP government, which emphasized the protection of workers, provision of universal services, and reduction of inequality. It also involves the transfer of some functions from the central government through special laws and the establishment of a regional government in charge of social welfare and healthcare for the municipalities in the region in an integrated manner. Reforms proceeded smoothly as they were implemented by municipal leaders, achieving financial stability and improving the quality of services, but consensus could not be reached for the transfer of authority from some ministries, and the project was terminated by the continued opposition of one participating municipality.

The case of South Karelia Healthcare District developing new services as a broad administrative region in the social welfare and healthcare district of Eksote was an effort of a declining peripheral region with unfavorable geographical conditions.

When the initiative was launched, the Center Party, which had its main support base in the rural area, was in power, and without a radical merger of municipalities, the PARAS reform could only determine the required population size of the supply units of administrative services. However, this led to the creation of the Eksote district, where hospital medical care, social welfare, and primary care were integrated. Eksote collaborated with local universities, introduced business management methods, used project-based funding to improve finances, and successfully developed new services and projects. This can be attributed to the financial stabilization of the fragile, peripheral areas shifted from the traditional central government-managed disbursement of grants to support municipalities to project-based financial assistance and regional-development-based financial support.

LAPE can be considered an example of introduction of a new regional service governing district system led by the central government. While the Center Party administration, which pledged to reform social welfare and healthcare by establishing new regions, faced issues in adjusting its interests, the Party's policy leaders in the field of child and family welfare drew up and steadily implemented bold reforms. Resistance to these reforms was diminished as issues in the field of child and family welfare had already surfaced and advanced cases had been accumulated; the broadening of social welfare and healthcare had already reached a common understanding as promised by the administration; and the maakunta, which had already been established as regional units, was used as a foundation, allowing a menu of reforms to be selected by the unit. However, there were no clear results on child and family support for children in a way that integrated social welfare, healthcare, and school education, which had been the original intention of LAPE. Although change agents were introduced to encourage collaboration and integration among professions and regions, the government's 4-year term ran out as the reform was realized, the administration changed, and SOTE was implemented before the outcomes of LAPE could be emerged.

The regional system reform aimed at the reorganization of local governments reached a certain conclusion with the establishment of alue through the SOTE reforms of 2021. The focused discussion over the reform of the local system since the 2000s failed to materialize as the Center Party, with its main support base in those regions, and the National Coalition Party, oriented toward liberalization and increased competitiveness, failed to gain support to establish regional blocs and reach a consensus on the liberalization of services. Marin's SDP focused on social welfare and healthcare based on existing regional administrative area markers of maakunta, which allowed smooth consensus formation. In addition, technological developments, such as the digitization of medical care, have become one of the driving forces for expansion to a wider area in an environment where constant efforts are required to reduce expenses given an aging population, which strengthens the theoretical argument. As seen in the three case studies above and the reform of the regional system as in PARAS, efforts toward regionalization were performed intermittently with trial and error, and established as the alue system by the SOTE reform.

After promoting a relatively loose centralized system of local self-government through a framework of institutions and subsidies to achieve a universal welfare state, Finland has reduced central government intervention and increased municipal discretion since the 1990s. In the first two reform cases, municipalities in disadvantaged areas proposed and implemented new reform plans for their survival. While the initial initiatives (the first) caused conflicts, the second took advantage of the changing local systems and financial support systems, and the original initiatives developed and spread to other municipalities.

While the local initiatives developed until the 2010s, the two initiatives of the 10 s and 20 s were top-down reforms implemented by the central government. Rather than taking the initiative, the central government followed and institutionalized the spread of joint governance practices at the municipal level and reinforced them.

In other words, the central government sometimes reduced its intervention and sometimes changed the framework through top-down initiatives, facilitating changes in the service provision structure of the welfare state. However, it can be interpreted that it is/was a facilitative process that encouraged spontaneous and autonomous change. This is because, rather than a strictly centralized institutional design, it created an environment that was tolerant of local government discretion and rather facilitated local government self-determination.

10.4.2 Final Reflections

Local governments in Nordic countries have considerable administrative and financial autonomy, similar in the sense that their local government forms an integrated part of the state, carrying out administrative work, while the central government exercises a certain degree of control. It has even been explained that the structure of a Nordic welfare state model is incomplete without depicting the central position of local self-government in the implementation of the welfare policies (Petersen et al., 2017).

While locating the path to the establishment of Finland's regional government in the context of local systemic reform, this chapter looked at changes in its external environment, such as EU membership and technological developments, and the transformation needs from individual circumstances such as declining peripheral regions, and described the structure and response of the actors involved in the reform. In the research on the formation and development of vocational training systems, as Thelen states, we can find a continuity rather than transformation (Thelen, 2012). The process leading up to the SOTE reforms in Finland described here is a continuum of change and can be regarded as an adaptation to the pressures that multiple environmental factors put on welfare state actors.

The SOTE reforms have led to discontent in individual regions over changes in services and the pressure to modify them. The SDP administration that introduced SOTE also backtracked, and the National Coalition Party administration worked to "modify" SOTE as of 2024. Thelen states, "When institutions are established, they are not universally welcomed by their surroundings and are not capable of adapting completely to their environment. Rather, they remain subject to ongoing conflict as actors fight over the form they should assume and the functions they should perform" (Thelen, 2012). Thus, the structure of welfare provision in Finland continues to evolve in a context of ongoing conflict.

Acknowledgments This research was supported by JSPS Grant-in-Aid for Scientific Research No. 19H04368.

References

Armingeon, K., & Bonoli, A. (2006). *The Politics of post-industrial welfare states: Adapting post-war social policies to new social risks*. Routledge.

Bonoli, G., & Natali, D. (2012). *The Politics of the new welfare state*. Oxford University Press.

Eksote. (2017). *The Eksote model: Building on the integration of social and health care services, May 2017*. South Karelia Social and Health Care District.

Esping-Andersen, G. (1989). *The three worlds of welfare capitalism*. Polity Press.

Esping-Andersen, G. (1999). *Social foundations of postindustrial economies*. Oxford University Press.

Heikkila, M., Hvinden, B., Kautto, M., Marklund, S., & Ploug, N. (Eds.). (1999). *Nordic social policy: Changing welfare states*. Routledge.

Hemerijck, A. (2013). *Changing welfare states*. Oxford University Press.

Kettunen, P., & Yabunaga, C. (2013). Political process of municipal amalgamations in Finland and Japan: Differences and similarities. *Japanese Journal of Northern European Studies, 10*, 25–34.

Kitayama, K. (2011). *Fukushikokka no seidohatten to chihoseihu—Kokuminkenkouhoken no seijigaku [Institutional development of the welfare state and regional administration: the political science of national health insurance]*. Yuhikaku.

Komamura, Y., & Tanaka, S. (Eds.). (2019). *Kensho. atarashii sehuti net. Seikatsu konkyusya jiritsu shienseido to Saitamaken Asupotojigyo no Chosen [Examination the new safety net: The system for supporting independence of the destitute and challenges of Saitama's Asport project]*. Shinsen-sha.

Korpela, J., Elfvengren, K., Kaarna, T., Tepponen, M., & Tuominen, M. (2012). Collaboration process for integrated social and health care strategy implementation. *International Journal of Integrated Care, 12*, e42. https://doi.org/10.5334/ijic.816

Myles, J., & Quadagno, J. (2002). Political theories of the welfare state. *Social Service Review, 76*(1), 34–57. https://doi.org/10.1086/324607

Nishioka, S. (2021). *Nihongata fukushikokka saihen no gensetsu seiji to kanryosei [Discourse politics and bureaucracy in the reorganization of the Japanese welfare state: "Countermeasures to the falling birthrate" in the family policies]*. Nakanishiya Shuppan.

Ota, S., Masuda, S., Tanaka, T., & Kamitubo, A. (1986). *Sawauchimura hunsenki [Diary of struggles in Sawauchi village]*. Akebi Shobo.

Owalgroup. (2019). *Lapsi- ja perhepalvelujen muutosohjelma (LAPE) -kärkihankkeen arviointi, loppuraportti*. https://stm.fi/documents/1271139/13111556/Loppuraportti+LAPE_arviointi+8.3.2019_final.pdf/3efbd6b7-c22f-ef66-b412-4b3b521d9512/Loppuraportti+LAPE_arviointi+8.3.2019_final.pdf

Petersen, K., Kuhnle, S., & Kettunen, P. (Eds.). (2017). *Hokuo fukushikokka ha jizoku kanouka? Tagensei to seisaku kyocho no yukue [The Nordic model: Still sustainable? Five exceptions and policy cooperation]*. Minerva Shobo.

Rose, L., & Ståhlberg, K. (2005). The Nordic countries: Still the 'promised land'? In B. Denters & L. Rose (Eds.), *Comparing local governance: Trends and developments*. Palgrave.

Sosiaali- ja terveysministeriö. (2019). *Sosiaali- ja terveysministeriön kärkihankkeiden arvionti yhteinen raportti [Overall report on the assessment of priority projects by the Ministry of Social Welfare]*, Sosiaali- ja terveysministeriö. http://urn.fi/URN:ISBN:978-952-00-4071-0

Sellers, J. M., & Lidström, A. (2007). Decentralization, local government, and the welfare state. *Governance, 20*(4), 609–632. https://doi.org/10.1111/j.1468-0491.2007.00374.x

Steinmo, S. (2010). *The evolution of modern states: Sweden, Japan, and the United States*. Cambridge University Press.

Taylor-Gooby, P. (ed.) (2004). New Risks, New Welfare: The Transformation of the European Welfare State, Oxford: Oxford University Press.

Thelen, K. (2004). *How institutions evolve: The political economy of skills in Germany, Britain, the United States, and Japan*. Cambridge University Press.

Thelen, K. (2012). Varieties of Capitalism: Trajectories of Liberalization and the New Politics of Social Solidarity. Annual Review of Political Science, 15:137–159. https://doi.org/10.1146/annurev-polisci-070110-122959

Valtioneuvosto. (2019). *Inclusive and competent Finland - A socially, economically and ecologically sustainable society*. Programme of Prime Minister Sanna Marin's Government 11 December 2019. Valtioneuvosto.

Valtioneuvosto. (2020a). *Faktalehti 001, Sote-uudistus – keskeinen lainsäädäntö tiiviisti, Valtioneuvosto*. [Factsheet].

Valtioneuvosto. (2020b). *Faktalehti 002, Sote-uudistus – keskeinen lainsäädäntö tiiviisti, Valtioneuvosto*. [Factsheet].

Valtioneuvosto. (2020c). *Faktalehti, Sote-uudistus – järjestämisvastuu ja monituottajuus, Valtioneuvosto*. [Factsheet].

Valtioneuvosto. (2020d). *Hallituksen esitys: Hyvinvointialueiden perustaminen ja sosiaali- ja terveydenhuollon sekä pelastustoimen järjestämisen uudistus*, Mediatilaisuus 8.12.2020, Valtioneuvosto.

Valtiovarainministeriö. (2014). *Kunnat turbulenssissa- Millainen on tulevaisuuden kunta? Tulevaisuuden kunta – asiantuntijatyöryhmän keskustelupaperi*, Joulukuu 2014, Valtiovarainministeriö.

Valtiovarainministeriö. (2015). *Kuntien tehtävät ja velvoitteet 2015. Täydennysraportti, Valtiovarainminisiteriön julkaisu 30/2015, Valtiovarainministeriö*. https://vm.fi/kuntien-tehtavat-ja-toiminta

Yabunaga, C. (2008). Finland-ni-okeru Chiikiseisaku-no Henyou: Kakusa shakai-no Shinkou-no Nakade [Rising social inequality: the transformation of of regional policy in Finland]., *Japanese journal of Northern European studies, 5*, 17–27.

Yabunaga, C. (2021). Development of welfare states' structural reorganization: Focusing on the establishment of new regional governments in Finland, 2021 Conference paper of the Japanese Association of Northern European Studies.

Yamada, M. (2006). *Finland fukushi kokka no keisei: Shakai sabisu to chihobunken kaikaku [Development of the Finnish welfare state. Social services and decentralization reforms]*. Bokutakusha.

Yokoyama, J. (2019). *Tenki ni tatsu Finland hukusikokka. Koureisyahukusi no henka to chihouzaiseichoseiseido no kaikaku [Finland's welfare state reaching a turning point: Changes in elderly welfare and a reform of the local financial adjustment system]*. Dobunkan Shuppan.

Chapter 11
Adaptation of Finnish Welfare State to a Post-Industrial Society: Practicing "The Consensus Model of Democracy" Through Formation of Diverse Coalition Governments

Yuriko Shibayama

Abstract This chapter explains the political mechanism of the Finnish welfare state adapted to a post-industrial society as one of the Nordic welfare states (Esping-Andersen, The three worlds of welfare capitalism. Polity Press, 1990) and countries with a coordinated market economy (Katzenstein, Small states in world markets industrial policy in Europe. Cornell University Press, 1985). Steinmo (The evolution of modern states: Sweden, Japan, and the United States. Cambridge University Press, 2010) argues that Sweden has several adaptive advantages that enable the coevolution of politics, economics, and social policy. However, Finland has many differences from Sweden in its conditions, which raises the question of how Finland achieves the current position. When strong presidential power ended in the 1980s, parliamentarianism began to function. Since 1983, stable 4-year governments of majority coalitions out of a multiparty system have been in power. Diverse coalition governments with no dominant party and different parties' combination are one of the characteristics of Finnish politics that bring resilience to its policies in a rapidly changing society. Higher education, and economic policies, especially science and technology, and information and communications technology policies developed since the 1960s, have been strongly integrated into the program of post-industrial welfare state since the 1980s. As Lijphart (Patterns of democracy. Yale University Press, 1999) argues for the possibility of a consensus model as a form of democracy in opposition to the Westminster model, the case of Finnish political mechanism provides policy flexibility in post-industrial society.

Keywords Finland · The consensus model of democracy · Multiparty system · Majority coalition governments · Social investment state

---

Y. Shibayama (✉)
Department of Nordic Studies, School of Cultural and Social Studies, Tokai University, Hiratsuka, Kanagawa, Japan
e-mail: ys@tokai.ac.jp

N. Tokumaru et al. (eds.), *Creative Co-evolution of the Economies and Welfare States in the Nordic Countries*, Evolutionary Economics and Social Complexity Science 32, https://doi.org/10.1007/978-981-97-8569-8_11

11.1 Introduction

The challenge for welfare states in post-industrial societies is to expand their capacity to respond to globalization and a knowledge-based society. The welfare state is more required to play the role of a "social investment state" with functions such as active labor market policies that encourage skills. Katzenstein (1985) argues that welfare state development is encouraged in countries with small open economies that are more susceptible to international markets. When business and labor are subject to forces beyond the domestic market, the pressure to control class conflicts over distribution through government intervention and the adjustment of interests becomes extremely strong (Katzenstein, 1985). He has conducted research on small European countries, including Norway, Denmark, and Sweden. However, the case of Finland has not been covered in his research.

Esping-Andersen (1990) utilized Katzenstein's ideas and classified welfare states into three types, and classified the Nordic countries into "social democratic regimes." Finland achieved this later. Hall and Soskice (2001) showed that there are varieties of capitalism (VoC) and he positioned Nordic countries such as Denmark and Sweden as coordinated market economies (CMEs), as opposed to the Anglo-Saxon model, a liberal market economies (LMEs). The Nordic welfare state, with its idea of universalism, has limited the influence of neo-liberalism, which also applies to Finland even more due to the timing of building welfare state in the country. Steinmo (2010), a researcher in the new institutional theory of comparative politics, incorporated evolutionary theory and developed an analysis comparing Japan, the United States, and Sweden. He clarified Sweden's adaptive advantage by describing the country as a "bumblebee," which can fly despite it looks heavy. He explained Sweden's coevolution of economics, politics, and social policy as an answer to one of the VoC theories. In this chapter, inspired by the researches above, Finland's case of adaptation to the welfare state in post-industrial time will be examined.

The main arguments of this chapter are as follows:

1. First, Finland has been adapting to a post-industrial social investment welfare state since the 1980s, based on its adaptation to basic social security for all citizens in the 1930s and the Nordic welfare state since the 1960s, although the process is quite different from that of Sweden.
2. Despite many differences with Sweden, Finland's "consensus democracy" functions with multiparty system and various coalition governments as a mechanism for quickly responding to crises and changes. This mechanism was embedded in the early twentieth century, but with the expansion of presidential powers during the Cold War, what had been dysfunctional came to the forefront.
3. In details, since 1980, Finnish politics has been characterized by a coalition government especially by oversized coalitions, with no dominant political party. Votes were distributed among three to four major parties. This means basically the biggest party forms a coalition with other major and smaller parties participating in the coalition. There are many patterns of coalition governments, also

parties emerged from new social cleavages. Those varieties of coalitions bring flexibility and resilience to the Finnish policies.

Lijphart (1999) argued for the diversity of democracy, and referred to the potential of the consensus model instead of the Westminster model. He often discussed Belgium and Switzerland as examples of consensus democracy, but Finland's case was not covered in detail. The reason behind of this was as Sartori (1976) has classified the party system, Finnish party politics have for a long time been recognized as an "extreme multiparty system" or "polarized multiparty system." This was due to the timing of the research when presidential power was strong due to the Cold War and governments were unstable.

From the 1980s onward—the post-Kekkonen era—"proportional representation system," a "unicameral system" embedded in the 1906 parliamentary reform, started functioning well. A spontaneous "multiparty system" has begun to emerge, with major political parties competing with each other and conducting various governments. There are three or four major parties, therefore no dominant party exist. The formation of coalitions varies. An oversized majority of governments is common in Finland (Karvonen, 2014). This chapter shows how these diverse multiparty systems and coalition government structures open to innovation and suitable for adapting to change and contribute to the adaptation of welfare state in post-industrial time. The key to Finland's adaptation to a post-industrial society is the interlocking of politics, and educational, economic, and social policies.

This study presents a new perspective based on the findings of several previous studies. Castells and Himanen (2002) and Miettinen (2010) analyze the "Finland model" from the perspective of the relationship between the development of information and communication technology and the welfare state. Castells and Himanen (2002) argue that information society has renewed its welfare state. Miettinen (2010) provides a detailed analysis of the Finnish case as a national innovation system, referring to important actors such as the Academy of Finland, Sitra, the Council for Science and Technology, and Tekes (the Agency for Technology and Innovation). Notably, he supports the idea that innovation policy flexibly adapted to Nokia's success rather than Finland's innovation policy being successful. Nokia's presence in Finland, which does not have as many large international corporations as Sweden, can be considered contingent, and it shows that making effective use of the company and its subsystems contributed to the construction of a welfare state in a post-industrial society. He also notes that as a small country between big powers, Finland has experienced numerous crises that have shaped its strong national identity.

The "Finnish model" has been reconsidered in the field of social policy since joining the EU. For example, Saari (2006) comprehensively presented Finnish policies in diverse areas such as the economy, employment, education, information society, and policies for a sustainable society, while adhering to Pierson's (2014) path dependence. However, this study does not discuss the political mechanisms that connect various policies. Kettunen (2019) argues that the meaning of the "welfare state" has expanded. In the evolution of the electoral and party systems in Finland, Sundberg (2002) insists that the parliamentary reform of 1906 was very modern and points out that the general framework of Finland's parliament and elections has changed little since it was originally designed. Considering Pierson's (2004) "Politics in Time," what was embedded in Finnish politics in its early years had a profound effect later on after they passed through a complicated route influenced by external factors.

Karvonen (2014) conducted a study on Finland's coalition government, and his research provides important implications for this chapter when considering how Finland's political characteristics influence consensus democracy—the formation and operation of governments and the direction of policies that respond to change. Lijphart (1999) has developed the idea of "the consensus model of democracy" toward "the Westminster Model of Democracy." While this research is based on comparative politics, drawing on the ideas of evolutionary theory, it raises the question of how Finland has become a post-industrial welfare state, despite various conditions different from Sweden, focusing on Finland's party politics and coalition government as a mechanism for promoting innovation and responding flexibly to change. This study argues how politics, policies, and diverse coalition governments enable adaptation in a post-industrial society.

The next section introduces the Finnish political and party systems. In Sect. 11.3, based on Steinmo's (2010) research, differences between Sweden and Finland are observed by examining Swedish adaptive advantages; subsequently, having understood the differences in Finland, the process of building Finland's welfare state is presented. Section 11.4 focuses on the characteristics of the coalition government since the 1980s; and Sect. 11.5, an analysis of adaptation of the welfare state in post-industrial societies out of the influence of diverse coalitions will be explained as quoting government programs with concrete cases. In conclusion, Finland's diverse coalition governments contribute to the coevolution of social, economic, and educational policies.

11.2 Finnish Political System and Party System

This section provides an overview of Finland's political system, including its semi-presidential system, party politics, and multiparty systems.

The history of parliament started when the Estates Assembly was convened as Finland became the Grand Duchy of the Russian Empire in the nineteenth century. The movement to raise nationalism began, and from the 1860s onward, political parties were born. In 1906, a unicameral, proportional representation parliament was established through parliamentary reform, giving men and women over the age of 24 the right to vote and be elected. Several political parties were formed before and after the establishment of the parliament. The first election was held in 1907.

A declaration of independence was issued on December 6, 1917; however, a civil war began in January 1918. When Finland became independent, the original plan was to invite the king from Germany; however, due to opposition from other countries, it was decided in 1919 that the country would become a republic. Consequently, the president became the head of state, creating a semi-presidential system. After independence, several political parties reorganized themselves.

Finnish political parties can be classified as (1) traditional major political parties; the National Coalition Party, the Liberal Party (dissolved after World War II), the Agrarian Party, the Social Democratic Party, (2) traditional small parties; Swedish People's Party and the Left Alliance (previously the Communist Party, and after World War II, the Finnish People's Democratic League), (3) relatively new political parties; Christian Democratic Party, Green Party and True Finns Party. The major parties' voter turnout is around 20%.

From the time the parliament was established to the present, Finnish politics have been based on a multiparty system. This also applies to the Nordic five-party system (currently an eight-party system). The first political party was launched during the cleavage on language issues. In relation to the Russian Empire, the Finns Party and Swedish Party split into the Old Finns Party (conservative) and the Young Finns (liberal) Party.

The second wave of the establishment of political parties made parties for the mass people. The Workers' Party was founded in 1899 (renamed to the Social Democratic Party in 1903). It was founded under the influence of socialist parties in Germany, Austria, Sweden, and other countries. At first, there was no clear distinction between socialism and social democracy. In 1906, several political organizations joined to form the Agrarian League.[1] One of the founder of the Agrarian League, Santeri Alkio, was originally a politician from the Young Finns (Mickelsson, 2015), and the Finnish Agrarian League had ideological roots that combined liberalism and conservatism (Shibayama, 2021). The result of the 1907 election, the Social Democratic Party won the largest number of seats, and it was a huge victory. At that time, in terms of population structure, the proportion of farmers was big, and the number of the Agrarian League expanded thereafter. In 1918, the Old Finns changed their name to the National Coalition Party and the Young Finns to the Progressive Party. Additionally, the Communists were officially separated from the Social Democratic Party.

Social cleavages ("the frozen"; Lipset & Rokkan, 1967) of Finnish political parties can be classified: (1) language (ethnicity), (2) capitalist and non-capitalist, (3) urban and rural areas. The Liberal Party and Agrarian League contributed significantly to Finland's decision to become a republic. This also applies to the Nordic five-party system, but there are some differences, such as the existence of language parties, the disappearance of the Liberal Progressive Party after World War II, and the stronger presence of the Agrarian League.

Finnish politics since World War II can be roughly divided into an era when the presidential system was strengthened, and an era when it was weakened and parliamentarianism was strengthened. The main political parties in the 1920s and 1930s

[1] Maalaisliitto (Agrarian League) was established in 1906, and renamed "Keskusta" (the Centre Party) in 1965. In this paper, "Agrarian Leage" refers to the earlier time, whereas "Centre Party" refers to the subsequent period. "Agrarian Party" refers to both the Agrarian League and the Centre Party time.

were the National Coalition Party, the Progressive Party, the Social Democratic Party, and the Agrarian League. Expansion of presidential power in the Cold War structure, the President Urho Kekkonen initially from the Agrarian League gained the power, on the other hand, the National Coalition Party was not appointed to the government, in the beginning of his time, the Social Democratic Party was also warned. However, the party gained a position in the government when Kekkonen discovered his personal relationship with some of the party's politicians (Häikiö, 1992). Sartori (1976) categorized and evaluated the Finnish party system of this period as a polarized multiparty system in his comparative studies of party politics.

In the 1980s, the post-Kekkonen era began, and with the next Mauno Koivisto and Martti Ahtisaari, presidential powers were reduced, and parliamentarism was strengthened. The constitutional amendment in 2000 significantly reduced presidential powers.

11.3 Condition to Form Nordic Welfare State in Sweden and Finland

In this section, the differences between Sweden and Finland's adaptive advantages based on Steinmo's research (Steinmo, 2010) will be clarified. He argues that Sweden has been admirably successful in adapting to the global economy and social change in the country, while maintaining its commitment to a progressive welfare state and an egalitarian society. Sweden and Finland, as Nordic welfare states (Esping-Andersen, 1990) and CMEs (Katzenstein, 1985), respectively, have a high level of income equality, the highest tax burden in the world, and the highest level of social expenditure worldwide while providing universal and comprehensive social policies. A high degree of equality between men and women was common (see Chap. 1 for further details).

First, based on Steinmo's (2010) analysis of Sweden's adaptive advantages, the differences in Finland's conditions are clarified. An overview of the Finland's welfare state of the early period, the period of development of the Nordic welfare state, and the period of the social investment state will be explained next.

11.3.1 Difference of Adaptive Advantages in Sweden and Finland

This study clarifies how Finland, a welfare state with different environments and conditions, was able to "fly" as another "bumblebee" (Steinmo, 2010). To this end, differences between Finland and its conditions were investigated. Although both are Nordic welfare states, Sweden and Finland have many differences. Steinmo describes Sweden's various adaptive advantages, such as proportional representation and compromise in politics and cooperation between labor and capital, and concludes that these factors create the coevolution of politics, the economy, and the welfare state. Many of these advantages do not apply to Finland, which has uniquely filled the gaps and differences.

Considering the historical backgrounds of Sweden and Finland, it is common that they are historically homogeneous countries located in the northern part of Europe, but in terms of current population size, Finland is a smaller country, with about half the size of Sweden. Another historical difference is that Sweden and Russia ruled the country for a long time. While Sweden has steel resources that have led to the rapid development of the steel industry, Finland's resources are mainly forest ones, so it cannot be said that it is rich in resources. Another big difference is that due to geopolitical differences, Sweden survived both world wars as a neutral and there was also a "coincidence" of wartime demand, but due to geopolitical and historical conditions, Finland after gaining independence, it has experienced a tragic civil war, and during World War II, it experienced two wars against the Soviet Union, starting with an invasion by the Soviet Union. Geopolitical conditions gave Sweden an adaptive advantage (Steinmo, 2010) but posed crises and challenges to Finland, forcing it into harsher conditions.

Furthermore, the symbiotic relationship between labor and capitalism based on the history of harmony and cooperation that Steinmo (ibid.) shows is progressing slowly in Finland. The civil war divided labor and capital, and the war with the Soviet Union overcame this division. Sweden is characterized by a high rate of unionization and concentration of economic power, and although it is relatively high in Finland, the rate of unionization remains lower than in Sweden.[2] Furthermore, the concentration of economic power that prioritizes resources in the hands of large companies is not observed in Finland, and the Rehn-Meidner model developed in Sweden has not been adopted. The government was extremely unstable during the Cold War, as the socio-democratic elite, who viewed political economy as an engineering problem and were growing in confidence, did not assume a dominant position in Finland. There was not a stable long-term government by the Social Democratic Party there.

In the process of confronting a highly competitive international economy, a "symbiotic relationship" was created between organizations representing capital and labor (Steinmo, 2010). The result was the development of a dynamic process of increasing returns. Steinmo analyzed that in Sweden, labor, capital, and the state formed the basis for a mechanism of mutual cooperation and advantage and this resulted in an extremely adaptable and flexible system. In summary, Sweden's adaptive advantages do not apply to Finland's. Next, the process of developments of the welfare state, how Finland can build a Nordic welfare state and form a CME accordingly under the different condition, will be described.

---

[2] OECD shows trade union density of Sweden is 65.2%, and those of Finland is 58.8% (OECD 2019). https://data-explorer.oecd.org/vis?df[ds]=DisseminateFinalDMZ&df[id]=DSD_TUD_CBC%40DF_TUD&df[ag]=OECD.ELS.SAE&dq=..&pd=2000%2C&to[TIME_PERIOD]=false&ly[cl]=TIME_PERIOD&ly[rs]=REF_AREA&vw=tb

11.3.2 *Path to Welfare State and Nordic Welfare State*

Finland has become a CME/Nordic social investment state because it has introduced universal social policies targeting all citizens and built a Nordic welfare state by raising the level of universalist welfare services, while also improving the level of welfare for wage earners. Here, how Finland, despite its different conditions and circumstances, developed stepwise and uniquely into a welfare state is observed. The process of adaptation of a welfare state is mainly divided into three stages: (1) the initial stage of gaining an early main social policy (from 1920s to the 1950s), (2) adaptation to a Nordic welfare state (from 1960s to 1980s), and (3) adaptation to the welfare state of a post-industrial society (from the late 1970s or the 1980s to the present).

11.3.2.1 Introduction of Early Social Policies

In the late nineteenth century, Yrjö Sakari Yrjö-Koskinen, founder of the Conservative Finns' Party, attended the German Society for Social Policy and conveyed his social policy ideas to Finland. After the inauguration of the parliament, the Social Democratic Party called for the introduction of social insurance in continental Europe, but in the 1910s, when the Social Democratic Party had the largest number of seats in parliament, Finland suffered severe financial setbacks on the eve of independence. The influence of the Social Democratic Party weakened as a result of the civil war, and the Agrarian League rejected the introduction of social insurance for wage earners. The discussion on social insurance was replaced by a discussion on the "national pension" by the Agrarian Union, and the Act of National Pension was enacted in 1937 (see Chap. 3 for details). In the conflict between the interests of urban and rural areas, income redistribution to rural areas was prioritized. As a characteristic, Finnish social policy did not start with a Bismarckian occupational system but instead became strongly embedded in the nature of Beveridgeian universalism, which targeted all citizens based on social rights.

This question can also be asked about how Finland adapted as a welfare state, but shows that when it acquired the characteristics of a welfare state, it strongly embedded universal elements. This is an important requirement for later acquiring the characteristics of a Nordic welfare state. It can also be said that in Finland, which had strongly introduced a flat-rate benefit system earlier, Bismarckian characteristics were weakly adopted (Baldwin, 1990).

11.3.2.2 Adaptation to Nordic Welfare State

The next question is how they have adapted to the Nordic welfare state. Although conditions are significantly different from those of Sweden, such as war experience and the absence of stable long-term governments, how can Finland develop a more comprehensive social policy after becoming an industrialized society after the 1960s?

After the war, with postwar reconstruction strengthening ties with Western European countries, and progress in industrialization, Finland's social policy gradually became "social democratic." Its seeds were observed in the 1960s and reached the level of the Nordic welfare state in the 1970s and the 1980s. This was not carried out by a political alliance centered on the Social Democratic Party, but by the efforts of the Agrarian League (from 1965, the Centre Party) as well. Furthermore, during the Cold War, presidential power increased, cabinet formation strongly reflected the president's intentions, and the president intervened in various policies. Economic growth and development of social policies are linked. From 1968 onward, labor-capital agreements proceeded, initially with the mediation of the president.

Discussions about social insurance and health insurance continued in the 1940s, and although a committee was set up to introduce health insurance in the 1950s, Prime Minister Sukselainen of the Agrarian League prioritized the national pension system from a funded system to a pay-as-you-go system in 1957 (See Chap. 3 for details). Social policy in Finland continues to be dominated by agrarian forces, which differs from Sweden, where the Social Democratic Party has taken a big initiative.

After Kekkonen was elected president in 1956, the Agrarian League strengthened its influence as the presidential party. On the other hand, the National Coalition Party and the Social Democratic Party began to realize their interests in other forms, and Finland's social policy became more eclectic. In 1960, an occupational pension was established reflecting the wishes of the National Coalition Party and the Social Democratic Party. With a compromise made by the Agrarian League, an occupational pension for short-term workers was introduced the following year. The health insurance system was debated over occupational and voluntary systems, and in 1963, a system that would cover all citizens was settled. Then separate set-ups were arranged for occupational health, and a complementary system was added in a similar way to the pension system. Unemployment insurance was also developed in combination with public and semi-public systems supplemented by businesses and insurance companies. In Finland, the national government was in charge of the universal system, and companies and insurance companies were mainly in charge of the income-based system; however, since all workers are compulsory to participate, it can be said that it is a semi-public system. This corporatism resulted in an increase in the standards of welfare services. However, the mechanism is more complex, and it can be said that they created a system significantly different from that of Sweden.

Additionally, Finland's transformation into an industrial society in the 1960s contributed to the establishment of the health insurance system and the expansion and improvement of welfare services. Although Finland was industrialized later than the Nordic countries, it did so at a very fast pace. The idea of building a Nordic welfare state was supported by the scholar Pekka Kuusi (1917–1989). He was also a politician, and the president of the alcohol monopoly corporation Alko. He published a book called "60's Social Policy" in 1961 (Kuusi, 1961). Based on the theories of Gunnar Myrdal, the book proposed an update to Finland's traditional social policy thinking at the time of its transition to an industrial society and proposed more comprehensive policies. Kuusi's words and ideas received wide media coverage and were mentioned by politicians and academics, which made huge impact on Finnish society and resulted in an agreement to build a Nordic welfare state (Saari, 1997; Shibayama, 2010; Tuomioja, 1996). His work was significant because it attempted to redraw Finnish social policies.

Furthermore, from the 1970s onward, cooperation between labor and capital, red and green, progressed, and the construction of a Nordic welfare state progressed from the 1970s to the 1980s. Smolander (2000) points out that the 1970s was a period of construction of Finland's version of the "People's home" promoted in Sweden in the 1930s. Changes in party politics included the transformation of the National Coalition Party and the compromise of the Social Democratic Party. The National Coalition Party began to incorporate the middle class. The Social Democratic Party was also compromised by giving up state-owned enterprise projects (Häikiö, 1992). Since 1960, the Centre Party has become a catch-all, comprehensive party, allowing farmers to respond to domestic needs. In the 1970s, there were many coalition governments between the Social Democrats and the Centre Party (the red-green coalition); however, this was due to President Kekkonen's influence.

11.3.2.3 Adaptation to Social Investment State

In Finland, education and science and technology policies, which were developed after the 1960s, were gradually integrated into the welfare state strategy. Presidential intervention was seen in various policies, and many decisions were made in a top-down manner. The coevolution of politics, the economy, and social policy has enabled the country to adapt to a post-industrial society. Awareness of education, science and technology, information society, and international competitiveness became the driving forces from the 1970s and 1980s onward. Also it can be pointed out that owing to late industrialization, welfare state construction, and economic growth, Finland was not strongly influenced by neo-liberalism in the 1970s.

In the 1970s, the Finnish People's Democratic League, which refrained from entering the government based on its policy of friendship with the Soviet Union, began to enter. President Kekkonen's leadership was not limited to the Centre Party, but he also began to establish a Social Democratic Party government and join the People's Democratic League as the governing party, and the variety of coalition governments began to increase. There were also growing voices of skepticism regarding a strong presidential system. Government management, which had been extremely unstable until the 1960s due to Soviet intervention, speculation, and related presidential intervention, gradually stabilized from the 1970s onward, and the duration of coalition governments became longer.

Since the 1960s, progress has been made in educational policies. Educational policy was strongly influenced by the Agrarian Party and the Finnish People's Democratic League, and an equal system was meant to develop nationwide (Pernaa & Tiitta, 2007). First, basic, compulsory education reform was implemented with the introduction of a 9-year comprehensive junior high school system in 1968, which was gradually implemented from 1972 to 1977 (Häikiö, 1992). There was also a focus on higher education policy, and universities were established in various places to promote regional development, such as the University of Oulu in 1958 and the University of Rovaniemi in 1979. In the 1980s and 90 s, the reform of the University of Applied Sciences accelerated. The University of Applied Sciences Act was enacted in 1987 (Pernaa & Tiitta, 2007). President Kekkonen also had a personal interest in the development of higher education and the restructuring of the Academy of Finland, which was established in 1939.

In 1967, to commemorate Finland's 50th anniversary of its independence, Sitra was launched at the initiative of the Bank of Finland (Särkikoski, 2007). Sitra has continued to contribute to the development of Finnish science and technology by changing its functions over time. In the late 1970s, new technologies emerged and the Technology Committee was established in 1979. From the 1980s onward, research funding increased and the new government launched Tekes in 1983. The importance of the knowledge, science, and technology industries has increased. Technology policy was first centered in Southern Finland, but a new base was established in Oulu (Pernaa & Tiitta, 2007).

In particular, expanding and maintaining the capabilities of the welfare state through cooperation between education policies, especially in higher education and industry, became an issue. Since the 1960s, science and technology policies especially in the information and communications industry and higher education policies have been developing. Both were aware of internationalization strategies. Castells and Himanen (2002) consider that the development of an information society has revolutionized the welfare state. The link between science and technology policy, especially information and communication technology, education policy, and social policy, has become important for the country's transition to a post-industrial society.

11.4 Finnish Coalition Government After 1980s

This section focuses on the formation of the Finnish coalition government in the 1980s and examines its characteristics.

11.4.1 Establishment of Majority Government

To date, Finland has 77 governments.[3] During the Cold War, as presidential power expanded, governments became short-lived and were replaced with new ones. The inauguration of the government was influenced by the president's wishes, with appointment politics and nepotism being the main factors. Most governments from the 1940s to the 1970s included the Agrarian Party. Occasionally, people outside parliament were cabinet leaders (Karvonen, 2014). Beginning in the 1970s, Finnish party politics began to change. The Social Democratic Party returned to the coalition because of Kekkonen's personal preferences.

Even until the 1970s, unilateral governments were an exception and since 1977, there has been only a majority government. In the 1980s, when President Kekkonen stepped down and Koivisto took over as president, the parliament's power was strengthened, and parliamentarism gradually began to function. A characteristic of Finnish politics since the 1980s is that since 1983, the government has generally continued for 4 years, although there have been changes in prime ministers and the departure and replacement of coalitions, and the Finnish government has shown stability.

In Finland, where the presidential system has weakened, the original systems of proportional representation with an open list, unicameralism, and multiparty systems have come to the forefront and the formation of majority coalition governments has become common. Regarding Finland's parliamentary and electoral system, Sundberg (2002) explained that a preparatory committee decided upon the inauguration of the parliament, in which men and women were given the right to vote, the parliament was unicameral from the beginning, and the election method was proportional representation (D'Hondt method). He evaluates this system as a very modern system at the time. It also shows that the overall framework of the system remained largely unchanged. While other Nordic countries have changed from bicameral to unicameral systems, Finland initially adopted a unicameral system (Sundberg, 2002).

Relations with the Soviet Union and the strong presidential power affected the size of political parties and their access to the government. As previously mentioned, the Agrarian Party had a large impact on Finnish party politics. After the 1980s, when the presidential power declined, parliamentarism and party politics began to function normally. The first was a majority coalition government. With major parties receiving approximately 20% of the votes, a single government is unlikely. Furthermore, Karvonen (2014) pointed out that Finland's coalition government was oversized.

---

[3] Finnish Government webpage: https://valtioneuvosto.fi/hallitukset-ja-ministerit

11.4.2 Coalition Government with No Dominant Party

Another major feature of Finland's multiparty system and coalition government is that there are only three or four major parties and no single party is dominant. Neither party has a majority nor is in a competitive situation. Consequently, the Finnish government often involves smaller parties as the largest party partners with other major parties but lacks a majority.

The largest party is not fixed, as it varies among the major political parties. Furthermore, there are various types of coalitions, including adjacent types, bridge types, and grand coalitions. Although there are many diverse political parties, the most effective political parties have the potential to participate in the government although their frequency may vary. Representing various voices, each party has the potential to enter government, meaning that almost none of the parties have remained in opposition for a long time. The main political parties include the National Coalition Party, the Centre Party, the Social Democratic Party, and the True Finns Party. Minor parties include the Swedish People's Party, Christian Democratic Party, Green Party, and Left Alliance.

A major change since the 1980s was that the National Coalition Party returned to becoming a key member of government. Kekkonen retained conservatives outside the cabinet. To attain majority status, cabinets during this prolonged period had to include the Social Democrats and the Centre Party (Karvonen, 2014). In 1987, the National Coalition Party government was formed for the first time since the war, and it selected the Social Democratic Party as its coalition partner. This combination was unique among Finland's coalition patterns and was known as the "red-blue government."

11.4.3 Analysis of Governments Since the 1980s

In Finland, no dominant party has been able to stay in power for a long period, with the maximum term being two consecutive terms of 8 years. The three major political parties, the National Coalition Party, the Social Democratic Party, and the Centre Party, are the largest. From 1983 to 1987, the Social Democratic Party government (coalition with the Centre Party, etc.); from 1987 to 1991, the National Coalition Party government (coalition with the Social Democratic Party, etc.); and from 1991 to 1994, which was affected by the collapse of the Soviet Union and the Centre Party. From 1995 to 2003, when Finland gained accession to the EU and EMU, a grand coalition government was formed, led by the Social Democratic Party (coalition with the National Coalition Party, the Left Alliance, and the Green Party etc.). From 2003 to 2011, it was the Centre Party government (from 2003 to 2007, it was in coalition with the Social Democratic Party, and from 2007 to 2011, it was in coalition with the National Coalition Party), and from 2011 to 2015, it was the National coalition government (with the Social Democratic Party). From 2015 to

2019, the Centre Party government (coalition with the National Coalition Party, etc. and the True Finns Party entered the cabinet for the first time); from 2019 to 2023, the Social Democratic Party government (coalition with the Centre Party, the Green Party, the Left Alliance, etc.); from 2023 onward, there will be a National Coalition Party government (with the True Finns Party, etc.), with diverse coalition patterns (see Table 11.1).

Here, we present three main coalition patterns of major parties—the National Coalition Party, the Centre Party, and the Social Democratic Party—there can be a coalition of two of the three largest parties: (1) Social Democrats and Conservatives (red-blue), (2) Center and Conservatives (bourgeois government), and (3) Center and Social Democrats (red-land coalition). Thus far, Finnish party politics are not left-right bloc politics. Karvonen (2014, p. 91) describes the features of coalition. First, Social Democrats and Conservative coalitions' common grounds are "urban-industrial coalition" and pro-EU. Potential tensions include labor market policies and taxation levels. The potential victims are of regional and agricultural interest. Second, Center and Conservative coalition's common grounds are "bourgeois coalition," private enterprise, limiting labor union influence, and potential tensions can be agricultural and regional subsidies, level of taxation, and potential victim is labor union. Third, Center and Social Democrats coalition's common grounds are "welfare coalition" and tax financed social security, and potential tensions could be regional policy, centralization vs decentralization (traditional conflicts in Finland), and potential victims can be corporate and high income taxpayers.

11.4.4 Small Parties and Oversized Coalition

Karvonen (2014) also points out that Finland has many oversized coalitions in international comparisons. As for the participation of minor parties, the pattern is similarly unorthodox from an ideological perspective. He refers to the reason that oversized cabinets are able to carry out the legislative and budgetary reforms included in these agreements. Corporatist consensualism has ushered in a new era of stability and cooperation in parliamentary politics. Cabinet stability was the political equivalent of a spirit of cooperation that had already existed in labor–capital affairs for about a decade. It can also be considered an opportunity for potential coalition parties—the expected utility of government is higher than the expected utility of opposition (Karvonen, 2014). In 1995, the Lipponen government formed the "rainbow government," which is a significant coalition. In 2011, the Katainen government formed a coalition of six parties, And then the Rinne and Marin governments formed five parties in the coalition. He also mentioned that an alternative explanation is that oversized cabinets have come to be seen as part of the pattern of "consensualism." If the two major parties do not reach a majority, another major party, or one or more minor parties, may be added to the government. Through this mechanism, various small parties or relatively new parties from new social

Table 11.1 Coalition governments in Finland since the 1983

			Major parties			Small parties					
Year	Government	Period	National coalition	Centre	Social democrats	True finns	Christian democratic	Swedish people's party	Green	Left alliance	Others
1983	Sorsa IV	6.5.1983–30.4.1987		○	●			○			○
1987	Holkeri	30.4.1987–26.4.1991	●		○			○			○
1991	Aho	26.4.1991–13.4.1995	○	●			○	○			
1995	Lipponen	13.4.1995–15.4.1999	○		●			○	○	○	○
1999	Lipponen II	15.4.1999–17.4.2003	○		●			○	○	○	○
2003	Jäätteenmäki	17.4.2003–24.6.2003		●	○			○			
	Vanhanen	24.6.2003–19.4.2007		●	○			○			
2007	Vanhanen II	19.4.2007–22.6.2010	○	●				○	○		
	Kiviniemi	22.6.2010–22.6.2011	○	●				○	○		
2011	Katainen	22.6.2011–24.6.2014	●		○		○	○	○	○	
	Stubb	24.6.2014–29.5.2015	●		○		○	○			
2015	Sipilä	29.5.2015–6.6.2019	○	●		○					
2019	Rinne	6.6.–10.12.2019		○	●			○	○	○	
	Marin	10.12.2019–20.6.2023		○	●			○	○	○	
2023	Orpo	20.6.2023–	●			○	○	○			

● = Leading party, ○ = Government party

cleavages joined the coalition. Larger parties must include smaller parties to gain a majority in parliament.

The National Coalition Party led the government in 1987, 2011, and 2023, and participated in the government in 1991, 1995, 1999, 2007, and 2015. The Centre Party led the government in 1991, 2003, 2007 and 2015 and participated in the government in 1983 and 2019. Social Democrats led the government in 1983, 1995, 1999, and 2019 and participated in the government in 1987, 2003, and 2011. In terms of small parties, the Swedish People's Party is a small party, but it has participated in almost all governments to safeguard the rights of the Swedish-speaking population. They are usually considered constructive cabinet players by the major parties (Karvonen, 2014). This differs from Switzerland and Belgium, where party conflicts over ethnicity are observed in terms of size and coalition (Lijphart, 1999).

The Green Party entered the government in 1995 for the first time but left the government in 2002 over a bill to expand nuclear power plants and joined the government in 2007, 2011, and 2019. The Left Alliance joined the government in 1995, 1999, 2011, and 2019. The Christian Democrats were part of the government in 1991, 2011, and 2023. In recent years, the True Finns Party has grown from a small party to one of the major parties, with a vote share of nearly 20%, using resentment against existing parties as the driving force for votes. They join the government in 2015 and 2023. As the Green Party and True Finns Party joined the government, multiparty systems provided avenues for new social cleavages.

As a summary, since the 1980s, Finnish politics has been characterized by parliamentarism, stability, and diverse coalition governments, and it is believed that these diverse coalition governments have created policy flexibility in the transition to a post-industrial society. The government programs since the 1980s have included new discourses, such as globalization, innovation, information society, entrepreneurship, new solidarity, climate change, sustainable society, information society sustainability, and circular economy, and the meaning of the welfare state has expanded.

11.4.5 Lijphart's Consensus Model of Democracy and the Case of Finland

Finland's political parties form coalitions, changing their combinations every 4 years. This indicates to the Red Queen hypothesis as Acemoglu has emphasized that it is difficult to remain within a narrow corridor of freedom and democracy (Acemoglu & Robinson, 2019). Finland seems to respond to crises and changes by changing its form of the government and continuing to move forward quickly while reaching out to various possibilities. Oversized coalition makes it easier to implement major reforms, whereas changes in the leading party and its partners allow access to various policies. Here the case of Finland is discussed from the perspective of Lijphart's "Patterns of Democracy" (Lijphart, 1999) and concrete cases of government programs will be analyzed in the next section. Changing of the combination of parties widen the possibilities of policies.

In his book, Lijphart highlights multiple patterns of democracy. Proportional representation creates a multiparty system in which a government is shared through a broad coalition. He described it as a multipolar consociational democracy, with each party acting as a corporatist intermediary to absorb and adjust opinions. He took issue with the identification of majority-rule democracy with general democracy in political science and focused on consensus democracy. His research has focused primarily on Switzerland and Belgium. He argues that majority-rule democracy, or the Westminster model, is exclusive, competitive, and antagonistic, while consensus democracy is inclusive, negotiating, and compromising. Lijphart saw consensus democracy as an alternative to majority-rule democracy (Lijphart, 1999).

Finland has all the features of the multiparty system, proportional representation, and unicameral system that Lijphart demonstrated, as well as a coalition with no dominant party, meaning that multiple parties are in balance. However, as already mentioned, the semi-presidential system may have made understanding of its multiparty system unclear due to its historical background. However as observed in the previous section Finland's party politics in the 1980s strongly show the characteristics of "consensus democracy." This supports the interlocking of political, economic, and social policies, and the ability to respond to change. This study argues that Finland's multiparty system and coalition government contribute to the operation of a flexible welfare state in a post-industrial society.

Having various parties in a coalition allows various opinions and approaches to be incorporated. Having a diverse perspective has made it possible to undergo rapid change, such as the end of the Cold War, crises, and joining the EU and EMU. New parties have also been incorporated into the multiparty coalition government system. Diverse voices and views are reflected in decision-making, creating diverse options and a new turnover in policies. Multiparty systems oversized by various types of coalition governments provide mechanisms for responding flexibly and tolerantly to crises and challenges.

11.5 Diverse Coalition Formation and Welfare State Policies in Post-Industrial Societies

Here concrete cases of the emergency of new ideas and policies are introduced. Government programs[4] after the 1980s indicate Finnish welfare state or welfare society, "science and technology," "innovation," "digitalization," "labor," "employment," "environment," and "climate change" and those words and themes appear repeatedly.

---

[4] Government Programs since 1917 in government webpage: https://valtioneuvosto.fi/historia-ja-rakennukset/hallitusohjelmat

As mentioned above, the government in 1987, which took over from the 1983 coalition of the Social Democrats and the Centre Party, was unique in that the National Coalition Party entered power and formed a government with the Social Democrats but not with the Centre Party, the so-called red-blue government. The pillar of the 1987 government was the development of an information science policy strategy that emphasized the importance of innovation.

In 1991, the Centre Party chose the National Coalition Party as its main partner and joined the Left Alliance. It continued its information science strategy and applied it to its EU membership following the end of the Cold War. The Social Democratic Party government in 1995 was formed immediately after Finland's accession to the EU and was called a rainbow government, as it included many parties except the Centre Party. It became a government that responded to major changes in EU accession and globalization. Castells and Himanen (2002) point out that the greatest characteristic of Finland is the rise of an information society and welfare state and state that the government was able to make bold policy decisions that paved the way for a powerful new science, technology, and economy in 1990. By joining the EU, Finland's identity was reaffirmed, and the identity of "Nordic welfare state" and "Finnish welfare state" was emphasized. In 1999, the Social Democratic Party and National Coalition Party emphasized innovation, employment, and solidarity. Interest in immigration has also increased with the progress of globalization, and for the first time, an immigration topic appeared in the government program.[5]

In the 2000s, the focus remained on employment and solidarity, but entrepreneurship became a new trend. Digitalization, climate change, and international competitiveness have also been emphasized. In 2003, the Centre Party government implemented the digitalization of social security (Kanta Service). In 2011, the National Coalition Party emphasized the importance of developing the skills and technology of most people.[6] The focus was on education policy, training in working life, and improving productivity through digitalization. Education and learning have become the major themes. They also began the SOTE reform.[7] In 2015, the Centre Party government conducted a social experiment on basic income for 2 years. Participation and education, welfare and health, bioeconomy, and digitalization were the pillars. In 2019, the Social Democratic Party government set targets to respond to rapid changes due to climate change, globalization, aging, population aging, and technological development. The government made high schools compulsory.

Overall, since the 1980s, new perspectives such as "environmental policy," "innovation policy," "transition to an information society," "sustainable society," and "creation of a creative economy" have been added to discussions of social

[5] Government program of Lipponen II government: https://valtioneuvosto.fi/-/67.-lipponen-ii-15.4.1999-17.4.2003-

[6] Government program of Katainen government: https://julkaisut.valtioneuvosto.fi/handle/10024/79792

[7] Reform of the health and social service system since 2011.

policy. Early trends were observed from the 1980s to the 1990s and have been accelerating since the 2000s. As modern social policies, such as digitalization in social policy, have begun to be implemented. The embedding of new ideologies and technological aspects can also be observed. The word "welfare" is now used in the context of a sustainable society, the use of technology based on the information society, and human resource development, and is now used to mean not only the continuation of basic security, but also a prerequisite for revitalizing the new economy, and people's happiness and well-being in the new economy.

11.6 Conclusion

Conditions in Finland were very different from those in Sweden, and the two countries share few of the adaptive advantages of coevolution that Sweden had. Welfare state construction processes were also quite different. In Finland, industrialization occurred even later and developed in almost the same way as post-industrialization, and there was a shift to a social investment state at roughly the same time as the construction of a Nordic welfare state. This chapter showed that the small country of Finland has diverse coalition governments and consensus democracies as mechanisms for responding to crises and adapting to changes quickly and dynamically.

Finland, which did not or could not build a thoroughly engineered system like Sweden, has been able to adapt to diverse possibilities by having many political parties, old and new, incorporate their ideas into the government and policies, make adjustments, and respond nimbly to the demands of the time. Coalition governments are not always successful, and there are cases such as the SOTE reform, where policies change from one government to the next, and systems are constructed in a patchwork manner that can lead to confusion; however, the point remains that they are a process of trial and error. In recent elections, the Centre Party has shrunk and populist politics have expanded, so bloc politics may also be possible in Finland in the near future.

When observing Finland through the lens of evolutionary theory, we can see that the current coalition government dates back to the parliamentary reform of 1906. Since then, due to special circumstances in which external factors and the expansion of presidential power strengthened the Agrarian Party and restricted left and right party, the country has developed a unique form of party politics—in other words, a repeated running of various overly powerful governments—and we can understand that various factors influence each other (Steinmo, 2010). Many political parties represent the interests of diverse ways of thinking and methods, and the government itself can be said to have high learning ability and capacity. They continue to try and error in the face of crises and pressure, and elections function as a barometer for evaluating the government, whereas opposition parties always calculate and act on the possibility of entering the next government. Katzenstein (1987) emphasized that in Germany, policy responses have progressed slowly and steadily through the catalysts of various political actors and the coordination between them, but looking at the case of Finland, we can observe gradual progress in the long term and the ability to quickly respond to new things in the short term.

In response to the challenges of the century, as argued by Steinmo (2010), Finland is absorbing the ideas of many actors and opening various options for a path to stable national survival. The background to Finland becoming a social investment state in the CME is its choice of a welfare state, a Nordic welfare state. As a social investment state, it continues to undergo trial and error, with differences in its methods and content, even among Nordic countries. Finland has become another bumblebee because it has unique conditions, such as a republic, semi-presidential system, and proportional representation system. It has taken on the characteristics of a Nordic welfare state in its own way, starting from social policies with strong elements of universalism, and has evolved to respond to globalization and the information society.

Acknowledgments This research was supported by a KAKEN grant (19K20532) received in FY2019–2023 and 19H04368 in FY2019–2023.

References

Acemoglu, D., & Robinson, J. A. (2019). *The narrow corridor: States, societies, and the fate of liberty*. Penguin Press.

Baldwin, P. (1990). *The politics of social solidarity, class bases of the European welfare state 1875–1975*. Cambridge University Press.

Castells, M., & Himanen, P. (2002). *The Information Society and the Welfare State: The Finnish Model*. Oxford University Press.

Esping-Andersen, G. (1990). *The three worlds of welfare capitalism*. Polity Press.

Häikiö, M. (1992). *A brief history of modern Finland*. University of Helsinki.

Hall, P. A., & Soskice, D. (2001). *Varieties of capitalism: The institutional foundations of comparative advantage*. Oxford University Press.

Karvonen, L. (2014). *Parties, governments and voters in Finland: Politics under fundamental societal transformation*. ECPR Press.

Katzenstein, P. (1985). *Small states in world markets industrial policy in Europe*. Cornell University Press.

Katzenstein, P. (1987). *Policy and politics in West Germany: The growth of a semisovereign state*. Temple University Press.

Kettunen, P. (2019). The conceptual history of the welfare state in Finland. In E. Nils (Ed.), *The changing meanings of the welfare state: Histories of a key concept in the Nordic countries* (pp. 225–275). Berghahn Books.

Kuusi, P. (1961). *60-luvun Sosiaalipolitiikka*. WSOY.

Lijphart, A. (1999). *Patterns of democracy*. Yale University Press.

Lipset, S. M., & Rokkan, S. (1967). *Party systems and voter alignments: Cross-national perspectives*. Free Press.

Mickelsson, R. (2015). *Suomen puolueet*. Vastapaino.

Miettinen, R. (2010). *The Finnish national innovation system: From technology to human capabilities* [In Japanese]. Shinchosha.

Pernaa, V., & Tiitta, A. (2007). *Sivistyksen ja tiedon Suomi*. Edita.

Pierson, P. (2004). *Politics in time: History, institutions, and social analysis*. Princeton University Press.

Saari, J. (1997). In Gunnar Myrdal's footsteps: Pekka Kuusi and the vision of scientific planning. In K. Pauli & E. Hanna (Eds.), *Models, modernity and the myrdals* (pp. 129–152). University of Helsinki, Renvall Institute Publications.

Saari, J. (2006). *Suomen malli -Murroksesta menestykseen?* Helsinki University Press.

Särkikoski, T. (2007). *Sitra Tulevaisuus tehtävänä*. Sitra.

Shibayama, Y. (2010). Social democratization of Finnish social policy: Focusing on Pekka Kuusi's "social policy in the 1960s". *The Waseda Journal of Social Sciences, 16*, 90–104.

Shibayama, Y. (2021). A study of Finnish Agrarian Party - The ideas of Santeri Alkio. *Japanese Journal of Northern European Studies, 17*, 67–77.

Smolander, J. (2000). *Suomalainen oikeisto ja 'kansankoti' : Kansallisen kokoomuksen suhtautuminen pohjoismaiseen hyvinvointivaltiomalliin jälleenrakennuskaudelta konsensusajan alkuun*. SKS.

Steinmo, S. (2010). *The evolution of modern states: Sweden, Japan, and the United States*. Cambridge University Press.

Sundberg, J. (2002). The electoral system of Finland: Old, and working well. In G. Bernard & L. Arend (Eds.), *The evolution of electoral and party systems in the Nordic countries* (pp. 67–100). Agathon Press.

Tuomioja, E. (1996). *Pekka Kuusi–alkoholipoliitikko,sosiaalipoliitikko,ihmiskuntapoliitikko*. WSOY.

Chapter 12
The Future(s) of the Welfare State

Aleksi Neuvonen

Abstract The article explores the future of the welfare state towards the 2030s and 2040s. The primary focus is on possible directions, tensions, and ethical dilemmas facing welfare states in the wider context of the development of human civilizations. The article first maps the current well-known tensions that institutions of the welfare states grapple with. It then advances to investigating the ethical foundations of the twenty-first century welfare state by examining such issues as growth dependency and people-centrism. It eventually re-evaluates the claim made by the great Finnish welfare state theorist Pekka Kuusi (from the 1980s) on the urgency of transform the prevailing worldview held in modern societies to better grasp humans as "children of the Earth" instead of mere "brain creatures." Thus the article suggests the discovery of a new basis for welfare states in the century characterized by poly/metacrisis and the era of Anthropocene.

Keywords Futures · Sufficiency · Narratives · Individualism · Anthropocene

12.1 Introduction

This article explores the future of the welfare state in the 2030s and 2040s. Or preferably, the futures of the welfare states: there is no single future, nor one welfare state. The future is open and contingent; it exists only as the expectations of people (Beckert, 2013). Historian Jenny Andersson has described the dual role of the future in contemporary culture as follows: The future appears to us both as (1) images of a coming tangible reality, resulting from regular, path-dependent developments, and as (2) a fundamental social construct, emanating only from the human mind as a result of imagination (Andersson, 2018).

A. Neuvonen (✉)
Demos Helsinki, Helsinki, Finland
e-mail: aleksi.neuvonen@demoshelsinki.fi

N. Tokumaru et al. (eds.), *Creative Co-evolution of the Economies and Welfare States in the Nordic Countries*, Evolutionary Economics and Social Complexity Science 32, https://doi.org/10.1007/978-981-97-8569-8_12

This duality is particularly characteristic when discussing welfare states and their futures: We have a strong tendency to emphasize the institutional continuities of welfare states, occasionally calling them "frozen landscapes" (e.g., Palier & Martin, 2007) that favor path-dependent development and are often resistant to new topics and models of solutions. Assuming this perspective might lead us to think that there is just one plausible future, or perhaps two polarized ("weak vs. strong," "traditional vs. reformed") ones regarding the development of the welfare state.

The welfare state is, however, also to a large degree a political narrative that emerged in significant use after the 1980s (Kettunen, 2019), weaving together a variety of ideals, institutions, policies, and notions of historic processes, as well as the experiences and expectations of citizens. Without these constructed, imagined aspects, the welfare state would eventually fall apart, reduced to hollow institutions that serve only managerial principles (such as efficiency or quality of each service function), with no overarching, societally transformative goals and purposes. Yet, if discrepancies between the narrative and the functioning of the current institutions grow too wide and deep, it results in tensions in both (past) experiences and (future) expectations (Koselleck, 2004) of people, jeopardizing eventually the legitimacy of the welfare state.

We need to acknowledge these three separate yet interlinked approaches to the future of the welfare state: (1) Institutions, (2) The narrative, (3) Experiences and expectations. This distinction could help in widening and clarifying conversations about the plurality of possible futures of the welfare state. Acknowledging the presence of imagined elements also helps introduce new and external drivers and emerging phenomena to a context often perceived as a closed, institutionalized system.

At the time of writing this article, the principle dominating all these layers of the welfare state is efficiency. This principle, echoing the ideal of the competition state (Kettunen, 2019), intends to provide a justification for the welfare state as an attractive environment for the most competitive businesses, especially under conditions of the so-called skills-based technical change (Benkler, 2018). The leading argument of this paper is that the future of the welfare state can be seen as something differing from this principle. At the moment, there is an emerging need to expand the frame of the welfare state from the nation-state and economic growth-oriented vantage point. The new frame would have to be more global and acknowledge the role of planetary boundaries (Rockström et al., 2009) in defining the future of the welfare state. In such a possible and imaginable future, sufficiency would have to take the position as the central principle guiding the development of the welfare state.

It is relevant to disclose and define, however, that this article is written for a book that focuses largely on different aspects of and cases on welfare states in the Nordic countries and Japan. Additionally, the writer of this article has extensively encountered and approached the welfare state in the context of Finland, with some experience in comparative studies between various European countries. Therefore, the emphasis is largely on the futures of the Finnish and Nordic welfare states, with some possible generalizations to other welfare states.

The structure of this article largely follows the above-mentioned Andersson's distinction between path-dependent development of institutions and social constructs on possible, imagined futures, resulting from an array of global drivers shaping the futures of humankind and welfare states as part of this wider whole. In other words, I will first briefly overview current endogenous challenges and narratives of welfare states during the decade of the 2020s, i.e., the well-known tensions the institutions of the welfare states grapple with now. I will then delve into the wider context of the welfare states and explore some key ethical dilemmas that require welfare states to renew their justification in the world towards the 2030s and beyond.

12.2 The Narratives of the 2020's Welfare State

Before exploring the futures of the welfare state, we need to provide an overview of the forces and pathways that characterize the current context of the welfare state, particularly its Nordic variant. Therefore, I will present some broad landscape-level drivers and historical narratives that define welfare states today.

The welfare state and its institutions originally emerged as a response to the ills and tensions of the Industrial Revolution (Allen, 2017). The decline of the industrial era has been a topic of discussion for the past half-century, starting in the 1970s, when the number of industrial jobs peaked in many industrialized countries, resulting in a gradual shift towards more varied patterns of employment. Oftentimes, discontent with the practices of the welfare state has been attributed to the discrepancy between the prevailing organizational industrial-era mindset and the expectations of contemporary people.

The Nordic welfare model, however, has been characterized by cornerstones such as universal health and education services and universal social security that covers the entire population in terms of minimum subsistence. The model has also included a strong housing policy and a labor market model based on agreements between large and powerful confederations of both labor unions and employer organizations, as well as government.

This bundle of universal (available to all citizens) welfare services and social security measures creates strong institutional inertia that is further strengthened by social norms favoring the welfare state, appearing in public opinion and political culture (Esping-Andersen, 1990). This has given rise to a narrative in which the welfare state is intertwined with an attempt to nurture stronger citizenship that entails higher levels of education and professionalization, as well as steps towards greater gender equality (Buchardt et al., 2013).

Over the past decades, this narrative has inevitably gained additional momentum from the high standard of living, and high levels of both objective and subjective well-being, and a well-performing economy. As a result, the Nordic model has come to be perceived globally as one of the most successful, if not the most successful, social models of this era (e.g., Fukuyama, 2014). So despite all the aforementioned changes in economic structures, production technologies, demographics, and overall maturity of its institutional setting, the Nordic welfare model has appeared as an adaptable and future-oriented mix of institutions, experiences, expectations, and narrative.

Currently, the vast majority of inhabitants in Nordic welfare states have their basic material needs met, meaning that life is no longer a constant struggle against scarcity. Hence, the purpose of the welfare state cannot be justified through a battle against the Five Giants (Want, Disease, Ignorance, Squalor, and Idleness) of the Beveridge report (Beveridge, 1942). Instead, non-material and subjective aspects of well-being have gained attention as issues on which the welfare state should focus (Diener et al., 2009). Moreover, the wealth and expansion of consumer society have raised people's expectations regarding the quality of services, making it more difficult for mass-produced public services to satisfy the wants and desires of many citizens.

Meanwhile, advances in life expectancy and declining birth rates have radically tilted demographic balances towards an aging population. The economic basis of welfare states has largely stood on the assumption of a steady or expanding supply of labor, leading to a so-called demographic dividend and resulting economic growth. In Finland in the 2020s, record-low birth rates are leading to a situation in which large social investments are becoming riskier due to the anticipated lack of demographic dividends in the future (Murto, 2022).

Furthermore, the default modes of public services and social security schemes were built around the needs of the working-age population and their families, with pensions and elderly care being specicif issues that also liberated capable adults for paid labor by reducing family caregiving responsibilities. Longer lives and the resulting prevalence of chronic diseases have shifted the emphasis in medicine and care towards longer and more expensive treatments, resulting in a worldwide cost crisis in healthcare systems. Additionally, the diversification of populations, not only ethnically but also in terms of the more personalized needs people recognize in themselves, has affected the logic and efficiency of public service provision, both in healthcare and education.

Welfare states emerged as part of the nation-building processes of the twentieth century. The coexistence of the welfare state with increasingly open and integrated markets and a globalized economy has long been an open question: Will global competition and states' decreasing control over the economy result in the eventual decline of the welfare state? Can industrial-era welfare states survive in an era of global production and value chains, where much of the production occurs in countries with lower labor costs? Can the rights and responsibilities of citizens stay in balance in an economy relying on labor mobility and constant immigration flows?

As a narrative, this transition appeared in the 1990s as a rhetorical shift to a "competition state" that leaned on a nationalistic story of the welfare state as a long-term national project (Kettunen, 2019). The story of competition states portrays economic competition between nations in which a central mission of the state is to enhance the skills and competencies of its citizens within a system of production (Koch, 2022).

It is possible to attribute the resilience of societies to the welfare state and its focus on developing broad capabilities among citizens, thus extending their capacity to move on to build new solutions in a dynamic context (Korhonen et al., 2017). Consequently, there seems to be a broad consensus among both political parties and citizens in the Nordic countries regarding the welfare state as an ideal that they wish to retain. However, what this entails, and which functions and institutions of the welfare state should be prioritized, remain debated.

In other words, the welfare state as a narrative prevails even as experiences and expectations of welfare states might vary, and certain institutions either remain the same or undergo reforms. The narrative is in the long run dependent on both experiences and expectations, as well as the performance of the institutions. To date, citizens´ trust in institutions in the Nordic countries has been exceptionally high, indicating that people still largely have positive expectations of the welfare state. This occurs despite public discourse often being dominated by experiences of disappointment and economic outlooks that predict rising costs, growing demand, and tighter budgets for the welfare state and its institutions.

It is quite possible that there can be a delay in how fast such experiences affect the narrative. The narrative, however, might still buffer these potential negative impacts and help build resilience and a longer future horizon for the welfare state: Citizens anticipate the welfare state to be a significant building block in society and everyday life in the foreseeable future (and hence adjust their behavior accordingly). Meanwhile, experts view the welfare state as a rather flexible framework that allows sufficiently wide exploration of new solutions that could potentially improve the functioning of the institutions.

12.3 Institutions and the Key Tensions of the Welfare State Towards the 2030s

I am now shifting from the currently prevailing narratives of the welfare state to the discourses on welfare state institutions and their futures. Narratives typically attempt to contextualize the welfare state within broader contexts and focus critical attention on the strengths and weaknesses of the model in relation to wider societal goals. The futures of the welfare state, however, are more typically discussed in terms of how its institutions cope with changing conditions.

When examining Finland as a case example and the discussions on the future of the welfare state and its institutions, the following questions apper to dominate:

- **Will the healthcare system maintain its quality at reasonable costs?** From the early 2000s to the 2020s, healthcare reform was the biggest and most debated political topic. The aim was to address the challenges posed by an aging population, regional disparities in healthcare access, and the escalating costs of medical services. A central feature of this reform, eventually finalized during PM Sanna Marin's coalition, was the attempt to consolidate the numerous small municipalities managing health services into larger, more efficient regional entities. Now, a little over a year after the new well-being services counties were formed, many regions are coping with severe budget deficits, while PM Orpo's coalition is taking tougher measures to balance public spending, with healthcare and its rising costs being the single biggest contributor to the growth of public debt. However, the reform and improved organization of the wellbeing services counties alone will not resolve the major challenges of the healthcare and other care systems. Health disparities and differences in life expectancy between socio-economic groups are wider in Finland than in many other Western countries. A report published by the Ministry of Social Affairs and Health in 2023 suggests seven measures to address these inequalities, with only one being focused to improvements in the healthcare system (Rotko et al. 2023). Instead, it suggests improvements in poverty policies, education, and policies related to diets and alcohol consumption. Furthermore, mental health and care in its various forms are becoming increasingly pressing issues and an area of great inequalities that do not fit easily into the industrial-era, siloed framework of the welfare model. As a 2024 report from a multi-stakeholder vision process coordinated by Demos Helsinki suggests, care should not be treated as a topic institutionalized to specialized organizations and professions but as a fundamental human activity that requires attention and continuous contextualization in various realms of society and culture (Demos Helsinki, 2024).

- **Can the education system maintain a high level of academic quality and social mobility for all?** The Finnish model of primary and secondary education has been widely celebrated—and justifiably so. The guiding principle of the "common school for all" reforms of the 1970s is that every child must have an equal opportunity to learn, regardless of family background, income, or geographic location (Sahlberg, 2021). The school system places equal emphasis on equality and excellence—good schools for all younth. Finland's ranking in the OECD's PISA exam has slipped slightly since the early 2000s, raising concerns about how well the primary school system can fare under changing conditions. The Finnish model was developed at a time when almost all pupils spoke Finnish or Swedish, and immigrant youngsters confront challenges that native students did not face. The gap between native and non-native students on the PISA exam is greater in Finland than in any other OECD country, and it persists into the second generation. These findings have led to broader concerns about segregation between schools in larger cities with substantial immigrant populations.[1] Learning disparities widen not only between native Finnish and immigrant populations but also among children from poorer and less educated families, especially boys, who seem to find it particularly challenging to progress in education. The promise of high-quality, tuition-free education for all is not as widely recognized as it was at some point in the welfare state's development. This is espe-

[1] His phenomenon has been recorded well in studies by Venla Bernelius and Sonja Kosunen (eg. Kosunen et al., 2022; Bernelius & Kosunen, 2023)

cially worrying as the number of jobs available for people with only primary-level education is in a state of continuous decline.

- **Is the social security system able to incentivize people to work, thus thereby contributing to the funding the welfare state?** The past three coalitions in Finland have made significant efforts to reform the social security system. This has been motivated by (a) the need to support labor supply and consequently alleviate labor shortages in certain sectors and (b) the moral concern that a group of people live solely on benefits, thereby hampering the legitimacy of the welfare state. This discourse became very visible, for instance, in the results of the BIBU research project (2017–2022),[2] which studied how the global flux of economic restructuring, urbanization, and migration is changing political capacities, interests, and emotions in various citizen groups. While support for the welfare state narrative and many public services is high and cuts across social classes and citizen groups, there seems to be frustration towards the idea that some people can live on benefits with little motivation to work and earn their own living. Similar sentiments seem to motivate the work of the SOTU committee, the current social security reform process in Finland. The committee has largely confined its work to optimizing benefits to encourage employment while practically sidelining various other aspects of social security (Saikkonen & Ilmakunnas, 2023). Several experts have expressed doubts, however, about whether such incentives and activation measures (e.g., cutting social benefits) would have any significant impact on increasing labor supply. They suggest that the majority of people currently outside the job market are very difficult to employ in sectors in urgent need of labor due to a multiple health problems, lack of education, or other complex issues.
- **Can labor market policy support the creation of good jobs, offering quality work life and decent income for the entire workforce?** High standards for the protection of employees in Finnish labour markets, upheld by legislation and collective bargaining agreements, have been considered to maintain fair and equitable working conditions in practically all workplaces. Despite the robust labor protections and strong welfare state, various factors have contributed to the growth of precarious employment. In recent years, and most likely in the near future, job creation will largely occur in service industries where many jobs are relatively poorly paid and reliant on immigrant labor. PM Orpo's coalition's attempts to amend the rules of labour markets are hitting hardest those with the weakest negotiating power and without protection from collective bargaining agreements. Furthermore, the growth of the platform economy, with companies like food delivery services and ride-hailing apps, has led to more gig and freelance work. While this phenomenon is global, in Finland, it has received special attention due to the success of Wolt, a Finland-based food delivery start-up unicorn. As independent contractors, Wolt couriers do not receive employment benefits such as paid sick leave, holiday pay, health insurance, or pension

[2] https://bibu.fi/

contributions. This lack of benefits further characterizes their work as precarious. The fact that one of the biggest success stories in recent history is leading to the mainstreaming of weaker working conditions raises concerns about how to maintain high standards of employee protection in the future.

- **How can housing policy prevent the cost of housing from becoming a bottleneck for starting a family or moving to a new location for a job?** Finland's housing policy is often highlighted as a successful model internationally, particularly due to its innovative approaches to tackling homelessness and ensuring affordable housing for its citizens. Finland adopted the "Housing First" model,[3] which emphasizes providing stable, permanent housing to homeless individuals as a first step, rather than making housing conditional on behavior changes or treatment programs. Furthermore, the Finnish government has shown strong commitment and provided significant funding to address housing issues. Currently, the polarization of housing markets between larger urban regions and declining areas presents significant challenges for the Finnish model of housing policy. In smaller towns and rural areas, the decline in house and flat prices has been steep, making it difficult for people to sell or obtain loans for major renovations. As a result, building in these regions has practically stopped. Meanwhile, housing markets in the largest urban regions have become a destination for speculative investors and are directly linked to the global financial markets. These developments are making many of the earlier policy measures ineffective and threaten to slow down social mobility by making it more difficult to move to a new location for a job. They also risk eroding earlier successes in preventing housing segregation and homelessness.

These questions largely reflect some of the traditional cornerstones of the welfare state interpreted as a safety net, and its capacity to cope in a context of changing demographics and economic structures. This outlook on the future of the welfare state builds largely on path dependencies and an endogenous view of welfare systems, paired with the most immediate external drivers affecting the conditions under which the institutions operate. The framing of these questions arises predominantly from the interpretation of the welfare state as a "competition state" (Kettunen, 2019), emphasizing such drivers as the balance of public budgets, the activation of labor, and the development of human capital.

Yet the above-mentioned questions define only one take on the issue, excluding a large number of drivers and topics. The dominant narratives on the welfare state, typically following the idea of a competition state, tend to distinguish between the nation-state as "internal" and the global as "external," thus categorizing some topics as less relevant for the welfare state and its legitimacy.

In the world of the 2020s, however, such a distinction between internal and external has become extremely ambiguous, if not problematic. This period has been

[3] See e.g. Housing First Finalnd (https://ysaatio.fi/en/housing-first/) or Finland's Zero Homeless Strategy: Lessons from a Success Story (https://oecdecoscope.blog/2021/12/13/finlands-zero-homeless-strategy-lessons-from-a-success-story/)

characterized by concepts like "polycrisis" (Adam Tooze) or "megacrises" (Daniel Schmachtenberger), which perceive either a multitude and interplay of various overlapping, global urgencies (poly) or a single, overarching systemic crisis posing a fundamental threat to the entire system (meta).

Both interpretations emphasize that governments and other organizations have been pushed to operate in a constant crisis mode, in a context in which reacting and navigating won't resolve these complex and multilayered problems. Yet building longer-term transition pathways and keeping stakeholders confident for an extended period is extremely difficult when people are burdened by deep and constant uncertainty in their everyday lives. This situation affects states, cities, and public organizations and their economic realities very directly: The poly/metacrisis appears as a need to react to yet another emergency, requiring new, unplanned areas of public spending, growing pressure on existing functions and their professionals, unexpectedly rapid changes in citizens' behaviors, and rising costs of many commodities, from labor to critical raw materials and various goods with long logistics chains, such as medical masks or microchips.

An easy, straightforward response to this emerging change in our operating environment would be to simply emphasize the role of the welfare state as a major source of resilience in uncertain times. A political implication then would be to let public spending on welfare states grow and to prioritize the resilience of institutions over economic efficiency. This kind of approach is commonly articulated with the support of Modern Monetary Theory (MMT), which suggests acceptance of higher levels of public debt and a more active role for the government in managing the economy as ways to govern and manage in a transformative period. Accepting such an approach would be a major shift in principles guiding the institutions of the welfare states. Furthermore, it would change the way the prevailing narrative on the welfare state builds legitimacy. Not surprisingly, the topic of public spending and debt forms once again the main political divisions.

This political disagreement alone suggests that the future of the welfare state in this environment of poly-/metacrisis is a much more complex and expansive topic than just a matter of stronger and better-resourced public institutions. It is not political polarization (regarding levels of public spending and public debt) alone, however, that necessitates deeper scrutiny of the ethical foundations and central conceptual assumptions behind the welfare state—their institutions, experiences, and expectations as well as narratives—as a prerequisite for sketching futures. Money, or levels of public spending on welfare institutions, typically guides us to perceive the future as a material continuation of the past and restricts our capacity to approach the future as open, consisting of a multitude of alternatives.

It is fair to assume that a debate on money embeds more complex questions regarding rights and responsibilities between groups of people and institutions, and overall on the extents of moral behavior. In other words, who and what issues should be considered when legitimizing actions and structures guiding actions? In a changing environment, the transformative aspect typically consists of alterations in these normative rules. These rules and moral responsibilities somehow bind the future by defining which alternative futures we can deem acceptable. This kind of moral consideration, however, requires human imagination, i.e., considering the future of the welfare state as an open, human-constructed issue that is not defined solely by the incumbent institutions and past experiences of their operations.

12.4 The Endgame of the Efficiency-Driven Welfare State?

It is fair to say that in the welfare states of the late twentieth and early twenty-first centuries, the legitimizing normative principles have increasingly centered around the principle of efficiency. The welfare state has been justified as an effective environment for businesses, resulting from the high skills of people, a high level of trust in society, well-functioning infrastructures and institutions, and overall stability and predictability. On the other hand, efficiency has also been the principle guiding the development of welfare institutions and their methods of delivery: the deployment of technological and social innovations, as well as better management practices and optimized institutional structures, should bring about better outcomes (healthier, better-educated, and happier people across the population) while keeping public spending at tolerable levels. In other words, the welfare state should follow the same rules as businesses operating under competition in markets, constantly needing to cut their costs while delivering better value for their "clients," i.e., citizens. This is yet another example of the welfare state being perceived as a competition state!

Efficiency as a guiding principle, however, has its limitations. Typically, there are limits on how much key resources (money, labor) can be reduced without seriously degrading the quality of expected outputs. This is not necessarily a problem as long as there is at least modest growth of available resources, i.e., economic growth and an excess of labor. Once these conditions are no longer present, it becomes difficult to meet earlier standards and expectations of people. To overcome such trade-offs, serious redesigns are needed. In the case of the welfare state, this implies renegotiations of rights and responsibilities between the state, citizens, and companies. In a very abstract sense, these could still be called efficiency gains, yet most metrics and scales of efficiency would have changed quite completely. In other words, the welfare state would eventually look quite different from the past. Perhaps the framework of its narrative would remain the same, yet many of its features would be very different. Furthermore, at least the institutions and the experiences and expectations of people would eventually be largely altered.

The future prospects for economic growth are relatively uncertain in many developed welfare states, including Finland, characterized by low fertility rates and high levels of prosperity. The direct drivers of economic growth, such as an increasing labor supply and investments in easily attainable productivity gains, are no longer present, nor are there easy methods for accelerating them in sight. Many of these countries have experienced extended periods of slow growth during the early decades of the 2000s, and the future does not seem to alter this situation.

It is hence necessary to consider the future of the welfare state through alternative approaches and scenarios that are not built solely on the principle of efficiency.

One prominent option is to sketch beyond-growth futures around the concept of sufficiency. Sufficiency would define what is socially enough for a decent standard of living (the floor) but environmentally not too much (the ceiling) (Raworth, 2017). The new principle, however, would not make the principle of efficiency obsolete altogether: Equity (as well as perhaps accountability) has been a central principle in the era characterized by efficiency. It is a matter of priority and the direction of dynamism.

12.5 The Two Ethical Dilemmas of the Twenty-First Century Welfare State

I shall now describe two ethical tensions that push the welfare state in new directions and force it to search for new sources of legitimation. The resulting new synthesis—the new dynamic balance between the welfare state and the wider forces surrounding it in our era—may be found around the principle of sufficiency. Other outcomes are, however, also possible. Adopting a new principle would give rise to new narratives about the welfare state, as well as gradually transform its institutions and citizens' experiences of them.

12.5.1 Growth Dependency of the Welfare State

Welfare states are essentially intertwined with economic processes aimed at the growing supply and demand of material goods, eventually resulting in economic growth.[4] Economic growth produces the wealth that the welfare state can redistribute and channel into investments contributing to the renewal of society and addressing its pressing problems. Furthermore, welfare states and their funding bases rely on high levels of employment among the working-age population, a feature strongly linked to economic growth. All in all, welfare states to date have been designed to be dependent on economic growth.

At least since the publication of the *Limits to Growth* report (Meadows et al., 1972), we've been faced with the question of how and whether economic growth as a global phenomenon can happen within planetary boundaries. This expanded awareness of the cumulative effects of human action has expanded the concept of justice to include intergenerational and global scales. Especially the climate movements that have appeared during the past decade, for example, Extinction Rebellion and Fridays for the Future, have built their messages around the moral argument that

[4] It can be argued that economic growth can happen without increases in material production by shifting towards immaterial consumption. This is, however, still merely a hypothetical prospect, with no global historical evidence of it happening in the real world. (Vaden et al., 2019)

currently young people, as well as future generations, are bound to suffer substantially more from the adverse effects of climate change than the generations currently in power.

The narrative of green growth has aimed at solving this dilemma by steering investments, market rules, and the overall emphasis of the economy towards renewing production and consumption practices to be ecologically sustainable. The idea of green growth intends to align with the established logic of the welfare state: investments contribute to the reproduction of labor power, the tax system and welfare state convert that into real living standards, and these improved economic and social conditions form a feedback loop to employment and productivity (Gough, 1979; Gough, 2022). This would result in a win-win situation in which young generations would again become wealthier than their predecessors while the climate crises would be resolved.

It is widely acknowledged, however, that there will be inevitable consequences of climate change even now. These consequences will exacerbate inequalities. Furthermore, the green transition in the economy, aiming at both climate mitigation and growth, will result in "prospective losers," i.e., people who will lose their jobs or face rises in living costs proportionally higher than average.

These emerging "green social risks" require new initiatives in social policy, especially as they might affect already vulnerable groups. This has given rise to the rhetoric of "climate justice," "just transition," and "green new deal" practices in high-level policy initiatives by the EU and its member states (Gengnagel & Zimmermann, 2022). The just transition approach aims to address the social impact of decarbonization, while the Green New Deal is intended to build synergies between a safer climate and welfare.

The scope of "Green New Deal" and "just transition" policies has been rather narrow so far. An illustrative example in Finland has been the social security reform process, initiated in parallel with the goal of making Finland a carbon-neutral society by 2035. There seems to be alignment on the necessity of making decarbonization just for all citizens, thus suggesting a need for policies securing distributive justice. There are also explicit statements suggesting that the adoption of more sustainable lifestyles should be fostered.

Despite these parallel policy priorities, the central welfare state reform has excluded all other goals than making a benefit system that better incentivizes people to seek paid labor. Subsequently, questions such as whether people should be required to accept jobs that accelerate climate change, what the emissions of welfare state institutions are, or what kind of consumption and resulting carbon emissions various benefits and services induce, were not considered in the preparatory work of the reform (Saikkonen & Ilmakunnas, 2023).

Sustainability transition is currently expanding its points of reference and meaning-making as a political issue, making it more systemic and complex and thus harder to handle. This process reveals linkages and interdependencies between various policy sectors and eventually breaks apart justifications of previously siloed discourses and solutions.

As an example, sustainability transition has become a highly securitized field of policy, primarily as a result of Russia's invasion of Ukraine and other growing geopolitical tensions that have undermined the foundational idea of interdependence of the globalized economy. Thus, the green transition in European countries is increasingly motivated by the urge to gain energy and resource independence. Put another way, European countries, their economic systems, and welfare systems have been dependent on Russian hydrocarbon exports.

Professor Veli-Pekka Tynkkynen has described Russia and its political model as "oil culture," a concept closely related to "petrostate," a widely used term for oil-exporting countries with highly concentrated economies. In a society of "oil culture," politics and structures of the society (institutional and geographical alike) are formed around the primary resources of the economy (i.e., hydrocarbons), always prioritizing functions of their extraction and trade, subsuming and dominating other fields of politics, and eventually forming long-lasting political path dependencies that favor an authoritarian mode of governance (Tynkkynen, 2019).

The oil culture has also shaped Russia's (as well as other petrostates') relationship with other countries, first and foremost with Europe, creating certain kinds of power structures between exporters and importers of the strategic resources (Tynkkynen, 2023). Within the conceptual framework of interdependence in the global economy, these relationships have resulted in a seemingly win-win situation. For European countries like Finland, modestly priced energy has enabled competitiveness in the export of resource-intensive products while also securing affordability of many basic goods (energy, housing, mobility, and food) for its citizens. This kind of "resource culture" of the welfare state, however, is very often excluded and neglected as a complex, difficult question when discussing the future of the welfare state.

The most pressing issue in this transition to energy independence is not whether we are bound to spend more money on energy in the future and eventually sacrifice fractions of our current living standards. The more fundamental question is about the justification of the welfare state: Our current model has been built on the low price of commodities that contribute directly to climate change and hence jeopardizing the prospect of well-being for future generations. Hence, the welfare state does not stand on very firm ground from the point of view of intergenerational justice. In addition, this very same dependence has been contributing to the growth of economic and political power of the Russian authoritarian regime that is using this power in acts of violence against Ukraine and its civilians. Hence, our current model of the welfare state requires re-justification from the perspective of global justice.

To be honest, this is neither a new nor unique issue. European states, their economies, and models of welfare have been built on the history of colonialism, still evident in most forms and structures of global trade. What we celebrate as the most equal and efficient societies and economies conceals behind them the oppression of people and unsustainable extraction of nature in the global south. This historical pattern has not ended. Critical natural resources, not only oil and gas reserves but also many minerals, are in the hands of a limited number of authoritarian countries and their state-owned companies. Looking at the future of the welfare state, what kinds of "resource cultures," i.e., dependencies on such powers, are we willing to maintain to foster our current nation-state-based economic structures and models of welfare?

Despite all these tensions and contradictions, the only future vision present in mainstream public discourse assumes that the welfare state will be supported by green growth, i.e., the narrative of the industrial-era welfare state will be continued.

Koch (2022) claims that the welfare state model based on GDP growth has run into severe trouble. So far, decoupling economic growth from material resource use and greenhouse gas emissions has failed, thus making a sustainable welfare state merely a theoretical entity. Therefore, we should consider meta-strategies beyond green growth, such as redirecting consumption to low-carbon goods and services or stabilizing the absolute levels of consumer demand (Gough, 2022).

These alternative meta-strategies would lift sufficiency to be the central principle guiding the development of the welfare state and subsequently deprioritize GDP growth as an overarching target (Koch, 2022). Such a shift towards sustainable welfare (Koch & Mont, 2016) or "a good life for all within planetary boundaries" (O'Neill et al., 2018) would require embedding welfare systems in ecosystems (Koch, 2022) but also setting an upper/outer boundary of material living standards (following the doughnut economy idea by Raworth, 2017) in the welfare state, thus targeting and guiding the behavior of affluent and influential groups (e.g., capping maximum income, taxing wealth). Such limitarianism would position social policies as a central tool for countering inequalities and conflicts emerging from decarbonization/sustainability transitions. Gough (2022), along with various other proponents of the sufficiency economy, suggests that the welfare state should be an active force redistributing the composition of consumption by raising the share of public consumption via introducing the so-called Universal Basic Services (UBS), covering such basic needs of citizens as education, health, housing, public transit, and sufficient access to the internet and telecommunications (Neuvonen & Malho, 2019; Portes et al., 2017).

12.5.2 Responsibilities in the Age of an Individual

As discussed already earlier in this article, the Nordic welfare model has emphasized the broad development of capabilities as a basis for individual freedom (Korhonen et al., 2017) and the development of citizenship (Buchardt et al., 2013). Citizens' dependence on family, professional organizations, or other kin-based structures has not been favored in welfare provision. The principle of universalism, i.e., welfare policies that grant social security and services to the entire population, aims at equal community membership for all citizens, occasionally through differentiated treatment of individuals (Saikkonen & Ilmakunnas, 2023).

This promise of universalism sets a high bar for the Nordic welfare states. The success of these societies, characterized by secular, post-materialistic, and highly individualized sets of values, can be attributed to the significant autonomy they grant to their citizens. The welfare state is a central vehicle in maintaining and advancing this narrative and these expectations.

Keeping these promises of the welfare state is a constant challenge. Everyday life in our societies, filled with a multitude of fast and continuous flows of cultural symbols and other forms of information traveling across the human population, constantly creates atypical situations experienced by people who reason that their needs escape the norm. The tradition of public service provision is still in mass production, or perhaps in mass customization. The imperative of constant improvements in efficiency, measured by various productivity metrics, tends to favor centralized modes of production and output efficiency over long-term impact. This creates friction between institutions and the experiences and expectations of citizens who, in other areas of their lives, are accustomed to a widening selection of products and services provided by private companies in global niche markets.

The welfare state, however, operates on a logic different from commercial exchange. It encompasses the freedoms and responsibilities of democracy, as well as an implicit duty for citizens to develop themselves in order to serve as a morally capable citizen and as a workforce. From this perspective, the welfare state is primarily about collective action, not about the transactional use of services. The inability to create this experience has led the welfare state to continuously produce disappointments and unmet expectations.

According to Gengnagel and Zimmermann (2022), the tenet of activating citizens' market positions in the labor market has grown stronger in European welfare states, partly replacing the previous focus on securing citizens' fundamental rights against market forces. This is partly explained by the urgent need to keep the narrative of equal opportunities through employment alive amidst the current transformation. For instance, Rodrick and Sabel (2019) claim that states should even expand their role in shaping job markets and accelerate the creation of what they call "good jobs" to counter the current trend of polarization between regions and social groups, driven by globalization of economies, growing role of metropolitan regions, and the adoption of AI, other digital tools, and advanced production methods.

Beyond workforce activation and its necessity in social cohesion, the welfare state ties together various worldview elements regarding how the world, society, and the economy operate and how a citizen should and could orient oneself as a human: regarding paid labor, education, bureaucracy, knowledge institutions, market functioning, personal health, and societal resilience. These cognitive norms of citizenship in the welfare state are rather implicit and subtle, except for the duty to paid work. In a liberal, individualistic culture, those norms do not guide towards health-sustaining solutions, mutual aid, or ecologically sustainable lifestyles.

The transformative forces of our time—green transition, digitalization (artificial intelligence, data economy, platforms), and economic globalization—create conditions in which citizens constantly face discontinuities in their lives, making it increasingly difficult to secure one's position through their own effort and activity alone. This makes the criteria defining deservingness (van Oorschot, 2000), i.e., social norms on who is entitled to support and under what conditions in the welfare state, be in constant flux. This emphasizes the role of the welfare state in indicating directionality in future development and providing support to its citizens. Coping in a rapidly changing context requires shifts in perspectives and is fraught with anxiety. The welfare state's "frozen landscape" orientation, however, has not adequately considered this knowledge and worldview component.

The current transformative issues enter areas thought to be within the domain of individual choices, preferences, and values—related to work and profession, consumption, and lifestyle patterns. New knowledge can set new norms: certain preferences (e.g., consumption of alcohol or sugar products, excessive amounts of time spent on social media) may appear suddenly so detrimental from a collective perspective that individuals' rights to pursue them should be limited.

This is not new; societies already restrict many individually preferred but collectively harmful activities. What people consider as their preferences are not always necessary for their flourishing: humans and their preferences are flexible, and we can find various meaningful ways to live and flourish. We often lack psychological freedom that would allow to shape our direction and life-altering decisions. Therefore, the welfare state, especially in this era of choice, material affluence, and the prevalence of a consumer attitude, needs a definition of freedom. Such freedom would stand on the idea of sufficiency as the central principle of the welfare state.

Gough (2022) claims that a theory systematizing universal human needs would be required to support a sufficiency-based economy and consequently a welfare model. Sufficiency does not fit well into theories based on individual utility-driven consumption demand and thereby monetary price structures. With the help of a theory of universal human needs, we could imagine conditions for the well-being of future generations, regardless of culture (Gough, 2022). Through this emerging normative framework, a set of upper limits and constraints are also defined, for example, for wealth that exceeds conditions for human flourishing, i.e., luxury consumption not possible for the entire population within planetary boundaries.

Over the past decade, the concept of a well-being economy has emerged as an attempt to operationalize the above-mentioned ideas related to sufficiency and a post-growth economy. Well-being economy sets human and ecological well-being as the primary goal of society and suggests shifting the focus in measuring the success of society from magnitudes of production and consumption (i.e., GDP growth) to metrics that better reflect fundamental social and ecological dynamics and their contributions to well-being (Fioramonti et al., 2022).

In other words, a well-being economy would transcend a) the nexus of economic growth and a growth-dependent system of welfare as prerequisites for successful policies supporting wellbeing in society, b) the idea that GDP growth is the best available proxy measurement for society-wide well-being, and c) an implicit assumption that well-being in society is a phenomenon appearing primarily on the level of individual citizens instead of wider socio-ecological systems. Various authors in Finland have also contributed to the development of the well-being economy (e.g., Häikiö & Hirvilammi, 2024) as well as new definitions of well-being in the context of a society (e.g., Salonen & Konkka, 2015; Salonen & Konkka, 2023). Finland as a nation has also joined the Wellbeing Economy Alliance, a leading global network of organizations and individuals working towards a Well-being Economy.[5]

Furthermore, such a perceptual change would also mark a change in welfare states' traditional relationship between the state and people: it would be a departure from the above-mentioned setting in which citizens and the state have mutual obligations in the form of an exchange of labor and welfare, and that responsibility would form the primary structure through which the state targets wellbeing. Otherwise, wellbeing is seen as belonging to a non-public sphere and relying on acts and motivations of individual citizens. The shift would acknowledge and make visible the necessity of relationships between people, people and communities, and people and other species in building sustainable well-being. Therefore, subjective well-being, in its various forms and ways of measuring it, would need greater attention, both from both citizens and decision-makers (Diener et al., 2009). This means that well-being would be understood as a much wider issue than previously, consisting of other dimensions than merely material ones. A welfare state would eventually move on to be a well-being state.

Building a new system of needs, freedoms, and responsibilities, and operationalizing them through a welfare/well-being state, will require new kinds of collective processes, forming a new deliberative democracy (Gough, 2022). Such new models of citizen participation should also contribute to a stronger interpretation of distributive and procedural justice. Transformative developments affect different demographic groups and generations in differing ways. Many investments related to constructing new infrastructure and institutions, requiring substantial public funds, demonstrate their benefits only over a longer term. Similarly, many ramifications of various contemporary practices and developments accumulate only gradually, favoring current generations and disfavoring future ones. Thus, it should be possible to balance benefits and detriments between generations and to create space for addressing long-term themes amid the pressure of acute issues, especially since people typically prioritize short-term losses over potential long-term benefits.

The metrics of well-being, as well as forms of new, participatory, and deliberative democracy, represent clear changes in the institutions of the welfare state. Even more than that, the step from a welfare state approach to a wellbeing state approach would be a significant change in expectations people have of the welfare state: wider structures for responsibilities and freedoms, shared notions on human needs, expansion from a state to global-multispecies systems, and new roles of a state in supporting socio-ecological transformations. Gradually, this all would also reshapes the narrative(s) of the welfare state to the conditions of the Anthropocene and multi-/metacrises, and the era beyond the "precipice" of the human future (Ord, 2020).

---

[5] https://weall.org/

12.6 Towards the Welfare State for the Children of the Earth

Pekka Kuusi is renowned as the reformer of the Finnish welfare state, particularly for the program outlined in his book *Social Policy for the 60s*, published in 1961 (Kuusi 1964). Later in his life, he published a book called *This World of Man* (Kuusi 1985), which explores the future of humanity, depicting in detail the evolutionary history of the human species and the civilization it has created. The central claim in Kuusi's later book is that we should perceive humans as an outcome of both biological and cultural evolution. Understanding these biological origins of the human species and its embeddedness in Earth's ecosystems is a necessary step in addressing the existential threats resulting from cultural evolution. Pekka Kuusi sketched a truly big history narrative of the past and future of humankind, akin to the works of Jared Diamond and Yuval Noah Harari a few decades later.

From the perspective of Kuusi's ecological thinking, the future of the welfare state depends largely on our ability to recognize and address basic human needs, as shaped and adapted over a long evolutionary history. According to Kuusi, humans, like all other species, are driven by four basic functions: seeking energy, needing shelter, reproduction, and gathering and processing information. Not surprisingly, these basic functions resemble the needs that welfare states are built to secure for their citizens. This evolution-based approach also suggests that institutions of the welfare state should be perceived as "adaptations" to conditions of a certain phase of cultural evolution. Hence, they must continuously adjust to changing needs arising from surrounding society and the changing behavior of people.

The threats Kuusi focused on in his analysis of the Zeitgeist of the 1980s included population growth, inequality between the poor and the rich, military tensions between the superpowers—particularly the threat of nuclear war—and the emerging issues of depleting natural resources and pollution. These themes continue to form, perhaps once again, a central part of the polycrisis of our times, shaping also the welfare state and its future. Alongside these, a series of newer existential threats has emerged, including the rapid and uncontrolled development of artificial intelligence, climate change, and the loss of biodiversity, the latter two resulting in irreversible changes in the planetary system, marking possibly a new geological epoch, the Anthropocene.

Kuusi synthesizes his central claim by suggesting that we should perceive humans as "children of the Earth," not merely as "brain-entities," and thus analyze and try to govern societies as something belonging to nature. Continuing this strain of thought, the narrative of the welfare state should not be too tightly anchored to human-created institutions alone, nor around values and moral duties of a certain era, nor around particular industrial structures. Rather the narrative of the welfare state should be capable of placing humans in the ecosystems in which their societies are embedded. Therefore, the future of the welfare state should not be explored within the confines of nation-states. Instead, such exploration should embark from the wider, global development steps of humanity and the challenges we as a species need to resolve urgently.

This endeavor to build a welfare state in which humans are understood as "children of the Earth" also involves the concept of sufficiency as a central principle of the welfare state. This sufficiency approach recognizes planetary boundaries as central determinants of the future of our societies and economy. Trying to adjust to the boundaries solely with the help of efficiency as the guiding principle will most likely fail. Most contemporary theories on the economy, based on consumer demand driven by individual utility, have been inadequate in prescribing policies that would enable the welfare state to cope with the planetary boundaries (Gough, 2022).

This World of Man by Pekka Kuusi portrays humans as a species that has evolved to be social beings, who not only seek their own good but also possess an urge to act for the benefit of their peers and their community. This fundamental need for community and helping others is a core values of the welfare state and should also play a central part in the future narrative of the welfare state.

Acknowledgments I would like to express my gratitude to Elina Hakoniemi (Demos Helsinki), Antti-Jussi Kouvo (University of Eastern Finland), and Arto O. Satonen (University of Eastern Finland), who read the first manuscript of this article and pointed me to various valuable sources, theories, and concepts that significantly improved the quality of my key arguments.

Funding The article was written as part of a research project that was funded by the Strategic Research Council of Finland (Grant No. STN/2023/358763, Sufficiency solutions for a resilient, green, and just Finland).

References

Allen, R. (2017). *The industrial revolution: A very short introduction*. Oxford University Press.

Andersson, J. (2018). *The future of the world. Futurology, futurists, and the struggle for the post cold war imagination*. Oxford University Press.

Beckert, J. (2013). Imagined futures: Fictional expectations in the economy. *Theory and Society, 42*, 219–240.

Benkler, Y. (2018). *The role of technology in political economy*. LEP Originals. https://lpeproject.org/blog/the-role-of-technology-in-political-economy-part-1/

Bernelius, V., & Kosunen, S. (2023). "Three bedrooms and a nice school" - Residential choices, school choices and vicious circles of segregation in the education landscape of Finnish cities. In M. Thrupp, P. Seppänen, J. Kauko, & S. Kosunen (Eds.), *Finland's famous education system: Unvarnished insights into Finnish schooling* (pp. 175–191). Springer.

Beveridge, W. (1942). *Social insurance and allied services*. His Majesty's Stationery Office.

Buchardt, M., Markkola, P., & Valtonen, H. (2013). Introduction: Education and the making of the Nordic welfare states. In M. Buchart, P. Markkola, & H. Valtonen (Eds.), *Education, state and citizenship* (NordWel studies in historical welfare state research) (Vol. 4). NCoE NordWel.

Demos Helsinki. (2024). *Hoivan uusi aika – Viisi kysymystä huolenpidon resursoinnista*. https://demoshelsinki.fi/wp-content/uploads/2024/04/Demos-Hoivan-aika-0704.pdf

Diener, E., Lucas, R., Schimmack, U., & Helliwell, J. (2009). *Well-being for public policy*. Oxford University Press.

Esping-Andersen, G. (1990). *The three worlds of welfare capitalism*. Princeton University Press.

Fioramonti, L., Coscieme, L., Costanza, R., Kubiszewski, I., Trebeck, K., Wallis, S., et al. (2022). Wellbeing economy: An effective paradigm to mainstream post-growth policies? *Ecological Economics, 192*, 107261. https://doi.org/10.1016/j.ecolecon.2021.107261

Fukuyama, F. (2014). *Political order and political decay: From the industrial revolution to the globalization of democracy*. Profile Books.
Gengnagel, V., & Zimmermann, K. (2022). Green deservingness, green distinction, green democracy? Towards a political sociology of a contested eco-social consensus. *Culture Practice & Europeanization, 7*(2), 292–303. https://doi.org/10.5771/2566-7742-2022-2-292
Gough, I. (1979). *The political economy of the welfare state*. Palgrave Macmillan.
Gough, I. (2022). Two scenarios for sustainable welfare: A framework for an eco-social contract. *Social Policy & Society, 21*(3), 460–472. https://doi.org/10.1017/S1474746421000701
Häikiö, L., & Hirvilammi, T. (2024). *Time ToBe transformative: Strengthening sustainable well-being and economic alternatives*. ToBe project Deliverable 1.5. https://toberesearch.eu/wp-content/uploads/2024/03/D1.5-Policy-brief-first-edition.pdf
Kettunen, P. T. (2019). The conceptual history of the welfare state in Finland. In N. Edling (Ed.), *The changing meanings of the welfare state: Histories of a key concept in the Nordic countries* (pp. 225–275). Berghahn Books.
Koch, M. (2022). Social policy without growth: Moving towards sustainable welfare states. *Social Policy and Society, 21*(3), 447–459.
Koch, M., & Mont, O. (Eds.). (2016). *Sustainability and the political economy of welfare*. Routledge.
Korhonen, S., Neuvonen, A., & Hokkanen, L. (2017). *The Nordic model is not about well-being – It is about capabilities*. Sitra. Retrieved May 23, 2024, from https://www.sitra.fi/en/articles/nordic-model-not-well-capabilities/
Koselleck, R. (2004). *Futures past: On the semantics of historical time* (Translated by K. Tribe). Columbia University Press.
Kosunen, S., Bernelius, V., Seppänen, P., & Porkka, M. (2022). School choice to lower secondary schools and mechanisms of segregation in urban Finland. *Urban Education, 55*(10), 1461–1488.
Kuusi, P. (1964). *Social policy for the sixties: A plan for Finland* (pp. 13–26). Finnish Social Policy Association.
Kuusi, P. (1985). *This world of man*. Bergamon Press.
Meadows, D., Meadows, D., Randers, J., & Behrens, W. (1972). *The limits to growth*. Potomac Associates.
Murto, R. (2022). *Puuttuvat puoli miljoonaa. Väestökato ja Suomen talouden tulevaisuus*. Otava.
Neuvonen, A., & Malho, M. (2019). *The next era of universalism. Moving beyond distribution*. Demos Helsinki. https://www.demoshelsinki.fi/wp-content/uploads/2019/02/180215_demos_next_era.pdf
O'Neill, D., Fanning, A., Lamb, W., & Steinberger, J. (2018). A good life for all within planetary boundaries. *Nature Sustainability, 1*, 88–95. https://doi.org/10.1038/s41893-018-0021-4
Ord, T. (2020). *The precipice: Existential risk and the future of humanity*. Bloomsbury Publishing.
Palier, B., & Martin, C. (2007). Editorial introduction. From 'a frozen landscape' to structural reforms: The sequential transformation of Bismarckian welfare systems. *Social Policy and Administration, 41*(6), 535–554.
Portes, J., Reed, H., & Percy, A. (2017). *Social prosperity for the future: A proposal for universal basic services*. IGP. IGP UCL. https://www.ucl.ac.uk/bartlett/igp/sites/bartlett/files/universal_basic_services_-_the_institute_for_global_prosperity_.pdf
Raworth, K. (2017). *Doughnut economics: Seven ways to think like a 21st-century economist*. Random House.
Rockström, J., Steffen, W., & Noone, K. (2009). A safe operating space for humanity. *Nature, 46*, 472–475. https://doi.org/10.1038/461472a
Rodrick, D., & Sabel, C. (2019). *Building a good jobs economy*. HKS Working Paper No. RWP20-001.
Rotko, T., Majlander, S., & Mesiäislehto, M. (2023). *Koko väestön terveys on yhteiskunnan menestystekijä: Ratkaisuja terveyserojen vähentämiseksi. Tieteellinen asiantuntijaryhmä terveyden eriarvoisuuden vähentämiseksi*. Sosiaali- ja terveysministeriön raportteja ja muistioita

2023:16. https://julkaisut.valtioneuvosto.fi/bitstream/handle/10024/164837/STM_2023_16_rap.pdf?sequence=1

Sahlberg, P. (2021). *Finnish lessons 3.0*. Teachers College Press.

Saikkonen, P., & Ilmakunnas, I. (2023). Reconciling welfare policy and sustainability transition – A case study of the Finnish welfare state. *Environmental Policy and Governance 34*(1), 53–64.

Salonen, A., & Konkka, J. (2015). An ecosocial approach to well-being: A solution to the wicked problems in the era of Anthropocene. *Foro de Educación, 13*(19), 19–34.

Salonen, A., & Konkka, J. (2023). Kansalaisten hyvinvointi kestävyyttä tavoittelevassa yhteiskunnassa. *Tiedepolitiikka, 47*(4), 23–38.

Tynkkynen, V.-P. (2019). *The energy of Russia: Hydrocarbon culture and climate change*. Edward Elgar. https://doi.org/10.4337/9781788978606

Tynkkynen, V.-P. (2023). Violent Russia powered by fossil fuels. In T. Jermalavičius (Ed.), *War and energy security: Lessons for the future* (pp. 3–9). International Centre for Defence and Security.

Vaden, T., Lähde, V., Majava, A., Toivanen, T. T., Eronen, J. T., & Järvensivu, P. (2019). Onnistunut irtikytkentä Suomessa? *Alue ja ympäristö, 48*(1), 3–13.

van Oorschot, W. J. H. (2000). Who should get what, and why? On deservingness criteria and the conditionality of solidarity among the public. *Policy & Politics, 28*(1), 33–48.

Glossary

Corporatism and industrial transformation In capitalist economies, as the out-dated, obsolete products are eliminated, new products are constantly being created and introduced, which Schumpeter called "creative destruction" as the essential process of capitalist economic development. The industrial transformation of capitalist economies can be properly understood as a process of creative destruction in which entrepreneurs introduce innovations, followed by the selection process in the market. However, industrial transformation can be smoother and faster if stakeholders negotiate beforehand where resources should be concentrated. In this context, the institutional configuration of corporatism can play a productive role, as Darius Ornston's study of "creative corporatism" shows (Ornston, 2012), where he found that Denmark, Finland, and Ireland were able to rapidly transform their industrial structure by creatively using their corporatist institutional framework.

Innovation system and innovation policy The concept of a National Innovation System (NIS), proposed by Christopher Freeman, was originally based on the Japanese experience until the 1980s. Finland was the first country in the world to adopt this concept as a basis for innovation policy in the 1990s. In particular, it was adopted as a basic idea for policy instruments to promote cooperation between industry, government, and academia. On the one hand, many argued that the economic success around the year 2000 could be explained, at least in part, by policies based on the concept of NIS. Others, however, argued that Nokia's success actually drove the economic success and criticized the emphasis placed on NIS-based policies. Particularly after the economic downturn following the crisis in Nokia's mobile phone business and the global financial crisis, subsequent governments adopted austerity measures, which also had a negative impact on the resources devoted to innovation policy.

N. Tokumaru et al. (eds.), *Creative Co-evolution of the Economies and Welfare States in the Nordic Countries*, Evolutionary Economics and Social Complexity Science 32, https://doi.org/10.1007/978-981-97-8569-8

Nordic model and social democracy Party politics in the Nordic countries is characterized by the Nordic five-party system, with the size of the social democratic forces being one of its characteristics. Walter Korpi (1978) focused on the actors and their intentions in constructing the welfare state and proposed the power resource theory. This work influenced Gøsta Esping-Andersen's typology of welfare states, where he classified the Nordic countries as social democratic regimes, which indicate that social democratic forces, that is, labour forces, played an important role in building the welfare states of the Nordic countries. On the other hand, Baldwin (1990) argues that not only the role of labour forces, but also solidarity between labour and agrarian forces, and between labour and bourgeoisie forces, was important in reaching an agreement to form a universal welfare state. More detailed research is being conducted into the process of the formation of the Nordic welfare state, showing that it was not simply due to agreements with workers alone, in other words, that social democracy supports the Nordic model.

Social capital The concept of social capital was proposed by American political scientist Robert Putnam, and it considers the ties between people within an organization to be "capital", in addition to cultural capital or economic capital. It argues that the efficiency of society can be increased by stimulating cooperative behaviour between people, such as "trust", "social norms", and "networks". In contrast to the United States, there is little evidence of a decline in social capital in the Nordic countries. It is argued that the high level of social capital in Scandinavian countries can be explained by high levels of economic equality, low levels of cronyism and corruption, and the dominance of non-discriminatory universal welfare programmes.

Social investment state Globalization and post-industrialization have brought new risks to the welfare state, and as a result, there has been growing attention being paid to employment welfare as a role and function of the welfare state. Importance has been placed on ensuring a stable supply of workers with high skills or in other words, human capital. There has been much discussion about moving from the welfare state to a social investment state. The social investment state differs from neoliberalism in that it aims to increase employment opportunities through the increase of research funding, education, and vocational training and to adapt to global competition and the knowledge economy. The meaning of the welfare state has expanded. Peter A. Hall and David Soskice (2001) have focused on the Varieties of Capitalism (VoC), positioning the Nordic countries as "coordinated market economies" and pointing out their advantages in innovation and advanced human resource development. In this context, social spending has been redefined as a form of productive investment, which has come to be known as "social investment".

Wage compression and industrial transformation The compression of differences in wage levels across firms and industries is called "wage compression". Wage compression promotes the industrial structural transformation of the economy in the following ways: When average wage rates are set at similar levels despite differences in labour productivity levels across firms and industries, profits in high-productivity firms and industries increase, while profits in low-productivity firms and industries are compressed. The result is that high-productivity firms and industries are encouraged to expand further, while low-productivity firms and industries are encouraged to contract, which promotes an increase in labour productivity in the economy as a whole. In the Nordic countries, wage compression has been achieved through centralized wage bargaining backed by strong trade unions. Although bargaining has become more decentralized in recent years, the degree of wage compression in the Nordic countries is still higher than in other industrialized countries.

Welfare provision Welfare provision refers to the system of programmes, services, and financial assistance provided by government or other institutions to support the well-being of individuals and families. Key aspects of welfare provision include the roles and relationships of government, civil society, markets, and households, as well as objectives, programmes, targets, client eligibility, financing, and delivery. As Esping-Andersen pointed out early on, one of the characteristics of the Nordic welfare states is that they are government-driven and have a high share of public expenditure in social spending compared to other industrialized countries. In addition, the Nordic countries have been characterized by an emphasis on in-kind benefits such as care and services rather than income support, investment type of benefits rather than compensatory benefits, and generous benefits for the working age population. The universal and egalitarian welfare state requires a degree of central government control or supervision over local governments to ensure their capacity to provide welfare services and to achieve universality. However, the state supervision is rather less and the autonomous local government with high discretionary power and capacity is also the characteristic of the Nordic welfare state.

Welfare universalism Welfare universalism refers to a principle of social policy in which welfare benefits and services are made available to all members of a society, regardless of income, wealth, or social status. This approach contrasts with means-tested welfare systems, where benefits are provided only to targeted recipients who meet certain economic criteria. While a selective approach may be seen as an effective way to invest resources in alleviating poverty, targeted services and benefits may stigmatize recipients and lead to benefit avoidance. Universal benefits and their unconditionality represent the generosity and egalitarian orientation of the welfare state and are found in countries with low-income inequality. In the Nordic countries, the notion that the universal welfare state covers the entire population is one of the key principles of the Nordic model and legitimizes the comprehensive welfare programmes. The ethos of equality, manifested in welfare universalism that reduces the social and economic risks of individual life, has been said to be visible in and reinforced by a more egalitarian culture. However, it has also been noted that the ideational turn from universalism to the idea of selectivism has been observed since the 1990s.

References

Baldwin, P. (1990). *The politics of social solidarity: Class bases of the European Welfare State, 1875–1975*. Cambridge University Press.
Hall, P. A., & Soskice, D. (2001). *Varieties of capitalism: The institutional foundations of comparative advantage*. Oxford University Press.
Korpi, W. (1978). *The working class in welfare capitalism work, unions and politics in Sweden*. Routledge.
Ornston, D. (2012). *When small states make big leaps*. Cornell University Press.

N. Tokumaru et al. (eds.), *Creative Co-evolution of the Economies and Welfare States in the Nordic Countries*, Evolutionary Economics and Social Complexity Science 32, https://doi.org/10.1007/978-981-97-8569-8

The manufacturer's authorised representative in the EU is Springer Nature Customer Service Centre GmbH, Europaplatz 3, 69115 Heidelberg, Germany. If you have any concerns regarding our products, please contact ProductSafety@springernature.com

Printed and bound by CPI Group (UK) Ltd, Croydon, CR0 4YY
30/09/2026
02225300-0011